Access to Economics

Access to Economics

Richard Ledward

Senior Lecturer in Economics
Staffordshire University, UK

TUDOR

First published in Great Britain in 1995 by
Tudor Publishing.
Sole distributors worldwide, Hodder and Stoughton (Publishers) Ltd., 338 Euston
Road, London, NW1 3BH

British Library Cataloguing in Publication Data
A catalogue record for this book is available from the British Library

ISBN 1 872807 11 9

1 2 3 4 5   95 96 97 98 99

Typeset in Times by GreenGate Publishing Services, Tonbridge, Kent
Printed and bound by Athenæum Press Ltd., Gateshead, Tyne & Wear.

Contents

Chapter One

The Nature of Economics

This book is the product of over 25 years of teaching economics to a range of students, both within the university sector and within secondary schools. Economics has, for some reason, become seen as a 'hard' subject among students, and the conventional wisdom is that economics is becoming a less and less popular choice in schools and colleges. This state of affairs is partly the result of the decline into which the economics profession has slipped, and partly the result of changes within the nature of the discipline.

The decline within the profession has followed from the failure of economic management over the last 20 years. In the post war period, 1945 to 1965, economists were held in high esteem because of the success which governments achieved in controlling unemployment and increasing output. Part of the success was attributed to the theories which the economics profession was offering government at that time. The rising unemployment of the 1970s, 80s and 90s seemed to show the weakness of economics, and the economics profession lost much of its reputation as an important instrument of government.

One of the problems which characterises economics is the fact that there is no accepted consensus as to which economic theories are 'correct'. Economists are famous for disagreeing, and there are many jokes told at their expense:

- For every two economists there are three opinions
- If all economists were laid end to end they would fail to reach a conclusion
- All governments are looking for a one armed economist, because he would be unable to say 'on the one hand..., but on the other...'

This failure to agree sets economics apart from other disciplines which claim scientific status. It would be very surprising if chemists or physicists disagreed about the basic theories in their disciplines, yet economists will offer a variety of explanations for most events.

One reason for this is the fact that economics has great difficulty in testing its theories. Most economic theories claim to establish a relationship between two variables, e.g. price and demand. In order to test this relationship, however, it is necessary to see how the two variables move against each other. Unfortunately it is never possible to observe these two variables reacting to each other, because there is always the possibility that they are being influenced by some other third variable. Thus all economic propositions contain what is known as a *'ceteris paribus'* clause, which says that two variables will be related in a certain fashion, other things being equal.

In the real world other things are never equal, and so any result can be explained by asserting that some other variable may have changed.

As an example, take the case of a demand curve. As we shall see later, economists usually argue that if the price of a product falls, the demand for the product will increase. In the late 1980s the price of houses in the UK fell, on average, by more than 20%. The demand for houses also fell, as evidenced by the drop in house sales. Does this experience cast doubt on the basic idea of lower prices increasing demand? Most economists would argue that the result can be explained by the fact that incomes fell during the period, as the economy entered recession, and that this reduced both the demand for houses, and their prices. This result might appear as common sense, yet a little thought will show that this sort of reasoning can explain any event, while at the same time maintaining the basic theory, due to the logic of *ceteris paribus*.

Normative and positive economics

If economics is to be considered as a science, it must put forward propositions which are testable, since this is normally taken as the basis of science. In order to be testable, economic theories must be expressed in such a way that an appeal to evidence is capable of determining the accuracy of the proposition. This is what is normally thought of as positive economics. Positive statements are statements which are capable of being tested against evidence.

Normative statements are statements which are expressions of opinion which cannot be tested against evidence. Thus the statement 'murderers should be hung' is a normative statement. If the statement was 'murderers should be hung because this would act as a deterrent to murder', this would be positive, since in principle one can appeal to evidence to see if capital punishment does act as a deterrent, by examining the incidence of murder in countries which have abolished, or introduced, the death penalty for murder.

The difficulties of testing theories do not affect the positive/normative distinction. The nature of a particular proposition depends upon whether the proposition is testable in principle.

Economics and realism

Economics is often criticised for being unrealistic. This usually means that the critic complains that economic theories are not accurate descriptions of how the world operates, and so cannot be an accurate analysis. This criticism is misplaced because it fails to understand the objective of economics.

Many economists see the discipline as one whose major purpose is to accurately predict the outcome of certain events. Thus, the example of the link between price and demand would be interpreted as trying to predict the impact on demand of a change in price. If prediction is the major goal of economics, then economic theories become instruments for generating predictions. If the predictions are borne out by experience, then the economic theory has done its job and can be thought of as a success.

An analogy which is often used is to compare an economic theory with a map. Suppose that you wish to travel from Manchester to London by road. A useful map would be one which showed the direction to access the motorway system and which showed the exits necessary to reach London. The map would not have to be to an accurate scale, and would not need to show all possible roads. If the traveller reached London, the map must have been sufficiently accurate to serve its purpose. Economic theories are sometimes seen in the same light. If predictive success is the yardstick which is to be used to judge the success of economic theories, the only valid test of the theory is to see whether it provides a valid prediction. If it does, it has served its purpose. That is to say, descriptive realism is **not** an important criteria for judging a theory.

Unfortunately, there is a problem with this approach. If the theory does predict accurately, the theory is confirmed and will be judged a success. If the prediction is not accurate, then there are always other factors which can be claimed to have spoilt the prediction. Thus, a false prediction will not be taken as a valid test of the theory, and so the theory will never be at risk.

Other economists stress that economic theories should not simply be engines of prediction, but that they should also provide valid explanations of economic events. In this case realism is an important property of theories because a theory which is a false description of the world cannot be a valid explanation of an event. Sometimes these two aspects of theories are difficult to disentangle.

Suppose that the economic theory is that a fall in price will increase demand. In one sense this is a prediction, since it predicts that a fall in price will increase demand. Some economists would also claim that it is able to explain an increase in demand. Demand will increase because of a fall in price. Thus, the explanation is simply the prediction written backwards. Other economists would want more from an explanation and would want to be told a story which explains why a fall in price will increase demand. If predictive accuracy is all that concerns the economist, there is no need to explore the causal link between price and demand.

Induction and deduction

Scientific enquiry is often described as either induction or deduction. The inductive method is based on the idea that the way to discover facts about the world is to gather data, and to look at the data to discover, or induce, something about how the data is connected. This has been called the 'bucket theory of knowledge' since facts are simply collected in a 'bucket' and examined.

The deductive method is the idea that all scientific theories begin as a hypothesis, or idea, which the scientist creates, and which is then tested against the evidence to see if the idea is valid. This method, the hypothetico-deductive method, starts with a hypothesis and then refers to evidence. The inductive method reverses this process.

Economist usually concentrate on the deductive method. The problems of testing which we have seen above mean that many hypotheses are able to survive simultaneously.

About this book

This book is an introductory text designed to give the reader an insight into the various areas and theories in economics. Mathematical reasoning has been kept to a minimum, and the major tool of exposition is the graph. The book is primarily theoretical in that the use of data is kept to a minimum, and only used when it aids the explanation of the theories. A grasp of economic theory is important both to students who wish to take examinations in the subject, and also to the general reader who wants to keep abreast of the economic debates which underlie most political discussions.

Each chapter has a set of five multiple choice questions at the end. These questions are there to give practice to people who may come across such tests in the future, to add a little interest to reading the text, and as part of the learning process. They have been designed to bring out the important points which have been made in the chapter. Quite often people do not see the relevance of certain ideas until they are forced to think about, and to answer specific questions.

Economics is an interesting and important subject. Almost every difference of opinion in politics is based upon a point of economics. This book is designed to promote understanding of these issues and to allow the reader to better participate in such discussions. Remember, however, that economic ideas are difficult and some would say impossible to test, and, therefore, one idea is just as likely to be true as is another. Tolerance is a necessary virtue of a good economist, as is humility. No-one has a monopoly of the truth, and economists have less than most.

Chapter Two

The Economic Problem

Key concepts

❏ The problem of scarcity of resources
❏ The concept of opportunity cost
❏ The nature of economic efficiency
❏ The advantages and weaknesses of the market economy in solving the problem of scarcity
❏ The advantages and disadvantages of a planned economy in solving the problem of scarcity
❏ The arguments for privatisation

Key words

Land, labour, capital. Opportunity cost, production possibility curve
Productive efficiency, allocative efficiency
Monopoly, merit goods, public goods, externalities, immobility. Privatisation

---

Definition

Economics is the study of how man can provide for his material well being. As such it analyses how the resources which are available to society can be used to produce those goods and services which will give the most benefit to society. Therefore, economics is often defined as the study of how scarce resources are allocated among competing ends. The rest of this chapter is devoted to explaining this statement.

Resources

The resources which are available to society are known as factors of production. These are normally classified under three headings:

- **Land** – all natural resources e.g. oil, gas, livestock, vegetation.
- **Labour** – all human resources e.g. workforce
- **Capital** – all man made resources. e.g. machinery, factories, roads.

The activity of combining all these factors together is referred to as *Enterprise* and is sometimes included as a fourth factor (although others consider this to simply be a form of specialised labour). *Enterprise* is undertaken by an entrepreneur, who accepts the risk of producing in advance of sales and in return receives *Profit*. The payments to the other factors are as follows:

- **Land** – receives payment in the form of **Rent**
- **Labour** – receives payment in the form of **Wages**
- **Capital** – receives payment in the form of **Interest**

Opportunity cost

Resources are limited in supply and people's wants are normally thought of as insatiable. This means that society always has a problem in choosing what to do with the available resources. This choice is at the centre of economics. Every time a decision is made to produce an item, we must forego the alternative which we could have produced. What we have given up is referred to as the Opportunity Cost of the item. If resources are scarce, a decision to use them in one way must involve a sacrifice in that they are no longer available for use in any other way. The phrase – 'There is no such thing as a free lunch' illustrates the idea. Time spent eating could be devoted to some other activity; resources used to provide the meal could have been used elsewhere. This is also sometimes referred to as the 'guns and butter' issue of economics. This is illustrated in the next section.

Production possibility curve (PPC)

Suppose that our economy is capable of producing two goods, which we will call Good X and Good Y. If all resources were devoted to producing Good X and none to Good Y, then the economy might produce OB of X. If all resources went on producing Y (and none on X) then we might be able to produce OA of Y. Combinations of X and Y which could be produced are shown by the line connecting A and B (the slope of this line will be discussed later). Thus, the curve AB shows the maximum amounts of output which can be produced by the economy, given its available supply of resources.

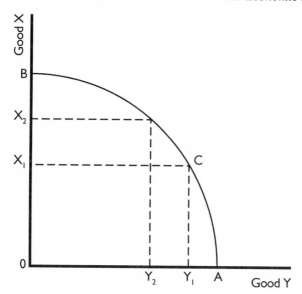

Fig. 2.1 *Production possibility curve*

Suppose we are at point C enjoying OX_1 of X and OY_1 of Y. If we wanted to increase the output of X to OX_2, we would have to cut the output of Y to OY_2. Thus, the opportunity cost of the extra units of X (X_1-X_2) would be the units of Y given up (Y_1-Y_2). If Good X were armament output (guns) and Good Y were consumer goods (butter), this gives the classic choice of guns or butter. The only way we could obtain more of both would be if the PPC shifted to the right. This can only occur as a result of technological change, increased productivity, or an increase in available resources.

Economists make much use of the concept of opportunity cost, since what economists are interested in is the output of goods and services which have to be foregone in order to produce something else From the point of view of an economist, the cost of, say, a heart transplant, is the other treatment which could be carried out using the resources tied up in the transplant. This is important to ensure that the resources are used in the best manner possible.

Scarcity

When resources are insufficient to satisfy all the wants of consumers, resources are said to be scarce. Thus, scarcity and choice are at the heart of economics. If goods are not scarce (air, bad eggs) then they normally fall outside the scope of economics since there are no choices which need to be made. Scarcity is sometimes referred to as THE economic problem and this problem faces ALL societies, from the most primitive to the most sophisticated.

Goods and services

The goods and services which an economy produces can be classified under various headings:

Consumer Goods: these can be classified as durable or non-durable. Not surprisingly, durables are those goods which are of use over a long period of time, (e.g. a refrigerator or a washing machine). Non-durables are those goods bought by consumers which last for a short period, (e.g. a meal). It is not always possible to make a clear distinction.

Producer or Capital Goods: these are goods which do not directly satisfy consumers' wants but which are required by firms for the production of goods in the future, (e.g. machinery).

Services: these constitute intangibles where no actual physical product is produced, (e.g. hairdressing, massages). These are examples of personal services. Commercial services are provided for firms by activities such as banking, insurance and communications.

What, how and for whom

The economic problem seen above is also sometimes referred to as the what, how and for whom problem.

- What to produce
- How to produce
- For whom to produce

All societies face this problem. It is important to remember that the problem is to use the scarce resources in a way which will make the society as well-off as possible. If this position can be reached, the economy is said to have managed an optimum allocation of resources. This can only occur if resources are used efficiently.

Efficiency

Efficiency in economics means using the scarce factors of production (land, labour and capital) in a way which maximises the welfare of society. Resources should never be wasted since they are scarce. There are two types of efficiency:

Productive Efficiency occurs when goods are produced using the least possible resources. It would be a waste of resources to employ 10 men to produce an item if it could be produced by 5. In terms of Figure 2.1, this means always operating on the PPC as this represents the most which the resources are capable of producing. Any point inside the PPC represents a situation where resources are not being employed as fully as possible, either because they are not employed at all (i.e. unemployment) or because they are not producing the maximum they are capable of producing.

Allocative Efficiency occurs when those goods are produced which give the consumers the greatest amount of benefit. It would be a waste of resources to produce something for which there is little or no demand. The benefit derived from a product must compensate for the use of the resources needed to produce it. In terms of Figure 2.1, this means choosing the position on the PPC which gives consumers the maximum benefit.

Economic systems

There are three main approaches which an economy can use to solve the economic problem of scarcity.

A Market Economy is where economic decisions are taken by individuals buying and selling goods and resources through a system of markets.

A Command (Planned) Economy is where a central planning agency decides what, how, and for whom to produce. This usually implies some form of government control

A Mixed Economy is where a combination of free markets and government control is used.

The market economy: what to produce

A free market economy is one where the decisions as to how resources are utilised are left to individuals who operate out of self-interest in an attempt to make themselves as well-off as possible.

In a free market all the factors of production are owned by private individuals. Economic decisions are taken by the interaction of market forces. Consumers will spend their income on the goods which give them most satisfaction, and consumers will exercise their choices in the market place. This is sometimes seen as a process of economic democracy where consumers vote for different products by spending income on them.

As the demand for some goods rises because of their popularity, this will put pressure on their prices to rise. Producers, who are assumed to be interested in maximising profits, will be encouraged to produce more of these products. Hence, more of those goods for which consumers have expressed a preference are produced. Production is said to have responded to price signals, which indicate those goods which should be produced, and consumer sovereignty is said to prevail. This process should lead to resources being used to produce those goods for which people are prepared to pay the most. This will lead to allocative efficiency since these must also be the goods which people want the most.

The market economy:
how to produce

This problem is solved because producers will be forced to use the least costly form of production to enable them to survive in a competitive environment. Thus, resources will be used as effectively as possible. This should lead to productive efficiency.

The market economy:
for whom to produce

This problem is solved by a market economy on the basis of ability to pay. Goods and services will go to those consumers able and willing to pay the market price. Critics of the market system often see this as an undesirable aspect of a market economy, since the distribution of income will determine the ability of different individuals or groups to enjoy the products available. Hence, the fruits of the market economy will not be shared equally among the members of society.

Supporters of the market mechanism will argue that this method of distribution holds the major attraction that it puts the goods and services into the hands of the people who want them most. Suppose that a bus arrives at a bus stop with only one seat available. There are ten people waiting at the bus stop. Who should obtain the seat? There are various ways of solving this problem of scarcity (i.e. wants exceed resources). Queuing is one solution. The market solution would be to auction the seat to the highest bidder, and this could be considered to be the allocatively efficient solution.

The logic behind this approach is to suggest that the amount a person is prepared to pay must reflect the benefit which that individual receives from the service. Hence, the person who is prepared to pay the most, is likely to be the person who wants the seat the most.

This market approach ignores the fact that not everybody will have the same ability to pay, and so wants may not be revealed by making people pay. Despite this objection, the idea that making people pay for items will force them to reveal how much they want the item is an important message which reliance on market forces transmits.

The market economy:
advantages

Most of the merits of a market economy stem from its efficiency in using resources. Thus, markets may achieve both allocative and productive efficiency.

Allocative Efficiency means that only those goods which are wanted by consumers are produced. The market satisfies consumer preferences. More than this, the goods which people want most will be the goods which they are prepared to pay most for. These will also be the goods which producers are interested in producing, since they will be the most profitable. As long as the price exceeds the cost of making a product, that product will be produced in a market economy. Resources will never be wasted by producing goods for which there is no demand.

Suppose that an entrepreneur is considering setting up in business and is undecided which of two products to produce. Each product would cost £5 to produce. The entrepreneur will choose that product which will make most profit. Other things being equal that will be the product which will sell at the highest price. This will also be the product which will confer most benefit on society, since the price that people are prepared to pay must reflect the benefit which they receive from the product. In fostering his/her self-interest, the entrepreneur is also creating the most benefit for society. **Productive Efficiency** is achieved by the desire to make profits, coupled with competition, since this will guarantee that firms will be forced to adopt the most efficient production techniques. Resources will never be wasted by a firm using more than is strictly necessary to produce an item.

Other advantages identified with a market economy are the freedom which it gives for people to exercise choices, the incentives which it gives for people to succeed, and the absence of interference by government in people's lives.

The market economy: disadvantages (failures)

Several factors may prevent markets from working properly. These factors are important since they provide the basis for much of the intervention which the government undertakes in a market economy.

Consumer Ignorance: if consumers are not fully informed about the products available, resources may not be used in the best fashion. Persuasive advertising is often seen as a dangerous form of interference with consumer sovereignty. This interferes with allocative efficiency.
Monopoly: if competition is absent, firms may not always respond in the desired fashion to changes in consumer demand. If the demand for a monopolist's product rose, the monopolist may raise the price, but not increase output. This would not achieve allocative efficiency, since higher prices should be a signal to produce more of the product. Competition would ensure that this occurred. Monopolies, therefore, interfere with allocative efficiency

The absence of competition may also enable firms to survive even if they operate at less than peak productive efficiency.

Merit Goods: the market will provide goods and services which are sold to only those able and willing to pay the price. If there are goods or services which it is decided should be available to everyone, such as health, education, and from which no-one should be excluded, then a price cannot be charged, and so the market could not be relied upon to provide all of the good or service. Hence, the state must provide.

Public Goods: some goods and services could not be provided by the market (e.g. national defence, street lights) since people would not be prepared to pay for them as they could not be denied the use of them. People would attempt to secure a 'free ride' by not paying, but still using the goods or services.

Externalities (Social Costs): the free market does not take into consideration the 'social costs' of a firm's activities (e.g. pollution of the environment). Thus production of an item may impose more cost on society than the benefit it gives. This is not efficient in terms of allocation.

Income Distribution: markets are usually seen as very efficient, but not always very fair.

Factor Immobility: resources may not be able to move between occupations or geographically in response to changing demands. Hence, the market may not produce the goods even if there is a demand for them. Allocative efficiency will not be achieved.

Unemployment: it is not clear whether reliance on market forces will achieve full employment. Hence, government may be forced to intervene. Similarly, problems with the balance of payments, or inflation, may require intervention in the market.

The command economy: advantages

Under this system, prices are normally controlled and the planners decide the quantity of the various goods which are produced and then send these instructions to firms who meet these targets. The decisions about what, how and for whom, are all solved by the planners. The major advantages are:

- Resources need not stand idle during a recession.
- Goods can be distributed according to need rather than by income.
- Social costs and benefits can be incorporated into decision making.

The command economy: disadvantages

The major disadvantages are:

- Goods may be produced which are not the ones which consumers want. The result being shortages of some goods and surpluses of others. This is allocatively inefficient.

- Resources will be wasted in attempting to discover what goods and services are required. The system will be very bureaucratic and, hence, use up valuable scarce resources. This is productively inefficient.
- Producers will have little incentive to produce efficiently, since their only requirement is to meet their production quotas.

The mixed economy

This is a characteristic of most modern economies. and while leaving much production in the private hands, it allows for a substantial role for government, mostly to overcome the examples of market failure given above. The only dispute is about the correct balance between the private and the public (government) sectors.

Since 1979 there has been a movement towards more emphasis on the private sector both in the United Kingdom and also in other parts of the world. The movement towards a market economy in Eastern European countries is an attempt to obtain the increased efficiency which market economies are seen to offer in solving the economic problem of scarcity.

Privatisation

Since 1979 many industries which were in the public sector have been privatised and sold to the private sector. Several reasons have been put forward to explain this process:

- To raise revenue for the government.
- To weaken Trade Union power, since unions in the public sector were seen as being too powerful.
- To increase share ownership.
- To increase economic efficiency.

This last point is usually seen as the most important. Efficiency would increase because of the reasons seen under the heading The Market Economy : Advantages, above. Critics of privatisation suggest that many of the privatised organisations are in non-competitive situations and, therefore, may act as monopolies and may, therefore, fail to achieve optimum efficiency. This problem has been recognised by the decision to appoint regulators to make sure that the companies do not abuse their position (e.g. Ofwat, Ofgas, Oftel). These industries were privatised as monopolies, partly to maximise their share price so as to raise as much revenue as possible for the government.

Summary

❑ All societies have limited resources.

❑ All societies have unlimited wants.

❑ Scarcity is sometimes referred to as THE economic problem.

❑ Opportunity cost is what has to be foregone in order to undertake a particular activity.

❑ Productive efficiency refers to producing goods with the minimum amount of resources.

❑ Allocative efficiency refers to producing those goods which maximise the welfare of society.

❑ Competitive markets guarantee efficiency.

❑ Planned economies may be inefficient.

❑ A mixed economy tries to overcome areas of market failure.

❑ Privatisation is an attempt to increase the efficiency of organisations in the public sector.

Multiple Choice Questions

1. Which of the following would you consider to be a merit good?

   A washing machine
   B motorway maintenance
   C defence
   D refuse collection

2. Which of the following will cause the Production Possibility Curve of a 2-good economy to shift outwards from the origin?

   A an increase in consumer demand
   B a fall in unemployment
   C an increase in output per worker
   D an increase in the price of both goods

3. Output of Goods in Units

Good X	0	20	40	60	80	100	120	140	160	180
Good Y	360	320	280	240	200	160	120	80	40	0

The figures above represent the production possibilities open to a 2-good economy. The opportunity cost of producing 20 units of good X is:

A 320 units of Y
B zero
C 20 units of X
D 40 units of Y

4. Economists refer to resources being scarce because:

A there are not many of them
B there are insufficient resources to meet our needs
C there are not enough to provide the goods and services which people want
D they are expensive

5. Externalities are thought of as an example of market failure because

A they are unpleasant
B goods may be produced which impose more costs on society than the benefit yielded
C they cause productive (technical) inefficiency
D they represent points outside the Production Possibility Curve

Elements of Demand

The market

A market is simply a meeting of buyers and sellers. Much of economic analysis is devoted to examining the way in which markets determine, and respond to, prices. This requires an examination of the factors which govern the behaviour of buyers and sellers, or, as economists put it, examining the factors determining demand and supply.

There is an old saying that if you can teach a parrot to say 'demand and supply' you have created a trained economist. There is always some element of truth in such stories, and the truth in this case is to the effect that most problems in economics can be examined by applying the rules of demand and supply, since in a market economy, it is market forces which determine and influence economic events.

Demand

When we refer in economics to demand, we are referring to effective demand, not how much people would like to have of an item, but how much they are trying to buy. Thus, it does not mean how much people need an item, nor what they would like to have. Demand represents what people are trying to buy in the market place during a particular period of time. Thus, the demand for motor cars in the UK might be 1.4 million cars per year. The demand for an item will depend upon many factors of which the following are usually seen as the most important .

- Price
- Price of Other Products
- Income
- Tastes
- Expectation of Price Increases
- Population

In order to be able to analyse how any one of these affects demand, we must assume that the other factors remain constant, otherwise it will be difficult to see the required relationship. This is referred to as the assumption of *ceteris paribus*, which, again, means other things being equal. The first relationship we discuss will be the way in which changes in price might effect demand.

The demand curve: demand and price

The relationship between demand and price is shown by a demand schedule. In Table 3.1 we illustrate a demand schedule for potatoes. Note that as price falls the demand for potatoes increases. The relationship between price and quantity demanded is therefore inverse. This schedule is shown in the form of a graph in Figure 3.1.

The demand curve shows how the demand for potatoes varies as the price of potatoes alters. At a price of £20 per tonne, the quantity demanded is 50 000 tonnes per month. If the price falls to £15 per tonne the quantity

Table 3.1 Demand schedule for potatoes

Price (£/ton)	Quantity demanded (000 tons/month)
30	25
20	50
15	75
10	125
5	200

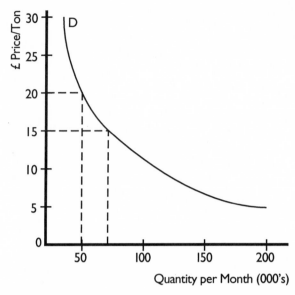

Figure 3.1 *Demand curve for potatoes*

demanded rises to 75 000 tonnes per month. Thus, a change in price is shown by moving along the demand curve. These movements are sometimes referred to as extensions or contractions in demand.

Demand curves are almost always drawn downward sloping from left to right, since lower prices are normally expected to boost demand. This is due to two reasons:

● As the price falls it will be substituted for other commodities which have now become relatively more expensive. This is known as the substitution effect of a price change.
● As the price falls it increases the real income of consumers who normally buy the good, since they now will have increased purchasing power. This increase in real income may lead to more of the good being bought. This is known as the income effect. (These effects are examined more fully in Chapter Eight).

Demand and the price of other goods

A change in the price of one good might affect the demand for another. The nature of the relationship depends on how the goods are connected; goods may either be substitutes or compliments.

Substitutes : if goods are substitutes, this means that consumers could buy one or the other, (e.g. tea and coffee). If the price of tea were to rise, one would expect this to increase the demand for coffee. This would cause the demand curve for coffee to shift to the right.

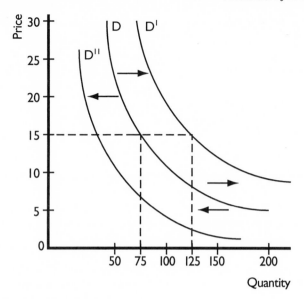

Figure 3.2 *A shift in the demand curve*

At the original price of 15, demand was 75. If the price of a substitute were to rise, this might stimulate demand to 125. Similarly, at all other prices, an increase in the price of the substitute would increase demand. Hence the whole demand curve shifts to the right by an amount equivalent to the extra demand created by people switching from the more expensive substitute. This is shown by the demand curve moving from D to D'. It is important when using demand and supply curves to remember that quantities are measured on the bottom axis. Thus, anything which implies an increase in the quantity demanded at all prices will shift the curve to the right.

Complements: these are goods where consumers buy one good and the other (e.g. cars and petrol). If the price of petrol were to rise we would expect this to affect the demand for cars. Higher petrol prices would reduce the demand for cars. Thus, if demand curve D in Figure 3.2 was now the demand curve for cars, an increase in the price of petrol would reduce demand at all prices, and so the curve would shift to the left, to curve D".

Demand and Income

Normally we would expect an increase in income to lead to an increase in the demand for all goods. This would result in their demand curves shifting to the right. However, there are a class of goods where an increase in income might lead to a fall in demand. These are goods which are only bought because they are all that people can afford, but when income rises people prefer to buy some alternative, superior product. These goods are known as **Inferior Goods**, usual examples being public transport, second hand clothes, cheap cuts of meat.

Upward sloping demand curves

Normally demand curves are always drawn downward sloping, indicating that at lower prices demand for a product will increase. There are two possible exceptions to this rule: neither are thought to be highly significant.

Goods of Ostentation: certain goods may only be bought because of their high price, and a lower price may cause people to believe that they are not receiving the necessary status from their purchase. It is not uncommon for antique dealers to find that they can sell certain items more easily when the price is raised. This behaviour is irrational and is usually ignored in economics, which normally assumes rational behaviour.

Giffen Goods: these are inferior goods where the income effect of a fall in price is so strong that it leads to less of the good being bought when its price falls. This effect was first noticed by Robert Giffen, a 19th century Irish economist, who noticed during the potato famine in Ireland that as the price of potatoes increased, the quantity of potatoes demanded increased.

The rationale for this behaviour is that since potatoes formed a large part of the household budget, the increase in price meant that there was less money available for meat and other foods. Thus, consumers were forced to buy more potatoes since they could no longer afford the alternatives. Try and trace through the way in which lower potato prices might reduce the demand for potatoes.

Both these factors might give rise to an upward sloping demand curve.

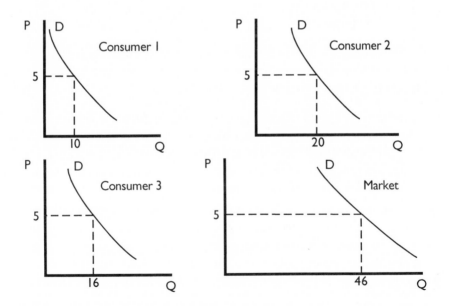

Figure 3.3 *Individual and market demand*

Market demand and individuals' demand

A demand curve can be drawn showing how the demand of an individual varies as the price alters, or a demand curve can be drawn showing the total demand for the product. The total curve is simply the individual curves added together. The total demand is the horizontal addition of each individual demand curve.

In Figure 3.3 on the previous page each consumer's demand at price 5 is added to give one point on the market demand curve. This can be done at every price to give a complete market demand curve.

Summary

- ❏ A market is a meeting of buyers and sellers.
- ❏ Demand refers to the quantity people are trying to buy.
- ❏ Demand depends upon price, income, price of other goods and tastes.
- ❏ Demand curves normally slope downwards i.e. lower prices increase demand, *ceteris paribus*.
- ❏ Demand curves will shift if demand changes because of any change in any of the other factors affecting demand.
- ❏ A shift to the right indicates an increase in demand, to the left a reduction.
- ❏ Market demand is the sum of the individual demands of buyers.

Multiple Choice Questions

1. What would an economist understand by 'the demand for houses'?
   - **A** the number of homeless people
   - **B** the number of people who own houses
   - **C** the number of people trying to buy houses
   - **D** the number of houses sold
   - **E** the number of people who need houses

2. Which of the following might shift the demand curve for beef to the right?
   - **A** an increase in the price of pork
   - **B** a fall in income
   - **C** a fall in the price of beef
   - **D** a fall in the price of pork
   - **E** health fears about eating red meat

3. A rise in the price of motor cars might cause the demand for one of the following to fall:

    A bus transport
    B bicycles
    C petrol
    D television sets
    E rail travel

4. Which of the following would you class as an inferior good?

    A a good which is unpopular
    B a good which has no close substitutes
    C a good which is preferred to all its rivals
    D a good which no-one buys
    E a good which people buy because it is all they can afford

5. The demand for a good is observed to rise. This might be explained by:

    A the price of a substitute falling
    B the price of a substitute rising
    C the product is an inferior good
    D the price of a complement rising
    E none of the above

Chapter Four

Elements of Supply

Key concepts

- ☐ The determinants of supply
- ☐ The nature of the supply curve
- ☐ Factors causing the supply curve to shift

Key words

Supply, price, profit, costs of production, goals of firms
Taxes, subsidies. Joint supply

Supply

Supply refers to the amount of a product which producers put onto the market in order to try and sell it. It is not the amount which is actually sold, since, if consumers do not wish to buy the product, it will remain unsold.

Determinants of supply

Suppliers are assumed to be interested in making profits, and, therefore, anything which affects the profitability of producing an item will alter the attractiveness of that item to producers and, hence, alter the amount which they are prepared to supply to the market. Thus, supply will depend upon many factors of which the following are normally seen as the most important:

- Price of the product
- Price of other products

- Costs of production
- Technology
- Goals of firms.

In order to analyse the impact of a change in any one of these, we again must assume that all other factors remain constant. This is the *ceteris paribus* assumption as seen in Chapter Three.

The supply curve: supply and price

The relationship between supply and price is shown by a supply schedule. In Table 4.1 we illustrate a supply schedule for potatoes. Note that as price falls the supply of potatoes will also fall, since potato production will now be less profitable and so some potato producers will switch production to some other, more profitable crop. The schedule is shown in the form of a graph in Figure 4.1 on the next page.

Table 4.1 *Market supply schedule*

Price (£/tonne)	Quantity supplied (000s / month)
30	150
20	100
15	75
10	50
5	0

Higher prices will encourage an increase in potato production, since producers will now see potatoes as a more attractive crop. The supply curve allows us to identify the quantity which will be supplied at each price. Thus, at a price of £20 per tonne, suppliers put 100 000 tonnes onto the market per month. This is shown as point A in Figure 4.1. If suppliers are trying to maximise profits, the usual assumption, this must imply that it is not profitable to produce more than this amount. Hence, the cost of producing extra potatoes must be higher than £20 per tonne. Thus, the supply curve is connected to the cost of producing extra output. This point will be expanded in Chapter Eleven.

It is important to recognise that the supply curve SS shows the affect of a price change on the quantity supplied. Thus if the price rose from £20 to £30 this simply causes supply to expand along the supply curve as shown by the arrows in Figure 4.1. Supply expands from 100 to 150, moving from A to B. The curve will only shift if supply changes without the price altering.

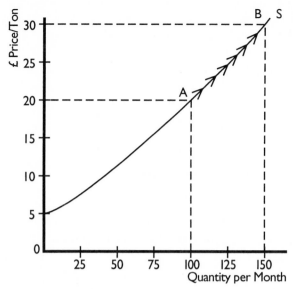

Figure 4.1 *Market supply curve*

Supply and the price of other goods

A change in the price of another good which the producer might deem more profitable could affect the supply of the good under consideration. Thus, if the price of carrots were to rise this might reduce the supply of potatoes since farmers might switch resources (land labour, capital) from potato production to carrots. This would cause fewer potatoes to be supplied at all prices and so would cause the whole supply schedule to shift to the left. This is shown by the shift from supply curve SS to curve SS' in Figure 4.2. The supply curve is shown as a straight line for ease of exposition. Thus at the price of £20, farmers were originally willing to supply 100 tonnes/month. The increase in the price of carrots might encourage farmers to grow more carrots, less potatoes, thereby reducing the market supply of potatoes to 75 tonnes/month.

Supply and the costs of production

If the cost of producing an item increases, this must, other things being equal, reduce its profitability. Hence an increase in the costs of production will cause the supply to fall. In Figure 4.2 the curve shifts from SS to SS''. Thus at a price of £20, instead of 100 000 tonnes being supplied, less will come onto the market, again shifting the supply curve to the left. There are two important ways in which costs of production can be affected by government action:

- Taxes
- Subsidies

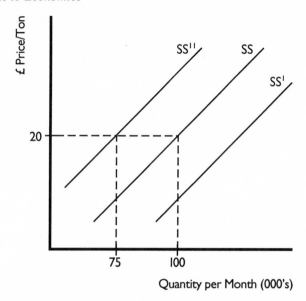

Figure 4.2 *The supply of potatoes following an increase in the price of carrots*

Suppose that a tax of £5 per tonne was put on potato producers. This means that instead of receiving the prices shown in Table 4.1 the producers were forced to pay £5 per tonne to the government. Thus, if the price was £20 the producers would only keep £15. Thus, instead of supplying 100 000 tonnes, producers would only put 75 000 tonnes onto the market, since £15 is all they will receive. To be encouraged to put 100 000 tonnes on the market, the producer would need to sell potatoes at £25 per tonne. Thus a tax on an item shifts the supply curve to the left. In fact the supply curve will shift vertically upwards by the amount of the tax. This is an important result which should be fully understood.

Conversely, if the government were to give a subsidy to potato producers, this would increase the attraction of producing potatoes and would cause the supply curve to shift to the right (SS to SS′ in Figure 4.2). The impact of taxes and subsidies will be considered in more detail in Chapter Twenty-Seven.

Supply and other factors

If any other factors change to cause supply to vary, while not affecting the price, this will also cause the supply curve to shift. The important point to remember is that since quantities are shown on the bottom axis, anything which increases quantity (other than a price change) will cause the curve to shift to the right. Anything which reduces quantity (other than a price change) causes the curve to shift to the left. Thus in Figure 4.2, a breakthrough in technology would increase supply to SS′, whereas bad weather would reduce supply to SS". If firms altered their behaviour (goals of firms) this would cause supply to alter.

Joint supply

When some goods are produced, it automatically results in the supply of other goods i.e. they are in joint supply. For example an increase in beef production increases the supply of hides. An increase in the supply of petrol increases the supply of other oil-based products produced in the oil refining process.

Summary

- ❑ Supply is the amount which producers are trying to sell on the market.
- ❑ Supply will depend upon the profitability of supplying the product.
- ❑ Higher prices will increase the supply, making supply curves slope upwards.
- ❑ Increased costs of production will cause less to be supplied at all prices shifting the supply curve to the left.
- ❑ Any factor, other than the price, which increases supply will shift the supply curve to the right.

Multiple Choice Questions

1. The supply of a product represents:
   - **A** the amount produced
   - **B** the amount sold
   - **C** the amount firms try to sell
   - **D** the amount consumers try to buy
   - **E** the amount bought

2. Which of the following will cause the supply curve of potatoes to shift to the left?
   - **A** an increase in the price of potatoes
   - **B** a fall in the price of carrots
   - **C** a fall in income
   - **D** an increase in potato picker's wages
   - **E** a subsidy to potato growers

3. Suppose that the price of a product has no effect upon the quantity which producers are willing to supply. The supply curve will be:

   A vertical
   B horizontal
   C upward sloping
   D downward sloping
   E impossible to depict

4. How will the supply curve for potatoes be affected by the government placing a tax on crisps?

   A the supply curve will shift to the left
   B the supply curve will shift to the right
   C the supply curve will be unaffected
   D the supply curve will become steeper
   E the supply curve will become flatter.

5 A supply curve is horizontal at a price of £5. This implies that;

   A none of the product will be supplied at a higher price than £5
   B people are prepared to pay £5 for the item
   C units of the product can only be produced for more than £5 each
   D units of the product can be produced for £5 each
   E supply is zero

Chapter Five

The Determination of Market Price

Key concepts

- The problem of scarcity of resources
- The determination of an equilibrium price in a market
- The impact on the price of a shift in demand
- The impact on price of a shift in supply
- The effect of price controls on markets

Key words

Equilibrium, excess demand, excess supply
Maximum price control, minimum price control

Market price

The price of a commodity is determined by the interaction of the forces of demand and supply. We can show that in a competitive market situation, the forces of demand and supply will cause the price to move to the point where the demand for the commodity just matches the supply. We can illustrate this by examining the market for potatoes seen in Chapters Two and Three and combining the demand and supply schedules. This is shown in Table 5.1 on the next page, whereupon the information is also displayed in graph form.

As we can see there is only one price where the demand and supply are equal. This is at a price of £15 per tonne. This is known as the equilibrium price.

Table 5.1 *Supply and demand schedules for potatoes*

Price (£)	Quantity demanded (tonnes/month)	Quantity supplied (tonnes/month)
30	25	150
20	50	100
15	75	75
10	125	50
5	200	0

Equilibrium price

Suppose that the price of potatoes was £20. As we can see from Table 5.1 and from Figure 5.1, at this price the demand for potatoes (50 tonnes per month) will be less than the quantity of potatoes sellers are trying to sell in the market (100 tonnes per month). Thus there is an excess supply of potatoes on the market. In terms of Figure 5.1 this excess supply is represented by the horizontal distance between the demand and supply curves at the price of £20. Sellers will be unable to sell all they would like, and so, the only way they could attempt to sell more would be to lower the price. Thus the price would not stay at £20 but would start to fall.

Suppose that instead of £20 the price was £10. At this price demand (125 000 tonnes per month) is greater than supply (50 000 tonnes per month).

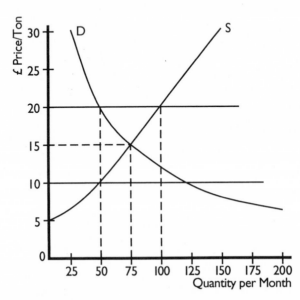

Figure 5.1 *Supply and demand curves for potatoes*

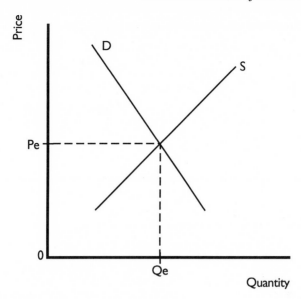

Figure 5.2 *Generalised supply and demand curves*

There will be a shortage of potatoes and this excess demand will put pressure on the price to rise. Hence, the price would not stay at £10 but would start to rise.

The processes at work will ensure that the price moves toward £15. When it reaches this position consumers are able to buy all that they require (75 000 tonnes per month), and sellers are able to sell all that they desire (75 000 tonnes per month). Neither buyers or sellers have any incentive to alter the price since they are both able to do what they want to do. Thus the price will stay at £15. This is known as the equilibrium price, since there are no forces at work causing the price to change. Equilibrium price is thus the price to which the market will always return, and, in terms of demand and supply curves, is always represented by the point at which the curves intersect.

More generally, the supply and demand framework is usually portrayed without actual figures on the axes, but instead using letters to denote price and quantity. In Figure 5.2 a market for a hypothetical commodity is shown with an equilibrium price of Pe and quantity Qe. If any factors cause the demand or supply conditions to change, the equilibrium will be disturbed and a new equilibrium formed.

Shifts in demand and market price

Suppose that in the market shown in Figure 5.2, there was an increase in consumers' incomes which caused an increase in demand. This would mean that at all prices consumers would be trying to buy more of the product. The demand curve will have shifted to the right. This is shown in Figure 5.3.

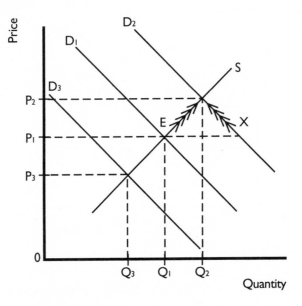

Figure 5.3 *Shifts in demand*

The original demand curve is shown as D_1 and the original equilibrium price is at P1. When the demand increases to D_2, there will be an excess demand at the original price, shown by the distance E X. This excess demand will put pressure on the price to rise. As the price rises, two things happen. First, demand starts to contract along demand curve D_1. Secondly, supply starts to expand along the supply curve as the higher price makes increased output more attractive to suppliers. These movements are shown by the arrowheads. Eventually, or very quickly in some markets, the price will arrive at P_2, at which point demand and supply are equal; the excess demand has been eliminated and the market has reached equilibrium at a higher price and quantity sold.

If something had caused demand to fall (e.g. lower income, a fall in the price of a substitute), the demand curve would have shifted to the left, causing price and quantity sold to fall, giving a new equilibrium at price P_3 and quantity Q_3.

Shifts in supply and market price

If supply conditions change so as to cause a change in supply, the equilibrium price will be disturbed. Consider the market for cars represented by Figure 5.4 on the next page.

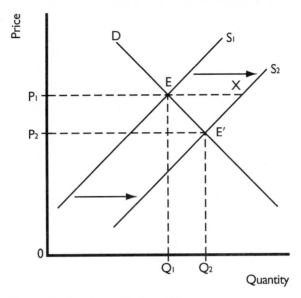

Figure 5.4 *The market for cars: shifts in supply*

Suppose that there is now an improvement in technology (perhaps the introduction of robots) which lowers the cost of producing cars. This will mean that more cars will be produced and put onto the market at all prices. Hence, the supply curve will shift to the right. At the original equilibrium price, P_1 there is now an excess supply of cars, shown by the distance EX. This will put pressure on the price to fall. As the price falls, demand expands from point E towards E′, along the demand curve. As price falls, supply will contract (because of reduced profitability) along the new supply curve S_2 towards E′. Thus E′ will be the new point of equilibrium, giving an equilibrium price of P_2 and quantity of Q_2. Thus price has fallen, and sales have increased because of an improvement in technology.

If a change occurred which caused supply to fall (e.g. increased costs of production, restrictions on foreign cars entering the UK), the supply curve would shift to the left, causing prices to rise and quantities sold to fall.

Price control and market forces

We have seen that left to market forces, prices will move to the point where demand equals supply and so create an equilibrium position where everyone is able to carry out their desired market transactions. There are occasions when non equilibrium prices are imposed upon a market. There are two main forms in which this can take place:

- Maximum Prices
- Minimum Prices.

Maximum prices: rent control

Maximum prices are designed to prevent prices rising above a certain level. Governments may attempt to keep the price of certain items below the level which would be determined if prices were left to the market. Thus in certain countries the price of food is controlled by the state and set at low levels to enable more people to afford food. In the UK the price of rented accommodation has been controlled by various Rent Acts, designed to enable tenants to afford rented accommodation. The impact of these measures is shown in Figure 5.5.

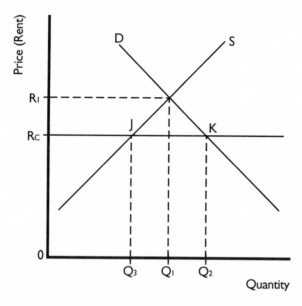

Figure 5.5 *Maximum price control (Rent control)*

The attempt to fix rents below the market level is shown by the price Rc. This stimulates the demand for rented accommodation to Q_2. The lower rents, however, make the supply of rented accommodation less profitable and so the supply falls to Q_3. This creates a shortage of rented accommodation shown by the distance JK or distance Q_2Q_3.

This is sometimes put forward as one explanation for the decline in the size of the private rented sector in the UK since the amount of rented accommodation available will fall from Q_1 to Q_3. This problem will be made worse if tenants are also given security of tenure which will make owning rented property less attractive. This will result in the supply curve shifting to the left, reducing rented accommodation even further.

One side effect of attempts to keep prices below their market (equilibrium) levels is that some demand will be unsatisfied. Some of these frustrated consumers might be willing to pay high prices for the product. This is likely to lead to a secondary or unofficial market where the forces of supply and demand will operate in response to the demand of consumers and the supply of people re-selling goods obtained legally in the controlled market, or obtained illegally elsewhere. This is best illustrated by the market for tickets for a very popular concert, or for tickets for an FA Cup Final. The tickets are sold at a price which often leads to some people being unable to obtain them. This must indicate that the price has been set below the equilibrium market price, since at an equilibrium price, demand and supply would be equal, and no-one would be unable to obtain a ticket as long as they were prepared to pay the market price.

Minimum prices: minimum wages

Minimum price controls are designed to prevent prices from falling below a certain level.

It is sometimes argued that government should introduce a minimum wage to prevent workers from being exploited by employers. This implies that wages are to be controlled at a level above the level determined in the market place. (If workers are already earning £100 per week when their wages are determined by market forces, it makes no sense to introduce a minimum wage of less than £100, since this would have no effect). The impact of minimum wages is shown in Figure 5.6.

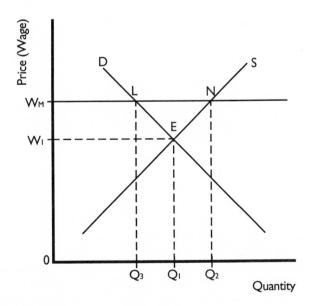

Figure 5.6 *The impact of a minimum wage*

At the minimum wage of Mw, the demand for workers has fallen from point E to point L. The supply of workers has increased from Q_1 to Q_2. Thus more people would like to work at the higher wage, but there are fewer jobs available and so employment will fall. If prices are set above equilibrium, demand will be less than supply. This explains why one of the major arguments against a minimum wage is the possibility of increased unemployment. The extent of the increase in unemployment will depend upon the slope of the demand curve for labour. This will be examined in Chapter Fifteen.

A similar problem arises within the agricultural policy of the European Union, since food prices are raised to provide farmers with higher incomes, which inevitably causes food surpluses that have to be removed from the market to prevent prices from falling back to equilibrium. This is achieved by intervention agencies buying the surplus, shown by the distance LN in Figure 5.6 (if this diagram is interpreted as representing the market for food within the European Union).

Summary

□   Excess demand will cause prices to rise.

□   Excess supply will cause prices to fall.

□   Price will settle at equilibrium; where demand equals supply.

□   An increase in demand shifts the demand curve to the right, resulting in a higher price and higher quantity sold.

□   An increase in supply shifts the supply curve to the right, resulting in a lower price and increased quantity sold.

□   The imposition of a price below the equilibrium reduces the amount sold and creates an excess demand.

□   The imposition of a price above the equilibrium reduces the amount sold and creates an excess supply.

Multiple Choice Questions

The diagrams A to E show the demand and supply curves of various industries operating in competitive markets. In each case P_1 and Q_1 represent the initial equilibrium position and P_2 and Q_2 the situation after a change has occurred

Diagrams A to E From the diagrams A to E, select that which illustrates the market described in questions 1 to 3.

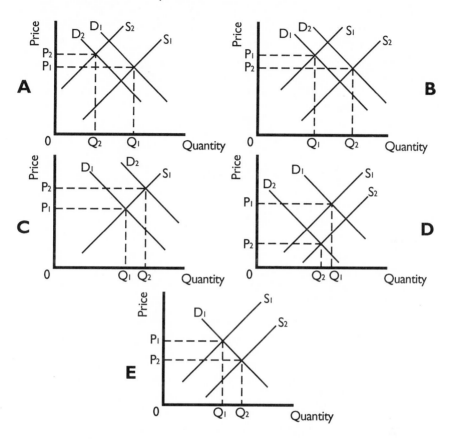

1. The market for coffee after an increase in the price of tea.

2. The potato market after a tax on crisps and a rise in potato pickers' wages.

3. A bumper harvest of carrots and health fears concerning the consumption of carrots.

4. The market price of a product is observed to rise and the quantity bought and sold is also observed to rise. If the normal forces of demand and supply operate, this could be due to:

   A demand falling
   B demand rising
   C supply falling
   D supply rising
   E none of the above

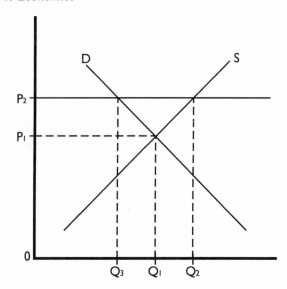

5. The diagram represents the market for butter. If the government wish to maintain a minimum price for butter of OP_2 then in the circumstances illustrated, it should:

    A   buy the quantity Q_1Q_3
    B   sell the quantity Q_2Q_3
    C   buy the quantity Q_1Q_2
    D   sell the quantity Q_1Q_2
    E   buy the quantity Q_2Q_3

Chapter Six

Elasticities of Demand

Key concepts

❏ The measurement of the impact of price changes on demand
❏ Factors affecting the impact of price changes on demand
❏ The measurement of the impact of income changes on demand
❏ The measurement of the impact of a change in the price of a complement or a substitute on demand
❏ The relationship between price changes and changes in expenditure
❏ The measurement of the impact of price changes on supply

Key words

Price elasticity of demand, income elasticity of demand, cross elasticity of demand
Inelastic demand, elastic demand, unitary elasticity
Inferior goods, positive elasticities, negative elasticities
Price elasticity of supply

Elasticities

Elasticities play an important role in economics and there are several types of elasticity. They all refer to how one variable responds to a change in some other variable. Thus, price elasticity of demand refers to how demand for a product alters when its price changes. Income elasticity of demand refers to how demand for a product alters when incomes change. Interest elasticity of demand refers to how demand alters when the rate of interest changes. These concepts are important because they all describe how one side of the market (the demand side) react to a change in some economic variable. This reaction has important consequences for how markets then reacts to changes in that variable.

Price elasticity of demand (PED)

This is defined as the responsiveness of demand to a change in price. Economists and businessmen are often interested in how consumers will react to a change in the price of a product. This is what price elasticity of demand (PED) attempts to measure.

The formula which is most often used to measure PED is:

$$\text{PED} = \frac{\text{Percentage (or proportional) change in quantity demanded}}{\text{Percentage (or proportional) change in price}}$$

Consider the information given in Table 6.1.

Table 6.1

Price (p)	Quantity demanded
6	100
5	200
4	300
3	400
2	500
1	600

Suppose that price falls from 5p to 4p. Using the formula :

$$\text{PED} = \frac{50\%}{-20\%} = -(2.5)$$

This states that the price elasticity of demand is – (2.5.) The minus sign indicates that a fall in price will be associated with an increase in the quantity demanded. Price elasticity of demand will always be negative so long as the demand curve slopes downwards. The value of PED simply says how much demand alters relative to the price. A PED of 2.5 says that demand changes 2.5 times as much as the price (in percentage terms). An elasticity of 0.5 would suggest that demand changes half as much as the price. In this case, a 10% change in price would cause a 5% change in demand.

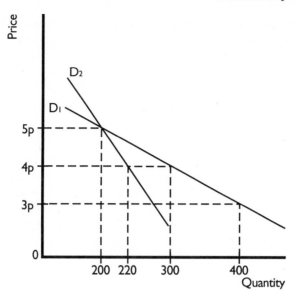

Figure 6.1 *Price elasticity and the slope of the demand curve*

The larger the value of PED, the larger the impact on demand of a given change in price. This has obvious implications for the slope of the demand curve. Consider the two demand curves shown in Figure 6.1.

At a price of 5p, demand is equal to 200 units on both curves. If price falls to 4p, demand in both cases will increase. Demand curve D_1 shows demand rising to 300. This is the example given earlier and gives a PED of 2.5.

Demand curve D_2 shows demand increasing to 220. This gives a PED of 0.5 (10%/20%). This suggests that the steeper the demand curve, the smaller the PED. However visual comparisons of PED can only be made if the demand curves are drawn to the same scale and the price changes are identical.

It is dangerous to take the slope of the demand curve as an indicator of PED, because the value of PED will vary along the demand curve, even if the slope remains constant. Consider demand curve D_1 above. If price falls from 4p to 3p, what will be the PED? The percentage change in price is 25% (1/4), whilst the percentage change in demand is 33.3% (1/3). This gives a PED of 1.33. So the value of PED varies along the demand curve despite the slope remaining constant. This makes the measurement of PED difficult if we wish to measure it over a range of the demand curve.

Consider what value of PED is obtained if the price in Table 6.1 rises from 3p to 4p (33.3%). Demand falls from 400 to 300 (25%). This gives a PED of 0.75. A different value of PED is obtained depending upon whether the price has risen or fallen. The usual solution to this problem is to suggest that the value of PED between prices of 3p and 4p is an average of the two values obtained. In the example above this yields a PED of 1.04. Measuring PED over a range of the demand curve gives what is known as 'arc' elasticity of demand.

Price inelastic demand

If the percentage change in price is greater than the percentage change in demand, the product is said to have an inelastic PED. This suggests that demand does not alter (stretch) very much. Mathematically this results in PED having a value less than one. There is a limiting case where price changes have no impact on demand. This would result in the demand curve shown in Figure 6.2. This is described as a perfectly inelastic demand.

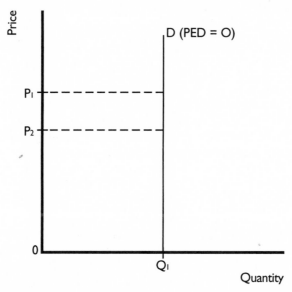

Figure 6.2 *Perfectly inelastic demand*

If PED < 1 (inelastic) this has important implications for the impact of price changes on the total amount of money spent on a product. Suppose that PED is 0.5 and that the price of the product rises from £1 to £1.50. Suppose that the current quantity demanded is 1000 units a week. What will happen to the total spending of consumers (which in turn represents the revenue received by the producer)?

The new demand will be 25% lower than the old (since the price change is 50% and PED is 0.5).

The original expenditure was $1000 \times £1 = £1000$
The new expenditure is $750 \times £1.50 = £1125.50$
Total expenditure has risen.

This result always holds if PED < 1. An increase in price increases the amount spent on the product. A fall in price will have the opposite result. Thus the following relationships always hold:

If PED < 1, then $\uparrow P \rightarrow \uparrow$ TR   TR = Total Revenue
If PED < 1, then $\downarrow P \rightarrow \downarrow$ TR

This has important implications for producers of products with an inelastic demand since it means that anything they can do to raise the price of their product will increase the amount of revenue which they earn. This explains the behaviour of OPEC (The Organisation of Petroleum Exporting Countries), when they cut oil production in 1974 in order to increase the price of oil. Many other producers of primary products, whose price elasticity of demand is low, have also attempted to reduce output in order to raise the price of their products.

Price elastic demand

If the demand for a product changes more than the price (in percentage terms) then the product is said to have an elastic PED. This will result in a PED of greater than one. Thus in Table 5.1 the fall in price from 5p to 4p (20%) leads to an increase in demand from 200 to 300 (50%) giving a PED of 2.5. Any change in demand which is a greater percentage than the price change will result in a PED of more than one.

The impact on expenditure is again important. In the example above:

The original expenditure was $200 \times 5p = £10$
The new expenditure is $300 \times 4p = £12$

Thus, if PED is greater than one (elastic) a fall in price raises total expenditure, and hence, the revenue received by the firm. An increase in price will lead to a fall in expenditure and hence revenue.

If PED > 1, then $\uparrow P \rightarrow \downarrow$ TR   TR = Total Revenue
If PED > 1, then $\downarrow P \rightarrow \uparrow$ TR

A limiting case is when a small change in price causes an infinite change in demand. This is shown in Figure 6.3 on the next page and is referred to as a perfectly elastic demand curve.

The figure illustrates that an increase in the price above P_1 leads to demand falling to zero, while at P_1, demand is infinite.

Unitary price elasticity of demand

If the percentage change in demand exactly equals the percentage change in price, PED will have a value of one. This is referred to as having unitary (or unit) elasticity. In these circumstances a change in price will have no

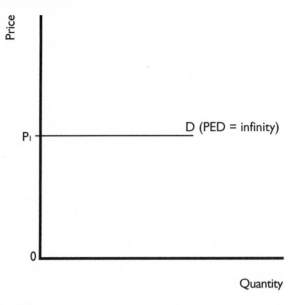

Figure 6.3 *Perfectly elastic demand*

effect on the total amount spent on the product, since the change in price will be offset by the change in demand.

Thus if price falls by 5% and the quantity demanded increases by 5%, the consumer is buying 5% more items but paying 5% less for each one. Expenditure will therefore be fairly constant.

Determinants of price elasticity of demand

PED is determined by the following factors.

- The availability of substitutes: the greater the number of substitutes the more elastic the demand. This is because if the price rises and there are alternatives available, consumers will switch to these alternatives. Thus the demand for a particular brand of petrol will be very high, but the demand for petrol as a whole will be very inelastic
- The proportion of income spent on the good : the smaller the proportion of income spent on the good, the less elastic the demand. Thus a 50% increase in the price of an item which sells for 2p will have a much smaller impact on demand than a 50% increase in the price of a £20 item
- Habit
- Time: it may take time for consumers to respond to a change in price, since it will take time to find alternative products.

Income elasticity of demand

Income elasticity of demand (YED), measures the responsiveness of demand to a change in income and is calculated as

YED = Percentage change in quantity demanded

Percentage change in income

Normally we would expect the demand for a product to rise if there was an increase in income. Hence YED will normally have a positive value (income and demand move in the same direction). Suppose a 10% increase in income caused a 5% increase in demand for a particular product. This yields a YED of 0.5. Thus, as long as YED is positive, an increase in income will cause an increase in demand.

However, there may be goods which, as income rises, fewer are purchased. This will be because these goods are bought if they are all that can be afforded. As income increases, superior goods are preferred. This type of good is known as an Inferior Good. The value of YED for an inferior good will be negative, since an increase in income causes a fall in demand. Possible examples of an inferior good are public transport, or cheap cuts of meat. If changes in income have no effect on demand, this gives a value of YED of zero. Thus, YED can be positive (normal goods) or negative (inferior goods), or YED can be zero.

Cross elasticity of demand

Cross elasticity of demand (XED) is defined as the responsiveness of the demand for one product to a change in the price of another. It is measured by the formula:

XED = % change in the quantity demanded of product A

% change in the price of product B

The value of XED will depend upon how the two products are related. If the two products are substitutes (tea and coffee), an increase in the price of tea would be expected to increase the demand for coffee, since some consumers will substitute coffee for tea. There will be a positive relationship between the price of one of the products and the demand for the other. Thus, if the price of tea were to rise by 10%, and the demand for coffee to rise by 5%, this would give an XED of + (0.5). Hence substitutes have a positive cross elasticity of demand.

If the two products were complements, (cars and petrol), we would expect an increase in the price of cars to reduce the demand for petrol. Hence the XED will be negative, since the value of the denominator (% change in price) will be positive, but the numerator (% change in demand for the other product) will be negative. Complements have a negative cross elasticity of demand. If the two products are not connected the XED will be zero.

Price elasticity of supply

Elasticity of supply (Es) refers to the responsiveness of supply to a change in price, and will be reflected in the slope of the supply curve (unless it happens to be a straight line from the origin, in which case the Es is always unity). It is calculated by the formula:

$$Es = \frac{\% \text{ change in quantity supplied}}{\% \text{ change in price}}$$

If supply is fixed and cannot be altered, the Es = 0. This would give a supply curve which was vertical.

One of the major factors affecting Es is the time period taken into consideration since this will have an important impact on the ability of an industry to respond to a price change. Three periods are normally distinguished:

● The market period when supplies sent to the market have already been determined
● The short run when existing firms can alter output
● The long run when new firms may enter, or existing firms change their scale of operations.

In Figure 6.4 there is an increase in the demand from D_1 to D_2.

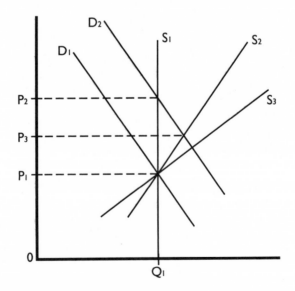

Figure 6.4 *Elasticity of supply over time*

In the market period supplies are fixed at Q_1 and supply is completely inelastic. For example if demand for oil suddenly increases, supplies on the market will be fixed and price will rise to P_2. After a period of time existing oil producers will increase production and the supply becomes more elastic, perhaps increasing to the position shown by S_2. This will cause the price to fall to P_3.

In the long run new oil fields might be developed and new producers may supply oil attracted by the higher prices. Supply becomes even more elastic, S_3 in Figure 6.4, and the price will have fallen back toward the original price. Thus over time the price of oil may not simply move from one equilibrium to another, but may in fact continue to vary as supply takes time to respond.

Es also depends upon the nature of the product and how easy it is to increase output. This is closely connected with how expensive it is to increase production, and, hence, how large a price rise is necessary to encourage output to expand. If it is very expensive to produce larger quantities, it will require a large price increase to raise output. Hence Es will be low. Thus the slope of the supply curve is related to the costs of production, and, in particular, how much it costs to alter output.

Summary

- Price elasticity of demand is the responsiveness of demand to a change in price. This is always negative, except for Giffen goods.
- An elastic demand is when PED > 1. In this case an increase in price will reduce total revenue.
- An inelastic demand is when PED < 1. In this case an increase in price will increase total revenue.
- Income elasticity of demand is the responsiveness of demand to a change in income; this is usually positive except for the case of inferior goods.
- Cross elasticity of demand is the responsiveness of the demand for one good relative to a change in the price of another. This is positive for substitutes and negative for complements.
- Elasticity of supply is the responsiveness of supply to a change in price. Time is an important factor.

Multiple Choice Questions

1. The price of a product rises from £1 to £1.20 and the quantity demanded falls from 2000 units a week to 1800 units a week. The elasticity of demand is:

    A – (20)
    B – (2)
    C – (0.5)
    D – (200)
    E – (10)

2. A firm sells 5000 items at a price of £5. If the price is increased to £5.50 and the price elasticity of demand for that particular price change is – (0.5) what will be the new sales level?

    A 5250
    B 250
    C 4750
    D 4950
    E 4500

3. The price of a product rises and consumer expenditure on the product remains constant. This implies that the price elasticity of demand is:

    A zero
    B less than one
    C more than one
    D one
    E infinite

4. The income elasticity of demand for a product has a value of + (0.5). This will mean that:

    A when income rises the quantity demanded falls
    B when price rises more of the product will be demanded
    C when income rises the quantity demanded rises
    D when price rises total expenditure rises.
    E none of the above

5. Evidence suggests that the cross elasticity of demand between coffee and tea has a value of + (0.5). This means that:

    A a 10% increase in the demand for tea will raise the price of coffee by 5%
    B an increase in the price of tea will increase the demand for coffee
    C a fall in the demand for tea will raise the price of coffee
    D a fall in the price of tea will increase the demand for coffee
    E tea and coffee are complementary goods

========== Chapter Seven ==========

Supply and Demand in Action

Key concepts

- ❐ The problems of agriculture caused by over supply
- ❐ Agricultural support schemes aimed at raising farm prices
- ❐ Producer agreements designed to raise prices; the example of OPEC
- ❐ Price adjustments when supply responds after a time lag: a dynamic model

Key words

Statics and dynamics
The Common Agricultural Policy (CAP), Cartels
The Cobweb model

Static and dynamic analysis

Most analysis using supply and demand curves consists of identifying an original equilibrium price, disturbing that equilibrium by changing some factor affecting demand or supply, and comparing the new equilibrium with the old. This procedure is referred to as an exercise in comparative statics, since it consists of comparing two equilibrium (static) positions. Dynamic analysis consists of trying to look more closely at the process by which the new equilibrium is achieved and so is concerned with the process of prices changing.

We will use the study of various commodity markets to illustrate ways in which elementary economic analysis can shed some light on current economic problems by using comparative static and dynamic analysis.

The farmer's dilemma: higher output reduces income

Most agricultural products have an inelastic demand. If farmers experience a good harvest, the supply of agricultural produce will rise. This will cause the price to fall. Will farmers be better or worse off?

The result depends upon whether the fall in price outweighs the increase in the quantity sold. This depends upon the price elasticity of demand. Suppose the good harvest has caused output to rise by 10%. If the PED is less than one (inelastic), then in order for consumers to be persuaded to buy 10% extra, the price will need to fall by more than 10%. This will result in less money being spent on agricultural products, reducing farmers' incomes. Thus any increase in the output of agricultural produce will make farmers worse off.

In a similar way, anything which causes the supply of agricultural produce to fall will lead to an increase in price which will compensate for the reduced quantity sold. Given that the supply of agricultural produce will vary because of the vagaries of the weather, prices will fluctuate and so will farmers' incomes, with incomes varying inversely with output.

The problem of a fluctuating income is made worse by the fact that over time, productivity in agriculture rises as new strains of produce are introduced and improved farming techniques are used. This means that the supply curve is continually moving to the right. Unfortunately for farmers, the income elasticity of demand for food is fairly low, and so the demand for food fails to keep pace with the increases in supply. This is illustrated in Figure 7.1 where the original equilibrium is at the price of P_1. However,

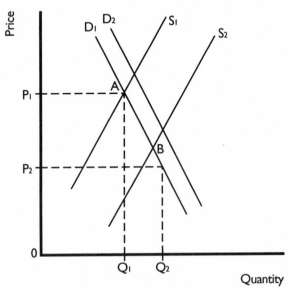

Figure 7.1 *Impact of increasing productivity in agriculture*

at a later date the price has fallen to P_2. The income of farmers at the original price is given by the area $OP_1A\,\hat{Q}_1$, The income after the changes is given by the area OP_2BQ_2. Income has fallen.

The above analysis suggests that, left to market forces, farmers are likely to suffer from fluctuating and declining incomes. To overcome this problem various schemes of agricultural support have been considered.

Buffer stock schemes: the Common Agricultural Policy

These schemes attempt to maintain farm incomes by means of a guaranteed or target price, which is maintained by means of a central agency which purchases stocks in times of surplus and re-sells them later during periods of shortage. This will ensure that the price of the produce remains stable at the target price. In order to increase farmers' incomes the target price is often set at a level which is above the level which would be determined by the free market. This implies that the target price is above the equilibrium and forms the basis of the Common Agricultural Policy (CAP) of the European Union. This is illustrated in Figure 7.2.

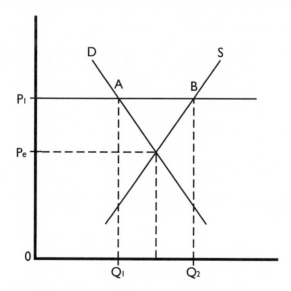

Figure 7.2 *Minimum prices and the CAP*

Left to market forces, the price of agricultural produce would be Pe. Suppose the target price is set at P_1. This price would result in demand being Q_1 and supply being Q_2, causing an excess supply of AB. In order to keep the price at P_1, the excess supply must be removed from the market by being purchased by the intervention agency. The high price will encourage farmers to continue producing Q_2 and so the intervention agency will have to keep purchasing the excess supplies.

These food stocks are expensive to maintain and a source of political embarrassment. In order to offload these stocks, they can be sold on the world market outside the EU at prices below the target price. This has the effect of reducing world prices below what they would otherwise be, and in turn reduces the incomes earned by farmers in the rest of the world. It is not difficult to see why the CAP is so unpopular in the areas of the world which rely on agricultural exports for their income.

Another solution to the problem would be to persuade farmers to grow less food, which would also raise the price, and so increase the amount of money spent on food. Various schemes have been introduced to try and achieve this reduction in supply.

In Figure 7.2 farmers receive an income of OP_1BQ_2. Consumers pay OP_1AQ_1 and so the area ABQ_2Q_1 represents income from the intervention agencies (which is raised from taxpayers in the EU). If this money could be spent encouraging farmers to limit output to Q1, it would avoid the problem of excess supplies. Thus farmers may be paid to take land out of production.

Producer cartels

Producers of products with an inelastic demand know that anything which raises their price will cause consumers to spend more on their product. This gives producers of these products an incentive to combine together to increase their prices. Higher prices will mean that less of the product will be sold and so a decision to raise prices is also a decision to reduce supply. In fact, if the product is one which is bought and sold in world markets, its price will be determined by demand and supply and so the only way producers can raise the price is to agree to reduce supply. This was achieved by OPEC (the Organisation of Petroleum Exporting Countries) in 1973/74 and 1979/80. Consider the position shown in Figure 7.3.

The original price is P_1 and sales are Q_1. The members of OPEC want to raise the price to P_2 and therefore agree to reduce supply, thereby shifting the supply curve to S2. This higher price more than compensates for the reduced quantity sold. (In 1974 the price of oil rose more than four-fold). This situation suffers from two major problems:

a) members of the cartel have an incentive to cheat and supply more than agreed.
b) the higher price may lead to increased supplies some time in the future which will trigger off price changes, which in turn may cause further changes in supply and so on. This is explored further in the section below.

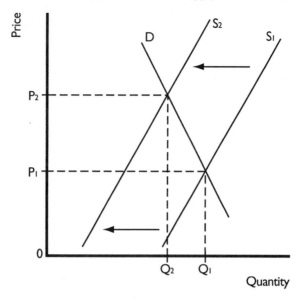

Figure 7.3 *OPEC and the price of oil*

Dynamic analysis: the cobweb model

There are many markets where a decision to increase supply cannot be taken immediately, but instead takes a considerable period of time. Thus if the price of the product changes, supply does not respond until some time later. This can cause the price to be unstable.

Suppose that the price of coffee rises. Coffee growers may wish to respond to this by growing more coffee. Given that it takes several years for coffee trees to mature, the increased supplies do not appear on the market until some years later. If most coffee growers have increased their acreage of coffee, the market will be flooded by the extra supply and coffee prices will fall. These low prices may force some coffee growers to reduce their planting, or perhaps to go out of business altogether. This may result in a fall in supply which in turn raises prices and the whole cycle may start again. This is illustrated in Figure 7.4 on the next page.

Assume that the supply curve represents what producers would like to put on the market in response to various prices, but that it takes a certain length of time for them to be able to alter their supply. In the case of agriculture this might be the time to grow a new crop, or to breed animals. This is shown by supply (S_t) being a function of last periods price (P_{t-1}). Demand will depend upon the current price (P_t). The market is initially in equilibrium at point E.

Assume that for some reason the price rises to P_1. (This may be due a temporary fall in supply. The resulting shift in the supply curve has not been shown to keep the diagram simple). In response to this higher price,

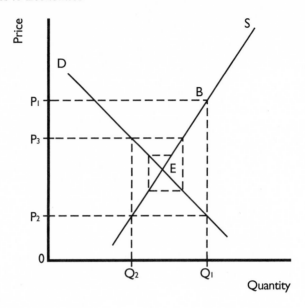

Figure 7.4 The Cobweb model

suppliers will be encouraged to increase their supply. They will try and produce the quantity shown by point B. However, because of the time lag in being able to alter supply , the increased output will not appear in the market until some time in the future. At this time supply will increase to Q_1. Because farmers must clear their stocks, the price must fall until consumers are prepared to buy Q1. This will only occur when the price has fallen to P_2, at which price demand is also Q_1. This low price might now prove very unattractive to producers, and so they react by planning to reduce supply to Q_2.

Next period only Q_2 comes onto the market and so a shortage of Q_1–Q_2 will occur. Prices will rise until demand falls to Q_2. This will mean a price of P_3 This higher price encourages supply to expand and price will then fall. The diagram indicates that the market will eventually return to the original equilibrium at point E. This diagram is often referred to as a cobweb diagram since the path of the price and quantity changes traces out a cobweb shape. Figure 7.4 shows a converging cobweb, since the price converges on its original level.

If the supply curve is drawn flatter than the demand curve, the cobweb will diverge as shown in Figure 7.5.

The explanation for this is that if supply responds a great deal to the price change, this will cause a large change in price when the market reacts, which in turn will cause an even larger change in supply and hence an even larger change in price, etc. Trace your way around the diagram starting at point A.

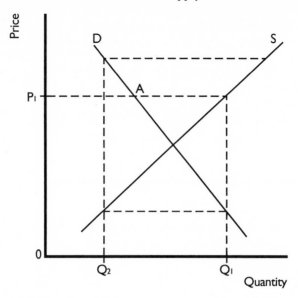

Figure 7.5 Diverging cobweb

The cobweb analysis has been applied to a variety of markets. It was first observed in the market for pigs in the USA and, so, is sometimes referred to as the 'hog cycle'. House prices may exhibit the same behaviour. High prices one year will encourage house builders and developers to expand their house building operations. When these new houses appear on the market they may depress house prices, which results in supply falling in the future as new estates become uneconomic to develop. This may lead to a shortage of new houses in the future which may raise house prices, so starting the process off again.

Similarly, the pay associated with some occupations is claimed to move cyclically (up and down). Suppose that computer programmers are in short supply and so recently qualified computer students are able to obtain well-paid jobs. This might encourage many people to train as programmers. When all these new programmers appear on the job market they may depress the pay of programmers. This may deter students from training for that occupation, so that at some time in the future there will be very few young programmers available. This might raise their pay and the process may begin again.

The problem experienced by OPEC referred to earlier arose from the fact, that, in the short run, the reduced output from OPEC members led to a dramatic increase in price. As time progressed, the high profits to be earned from oil production caused the supply of oil from a variety of sources to increase. Most of North Sea oil production would not have been profitable without the price increase. When these new oil supplies reached the market, the price of oil began to fall. Now the members of OPEC were faced with a different position. In order to keep the price high, they were forced to cut their oil production. This reduced their incomes and so gave the members of OPEC a great incentive to cheat on their production quotas. Non OPEC oil producers were quite happy to pump oil as fast as they could to capitalise from these high prices and so the price of oil continued to fall.

Thus a decision in the 1970s by OPEC to raise the price of oil has put forces in operation which have led to an increase in oil production and a fall in oil prices. In the 1970s there was considerable talk about an energy crisis and how oil would run out by the end of the century. The events of the last two decades provide proof of how powerful the market can be in overcoming the problem of scarce resources.

Summary

- ☐ If demand is inelastic, higher prices will increase the revenue of producers.
- ☐ Increases in supply reduce revenue for suppliers of products with an inelastic demand.
- ☐ Agricultural support schemes are designed to raise farmers' incomes.
- ☐ Higher incomes require higher prices, which will cause excess supplies.
- ☐ Producers of products with inelastic demand have an incentive to combine together to reduce supply.
- ☐ These producer agreements tend to be unstable.
- ☐ If supply only responds after a time lag, any disturbance from an equilibrium might cause prices to continue to fluctuate, causing the cobweb effect.

Multiple Choice Questions

1. If the demand for a product is price inelastic, and the price falls, the amount spent by consumers will:

   A   fall
   B   remain constant
   C   rise
   D   depend upon how supply responds
   E   depend upon the value of the elasticity of demand..

2.

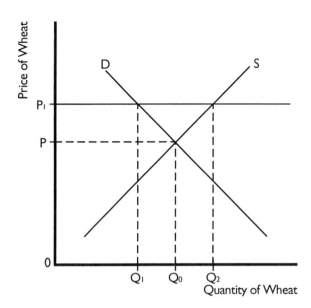

Consider the market situation shown in the diagram. If the authorities wanted to keep the price of wheat at OP1, it would have to:

A sell the quantity $Q_1 - Q_2$
B sell the quantity $Q_1 - Q_0$
C buy the quantity $Q_1 - Q_2$
D buy the quantity $Q_1 - Q_0$
E buy the quantity $Q_0 - Q_2$

3. What would be the effect on the market for potatoes of an increase in the rate of tax on crisps?

A price would rise and quantity sold would rise
B price would fall and quantity sold would rise
C price would rise and quantity sold would fall
D price would fall and quantity sold would fall
E no effect

4. The fact that the demand for FA Cup Final tickets exceed the supply indicates that:

A the market price is above equilibrium
B the demand for tickets is inelastic
C the supply of tickets in limited
D the market price is below equilibrium
E the market price is the equilibrium price

5. The demand for a product is given by the equation D = 100 – 5p (where p = price in pence). Supply is given by the equation S = 5p. The equilibrium price and quantity will be:

A   5p and 10 units
B   10p and 10 units
C   10p and 5 units
D   5p and 50 units
E   10p and 50 units

Chapter Eight

The Theory of Consumer Demand

Key concepts

- ❑ How consumers spend their income to maximise their welfare
- ❑ The reason why consumers buy more when the price of a product falls i.e. why the demand curve slopes downwards
- ❑ How economists analyse the impact on consumers of a change in their income

Key words

Utility, diminishing marginal utility, the equi-marginal principle.
Indifference curves, budget line, consumer equilibrium.

The Demand Curve

In this chapter we will examine the theory which lies behind the simple demand curve. This curve, which was introduced in Chapter Three, is drawn on the assumption that a lower price for a product will cause its demand to increase. This seemingly obvious situation can be explained by examining the behaviour of an individual consumer when deciding how to spend her income.

Consumer utility

Consumers are assumed to be interested in maximising their welfare and they will spend their income so as to make themselves feel as well-off as possible. Economists refer to this as consumers trying to maximise their utility.

Utility is a word which attempts to describe the satisfaction which people receive from the products that they obtain. It does not mean usefulness, since some people might obtain much satisfaction from owning a diamond, which has very little use.

The demand curve tells us how much people are prepared to pay in order to buy particular quantities. Common sense tells us that this must depend upon how much utility the product gives to the consumer. A crucial distinction must be made between two concepts: **total utility** and **marginal utility**.

Total utility refers to the total amount of satisfaction which a consumer derives from the total amount of a product which she has bought.
Marginal utility is the extra utility which is obtained from an extra unit of the product.

Consider the Table 8.1. The figures show the total utility which a consumer obtains from purchasing various quantities of a product. This type of analysis assumes that people can put an actual number on the utility obtained, and these numbers are sometimes referred to as **utils**. Whether or not this is a realistic assumption, we will consider later.

Table 8.1

Unit	Total utility	Marginal utility
1	60	60
2	115	55
3	165	50
4	210	45
5	250	40
6	285	35
7	315	30
8	340	25

The table shows that as more of the product is obtained, so the consumer feels better off. However note what has been happening to the marginal utility. This has been falling. This reveals a fundamental assumption of consumer theory which is that the more one has of a particular product, the less satisfaction is gained from obtaining an extra unit. This is known as the law of diminishing marginal utility. If we were to graph the marginal utility curve we would obtain a diagram like Figure 8.1.

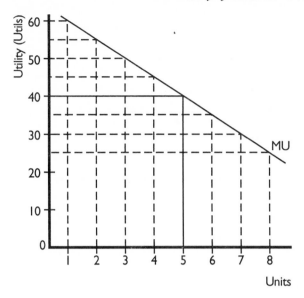

Figure 8.1 *Marginal utility schedule*

Suppose that the utils were expressed in money terms (or the utility of money was expressed in utils), and that £1 = 20 utils. This would allow us to predict how many items an individual consumer would purchase at any particular price. Suppose the product cost £2 (40 utils on our scale) . The consumer would be prepared to buy 5 units. This is because the 6th unit only gives 35 units of utility, but requires giving up 40 units in the form of money.

If the price of the product fell, the consumer might be prepared to buy the extra unit, and, so, more is demanded at a lower price. This is the basic relationship which we are trying to understand. This suggests that consumers will continue buying a commodity up to the point where the last unit purchased gives just as much satisfaction as the amount of money which must be spent to obtain it. Given the law of diminishing marginal utility, this implies that lower prices are necessary to persuade consumers to buy more of a product. The demand curve slopes downwards.

The Equi-Marginal principle

The above analysis suggests that consumers will spend their income on a product up to the point where the price equals the marginal utility. What happens if the consumer is dividing her income between several products, and it is not large enough to allow this point to be reached?

Given that the consumer is assumed to be trying to maximise her utility, she must allocate her income in such a way as to make it impossible to obtain more utility by switching money from one product to another. This means that the last unit of money spent on each product must yield exactly the same amount of utility, otherwise income will be switched from the product yielding less utility to the product yielding the most. This is known as the equi-marginal principle and will lead to the consumer maximising her utility when the following relationships hold:

$$\frac{MU_A}{P_A} = \frac{MU_B}{P_B} = \frac{MU_C}{P_C} = \frac{MU_D}{P_D} = \quad \cdots\cdots\cdots$$

where MU_A= marginal utility of A, and P_A is the price of A

Each of these terms represents the utility gained from the last unit of money spent on each item. Thus, if item A costs 50p and the last unit yields a marginal utility of 100 utils, then each penny spent on that last unit has yielded 2 utils. The maximisation of utility requires that this situation exists for all other products, because if it did not – if the last penny spent on B gave more than 2 utils – then extra pennies should be spent on B and not on A. (This assumes that products are infinitely divisible).

This analysis might appear a little far-fetched, but the logic is clear. When you enter a shop and are deciding how to allocate your income between various products you will be comparing their prices with the benefit that you feel you will derive from the product. If you are undecided between two which are of equal benefit (utility) you will buy the cheapest. To be encouraged to buy a product which is twice the price of another, you must be convinced that it yields at least twice as much utility. This is the type of behaviour seen above.

Suppose that the price of A fell. The ratios shown above would no longer be equal. The last penny spent on A now yields more utility than before. This will encourage the consumer to spend more pennies on A and less on other products. As the demand for A increases, the marginal utility of A falls, until the ratio is once again equal to that of the other products. This suggests that a fall in the price of A will increase the demand for A. The demand curve slopes downwards.

Rationality and advertising

A consumer is said to be rational if the actions she takes are designed to permit her to achieve her objective. The consumer's objective is assumed to be to maximise her utility (satisfaction). A rational consumer will therefore always act in a fashion consistent with the behaviour shown in the section The Equi-Marginal Principle above, since this will lead to her receiving the maximum amount of utility.

How will advertising affect the situation? Advertising is designed to persuade consumers to buy one product instead of another. The advertiser is attempting to influence the marginal utility which consumers perceive as being derived from the product. If the advertising is successful, the consumer will experience an increase in the marginal utility derived from buying the product. In order to maximise utility the consumer will buy more of this product and less of another. The consumer is still acting rationally, in the belief that her utility will increase by purchasing more of the advertised product. Whether this belief is realised or not is irrelevant to the idea of rationality.

Income and substitution effects

Any fall in price will influence the consumer in two ways. First, a fall in price will affect the consumer because she will always have an incentive to buy more of a product whose price has fallen in preference to other products since it now represents better value in that more utility can be gained by spending an extra unit of money on the product. This is what the exercise in the section The Equi-Marginal Principle above, is demonstrating. This is known as the substitution effect, and the substitution effect will always encourage a consumer to buy more of a product as its price falls. Marginal utility analysis concentrates on this effect.

Secondly, the price fall has the effect of increasing the purchasing power of the consumer. If she bought the same quantities as before, then there will be some money left over. This is known as the income effect, and one would normally expect this increase in income to increase the demand for all goods including the one whose price has fallen. Thus, the income effect will normally encourage more of a product to be bought as its price falls.

There is an exception to this with inferior goods. As we saw in Chapter Three, if people buy a good because it is all they can afford, but would prefer to buy a better product, the increase in income represented by the fall in price may encourage the consumer to buy more of a superior product and so may reduce the amount demanded. This effect cannot be analysed via marginal utility analysis.

These two effects together determine the price effect. For normal goods they both work in favour of the product whose price has fallen. Hence, a fall in price increases demand. The demand curve slopes downwards. If the product is an inferior good, the demand curve will still slope downwards if the substitution effect is more powerful than the income effect. If the product is an inferior good and the income effect is greater than the substitution effect, a fall in price will reduce demand. This would yield an upward sloping demand curve. The product would be a Giffen good.

Indifference curves

One problem with marginal utility analysis is that it only refers to the substitution effect of a price change. It cannot analyse income effects.

Indifference curve analysis allows this to be done.

Indifference curves represent different combinations of goods available to a consumer yielding the same levels of total satisfaction. An indifference curve shows combinations of two products between which the consumer is indifferent, or which yield the same level of utility. Table 8.2 represents different combinations of two goods A and B which yield the same level of satisfaction to the consumer.

Table 8.2 *Combinations of goods giving equal utility*

Good A	Good B
35 units	5 units
20 units	10 units
10 units	20 units
5 units	35 units

Table 8.2 suggests that the consumer will achieve a certain level of utility from receiving 35 units of A and 5 units of B. As the consumer obtains less of A, to keep her utility constant she will need to receive more of B. The figures in Table 8.2 suggest that losing 15 units of A (from 35 to 20 units) will just be compensated for by receiving 5 extra units of B, (from 5 to 10 units) This is shown in Figure 8.2. This gives a marginal rate of substitution of A for B of 3:1 (at this point).

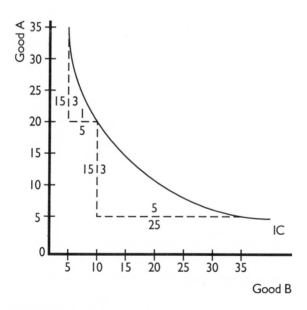

Figure 8.2 *An indifference curve*

As the consumer obtains less of good A she will need more of B to compensate for giving up another 15 units. This is known as showing a falling marginal rate of substitution. In Table 8.2 she needs 25 units of B to compensate for losing 15 extra units of A when her initial consumption of A is now only 20 units. Thus, to reduce from 20 to 5 requires an increase in B from 10 to 35. The marginal rate of substitution has fallen to 3:5. Thus, the indifference curve will slope downwards and be convex to the origin. This is known as showing a diminishing marginal rate of substitution. In order to be compensated for giving up an extra unit of a product which is scarce, the consumer needs to receive a larger gain in terms of the other product which is more plentiful.

Figure 8.2 represents combinations of A and B which yield a particular level of utility. Different levels of utility will be received by other combinations. For example, if the consumer received more of both products, she must be experiencing a higher level of utility. Thus the consumer is faced with an indifference map showing combinations of the two goods yielding various levels of utility. This is shown in Figure 8.3. The further the indifference curve is away from the origin, the higher the level of utility which it represents, since it represents larger combinations of the two goods. Thus, IC_2 shows combinations yielding a particular level of utility, that level being greater than the level shown by IC_1.

If we assume that the consumer is interested in maximising her utility, the consumer will try and achieve the highest level of utility possible, given her income and the prices of the two goods.

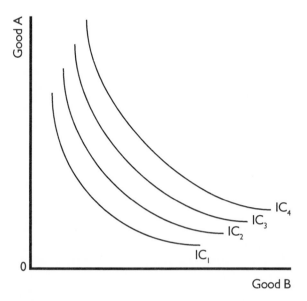

Figure 8.3 *Indifference curves*

The income constraint budget line

The ability of the consumer to purchase the two products depends on two factors: the consumer's income and the prices of the two goods. Suppose that the income of the consumer is £40 and that the price of good A is £1, and the price of good B is £2. Table 8.3 shows some of the possible combinations of A and B which the consumer could buy.

Table 8.3 Possible combinations of A and B affordable; the budget line

Good A	Good B
40 units	0 units
30 units	5 units
20 units	10 units
10 units	15 units
0 units	20 units

If this data is shown graphically, we obtain the consumer's budget line, shown in Figure 8.4.

Thus when all income is spent on B, the consumer can buy 20 units. If all income (£40) is spent on A, 40 units can be bought. The budget line shows all combinations of A and B which the consumer could purchase, e.g. 20 units of A and 10 units of B. The consumer will choose that combination which yields the highest level of utility. To identify this point we need to superimpose the budget line on the indifference curve map.

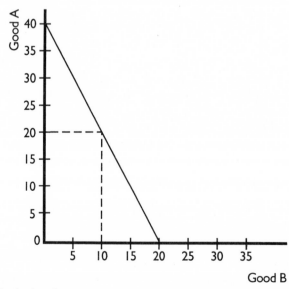

Figure 8.4 The budget line

Consumer equilibrium

Figure 8.5 shows the equilibrium for this hypothetical consumer. The line AB represents the original budget line Point E is the combination of the two goods, which the consumer can afford, which will allow her to reach the highest indifference curve IC2. The consumer is faced with an indifference curve map which shows an infinite number of indifference curves each one representing a different level of utility. In Figure 8.5 only three indifference curves are drawn. Thus, IC2 shows combinations yielding a higher level of utility than IC1, and IC3 higher than IC2

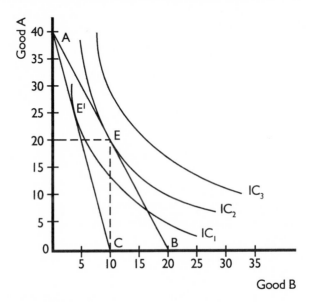

Figure 8.5 *Consumer equilibrium*

This suggests that the maximum amount of utility is obtained when the consumer buys 20 units of A and 10 units of B. Consumer equilibrium is always where the consumer's budget line is tangential to an indifference curve, since this must represent the highest indifference curve it is possible to reach. Thus in Figure 8.5 it is impossible to achieve the level of satisfaction shown by IC3, but it is just possible to reach IC2.

Price changes and consumer equilibrium

If the price of good B were to increase, this would alter the position shown in Figure 8.5. The possible combinations of A and B which could be bought would alter. If all the income were spent on B, the consumer would not be able to buy 20 units. Suppose that the price of B rose to £4. If all the income were spent on B, the consumer could now only buy 10 units. If all the income were spent on A, the consumer could still buy 40 units. Hence the budget line pivots to position AC shown in Figure 8.5. The new equilibrium for the consumer is at point E′, suggesting that the increase in the price of B has led to less of B being bought, and more of A being bought.

The slope of the budget line represents the relative prices of the two goods A and B. Thus in Figure 8.4 the slope is given as 40/20, that is, the price of A is half that of B. If the relative prices alter, so will the slope of the budget line. Thus, when, in Figure 8.5 the price of B rises, the slope of the budget line increases to 40/10.

Income changes and consumer equilibrium

A reduction in income will prevent the same quantities of both goods being bought. Since relative prices have not changed, the budget line has the same gradient, but now shows less of both goods being affordable. Thus the budget line will shift inwards.

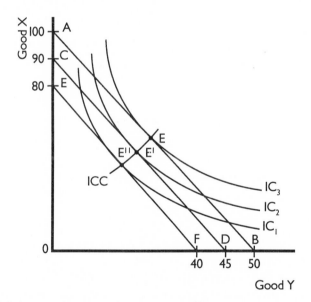

Figure 8.6 *Income changes and consumer equilibrium*

Suppose income is £100 and Good X costs £1, and Y costs £2. The consumer can buy 100 units of X and no Y, or 50 units of Y and no X. The budget line is shown as the line AB. Equilibrium is at E. If income falls to £90, the budget line will shift to CD, showing that 90 of X (and no Y) or 45 of Y (and no X), could be bought. The new equilibrium will be at point E′, which suggests that a fall in income has led to less of both goods being purchased. This would suggest that both goods are normal goods.

As household income changes, parallel shifts in the budget line occur, and for each level of income there will be an equilibrium point at which each budget line is tangent to an indifference curve. This means we can trace out the impact of successive changes in income on the demand for products. This is shown in Figure 8.6, where changes in income are represented by the three budget lines. If the equilibrium points are joined together, this yields an income consumption curve (ICC). Figure 8.6 shows two normal goods, since increases in income cause the demand for both to increase.

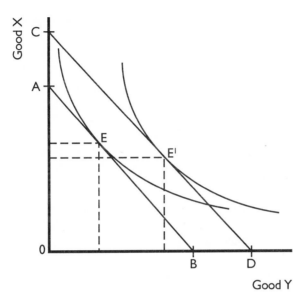

Figure 8.7 *An inferior good*

The original income gives a budget line AB and equilibrium at E. The increase in income moves the budget line to CD and a new equilibrium at E'.

Figure 8.7 illustrates conversely, an ICC for an inferior good. Increases in income cause the demand for good X to fall, and Y to rise. Good X must therefore be an inferior good while Y is a normal good.

Income and substitution effects

We can use indifference curve analysis to show that the reaction to a change in price is made up of two effects; the income and substitution effects. Suppose that in Figure 8.8, the consumer is initially in equilibrium at point E and that the price of good B increases. The budget line swings to position AC. The consumer moves to point E'. We know that the

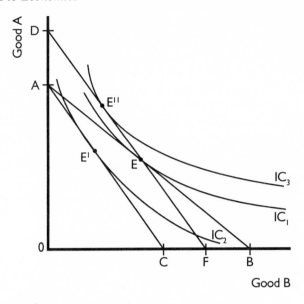

Figure 8.8 *Income and substitution effects of a price change*

consumer has reacted to two effects. The increase in the price of B has made A more attractive (the substitution effect) and at the same time the consumer's purchasing power has fallen, so long as some B is consumed (the income effect). We can attempt to isolate these two effects.

Suppose that the consumer's income was increased until she could purchase exactly the same combination of goods at point E, but at the new prices shown by the slope of AC. This yields the hypothetical budget line DF. This means that the reduction in income has been compensated for, and, if the consumer buys any combination other than the one shown by point E, she must be reacting solely to the change in prices. Thus any movement from E must now be because of the substitution effect alone, since the reduction in purchasing power has been overcome.

We can see from Figure 8.8 that the consumer would not stay at point E. This is because it is possible to rise onto a higher indifference curve at point E". This must be the case since equilibrium requires that the budget line is tangent to an indifference curve. Since the budget line now has a steeper slope it cannot be a tangent to IC_1 at point E. The movement from E to E" must be because of the substitution effect and the movement from E" to E' must be the income effect.

The substitution effect has led to more of A being bought and less of B. This is the expected result. The substitution effect always encourages a consumer to buy more of the product whose price has fallen. The income effect (movement from E" to E') shows that less of both goods are bought. Hence both these goods are normal goods.

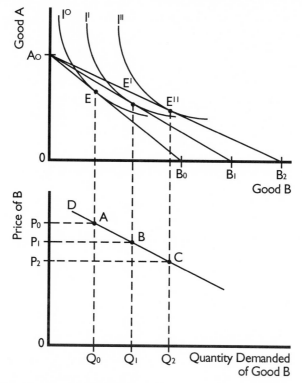

Figure 8.9 *Deriving the demand curve*

The demand curve

Indifference curve analysis also allows a demand curve to be derived. Again consider two goods A and B. The price of A is held constant, while the price of B is allowed to fall. This is illustrated by the upper segment of Figure 8.9, where the price of good B falls, producing three equilibrium points, E, E' and E'', with more of good B consumed as its price falls. The falling price swings the budget line from B_0 to B_1 to B_2. In the lower segment of the figure the quantity demanded of good B is related to its price. By joining the corresponding intersections A, B and C, we can derive the downward sloping demand curve for B. Indifference curve analysis thus allows a demand curve to be obtained, and economists use this form of analysis to describe the behaviour of economic agents when they are faced with factors which affect the price or income possibilities.

Consumer surplus

When consumers purchase a given quantity of a product at a particular price, they will obtain some units of the product at a price below what they would have been prepared to pay. This excess is known as consumer

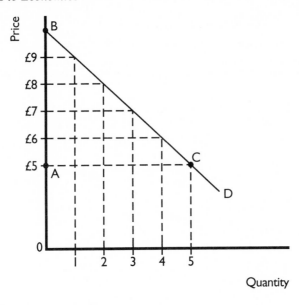

Figure 8.10 *Consumer surplus*

surplus. Consider the demand curve shown in Figure 8.10. At the price of £5, consumers are prepared to buy five units. The demand curve suggests that the first unit of the product is so important to the consumer that she would be prepared to pay £9 to buy it. The first unit must therefore confer at least £9 worth of benefit to the consumer. Similarly, for the second unit, she would be prepared to pay £8, and so on. Thus the consumer is obtaining benefit to the value of £9 + £8 + £7 + £6 + £5 = £35 from the five units she is buying. The consumer is only paying £25 and is thus receiving a surplus of £10. In Figure 8.10, this area is shown as the triangle ABC.

This is an important proposition. Whenever consumers buy more than one unit of a product at a given price, it is inevitable that some consumers are obtaining the product at a price below the maximum that they would be prepared to pay. The size of the consumer surplus depends primarily upon the price elasticity of demand for the product.

Multiple Choice Questions

1. If marginal utility diminishes as more of a product is purchased, a consumer will be in equilibrium when:

   A   the last unit of X purchased gives the same utility as the last unit of Y
   B   the total amount of money spent on each product is the same
   C   each penny spent on X gives the same utility as each penny spent on Y
   D   the last penny spent on each product gives the same utility
   E   the last penny spent on each product gives zero utility

2. Diminishing marginal utility implies that:
   A extra units of a product give more utility than previous units
   B total utility declines as more of a product is bought
   C as more of a product is bought, additional units give less and less utility
   D extra units of a product reduce total utility
   E in equilibrium consumers will obtain zero utility from an extra unit of the product

3. A consumer is faced with a situation where, having spent all his income on the two goods, the ratio of price to marginal utility for good X is 2:1 and the ratio of price to marginal utility for good Y is 3:1. In order to increase total utility the consumer could:
   A buy more of X and less of Y
   B buy more of Y and less of X
   C buy less of Y and X
   D buy less of X
   E buy more of both

4. In the indifference curve diagram below a price change has shifted the budget line from AB to AC. The consumer equilibrium has moved from point D to point E. The diagram suggests that:
   A the price of good X has risen
   B the quantity bought of good X has increased
   C good X is an inferior good
   D good Y is an inferior good
   E good X is a normal good

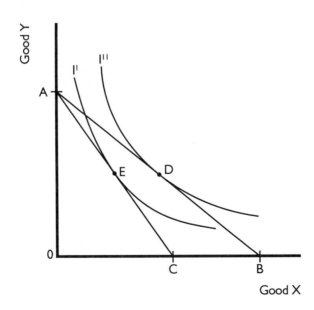

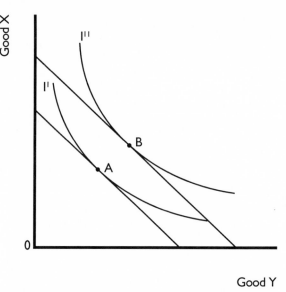

5. Consider the indifference curve diagram. The change in the equilibrium
    from point A to point B indicates:

    A   the price of good X falling by 10% and the price of good Y rising
    B   the consumer's income falling
    C   the price of good X and good Y falling by 20%
    D   good X being an inferior good
    E   the consumer's welfare having fallen

Chapter Nine

Costs of Production

Key concepts

- ❏ The behaviour of costs of production in the long and the short run, as output varies
- ❏ The shape of average, marginal and total cost curves

Key words

Long run, short run, the law of diminishing returns
Fixed costs, variable costs, total costs, average costs, marginal costs. Normal profit. Economies of scale

Supply

We saw in Chapter Four that the supply curve is based on the assumption that firms are interested in maximising profits. The theory of supply analyses this process in more detail and permits the supply curve to be obtained. The output which a firm is prepared to put on the market will depend upon two major factors. The behaviour of costs of production – how much it costs to produce an item – and the amount of revenue which the firm receives from selling that item. In order to understand the behaviour of firms we need to examine the behaviour of costs and revenue. This chapter will examine the behaviour of costs of production as firms make their output decisions.

The long run and the short run

It is convenient to define two time periods in which firms have to make their output decisions.

The short run is defined as that period of time in which at least one factor of production is fixed. This implies that the firm is faced with some sort of constraint in its output decisions, such as a fixed factory size, or a fixed quantity of machinery.

The long run is that period of time in which all factors of production can be varied and therefore the firm can alter everything. There will not be any capacity constraints.

Cost of production in the short run

Fixed costs (FC) refer to the costs of those factors of production which cannot be altered. They remain constant regardless of the level of output. Examples of fixed costs (FC) include rent, business rates, and interest on debts. The reason these are known as fixed costs is not that they can never change, but that they do not vary with output.

One ingredient in fixed costs is a concept known as Normal Profit. This refers to the amount of profit which a firm must make in order to make it attractive for the firm to remain in business. In the same way that a labourer must be paid a certain sum to encourage him to work, the entrepreneur must earn a certain sum if the firm is to continue. This sum is known as normal profit and is included as a cost to the firm. The size of normal profit will depend upon how much an entrepreneur can earn in his next best occupation:

Variable costs (VC) are costs which do vary with output. Examples of such costs include raw materials, power, and wages. (How variable labour costs are, depends on the difficulty of altering the numbers employed by the firm).

Total costs are the sum of fixed and variable costs:

$$TC = FC + VC.$$

These costs are shown in Figure 9.1. Note that the Total Cost is the vertical sum of the Fixed and Variable Costs. When output is zero, the firm is still faced with fixed costs, shown as OC is Figure 9.1. The slope of the total cost curve is explained in the section, The Law of Diminishing Returns, below.

Average costs are the costs per unit. This is obtained by dividing the total cost figure by the relevant level of output.

Average fixed cost is total fixed cost divided by output $AFC = FC/Q$. Thus, if fixed costs are £1000 and output is 50 units, the average fixed cost is £20.

Average variable cost is total variable cost divided by output: $AVC = VC/Q$

Average total cost is total cost divided by output: $ATC = TC/Q$ and average total cost is the sum of average fixed and average variable cost: $ATC = AFC + AVC$.

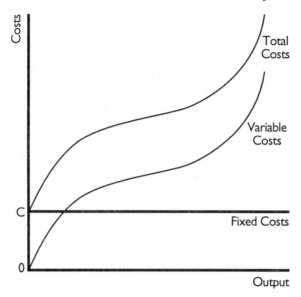

Figure 9.1 *The total cost curve*

Figure 9.2 illustrates these average cost curves. Because FC is constant, as output increases AFC declines. Average variable cost is normally shown as falling at first, but then eventually rising, yielding a U-shaped curve. This is because of an economic proposition known as the law of diminishing returns.

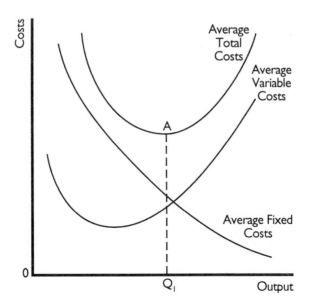

Figure 9.2 *Average cost curves*

The law of diminishing returns

This states that as more of a variable factor is applied to a fixed factor, eventually the returns to the variable factor will fall. This means that when a firm attempts to increase output, in the short run it can only achieve this by applying more of its variable factors (labour perhaps), to its fixed factors (number of machines, a fixed factory size).

Eventually capacity constraints are bound to make it very difficult to squeeze more output out of these fixed resources. This means that eventually the cost of employing the extra variable factors will rise faster than the extra output which these resources are capable of producing. Hence average variable costs will start to rise as costs rise faster than output. This yields the average cost curves shown in Figure 9.2. Eventually the rising AVC more than compensates for the falling AFC and so the ATC curve is also U-shaped. This implies that after a certain point, costs start to rise faster than output. The total cost curve thus becomes steeper, which explains the slope of the total cost curve in Figure 9.1.

The optimum output is sometimes identified as the output which can be produced most efficiently, or at least cost. This is the output where the ATC is at a minimum, at the lowest point on the ATC curve, shown as Q_1.

Marginal costs

Marginal cost is another aspect of costs which plays an important role in economics. Marginal cost refers to the cost of producing one extra unit. Given what we have seen concerning the law of diminishing returns it is not surprising that the cost of producing extra units start to rise after a certain point. Table 9.1 shows the cost of producing different output levels.

Table 9.1 *Costs (£) and output*

Q	FC	AFC	VC	AVC	TC	AC	MC
0	30		0		30		
1	30	30	15	15	45	45	15
2	30	15	24	12	54	27	9
3	30	10	30	10	60	20	6
4	30	7.5	38	9.5	68	17	8
5	30	6	50	10	80	16	12
6	30	5	72	12	102	17	22
7	30	4.5	110	15.7	140	20	38

Fixed costs are shown as always equal to £30. Variable costs rise with output, but display diminishing returns after the third unit is produced. Marginal cost is shown as the increase in total cost when output increases by one unit. The marginal and average cost curves are plotted in Figure 9.3.

When plotting the marginal cost curve it is important to realise that the marginal cost is the cost associated with a change in output, and, so, in Table 9.1, the cost of moving from one unit of output to the second unit is shown as £9. This means that in Figure 9.3 the marginal cost of £9 is plotted against the output level 1.5, since this is the mid-point between unit one and two. Similarly the marginal cost is plotted against the mid-point values for all other output levels.

There is an important mathematical relationship between the average and the marginal cost curves. When the average cost is falling, it is being dragged down by the marginal cost being below the average. When the average is rising it is because the marginal is pulling it up.

This can be explained by using the analogy of marks in an exam. If your average is 60%, and you then take another exam, if the marks in this next exam (the marginal exam) is above your average, your average will rise. If your average falls, this must be because your marginal exam result was below your average. If the average is falling, the marginal must be below the average. If the average is rising, the marginal must be above the average. Thus, both the average and marginal cost curves are depicted as falling and then rising (because of diminishing returns), with the marginal cost passing through the lowest point of both the average variable cost curve, and the average total cost curve.

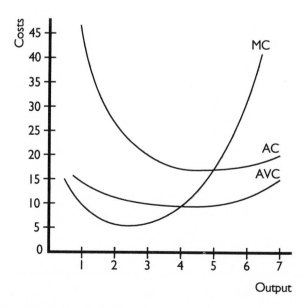

Figure 9.3 *Marginal and average costs*

The long run

The cost curves we have seen so far are applicable to firms operating in the short run when some factor of production is fixed and the firm is thus faced with some constraint on its output. This gives rise to the idea of diminishing returns. In the long run the firm is able to vary all its factors of production to avoid any constraints on its activity. The idea is that in the long run a firm will be able to build a larger factory, install more machines and so overcome the capacity constraints. Suppose that the firm is currently operating at an output of Q^1 in Figure 9.4, and is faced with the short run average cost curve shown as $SRAC^1$ If the firm now wished to expand output to Q^2, the firm would be forced to operate at a higher average cost, because of the law of diminishing returns, given that in the short run it is faced with some capacity constraints.

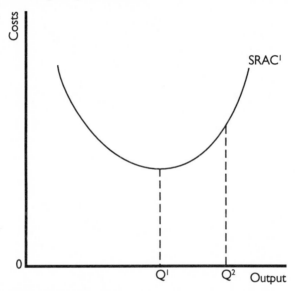

Figure 9.4 *Average costs and output*

It might make more sense for the firm to build a larger scale plant, which, when it was operating most efficiently, was capable of producing Q^2. The key question to answer is, will this larger scale plant operate at the same level of efficiency as the smaller one, or will it be more, or less efficient?

Economies of scale

In the long run the firm can alter its scale of production. Suppose that the firm is faced with the position shown in Figure 9.4 and wishes to build a plant which can produce Q^2 as efficiently as possible. This new plant will have a short run cost curve associated with it, shown as $SRAC^2$ in Figure 9.5.

This new plant is shown as being able to produce more cheaply than the original plant. This is because larger scale organisations are usually seen as having cost advantages which are not available to smaller firms. These advantages are referred to as economies of scale. As the scale of the firm increases even further, additional economies of scale are enjoyed and so the SRAC curves continue to be lower than the previous ones.

Eventually there must come a point where all the advantages of size have been exhausted, and constant returns to scale occur, shown by the SRAC curves beyond Q^4 in Figure 9.5. As size increases even further, it is possible that there may come a point where the firm starts to become less efficient because of its size. This is normally explained in terms of some sort of loss of managerial control. This is shown beyond output Q^6.

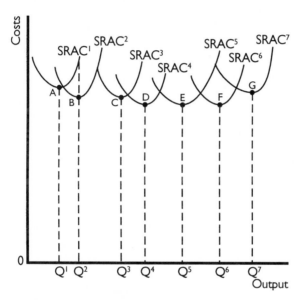

Figure 9.5 *Average cost in the long run*

Economies of scale can occur for a variety of reasons:

Technical economies: Larger firms have a greater scope to practice division of labour, and specialisation can be carried out to a higher degree. This facilitates the introduction of more machinery and specialised equipment, which raises productivity.

Managerial economies: Larger firms can employ more specialised management, leading to a higher level of efficiency

Purchasing economies: Larger firms can buy their raw materials in bulk and in return take advantage of larger discounts from suppliers.

Marketing economies: Larger firms can make more effective use of their sales force. Administrative costs do not rise in proportion with order size and so costs per item are smaller. Larger firms can make more use of effective advertising.

Financial economies: Larger firms may be able to obtain finance at more favourable rates than smaller firms.

Risk-bearing economies: Larger organisations may be able to diversify and so avoid some possible risks.

Indivisibles: Often firms must employ some minimum amount of a certain factor of production regardless of the level of output. If output doubles, it may not be necessary to double the number of telephones or the number of receptionists. Hence, costs per unit fall.

Multiples: A large output may be necessary to allow machines which have different capacities to operate together at their maximum levels.

The advantages discussed are examples of internal economies of scale, which arise from an increase in the scale of operation of a particular firm.

Long-run average costs

Given the possible cost curves associated with various output levels shown in Figure 9.5, the firm is faced in the long run with all the possibilities shown. If the firm wished to change output to Q^4, it would make sense to build the scale of plant having the cost curves shown as $SRAC^4$. Similarly, output Q^5 requires the scale shown by $SRAC^5$. In the long run the firm has many possible cost output combinations open to it. The lowest possible cost of producing the various outputs will be given by the locus of the points A, B, C, etc. This is often referred to as the envelope curve and is shown in Figure 9.6.

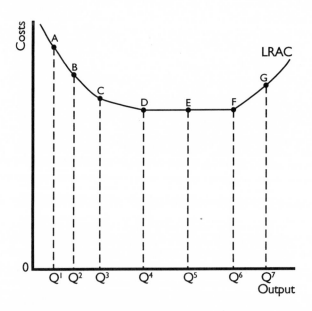

Figure 9.6 Long run average cost curve

This envelope curve is the long run average cost curve facing the firm, since it shows the minimum cost associated with producing various output levels, when the firm is able to vary all its factors of production. This is what is meant by changing the scale of operations.

The long run average cost curve is U-shaped, just like the short run cost curve, but for different reasons. The short run curve is U-shaped because of diminishing returns, caused by having some factors of production fixed. The long run curve is U-shaped because of economies and diseconomies of scale.

Summary

- [ ] The short run is that period of time when at least one factor of production is fixed.
- [ ] The long run is that period of time in which all factors of production are variable.
- [ ] Fixed costs do not vary with output.
- [ ] Normal profit is the return which the firm must make to keep it in business, and is included as a cost of production.
- [ ] In the short run, the behaviour of costs is governed by the law of diminishing returns.
- [ ] Short run average cost curves are U-shaped.
- [ ] Short run marginal cost curves are U-shaped and pass through the lowest point of the average cost curve.
- [ ] In the long run, the behaviour of costs is governed by the existence of economies or diseconomies of scale.
- [ ] Long run cost curves are U-shaped if economies and diseconomies of scale exist.
- [ ] The cost curves described in this chapter apply to all firms, regardless of the type of competition which they face.

Multiple Choice Questions

1. The short run is defined as:
    A   that period of time in which all factors of production are fixed
    C   that period of time in which all factors of production are variable
    C   that period of time in which at least one factor of production is fixed
    D   that period of time in which all costs are variable
    E   that period of time in which fixed costs decline with output

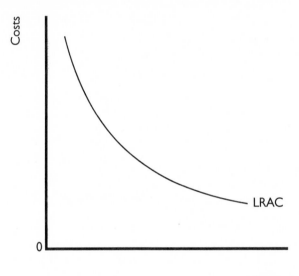

2. Consider the long run average cost curve shown in the diagram. This illustrates:
    A   the law of diminishing returns
    B   fixed costs falling as output increases
    C   diseconomies of scale
    D   falling marginal costs
    E   economies of scale

3. The fixed costs faced by a firm are £10 000 per annum. At a certain level of output, average total cost is £5 and average variable costs are £3. What is the level of output which the firm is producing?
    A   10 000
    B   2000
    C   20 000
    D   5000
    E   3333

4. When average variable costs are rising, the marginal cost must be:

A also rising
B less than average variable cost
C more than average fixed cost
D equal to average variable cost
E more than average variable cost

5. Consider the information in the table below, which shows the amount of capital and labour required to produce particular levels of output by a firm operating in the short run.

Output	Capital employed	Labour employed
100	100	100
200	210	190
300	330	270
400	460	340
500	600	400

The figures indicate:

A increasing returns to capital and labour
B constant returns to both labour and capital
C increasing returns to labour and decreasing returns to capital
D decreasing returns to labour and increasing returns to capital
E economies of scale

Theory of the Firm

Market structures

Producers may operate in a variety of different competitive environments. Economists usually distinguish between the following situations:

Perfect Competition: This refers to a situation where competition is as complete as possible. There will be many firms, all producing identical products. This implies that no one firm can have any sort of control over the market for the product.

Monopolistic Competition: This is a situation where there are many firms producing similar products, but there is a degree of product differentiation. Thus there is some competition, but firms do have some control over their market. Many branded goods fall into this category (petrol, chocolate bars).

Oligopoly: This is referred to as competition among the few. It is characterised by a few large firms dominating the market for a particular product.
The brewing industry is often quoted as an example. The significant factor
about these markets is that the firms all recognise that they are inter-
dependent. A decision by one is likely to bring about a reaction.
Duopoly: This is a situation where two firms control a market.
Monopoly: A situation where one firm provides the total output for a
market.

Each of these different market structures will constrain and influence the
behaviour of firms within the market. The theory of the firm is the title
given to that area of economics which investigates this behaviour.

The goal of firms

In economics all firms are assumed to be interested in maximising profits.
This is the key assumption which allows economists to analyse how firms
will react to various events. It is always assumed that firms will react in the
way which is most profitable. In terms of the output decisions of firms,
they will produce up to the point where it becomes unprofitable for any
more to be produced. In order to identify this position it is necessary to
investigate what determines profits and how this is affected by output
decisions.

Profit

As we saw in Chapter Nine, normal profit is included in the costs of the
firm. Profits in excess of normal profit are known as 'super normal profits'
and will be the difference between costs of production and revenue. We
saw in Chapter Nine that in the short run the total cost curve of a firm has
the distinctive shape shown in Figure 10.1 (TC).

After a certain point costs start to rise faster than output because of the
law of diminishing returns (perhaps best thought of as bottlenecks in
production). Suppose that the firm could sell all of its output at a constant
price. Total revenue would simply be output multiplied by the price:

$TR = P \times Q$

and this would be represented on the graph as a straight line rising with
output.

We can see from Figure 10.1 on the next page that profits will be
maximised at the point where the vertical gap between TR and TC is
greatest. This is at an output level of OX. If the price of the product were
to rise, the TR line would become steeper and the profit maximising output
would increase. This diagram is only applicable to a situation where
increased output is sold at a constant price.

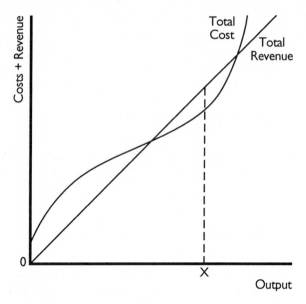

Figure 10.1 *Total cost, total revenue, profit*

In order to allow us to see this profit maximising output more clearly it is usual to present the information in Figure 10.1 in a slightly different manner. Instead of using total cost and total revenue curves, it is useful to use average and marginal concepts.

Average and marginal costs

We saw in Chapter Nine that short run average and marginal cost curves are U-shaped (because of the law of diminishing returns) and that long run cost curves are U-shaped because of the presence of economies and diseconomies of scale.

Average and marginal revenue

Average revenue is simply total revenue divided by output. Thus, if five items are sold and they yield a total revenue of £20, the average revenue is £4 per item. This must also have been the price at which the five were sold. Thus, if items are all sold at a single price, the average revenue is simply the price at which they are sold. In diagrammatical terms, the average revenue curve is the demand curve for the product, since this also shows the price at which certain outputs can be sold. Consider Figure 10.2, which is on the next page.

The demand curve shows that at a price of £4 the demand for the product is five units. Thus if the firm faced by this demand curve is producing five

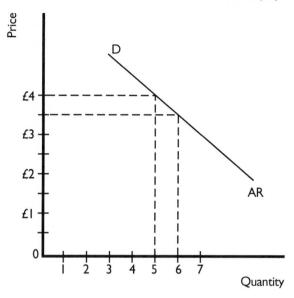

Figure 10.2 *The demand curve and average revenue*

units, the maximum price that it could charge would be £4. Thus the maximum amount of revenue it could obtain would be £20. In other words at an output of five units, total revenue would be £20. Average revenue would be £4 per unit, which is in fact the price at which they are sold. If output rose to six units, the demand curve suggests that the price would have to fall to £3.50 in order to sell the output. Hence total revenue would be £21, and average revenue would be £3.50 per unit sold. The demand curve is the average revenue curve since it shows the price at which the various levels of outputs can be sold.

If firms are interested in maximising profits, they must continually decide whether it is worthwhile producing extra units of their product or whether they should reduce output. In economists jargon, they are always making decisions at the margin. The production of a unit of a product is only profitable if that unit adds more to revenue than it adds to costs.

We have already seen that the addition to total cost is known as the marginal cost of an item. The addition to total revenue which accrues from producing (and selling) an extra unit is known as marginal revenue. If extra units of the product can be sold at a constant price, then the marginal revenue is simply the price. This, however, is not the usual case.

Consider the demand curve shown in Figure 10.2. In order to sell the extra output the price had to fall from £4 to £3.50. Thus the extra unit sold caused total revenue to only rise by £1. The extra unit only produced £1 extra revenue. This is known as the marginal revenue of producing an extra unit. Marginal revenue is the addition to total revenue from producing (selling) one extra unit.

The mathematical relationship between average and marginal concepts is the same for revenue as it was for costs. If the average revenue is falling (the demand curve sloping downwards) the marginal revenue must be less than the average. This is shown in Figure 10.3.

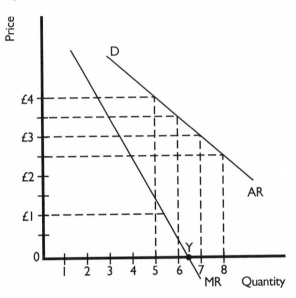

Figure 10.3 *Average and marginal revenue curves*

An output level of six has a marginal revenue of £1, but an average revenue of £3.50 The increase in output from five to six has increased revenue by £1 and so the sixth unit has a marginal revenue of £1. To be strictly accurate the £1 arises from the movement from five to six and so should be shown plotted against the mid point 5.5. This is the same idea that we saw when plotted the marginal cost curve in Chapter Nine. A fall in price to £3 would allow sales to rise to seven units. Total revenues would stay at £21 and so marginal revenue would be zero. This is plotted against the point 6.5.

Marginal revenue and elasticity of demand

In the example above, a fall in the price of the product from £4 to £3.50 led to the demand rising from five to six units. We can calculate what price elasticity of demand that represents. The percentage change in price is 12.5 and the percentage change in demand is 20. This yields a price elasticity of demand of 1.6. Since this value is greater than one, this indicates that demand is elastic.

As we saw in Chapter Six, when demand is elastic, a fall in price causes the total amount of money spent on the product to rise. From the point of view of the producer total revenue will rise . Hence marginal revenue is positive. This gives us an important result. If marginal revenue is positive, the price elasticity of demand must be greater than one.

In Figure 10.3 the marginal revenue is positive up to the output level OY. Beyond this point marginal revenue becomes negative. If the price falls to £3 and the quantity sold rises to 7. Total revenue stays at £21. There has been no increase in total revenue and so elasticity must be equal to one for the price movement from £3.50 to £3. Calculating the elasticity yields a value of 1.17 for this movement.

As we saw in Chapter Six elasticity over a range of the demand curve is more accurately measured by taking an average of the two figures obtained by calculating elasticities for the movement in prices in both directions. (This is connected with the idea of the marginal revenue being plotted against the mid point.) The value for the price change from £3 to £3.50 is 0.86. The average value is therefore 1.03. Thus, at the point where marginal revenue is zero, the price elasticity of demand is equal to one.

Beyond OY marginal revenue is negative. This means a further fall in price reduces total revenue. Suppose the price fell to £2.50 and demand rose from seven to eight. Total revenue has now fallen to £20. Price elasticity of demand must be less than one. My calculator suggests that it will be somewhere between 0.86 and 0.625. This is an important result. Given a straight line demand curve, elasticity falls as we move down the curve, and at some point demand becomes inelastic. At the output where the marginal revenue curve cuts the bottom axis, price elasticity of demand is equal to one.

Profit maximisation

If producing an extra unit adds more to revenue than it does to costs, that unit is profitable to produce. In other words, if the marginal revenue exceeds the marginal cost that unit should be produced. If marginal revenue is less than marginal cost, the unit is making a loss and should not be produced. If units are profitable to produce, firms will produce units up to the point where marginal cost just equals marginal revenue. Thus profit maximisation occurs at the point where marginal cost equals marginal revenue. This is a fundamental proposition in economics. Firms always maximise profits by producing at the point where marginal cost equals marginal revenue.

Summary

❏ Economists categorise market structures in terms of the degree of competition.

❏ All firms are assumed to be attempting to maximise profits.

❏ Normal profit is the profit that the firm needs to make in order to keep it in business. It is thought of as a cost which must be covered, and, so, is included in total costs.

❏ Profit is the difference between total cost and total revenue.

❏ Average and marginal cost curves are U-shaped

❏ Average revenue is the price at which the output is sold.

❏ Marginal revenue is the addition to total revenue from producing one extra unit.

❏ Marginal revenue is related to price elasticity of demand: if marginal revenue is positive, demand is elastic. If marginal revenue is negative, demand is inelastic. If marginal revenue is zero, demand has unit elasticity.

❏ Profits will always be maximised when marginal revenue equals marginal cost.

Multiple Choice Questions

1. Marginal cost is defined as:
   A the revenue gained from producing one extra unit
   B the change in fixed costs associated with producing one extra unit
   C the change in variable costs associated with producing one extra unit
   D the cost which just makes it worthwhile to stay in business
   E an unimportant cost

2. Firms will always maximise profits when they operate at the output, where:
   A marginal revenue is zero
   B marginal cost equals average revenue
   C average cost equals marginal revenue
   D average cost equals average revenue
   E marginal cost equals marginal revenue

3. When the law of diminishing returns begins to operate, the total variable cost curve will:
   - **A** Fall at a decreasing rate
   - **B** Rise at a decreasing rate
   - **C** Rise at an increasing rate
   - **D** Fall at an increasing rate
   - **E** None of the above

4. Which of the following statements about the fixed costs of a firm are incorrect?
   - **A** as output increases average fixed costs fall
   - **B** as output increases fixed costs remain constant
   - **C** marginal fixed costs are zero
   - **D** fixed costs become variable in the long run
   - **E** none of the above

5. A firm agrees to spend £1 million on an advertising campaign. This must lead to an increase in the
   - **A** average fixed cost
   - **B** average revenue
   - **C** average variable cost
   - **D** marginal cost
   - **E** marginal revenue

Chapter Eleven

Perfect Competition

Key concepts

❑ The characteristics of perfect competition
❑ The nature of demand in perfect competition
❑ Conditions necessary for profit maximisation in perfect competition, in the long run and the short run
❑ The derivation of the firm's supply curve in perfect competition

Key words

Price taker. Perfectly elastic demand, shut down point, equilibrium of the firm
Super normal profits

Perfect competition defined

Perfect competition is defined as a situation where several conditions exist:

● **Freedom of entry and exit**: new firms can always enter the industry and existing firms can always leave.
● **Homogeneous product**: all firms produce an identical product.
● **Many buyers and sellers**: no one individual can influence the market.
● **Perfect communications**: everyone knows what is happening in all parts of the market.

Given these conditions, all firms must be price takers. They must accept the ruling market price, since any attempt to sell their product for a higher price than other firms are charging will result in the demand for their product disappearing.

Although it is difficult to think of a market which satisfies all the conditions set out above, there are circumstances in which the conditions are a good approximation. For example much of agriculture is characterised by many producers, producing identical produce, and farmers can always switch production into different crops. Thus, the market for carrots is highly, (perfectly?), competitive.

Try not to think of the analysis which follows as an accurate description of how firms and industries operate, but instead try and appreciate that the analysis attempts to explore what would happen if the competitive environment was perfect. We are attempting to discover the implications of competition, rather than offering a description of how particular industries behave. Occasionally we will refer to particular examples of behaviour to illustrate points we are making.

The demand curve for a firm in perfect competition

Since the firm is a price taker it is forced to accept the ruling market price. Thus the individual firm has no control over the price which it can charge for its product. The price is determined by the forces of demand and supply in the market. At this price any one firm can sell any output it wishes, since any one firm is an insignificant part of the total market. Thus a carrot farmer can always sell his output at whatever the market has determined as the market price. In diagrammatic terms this implies that the demand curve facing the firm is horizontal at the market price. Any attempt to charge a higher price will result in the demand falling to zero. This is shown in Figure 11.1, which is on the next page.

Since the firm can sell all its output at the same price, this means that the marginal revenue is also equal to this price. Thus if the price of carrots is 40p per kilo, any farmer can sell more carrots at this price. Hence he will receive 40p for every extra kilo which he produces. This is why the demand curve in Figure 11.1 is labelled price = MR. As we saw in Chapter Ten, the price is also identical with the average revenue and so the line is also labelled price = MR = AR. In order to identify the position where the firm would be maximising profits, we need to look at what is happening to costs of production and profitability.

Profit maximisation in the short run

In the short run, cost curves will be U-shaped because of the law of diminishing returns. Given the price, which has been determined in the market, firms will attempt to achieve the position of maximum profits. As

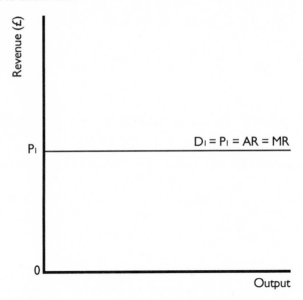

Figure 11.1 *The demand curve for a firm in perfect competition*

we saw in Chapter Ten, this is always at the point where marginal costs equal marginal revenue. Such a position is shown in Figure 11.2.

The price is shown as P. This gives an AR of P as shown by the horizontal demand curve. This means that the firm will receive P for every unit it produces. As we saw above, if all units can be sold at this price, including any extra which the firm produces, this is also the marginal

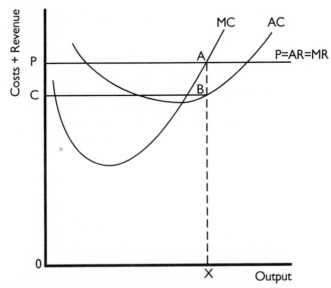

Figure 11.2 *Profit maximisation in perfect competition*

revenue. This obviously means that as long as the cost of producing extra units is less than P, it will be profitable to continue producing those units.

As soon as the cost of producing extra units (marginal cost) exceeds the extra revenue gained (marginal revenue), extra production becomes unprofitable. Hence, profits will be maximised at an output level of X units, at the point where marginal cost equals marginal revenue.

We can now examine the profit situation. Total revenue is given by: Price × Quantity Sold, which is represented by the area OPAX (OP × OX). Total costs are given by: Average Cost × Quantity Produced, which is represented by the area OCBX. Hence profits are represented by the area CPAB.

The situation depicted in Figure 11.2 is of a firm making profits. These are super normal profits, since as we saw in Chapter Nine, normal profit is considered to be a cost of production, and so is included in the average cost curve. This can only be a short run equilibrium because firms in perfect competition always experience freedom of entry and exit. This has implications for the ability of firms to earn profits in excess of the minimum needed to keep them in business (which is what is meant by normal profit).

Profit maximisation in the long run

In the long run, firms in perfect competition cannot earn more (or less) than normal profit. If firms do earn high profits, this will attract new firms into the market, and this will reduce the price of the product, and the profits of all firms in the industry. Figure 11.3 illustrates this process.

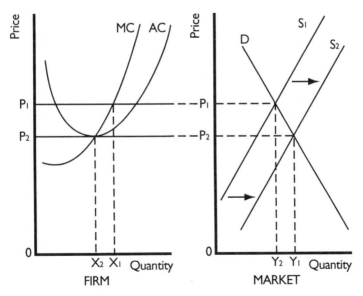

Figure 11.3 *Equilibrium in perfect competition*

In Figure 11.3 we show the position in both the firm and in the total market. Price is P_1. The individual firm's output is X_1 and the total output for the industry (made up of many firms) is Y_1. As we saw in the section on short run profit maximisation, the firm is making super normal profits. This will attract new firms into the industry and this will increase the total supply. The market supply curve will shift to the right, lowering the price. This process will continue until there is no longer any incentive for new firms to enter. This will occur when the price has fallen to P_2 and each firm will produce X_2. This is a very significant result.

Competition ensures that firms in perfect competition always operate where their average costs of production are at their lowest. This is what we referred to in Chapter Two as productive efficiency. A moments thought will demonstrate the common sense of this result. If there is a high degree of competition, firms will be forced to be efficient. Inefficient firms (those operating where their costs of production are higher than others), will be unable to survive. Thus, the long run equilibrium for a firm in perfect competition will be when it is producing at the lowest point of its average cost curve. This is also at the point where marginal cost equals marginal revenue.

This result can be illustrated as follows:

profit maximisation requires that MC = MR
normal profits require that AC = AR (total cost = total revenue)
in perfect competition AR = MR
thus in equilibrium MC = MR = AR = AC

The only point where this is satisfied is at the point where the AC and MC curves intersect, that is at average costs lowest point.

The above analysis suggests that in the long run firms in perfect competition cannot make super normal profits, (profits in excess of the normal level necessary for the firm to survive). We can also show that it is also impossible for the form to make losses in the long run, since this will cause some firms to leave the industry, which will raise the price and restore the long run equilibrium.

This point has important implications for allocative efficiency. If the demand for a product were to increase, in perfect competition, the price would rise. (The market demand curve would shift to the right.) This would enable firms in the industry to make super normal profits. These profits would attract new firms into the industry, which would drive the price back down. In the long run, the price would revert to its initial position, and all that would have happened is that output of the industry would have increased by an amount exactly equal to the increase in demand. This is a very powerful result.

Shut down point: making losses in the short run

Suppose that the market price of the product was less than the minimum level to which costs could be reduced. In Figure 11.4 this is shown by the AR = MR = Price being equal to P1. Profit maximisation (loss minimisation) will still be at the point where MC = MR. This is shown as being at output X1.

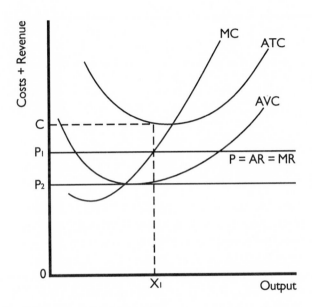

Figure 11.4 *Losses in perfect competition*

Now total revenue is equal to $OP_1 \times OX_1$ (price × quantity). At output X_1, average cost is C, and so total cost is $OC \times OX_1$ (average cost × quantity). Total costs are greater than total revenue and so the firm is making a loss. What will determine whether or not the firm continues in business? It all depends on whether the firm is able to cover its variable costs. If total revenue is sufficient to cover the variable costs of production, it is profitable for the firm to remain in business, **in the short run**.

Consider the case of a hotel which is considering whether or not to open for business during the winter months. Suppose that it has to pay £10 000 during this period in the form of rent, maintenance costs, business rates, caretaking. These are fixed costs and have to be paid even if the hotel does not open. If the hotel remains open for business it will incur extra cost, in the form of labour, raw materials, power, etc. Suppose that these extra costs (which are variable costs, since they depend upon the hotel operating) amount to £25 000. The revenue which the hotel will generate is estimated to be £30 000 during the winter period. Total costs are £35 000. Would you advise the hotel to open?

If the hotel opens for the winter period, it will lose £5000. If it closes for the winter period it will still have to pay £10 000 in fixed costs. Thus it will be £5000 better off by opening, even though it will still be making a loss. This illustrates the basic proposition; it will be profitable for a firm to remain in business, even if it is making a loss, if the firm is able to cover its variable costs. This means that the firm will continue to operate as long as the price of the product is higher than its average variable cost.

In Figure 11.4 we have shown three cost curves, average total cost, average variable cost and marginal cost. The minimum price which this firm could afford to keep operating at is P_2. If the price fell below this level, the firm would be unable to cover its variable costs and so would cease trading. If the revenue from operating the hotel fell below £25 000, it would not be sensible for the hotel to open.

Losses in the long run

In the long run firms must cover all their costs, both fixed and variable. This is consistent with what we saw in the previous section, since in the long run all costs become variable, and so the need to cover variable costs requires that all costs are covered. Thus in the long run some firms are forced to leave the industry, which will have the effect of shifting the industry supply curve to the left, thereby raising the price. This process will continue until surviving firms are once again just making normal profit. This will be back at the lowest point of the average cost curve. It is the freedom of firms to enter and leave the industry which produces the result that the long run position of firms in perfect competition occurs when they are just making normal profit.

This result shows the attraction of perfect competition: firms produce where their costs are minimised. This means that goods are produced as efficiently as possible. Secondly, the consumer is able to purchase the good at a price which is equal to its cost of production, both its average cost and its marginal cost. We shall see the significance of this result, in terms of allocative efficiency, in later chapters.

The supply curve in perfect competition

The supply curve shows the amount that will be put onto the market at various prices. The supply curve for the firm shows how much the firm will produce at various prices. At any particular price, the firm will produce up to the point where marginal cost just equals the price (since price is identical with marginal revenue). Thus the firm will produce where the

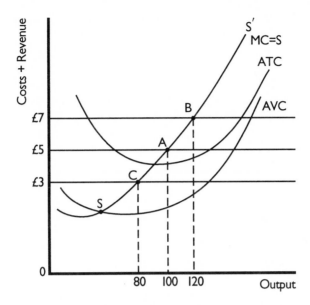

Figure 11.5 *The supply curve in perfect competition*

price line cuts the marginal cost curve. If the price rises, the new output will be where the new price cuts the marginal cost curve. Hence the marginal cost curve is the firms supply curve. This is shown in Figure 11.5.

At a price of £5 the firm will produce 100 units, shown by point A. If the price rises to £7 the output increases to 120 units, shown by point B. At a price of £3 the output falls to 80 units, shown by point C. The points showing the output produced at the various prices are being traced out by the marginal cost curve. This is another very significant result. In perfect competition the firm's marginal cost curve is also the firm's supply curve. It is important to remember that the firm will only produce at all if the price is above the level necessary to cover variable costs, thus it is only the portion of the marginal cost curve which is above average variable cost which constitutes the supply curve. Thus in Figure 11.5 it is the portion of the marginal cost curve marked as SS′ which represents the firm's supply curve.

Summary

❏ Perfect competition occurs when there are many firms, making an identical product, with freedom of entry and exit and perfect communications.
❏ All firms are price takers, and the price is determined by the forces of supply and demand, in the market.
❏ The demand curve for a firm in perfect competition is perfectly elastic; thus AR = MR.
❏ Profit maximisation occurs when MC = MR.
❏ In the short run firms may make super normal profits, or losses.
❏ In the long run freedom of entry and exit ensures that profits are normal.
❏ In the long run, firms are forced to operate at the lowest point on their average cost curve; they are forced to be productively efficient.
❏ Consumers can buy the product at the lowest price possible and at a price which equals the average and marginal cost of production.
❏ In the short run firms will keep operating, even if they are making a loss, so long as they are covering their variable costs.
❏ The firm's supply curve in perfect competition, is the portion of the MC curve which is above the average variable cost curve.

Multiple Choice Questions

1. The demand curve facing a firm in perfect competition is horizontal because:

   A   the firm can produce goods at a constant cost
   B   the firm cannot sell goods at a lower price
   C   the demand for the firm's output is perfectly inelastic
   D   the firm can always sell extra units at the current market price
   E   the firm does not want to cut its price

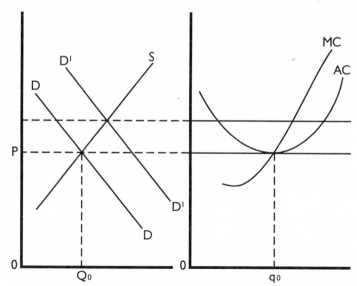

2. Consider the diagram above which illustrates the position of a firm and the industry, in perfect competition. The initial market demand is DD, establishing a price of OP. Demand rises to D'D'. What will be the long run impact on price and output of the firm shown?

   A price will rise and output will rise
   B price will rise and output will fall
   C price will fall and output will rise
   D price will fall and output will fall
   E price and output will be unchanged

3. The supply curve of the firm in perfect competition is:

   A the firm's average variable cost curve
   B the portion of the marginal cost curve which is above the average variable cost curve
   C the marginal revenue curve
   D the average revenue curve
   E marginal fixed costs

4. Which of the following total revenue curves in the diagram on the next page relates to a firm in perfect competition?

   A
   B
   C
   D
   E

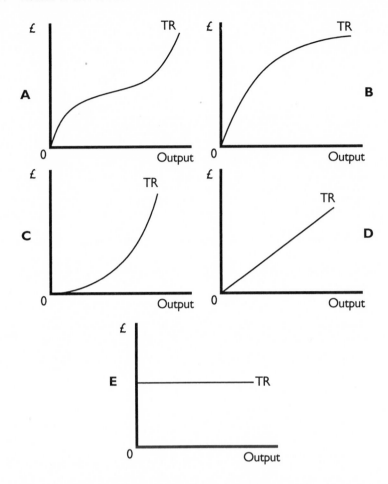

5. A firm in perfect competition receives £100 from selling 10 units. Given the following information on costs of production, what output level would allow the firm to just make normal profits?

$$TC = 150 + 5Q$$
Where: TC = total costs
Q = units of output

A 100 units
B 10 units
C 5 units
D 20 units
E 30 units

Monopoly

Monopoly defined

Monopoly is a situation where the total market for a product is provided by one producer. The legal definition in the UK is where one producer is responsible for 25% of the total market, but the economic analysis of monopoly examines the case of one producer having total control over the market for the product. This implies that other firms are not able to enter the market because of barriers to entry. These normally take the form of some sort of cost advantages which are available to the monopolist, but which are not available to newcomers. The most likely reason for this is the existence of economies of scale which require a producer to obtain large sales in order to reduce costs to the minimum possible. If the level of sales required is over 50% of the total market, the market will only be able to support one firm. A monopoly will result. Existing monopolies may try and erect barriers to entry, by taking actions which would make it very expensive for new firms to compete. Heavy advertising expenditure is one such activity. The following analysis assumes that a firm has the power to keep new entrants out of the market, and can, therefore, act as a monopolist.

The demand curve in monopoly

Since a monopolist is the sole supplier of the product, the demand curve facing the monopolist is also the demand curve facing the market. As we saw in Chapter Two the market demand for a product will be downward sloping. At any particular price there will be a limit to how much the firm can sell (unlike perfect competition where the firm is such an insignificant part of the market that any one firm can sell all that it wants to at the ruling market price). This is shown in Figure 12.1, where the firm is able to sell 10 units per week at a price of £1.

In order to expand sales beyond this point, the monopoly will have to drop its price. In Figure 12.1, in order to increase sales to 11 units, the price must be reduced to 95p so that an extra consumer can be encouraged to buy the eleventh unit. Thus when selling 10 units a week, the firm can charge £1, but must drop the price to 95p in order to sell 11 units. Thus at an output of 10 units total revenue is $10 \times £1$, which is £10. Average revenue is £1 per unit. At an output of 11 units average revenue is 95p per unit.

As we saw in Chapter Ten, the demand curve is the average revenue curve, since it shows the price which must be charged in order to sell particular levels of output. This is shown in Figure 12.1 by labelling the curve D = AR.

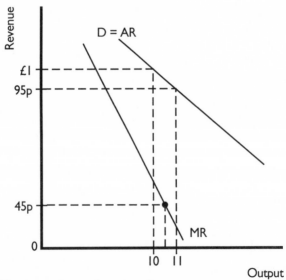

Figure 12.1 *The demand curve in monopoly*

The marginal revenue curve

In the example in the demand curve section, the increase in sales of one extra unit from 10 to 11 units increases total revenue from £10 to £10.45. Thus the extra unit has only generated 45p extra revenue. The marginal revenue from selling this extra unit, which is how marginal revenue is defined, is 45p. This result, which we saw in Chapter Ten, comes about because in order to sell the extra unit, not only is the price of that unit reduced (to 95p) but so is the price of all the other units which are being sold. Thus the firm has gained 95p from selling the eleventh unit, but has lost 5p from all the other ten units sold, giving the total benefit as 45p.

This result is basic. When the demand curve (average revenue curve) is downward sloping, the marginal revenue curve always lies below it. This is analogous to the example of exam marks used in Chapter Nine. When the average is falling it must be because the marginal is less than the average. Thus the demand curve in Figure 12.1 has a marginal revenue curve associated with it, shown as MR. The eleventh unit gives an average revenue of 95p but a marginal revenue of 45p. Again, as we saw in Chapters Nine and Ten, when plotting the marginal value, it is plotted against the mid point since it represents the increase in total revenue from increasing output from 10 to 11 units.

Short run profit maximisation

As we saw in Chapter Ten, profit maximisation always occurs when the firm is equating marginal cost with marginal revenue. Thus in order to identify the profit maximising output, we need to put the average and marginal cost curves onto Figure 12.1. This is shown in Figure 12.2.

Profit maximisation will occur at the point where MC = MR. This is at the point labelled A, which yields an output level of X units. If the firm were to produce beyond this point, the cost of producing extra units (marginal cost) would exceed the revenue gained from those extra units (marginal revenue). In order to identify the price at which this output can be sold we need to refer to the demand (average revenue) curve, as this tells us the price at which outputs can be sold. The price in this case is P.

The profit which the firm is making will be the difference between total revenue and total costs. Total revenue is given by the area OPBX. (Price times output.) Total costs are given by average cost times output. This is represented by the area OCDX. Profits are therefore represented by the area CPBD. Thus in the short run the monopolist can earn super normal profits.

Long run profit maximisation

It is easy to deal with long run profit maximisation in monopoly. Since new firms are unable to enter the market, there is no reason why the short run

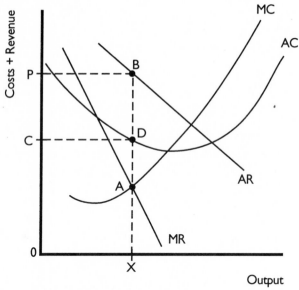

Figure 12.2 *Equilibrium of the firm in monopoly*

position should be disturbed. The firm can continue to earn super normal profits, and charge a price in excess of the costs of production, because there is no competitor able to bring the price down. Thus the situation shown in Figure 12.2 is also the long run position for a firm in monopoly.

Perfect competition and monopoly

Now that we have derived results for the long run equilibrium of firms in both perfect competition and in monopoly, we can see the implications of both for the economy in terms of how they impact on the economic efficiency of the market, and on the implications for consumers. In Figure 12.3 we show the position for a hypothetical product which is produced under conditions of perfect competition.

The price under perfect competition will be Pc and output Xc. Price and output are determined in the market place by the forces of demand and supply. The supply curve is labelled S = MC because we saw in Chapter Eleven, that the supply curve for the firm in perfect competition, is the firm's marginal cost curve. Thus the supply curve for the industry is simply the addition of all the supply curves of the firms and so is also the sum of the individual marginal cost curves.

Suppose that this industry now came under the control of one producer who could control the output of all the firms. In other words the industry becomes a monopoly and is able to keep out competition. How would a monopolist react given the situation in Figure 12.3?

In order to identify the profit maximising output, the marginal revenue curve needs to be drawn. This is relevant for the monopolist, but not for

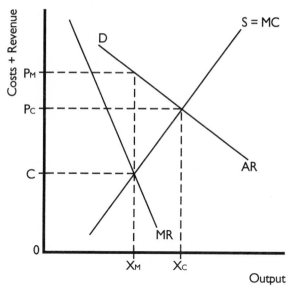

Figure 12.3 *Perfect competition and monopoly compared*

firms in perfect competition. The reason for this is that the firms in perfect competition have no control over their price, they must charge the market price. Thus as far as the individual firm in perfect competition is concerned, the price is given and thus marginal revenue for the firm is simply equal to the price.

At the industry level, however, the industry cannot sell all it wants at a set price, because the total market is given by the market demand curve, and so the extra revenue gained from increasing the industry output is less than the price charged, because of the need to cut the market price when industry output increases. Thus the industry faces a marginal revenue curve as well as the supply and demand curves shown in Figure 12.3.

Now that the industry is monopolised, the supply curve becomes the firm's marginal cost curve. The market demand curve is the monopolist's average revenue curve and the associated marginal revenue curve is shown as MR. Profit maximisation will now occur at an output level of Xm, which will yield a profit maximising price of Pm. This gives the classic case against a monopoly. Output will always be lower, and price will always be higher than for an industry which is competitive.

Arguments against monopoly

The main argument against monopoly is the problem it may create for the optimum allocation of resources. This is normally expressed in terms of interfering with allocative and productive efficiency. In perfect competition the firm would be at the lowest point on its average cost curve, while in monopoly, in order to increase the price, the firm will reduce output.

This means that the firm sells the last unit produced at a price which exceeds the actual cost of producing that unit. Hence the economy does not achieve allocative efficiency, since price does not equal marginal cost.

In Figure 12.3 the consumer is prepared to pay Pm for the last unit bought. It would only cost the firm C to produce an extra unit (marginal cost) and so it would be an efficient use of resources to allow an extra unit to be produced. However it is not in the interests of the monopolist to produce the extra unit since it will reduce his profits because of the need to reduce the price of all other units produced. This means that resources are not allocated so as to make consumers as well-off as possible. This is not allocatively efficient.

Productive efficiency might be impaired because the monopoly could survive even if it did not keep its costs at the minimum possible, since there are no competitors to undercut the monopolist. Hence there is no guarantee that a monopolist will produce as cheaply as possible and hence need not achieve productive efficiency.

Arguments for monopoly

Figure 12.3 can also be used to show the classic argument in favour of monopoly. As we saw in Chapter Nine, as firms become larger they may experience economies of scale. This will mean that a large firm may be able to produce more efficiently than a small firm. In terms of Figure 12.3, when the competitive industry becomes monopolised, if economies of scale occur, the marginal cost curve might shift downwards, reflecting the reduced costs of production. If this reduction is large enough, it is possible that costs and price may be below the competitive level. This idea is always used to defend the monopoly position enjoyed by a monopolist. They will always claim that they need to be a monopolist in order to be large enough to be able to take advantage of all the available economies of scale. Whether this is a valid arguments depends primarily on the concept of Minimum Efficient Scale (MES).

Minimum efficient scale

Suppose that in Figure 12.4 the long run average cost curve has the shape shown by the curve labelled LRAC. This indicates that the firm can enjoy economies of scale up to the output level OX.

This output level represents the lowest output which allows the firm to operate at its lowest costs of production. This is thus the minimum size which the firm needs to be to operate at maximum efficiency. The output level OX is referred to as the Minimum Efficient Scale. Suppose that this scale required an output of 10 000 units a week. In order to operate at the lowest possible cost, the firm needs to sell 10 000 units a week. If the total sales of this product were less than 20 000 units a week this industry would

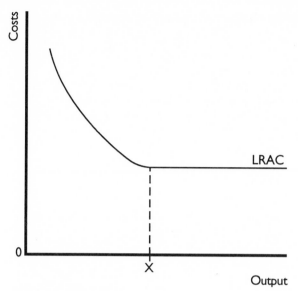

Figure 12.4 *Minimum efficient scale*

only be able to support one firm, since it would be impossible for two firms to achieve the MES. This would create a monopoly, and industries where this might arise are known as natural monopolies. Thus the size of the total market in relation to the MES is a crucial factor in determining the degree of competition which will exist in an industry.

Price discrimination

We saw in the section on the marginal revenue curve that, in monopoly, marginal revenue is always less than average revenue because of the need to lower the price of all units in order to attract extra customers. Price discrimination occurs when a producer tries to keep the price to some consumers high, while reducing the price to others. In order for price discrimination to be possible, the two markets have to be kept separate, to prevent goods from the lower-priced market being resold at a higher price, and the firm practising the price discrimination has to be a monopolist, to prevent competitors entering the higher priced market.

In order for price discrimination to be profitable, the consumers in the two markets must have different reactions to price changes. Their elasticities of demand must be different. The logic of price discrimination is easy to understand. Suppose that a firm was producing 20 units of a product and was selling ten in each of two markets at a price of £10 in each market, giving a total revenue of £200. An economic consultant tells the firm that the elasticity of demand in market A is 2 and in market B is 0.5. In order to sell an extra unit in A the firm would need to lower the price by 5% (since one unit represents a 10% increase in sales). This would generate revenue of £9.50 × 11, which equals £104.50. In market B the firm now has only nine units to sell, for which it can charge £12 (% change in quantity is 10, % change in price is 20, giving a price elasticity of demand of 0.5). This would generate revenue of £108. On the basis of this oversimplified example, simple price discrimination increases revenue from £200 to £212.50. This gives the basic result that if a firm is able to practice price discrimination, it will charge the higher price in the market with the less elastic demand. (As an exercise in elasticities calculate what would have happened to total revenue if the firm had tried to sell the extra unit in market B and one less unit, at a higher price, in market A.)

In order to examine price discrimination more closely, and also to identify what is the profit maximising output and sales in both markets we need to examine the behaviour of costs and revenues. This is shown in Figure 12.5. The first two graphs show the demand curves for the product in the two markets. The demand curve in market A is drawn with a steeper slope, representing a lower price elasticity of demand at any particular price, given that the scales and axes on the two graphs are the same. Each demand curve has a marginal revenue curve associated with it. The third graph represents the combined market which is derived by simply adding the two market demands together. There is a marginal revenue curve associated with this combined demand.

In order to identify the profit maximising output the marginal cost curve is also shown on the combined graph. The profit maximising point is again where marginal cost equals marginal revenue. This gives a total output of OX at a marginal cost of OC. The monopolist now has to decide how to split this output between the two markets. This is achieved by equating

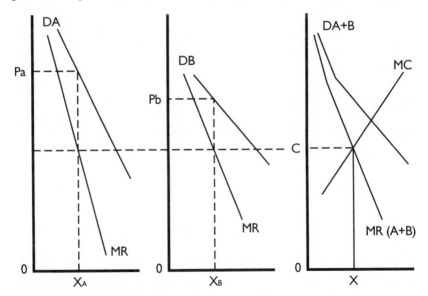

Figure 12.5 *Price discrimination*

marginal cost with marginal revenue in both markets. This gives an output of OXa in market A and OXb in market B. Price in market A will be Pa, and in market B it will be Pb. This reinforces the result we saw earlier. The price will be higher in the market with the less elastic demand.

Price discrimination is an accepted part of pricing in many areas of business. Rail fares are more expensive at certain times of the day, fares are reduced for certain categories of passengers. Thus business travellers who have to travel at particular times will have to pay more than people who can travel later in the day. The markets are kept separate by the time at which the train departs. It is often argued that the price of new cars in the UK is higher than on the continent. This is explained by the lack of competition for UK sales (given that cars drive on the 'wrong' side of the road when compared with cars made in Europe), and may also reflect the lower price elasticity of demand for cars in the UK.

The supply curve in monopoly

It is important to understand that in monopoly there is no such thing as a supply curve. Remember that a supply curve shows the way in which output responds to a change in price. In monopoly the firm can control either the price or the quantity sold. Thus it is not possible to talk about a monopolist reacting to a change in price, since it is the monopolist who determines the price. A monopolist will not sell different outputs at various prices. He determines the price at which his output will be sold. The monopolist is a price maker, not a price taker, and so it is not possible to draw a relationship between the price of the product and the output which the monopolist produces. Given the cost conditions facing the monopolist and the demand curve facing him, there will only be one profit maximising price and output. Thus a supply curve showing various possible combinations of price and output does not exist.

Monopoly and the government

The existence of monopoly is a threat to both productive and allocative efficiency and this has led virtually all governments to adopt controls over industries where firms have obtained a monopoly position. This control has usually taken one of three forms:

- Anti monopoly legislation may give the courts the power to dissolve an existing monopoly into a larger number of independent companies. This is the basic attitude taken in the USA. This is based on the belief that monopolies are inherently undesirable and that competition is to be encouraged at all times.
- The UK approach is to attempt to regulate the behaviour of the monopolist. Thus the monopoly is allowed to persist, but the govern-

ment ensures that it does not act against the public interest. This may take the form of a referral to the Restrictive Practices Court which investigates practices that restrict competition, or a referral to the Monopolies and Mergers Commission that may prevent a merger from taking place altogether if it might create a monopoly.

- The government may actually directly control the industry, especially if it is a natural monopoly. This was one of the principles which lay behind nationalisation.

The drive towards privatisation has led to most of these industries being re-privatised, but the need to control their monopoly power explains why virtually all the privatised concerns have government-appointed regulators who control the prices which can be charged. Thus, British Gas is regulated by Ofgas and power generation by Ofelec. The existence of these regulators is an implicit recognition of the dangers of allowing firms with monopoly power to operate without control in a market economy.

Summary

❐ Monopoly exists where there is one producer of a product. The monopolist faces a downward sloping demand curve. The monopolist's marginal revenue curve will lie below the demand curve.

❐ Profit maximisation occurs where marginal cost equals marginal revenue. Monopolists can make super normal profits both in the short run and in the long run.

❐ Compared with perfect competition, monopolists will produce less and charge a higher price, unless economies of scale exist.

❐ A natural monopoly is one where economies of scale will not permit more than one firm in an industry.

❐ The number of firms in an industry will depend upon the Minimum Efficient Scale of firms compared with the total market.

❐ Price discrimination is possible for a monopolist that sells in two separate markets. Price discrimination is profitable if the price elasticities of demand are different in the two markets.

❐ Price will be higher in the market with the less elastic demand.

❐ A supply curve cannot be drawn for a monopolist.

❐ Almost all governments adopt some form of control over monopolies.

Multiple Choice Questions

Elasticity And Revenue Calculations (Price Discrimination section)
To sell an extra unit in market B would require a price fall of 20%
(£10 to £8)
Selling one less unit in A would enable price to increase by 5%
(£10 to £10.50)
The new total revenue would be £88 + £94.50 = £182.50.
Total revenue would have fallen by £17.50

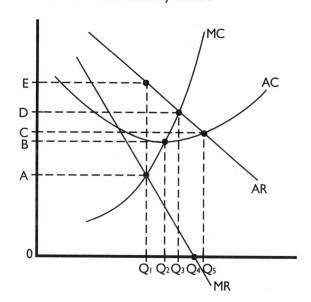

The diagram represents the cost and revenue curves of a firm in monopoly.

1. What is the profit maximising price?

2. What output would the monopolist produce if interested in maximising
    total revenue?

3. In the absence of economies of scale, a monopolist, when compared to
    an industry in perfect competition will:
    A produce more and charge a higher price
    B produce less and charge a higher price
    C produce more and charge a lower price
    D produce more and charge a higher price
    E produce the same and charge the same price

4. Which of the following is not necessary for price discrimination to be practiced profitably in two different markets?

   A   the different markets have different elasticities of demand
   B   the markets must be separable
   C   the marginal costs must be different in each market
   D   the producer must be a monopolist
   E   a higher price to be charged in the market with less elastic demand

5. A monopolist can sell 10 units of his product at a price of 50p each unit. An economist informs him that demand at this price has a price elasticity of demand of – (2.0). What would be the value of marginal revenue if the monopolist cut his price to 47.5p?

   A   47.5p
   B   50p
   C   22.5p
   D   0
   E   impossible to calculate

Chapter Thirteen

Monopolistic Competition

Key concepts

- ☐ Short run and long run profit maximisation in monopolistic competition
- ☐ The role of non price competition

Key words

Excess capacity, advertising, non-price competition

Monopolistic competition defined

Monopolistic competition is sometimes defined as competition among the many. The basic idea is that there are many firms all producing very similar, but not identical products. Thus there is a high degree of competition, but it is not perfect. Individual firms do have some control over the price of their products, since their customers may be prepared to pay a little more for a particular firm's product. Thus firms do enjoy some consumer loyalty, but given the high degree of competition, the price elasticity of demand for one firm's product will be very high. If price rises too much, the demand will disappear as customers switch to a competitor's products. There is also assumed to be freedom of entry and exit.

Short run profit maximisation

Profit maximisation will always occur where marginal cost equals marginal revenue. In the short run, the analysis of monopolistic competition is similar to that of monopoly. with the only difference being that the demand curve will be very elastic. This is shown in Figure 13.1. The profit maximising price is OP and output is OX.

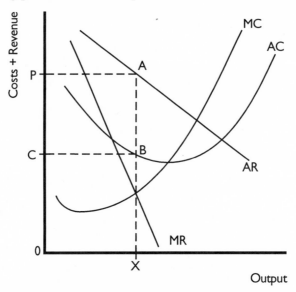

Figure 13.1 *Profit maximisation in monopolistic competition*

As we can see in Figure 13.1, the firm is making super normal profits equal to the area CPAB. Since there is freedom of entry and exit, this position is temporary, because new firms will be attracted into the industry. This will reduce the demand for all firms in the industry and all their demand curves will shift to the left. This process will continue until there are no longer any super normal profits to be earned.

Long run profits in monopolistic competition

The process described above will continue until all firms are earning normal profits. This will be when total cost equals total revenue (thus AC = AR) and at the same time marginal cost will equal marginal revenue. The only position where these circumstances will occur is when the demand curve is just a tangent to the average cost curve. This is shown in Figure 13.2.

Thus output is OX and price equal to OP. This result may appear a little contrived, but it simply states that in a situation where there is a high degree of competition, firms will be forced into a position where they have to price their product at a price equal to their average costs of production, and will be unable to make large profits. The other prediction which comes

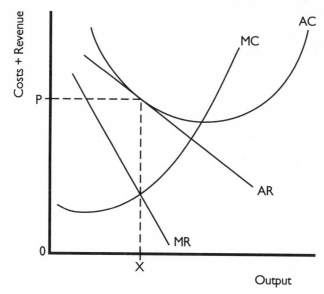

Figure 13.2 *Long run equilibrium in monopolistic competition*

out of this analysis is that firms will operate at an output level which is below the level necessary for them to minimise their costs of production. This is sometimes referred to as the prediction that monopolistic competition will be characterised by the existence of excess capacity within firms in the industry. This simply means that firms could produce more, at lower costs of production, but that they are unable to obtain large enough market shares for this to be possible.

Non-price competition

In monopolistic competition, firms always have an incentive to try and shift their demand curve to the right. This will enable them to make short run super normal profits. Firms will attempt to engender consumer loyalty, or to create brand loyalty since this will enable them to make short run profits and may delay the entry of new firms that might compete, driving these profits away. Firms recognise that they do have some control over their own market and will attempt to exploit this to the maximum. Thus advertising will be a characteristic of monopolistic competition.

   In perfect competition, advertising has no part to play since each firm can already sell all it wishes at the ruling market price. In monopoly, advertising may exist in an attempt to boost profits even higher, but since there is no competition, advertising is not always aimed at winning customers away from competitors, but at keeping out competition.

Summary

❏ Monopolistic competition is competition among the many.
❏ Firms have some control over their own market. Thus their demand curves are downward sloping.
❏ Competition ensures that profits in the long run are normal. (i.e. price in the long run equals the average cost of production).
❏ In long run equilibrium, firms will produce at an output below the level where average total costs are minimised. This is known as the excess capacity theorem.
❏ Price will be higher than that charged in perfect competition.
❏ Price will exceed marginal cost.
❏ The industry may be characterised by heavy advertising.

Multiple Choice Questions

1. Which of the following is not associated with monopolistic competition?
   A freedom of entry and exit
   B many firms
   C firms facing an elastic demand
   D long run super normal profits
   E advertising

2. In the long run, firms in monopolistic competition only earn normal profits, because:
   A they cannot produce at average costs lowest point
   B demand for their product is price elastic
   C firms must spend money on advertising
   D economies of scale exist
   E there is freedom of entry and exit in the industry

3. Firms in monopolistic competition face a demand curve which is:
   A perfectly inelastic
   B elastic
   C unit elastic
   D perfectly elastic
   E inelastic

4. In the short run, if a firm in monopolistic competition experienced an increase in its variable costs, this would be associated with:
   A an increase in output, and increased total revenue
   B an increase in output, and reduced total revenue
   C a reduction in output, and increased total revenue
   D a reduction in output, and reduced total revenue
   E none of the above

5. In the long run, in monopolistic competition, average cost will be equal to:
   A marginal cost
   B average revenue
   C marginal revenue
   D total cost
   E total revenue

Chapter Fourteen

Oligopoly

Key concepts

❏ The reason for price rigidity in oligopoly
❏ The impact of uncertainty on profit maximisation
❏ Possible strategies for combating uncertainty in oligopolistic markets

Key words

Kinked demand curve, zone of discontinuity
Game theory, pay off matrix, collusion, price leadership

Oligopoly defined

Oligopoly is often referred to as competition among the few. It is a situation where a few large firms dominate the market. The distinctive feature of oligopoly is that all firms recognise their interdependence and know that any decision by one of them will have an impact upon the others. Thus firms will expect their competitors to react to any decision which they make. This means that firms must be very careful when they are deciding upon their output and pricing strategies since they must try and take into account the likely reaction of their rivals. This is in contrast to perfect competition where each individual firm no control over the product, and where an individual firm's behaviour has no implications for other firms because the market is so large in relation to the individual firm.

In monopoly, the firm has no competitors and so can ignore the effect of its decision upon others. In monopolistic competition, because of the large number of firms, any one firm can behave independently of the others, since competitors need not react to their decisions. In oligopoly, by contrast, because of the small number of firms the reaction of competitors becomes a crucial factor in determining the behaviour of firms. This has the result that price competition becomes very risky for firms in oligopoly. This is often illustrated by reference to the 'kinked demand curve' facing an oligopolist.

The kinked demand curve

Consider the position shown in Figure 14.1 which shows the demand conditions facing an oligopolist.

If the current price is OP_1 the firm can sell OX_1 units. Suppose that the firm is considering reducing the price of its product to OP_2. If other firms in the industry react to the price cut, and also reduce prices, the firm will pick up very few extra sales. Its demand curve will be very inelastic. This is shown by the small increase in sales to OX_2. On the other hand, if the firm were to raise its price to OP_3, its competitors might react by keeping their price constant. This would result in this firm losing a lot of sales. Demand would be highly elastic, shown by the large fall in demand to OX_3. Thus the demand curve facing the firm kinks at the current market price.

This simply means that the firm in oligopoly faces two demand curves. One is the demand curve when all firms change prices together (D'D'), the

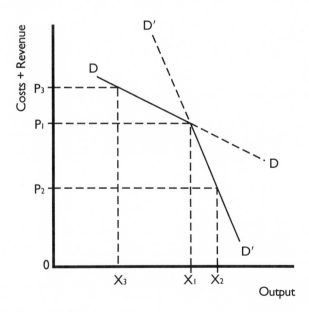

Figure 14.1 *The kinked demand curve in oligopoly*

other the demand curve facing the firm when it is able to change its price relative to that of its competitors (DD).

This makes the results of a change the price very uncertain. The outcome depends crucially on the reaction of other firms. Figure 14.1 shows an unfavourable outcome for this firm, and this will be the outcome which the firm must guard against. Hence price competition becomes very difficult, since the outcome is uncertain. This problem means that firms in oligopolistic markets will be reluctant to engage in price competition since this may result in all firms in the industry reducing their prices, which will damage the profitability of all of them. This is sometimes referred to as a price war, as all firms chase each other's prices downwards.

This feature of oligopoly may mean that an increase in an oligopolist's costs of production may have no effect on the price or output of the oligopolist. This is because the 'kink' in the demand curve, which is also the average revenue curve, creates a zone of discontinuity in the firm's marginal revenue curve. This is shown in Figure 14.2.

If the marginal cost curve (MC) cuts through the marginal revenue curve at output OX, the profit maximising price will be OP. Even if the marginal cost were to rise to (MC′), as long as it still equalled marginal revenue in the 'zone of discontinuity' (AB), the profit maximising output would still be at OX, with price OP. Thus the increase in costs will simply reduce the level of profits which the firm is making, and will have no impact on the price of the product.

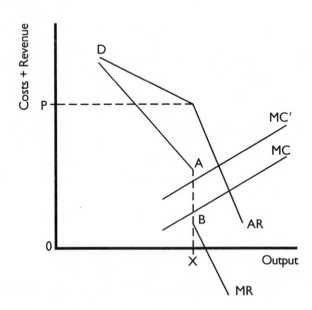

Figure 14.2 *The marginal revenue curve in oligopoly*

Non-price competition

The dangers of price competition means that firms will attempt to compete in ways which reduce the danger of a price war. This is known as non price competition. This can take various forms:

- **Advertising**: firms may spend resources trying to expand their sales by persuading consumers that their product is better than that of competitors;
- **Packaging**: firms may try and improve the image of their product through attractive packaging;
- **Sales promotions**: firms may resort to free gifts, or special offers to attract new customers.

Thus oligopoly is normally characterised by the existence of non-price competition. The important point to remember is that price cutting is the last thing firms want to encourage since this may lead to a price war which may benefit the consumer, but which harms the firms in the industry.

Game theory

In order to analyse the problem of inter-dependence, economists have made use of the field of game theory. This is an area of theory which tries to shed light on the problems of making decisions in a situation where the outcome of one player's actions depends upon the behaviour of another player. The most commonly used example is the game known as 'the prisoner's dilemma'.

Suppose that two individuals are captured by the police and are accused of a criminal offence. They are questioned, and the police inform them separately that if one confesses, and incriminates the other, that lenient treatment will be forthcoming in the courts. If the other person confesses but one continues to plead innocence, the other person will be treated leniently, but one will receive a heavy sentence. If both confess, they will both be treated less harshly than if they waste the court's time by pleading innocence. The suspects know that the police have very little evidence and that if they both refuse to confess, they stand a good chance of being acquitted. How should the suspects behave? This is the prisoner's dilemma.

This problem is often represented by the decision matrix shown in Figure 14.3.

The numbers in the matrix represent the length of sentence (in years) which individual A is likely to receive, given the behaviour of individual B shown on the top row. Thus if A confesses and B does not, A will receive a six-monthly sentence. If A does not confess and B does, A will receive a two-year sentence. If they both confess, A (and B) will receive one-year sentences. If neither confesses, both will be acquitted. How should A behave?

B A	Confess	Not Confess
Confess	1 Year	6 Months
Not Confess	2 Years	0

Figure 14.3 *The prisoner's dilemma: pay-off matrix*

If A is interested in ensuring that he avoids the worst possible outcome, he is said to be risk averse, and he will confess, since the worst that can happen is that he will receive a one year sentence. B will also confess, for the same reasons. Thus both confess, which is not the best outcome from either point of view. Thus decisions taken under conditions of uncertainty have led to a situation where both decision takers could have been made better off, but in order to protect themselves, they take rational decisions which result in a sub optimal position.

This example is useful since it illustrates the dangers involved in making decisions when one is not sure of the likely behaviour of other players, whose decisions have implications for the outcome of the game. Suppose the decision is whether to spend more money on advertising. If advertising is not undertaken, the danger is that other firms will advertise, and the sales of the firm not advertising will suffer. Thus all firms will have an incentive to advertise. It is likely that all firms would be better off if they all refrained from advertising, since this would not have any appreciable impact on total sales and would reduce their costs. The desire to ensure that they minimise the maximum risk they take (known as the minimax principle), will result in a sub-optimal position for all firms. In order to avoid such problems, the players in the game must be able to communicate with each other.

Collusion

Because firms recognise their mutual inter-dependence, they always have a great incentive to collude and to agree pricing and other decisions among themselves. Such agreements are normally illegal since they represent a restriction on competition. Economists often argue that such agreements are likely to fall apart very quickly because of the incentive which any one member of the agreement has to cheat on the decisions which they have agreed.

Suppose that producers agree to cut their output so as to raise the price of their products. If this policy is successful, price will rise. This will give all the firms an incentive to produce and sell more because of the higher price received. If all firms cheat, the price will fall and the agreement will have had no effect.

It was this line of reasoning which led many economists to argue that OPEC, (the producers cartel in oil production), would have little impact on the price of oil, because individual members would always have an incentive to exceed their production quotas, in order to increase revenue. Those same economists are still waiting for this breakdown to occur almost 40 years after OPEC was formed!

Price leadership

Another form of collusion occurs when firms engage in price leadership. This is said to occur when the dominant firm in an oligopolistic industry takes the lead in changing prices, and all the other firms follow suit. This can be because of two situations: either the dominant firm is in a position to exert control over the others because of some competitive advantage which it has acquired, perhaps because of economies of scale, or because all the firms in the industry have agreed, either formally or informally, that the pricing decisions are to be taken by the price leader and that they will all follow.

Firms in the industry may take it in turns to be the first to raise prices, certain in the belief that their competitors will all do likewise. This enables firms to behave as monopolists, since they will all be able to guarantee that their competitors will behave in the same way that they behave. It is sometimes argued that the major petrol producers operate in this fashion, and that they all tend to change petrol prices in unison.

Summary

❏ Oligopoly refers to competition among the few.
❏ Firms in oligopoly recognise their inter dependence.
❏ Price competition will be very dangerous since it may lead to a price war.
❏ Prices will be 'sticky' in oligopoly.
❏ Firms in oligopoly will engage in non-price competition.
❏ Uncertainty may lead to sub-optimal results.
❏ Firms in oligopoly will have an incentive to collude with each other to avoid competition.
❏ Collusion may be formal (illegal) or informal and may take the form of price leadership.

Multiple Choice Questions

1. Which of the following is a feature of oligopoly?
   A many large firms
   B price competition
   C non-price competition
   D homogeneous product
   E inelastic demand

2. If a firm in oligopoly were to cut its price in order to increase sales, but other firms in the industry kept prices constant, the kinked demand curve suggests that:
   A profits would rise
   B sales would fall and revenue would fall
   C sales would rise and revenue would rise
   D profits would fall
   E sales would fall and revenue would rise

3. 'Many firms producing a similar product'. This is a description of:
   A perfect competition
   B monopolistic competition
   C oligopoly
   D monopoly
   E duopoly?

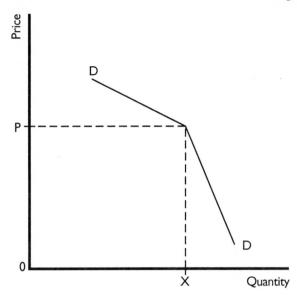

4. If a firm is currently charging the price OP and is faced with the demand curve shown above, it is likely that the industry in which it operates is characterised by:

    A   economies of scale beyond output OX
    B   stable prices
    C   freedom of entry and exit
    D   an inability to make long run super normal profits
    E   diseconomies of scale beyond output OX

5. If a firm wishes to maximise total revenue, it should always operate where:

    A   marginal cost equals marginal revenue
    B   average cost equals average revenue
    C   marginal revenue is positive
    D   demand is inelastic
    E   none of the above

Chapter Fifteen

Payments to Factors: Wages

Key concepts

- ❏ Factors affecting the demand and supply of labour. The market determination of the wage rate.
- ❏ Reasons for differences in wages.
- ❏ The impact of trade unions and minimum wages in the labour market

Key words

Marginal product, marginal revenue product, marginal productivity theory of wages.
Non competing groups, non pecuniary advantage, imperfect labour market. Wage differentials.
Unionised sectors, elasticity of demand for labour. Minimum wage.

Factor prices

In a competitive market economy the prices of goods and services are determined by the forces of demand and supply. The price of factors of production is also based on demand and supply. It is assumed that firms will demand factor services up to the point where it will not be profitable to employ any more. The supply of factor services will depend upon how much of the factor is offered for sale at various prices. We shall take the price of labour as an illustration of the process.

The supply of labour

Labour supply refers to the amount of labour which individuals are prepared to offer to employers. This is normally thought of as depending upon the wage that can be earned. The normal assumption is that as wages rise, more labour will be offered. Thus the labour supply curve is represented by the line S_L in Figure 15.1

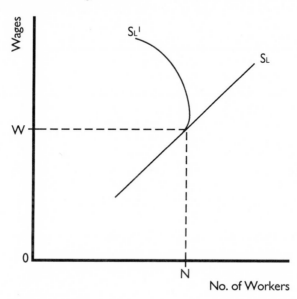

Figure 15.1 *The labour supply curve*

This suggests that as wages rise, more labour is supplied. The reason for this is that the higher wages will make people more prepared to work for this particular employer, rather than working elsewhere, or perhaps encourage people to enter the labour market who previously were content to not work and who preferred leisure. This is the substitution effect of the increase in the price of labour.

As we saw in Chapter Three, a change in price always has a substitution effect and an income effect. The substitution effect will always increase the supply of labour as wages rise, since work is now more attractive than leisure. The income effect may work in the opposite direction. As wages rise, workers experience an increase in their incomes. If work is seen as an inferior good (something which is undertaken because people are unable to afford leisure) the increase in income might result in people either working less, or other members of the family being able to give up work. If this were the case the labour supply schedule might be backward sloping as shown by S_L'. This possibility is sometimes referred to as a backward bending supply curve of labour. It suggests that as wages rise up to the level OW, labour supply expands. When wages rise above OW, the income effect encourages people to take more leisure, and labour supply starts to fall. This idea has most relevance when applied to the total supply of labour, rather than the supply to any particular employer.

This concept of a backward bending supply curve of labour has important implications. Suppose that the government is considering raising the rates of income tax. Many critics of income tax would argue that this is likely to act as a disincentive to effort in that the higher tax will discourage people from working. In effect this is arguing that a fall in wages will reduce the labour supply. This must therefore assume that the substitution effect of the wage reduction (which would tend to make leisure more attractive) is more powerful than the income effect (which would require people to work more to retain their income). There is no logical reason why this should be the case.

The only way to answer the question about the disincentive effects of income tax is to examine how people actually behave. The evidence on this is very unclear. As many studies have shown people working more following a wage cut, as have shown people working less after a wage cut. The controversy over whether income tax increases reduce the incentive to work cannot be solved by looking at the evidence currently available.

Despite this controversy, the assumption is normally made that the supply curve of labour is upward sloping. If we are talking about the supply of labour to a particular occupation, or a particular firm, this is a sensible assumption, since labour will be able to substitute other forms of employment for the one where the wage has fallen. It may not be a sensible conclusion when discussing the total supply of labour. This is an important point. It is very dangerous to extrapolate the supply curve for a particular firm into the supply curve for labour as a whole. Despite this danger, this is invariably what happens, as we shall see later.

The demand for labour: marginal productivity

Firms are assumed to be interested in maximising profits. Thus the amount of labour they demand will depend upon the profitability of employing extra workers. This will depend upon the difference between the cost of employing workers (the wage rate) and the value of what the worker is capable of producing for the firm. Thus the demand for any factor of production is a derived demand. Labour is only demanded because of a demand for the product which labour is producing.

Suppose that the firm is currently employing ten workers and is considering whether to employ an eleventh. It will compare the wage (say £100 per week) with the value of what the eleventh worker would produce in a week. This will depend upon two factors: the amount of extra output which the worker produces (known as the worker's marginal physical product: MPP) and the additional revenue which that output produces. The value of this extra output is known as the marginal revenue product (MRP) of the worker, or it is also known as the value of the marginal product (VMP).

In perfect competition, when extra units of the product can all be sold at the current market price, the MRP is calculated by multiplying the marginal physical product by its price. Thus:

MRP = Price × MPP.

Suppose the eleventh worker would increase output by 22 units a week and that these units sell at £5 each. The MRP is equal to £110 per week, and it is thus profitable to employ the eleventh worker. What about employing a twelfth? Again the decision depends on the MRP. If the price remains constant, the behaviour of the MRP depends upon the marginal physical product of the twelfth worker. It is normally assumed that the MPP does not remain constant as more workers are employed.

As we saw in Chapter Nine, in the short run, as more labour is employed there will eventually come a point where diminishing returns set in. This means that the marginal product of labour will start to fall. Suppose that the twelfth worker only adds 21 units a week to output. The MRP will now be £105 per week and again the twelfth worker will secure employment. If the thirteenth produces 20 units a week she will also be employed, but if the fourteenth has a MPP of 19, and thus a MRP of £95 per week, the firm will not offer employment. This is shown in Figure 15.2

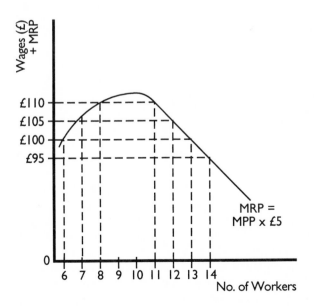

Figure 15.2 *Demand curve for labour: the marginal revenue product*

At a wage of £100 per week the firm employs 13 workers. If the wage rose to £110 per week the firm would only employ 11 workers. If the wage fell to £95 per week, the firm would demand 14 workers. Thus the firm's demand curve for labour is the curve which traces out the value of the workers' marginal product – it is the MRP of labour.

Note that if the MRP curve rises in its initial stages (before diminishing returns set in), the firm will employ beyond the point where the wage equals the MRP, if the MRP is rising. Thus in Figure 15.2, at a wage of £100, the MRP of the sixth worker is £100, but since the seventh has a larger MRP, it obviously makes sense to employ more than six people. Thus the demand curve for labour is only the downward sloping part of the MRP schedule.

Thus the demand curve for labour is the MRP curve, and in perfect competition, it is derived from the price of the product and the marginal product of workers. These are the only two factors which affect the position of the labour demand curve. If the price of the product rose the MRP curve would shift to the right. If the MPP of labour increased, this would also shift the curve to the left.

In any other form of competition, other than perfect, the MRP is **not** simply MPP × Price: Suppose that a firm is producing 100 units from employing five workers, and is able to sell the units for £5 each. Total revenue is £500. A sixth worker will produce ten extra units, but in order to sell all the 110 units the price may have to fall to £4.90. The MRP is **not** 10 × £4.90. The new total revenue will be 110 × £4.90, which is £539. The MRP is therefore £39. The 10 extra units only generate £39 extra revenue. This result alters the arithmetic of MRP but does not alter the basic idea that the demand for labour is determined by the productivity of labour, and the revenue which is generated by the additional output.

Wage determination: the marginal productivity theory of wages

Wages will be determined by the forces of demand and supply. Figure 15.3 shows the labour supply and demand curves for a employment in a particular occupation. The demand curve is simply the addition of the individual demand curves for the firms engaged in the industry. The equilibrium wage is shown as £100 per week. At any wage below this level, the demand for labour exceeds the supply and so wages will rise. At any wage above £100, supply exceeds demand and so wages will fall.

According to this theory, wages will rise if either the demand curve shifts to the right, or the supply curve shifts to the left. As we saw in the section on the demand for labour: marginal productivity, there are only two reasons why the demand curve might shift, either because the price of the product has risen, or labour has become more productive. Thus these are

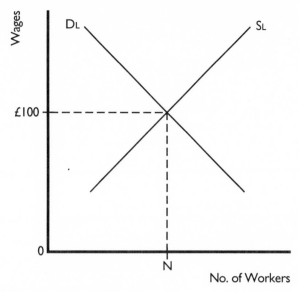

Figure 15.3 *Labour market equilibrium*

two reasons why wages might rise. The only other reason that wages might rise is if something occurs to reduce the supply of labour in that occupation e.g. other occupations might attract workers away, people with the necessary skills might retire.

This theory predicts that workers in any occupation will be paid the value of their marginal product. Thus wages are determined by market forces. Workers receive the 'correct' reward for their labour. Workers are not exploited because their wages are determined, not by the employer, but by the value placed upon them by the market.

Wage differentials

'If all people were the same, and all jobs were the same, and labour markets were perfect, all wages would be the same'.

This statement holds the key as to why different occupations are paid different levels of wages. If all people could perform all tasks equally well (if all people were the same) then as soon as one occupation started offering higher wages than any other, people would leave the low wage occupation (raising the wage) and enter the high wage occupation (lowering wages there). Wages would therefore equalise. In order for this process to work, people must be able to freely move between different labour markets. This is what is meant by labour markets being perfect. The requirement that all jobs be the same is the idea that unpleasant jobs should have to offer higher wages to persuade workers to take the job. As we shall see this does not appear to hold in practice.

If we wish to explain wage differentials we must examine more closely, why the conditions in the statement may not hold:

Non-competing groups: All people are not the same. If there are only a few people capable of performing a particular task, then the supply of labour in a particular occupation may be limited. If this is coupled with those workers having a high marginal revenue product, they will receive high wages. Thus all workers cannot compete for all jobs.

One of the major reasons for this inability to compete is because of the educational background of workers. Education and training will permit some workers to be eligible for certain occupations which are closed to those without that background. This is often one of the reasons put forward to explain the fact that female wages tend to be less than male wages. If women are denied equal opportunities in education and training, they will not be able to compete for better paid work.

Non-pecuniary advantage: All jobs are not the same. It is usually argued that if two occupations require the same skills, but one job is much more pleasant than the other, the less pleasant will have to offer a higher wage in order to overcome its unpleasantness. In terms of demand and supply, the supply curve will be shifted upwards, since people will need to receive higher wages to persuade them to undertake the job.

A possible example of this might be the high wages which have to be paid to workers producing oil in the North Sea. The dangers and inconvenience of such work mean that high wages are necessary to encourage workers to fill the jobs. Unfortunately, experience suggests that this cannot be an explanation for most wage differentials, since it is common to find the well-paid jobs also offering the more pleasant working conditions.

Imperfect labour markets: In order for workers to be able to compete for jobs, there must be freedom of entry and exit in the labour market. Thus, even if workers possess the necessary skills to enter a particular occupation, if there are barriers to entry into that occupation, the supply of labour will be restricted. It is often argued that many professions erect barriers to entry by insisting that entrants undergo some form of low-paid apprenticeship, or be forced to pass entrance examinations, where the pass rate is controlled by the profession.

Many occupations are in the public sector (teachers, nurses) and in these cases the laws of supply and demand may not apply, because these institutions are not profit maximisers and so will set wages with other objectives in mind. Another source of imperfection is that some occupations have wages fixed by other than market forces. Thus, some executives determine their own salaries, and so it is not surprising that they often appear to be very highly paid. These executives can be secure in the knowledge that competition for their jobs will not result in an excess supply of labour.

One other important source of labour market imperfection is the existence of trade unions, which may be successful at raising wages above the equilibrium level.

The conclusion from this section is that if the supply of labour to a particular occupation is limited, then, if this is coupled with a high marginal revenue product for those workers who are employed, those workers will enjoy high wages.

Trade unions and wage bargaining

Trade unions are normally analysed as trying to raise the pay of their members. This is sometimes referred to as a process of collective bargaining where unions and employers bargain over the wage level which is to be set. If unions are successful in raising the wage levels of their members, this will have the effect of causing the wage to rise above the market-clearing level. This is shown in Figure 15.4.

The market wage is at OW, but unions are successful in bargaining the wage rate up to the level OZ. The impact of this wage increase will depend upon the elasticity of demand for labour. Employers will only offer employment of ON, thus union members will experience a loss of jobs equivalent to the distance NQ. Sometimes the union may be able to bargain with the employer such that the employer promises to keep employment at pre-settlement levels, which would indicate a position such as point A.

The power of trade unions depends upon the extent to which they are able to raise wages without losing jobs. To a large extent this depends upon

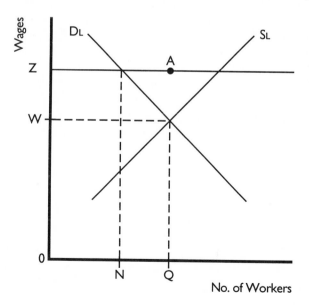

Figure 15.4 *Trade unions and increased wages*

the elasticity of demand for labour, since this will indicate the effect on jobs of a given increase in wages. This will be considered further in a moment.

The impact of trade unions can also be assessed in terms of the affect of trade union activity on the non-unionised sector. Consider the two labour markets shown in Figure 15.5.

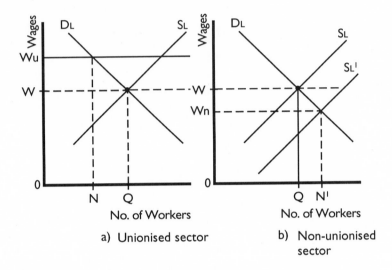

Figure 15.5 *Union activity on unionised and non-unionised sectors*

Figure 15.5 shows the initial equilibrium in both sectors prior to trade union activity. Wages in both sectors are the same at the level shown as OW. Suppose that sector (a) becomes unionised and wages are raised to the level OWu. This will have the effect of reducing employment in this sector to the level ON. In the non-unionised sector, workers who have been made unemployed in sector (a) will enter, causing the supply of labour to increase to SL^1. This will have the effect of reducing wages to OWn, but expanding employment to ON^1. Thus unions are sometimes accused of reducing employment in the unionised sectors of the economy, and of reducing wages elsewhere.

The elasticity of demand for labour

The power of trade unions will depend crucially on their ability to raise wages without causing great unemployment among their members, and of course on their ability to attract a large proportion of workers in an industry into the union. The first of these depends upon the extent to which a rise in the price of labour causes a reduction in the demand for labour. This is the concept of price elasticity of demand. This will be affected by the following factors:

The availability of substitutes. If it is easy to replace workers with machinery, the elasticity of demand for labour will be higher. This will depend upon the nature of the work being undertaken. If waitresses become more expensive to employ, one would expect more restaurants to become self-service. If car workers become more expensive, the move towards the increased use of robots would accelerate.

The proportion of costs represented by labour. If the cost of workers is a small proportion of the firm's total costs, an increase in wages will have less impact than if the wage bill was a major element of costs.

The elasticity of demand for the product. The demand for labour is a derived demand, since it depends upon the demand for the product. If the product has a very inelastic demand, employers will have little difficulty in passing any cost increase onto the consumer, and so an increase in wages may not have much impact on employment. In terms of the labour market diagram, the demand curve for labour (its MRP) will be very inelastic.

The elasticity of demand for labour is also of crucial importance in determining the impact on employment of the introduction of a minimum wage, since this also pushes wages in certain occupations above the level set by the free market.

Minimum wages

In Chapter Five we saw the diagrammatic representation of the impact of a minimum wage. The elasticity of demand for labour will determine whether or not the higher wage causes an increase in unemployment in particular occupations. The introduction of a minimum wage will also have other implications for the economy.

Inflation may be affected if firms react to the higher wage by increasing prices. This effect will be reinforced if other workers demand wage increases in order to maintain their wage differentials with those workers benefiting from the minimum wage.

Increases in the minimum wage will put extra purchasing power in the pockets of low paid workers. This increased spending might boost the total level of demand in the economy, and this might encourage firms to employ more workers.

Summary

❑ The payment to all factors of production is assumed to depend upon the forces of demand and supply.

❑ Wages are determined by the supply of, and the demand for, labour.

❑ The supply of labour is assumed to be a positive function of the wage rate.

❑ An increase in wages will increase labour supply if the substitution effect of a wage increase outweighs the income effect.

❑ The demand for labour depends upon the value of the marginal product of labour. This is known as the marginal revenue product.

❑ Wages will adjust to equate the demand and supply of labour.

❑ This is known as the marginal productivity theory of wages.

❑ Wage differentials must be because people differ, or jobs differ, or labour markets are not perfect.

❑ The elasticity of demand for labour will determine whether an increase in wages, above the market equilibrium, causes unemployment.

❑ Trade unions may increase wages in certain sectors, but this will reduce employment, and also reduce wages in the other sectors of the economy.

Multiple Choice Questions

1. Consider the labour market position shown in the diagram on the next page. The effect of introducing a minimum wage of OZ will be;

  A increase employment by XX_1
  B reduce employment by X_1X_2
  C reduce employment by XX_1
  D increase employment by XX_2
  E reduce employment by XX_2

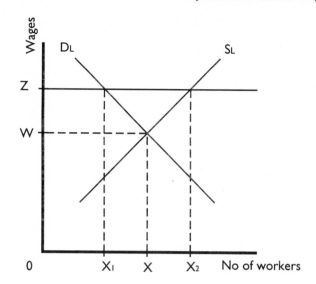

2. Which of the following will cause the demand curve for a labour to shift to the right?

   A an increase in the wage rate
   B an increase in labour productivity
   C a fall in the price of capital
   D a reduction in the supply of skilled workers
   E a fall in the price of the product

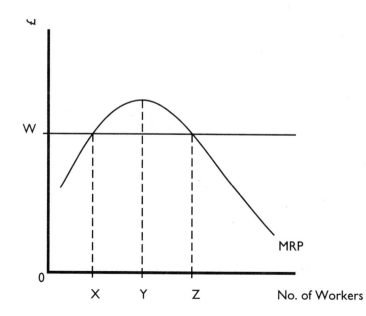

3. The diagram on the previous page shows the marginal revenue product curve for labour. At a wage rate of OW, the demand for labour would be:

   A OX
   B OY
   C XZ
   D OZ
   E more than OZ units of labour.

4.

units of labour	1	2	3	4	5	6	7	8	9
output	100	180	250	310	360	400	430	420	410

The table shows the weekly output which can be produced by a firm using various quantities of labour, which represents the only variable cost faced by the firm. If the firm is in perfect competition and can sell its product for £5 per unit, what will be the maximum employment level if the wage rate is £200 per week and the firm wishes to maximise profit?

   A 2
   B 4
   C 6
   D 8
   E more than 8

5. According to the marginal productivity theory of wages, which of the following would cause the wage rate of bricklayers to rise, and the employment of bricklayers to fall?

   A An increase in the price of property
   B An increase in the productivity of bricklayers
   C A fall in the productivity of bricklayers
   D An increase in the supply of bricklayers
   E A fall in the supply of bricklayers

Chapter Sixteen

The Return to Land: Rent

Key concepts

❏ Factors affecting the demand and supply of natural resources (land).
❏ Rent as a payment to land.

Key words

Transfer earnings, economic rent, quasi rent

The return to land: rent

Land is defined as all natural resources. The term was first developed with respect to land in the sense of agricultural land and it is this analysis which we will follow. Like the return to labour – wages – the idea is that land receives payment based upon its marginal productivity. As more and more land is used to produce agricultural produce, it is reasonable to assume that the productivity of land will fall. The most productive land will be used first and then as more land is used, the quantity of produce which it produces will fall. Thus the marginal physical product of land will decline. This will yield a MRP curve for land as shown in Figure 16.1.

When OX acres of land are in production the value of the output which the last acre produces is shown as £100 per annum. This will be based upon the value of the extra output which this last acre produces. If a further acre of land is brought into production, increasing land use to OY, the value of the extra output which it produces falls to £80 per annum. If the price of land – rent – is £100 per annum, then only OX acres will be demanded,

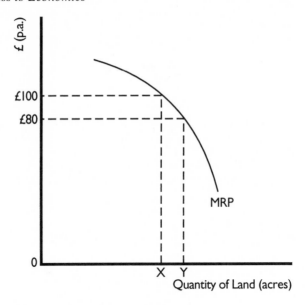

Figure 16.1 *The marginal productivity of land*

since the next acre yields less revenue than the rent. Thus as with the demand for labour seen in the previous chapter, the value of the marginal product of land, the MRP, is in fact the demand curve for land. Thus the simple idea is that the demand for land will depend upon the value of what it is capable of producing for the land user.

The supply of land

One distinctive feature of land is that it has no costs of production associated with its supply. Since it is a natural resource, the land will be available regardless of the price which it commands. Even if the price falls to zero, the land will still exist. This means that the total supply of land is fixed, and can be shown as a vertical supply curve. This implies that the price of land is solely determined by the demand for land. Consider Figure 16.2.

The supply of land is fixed at OQ. If the demand for land is given by the MRP curve DD, the land will command a price of OP. This price is referred to as the rent, since it is the price which the landowner could charge a tenant farmer for the land. Suppose that the price of agricultural produce was to rise. The demand for land (its MRP) would rise. This would shift the demand curve to DD', and the rent which could be charges would rise to P_1. This increased rent would accrue to the landowner as increased income, without the landowner actually doing anything to deserve such a windfall. This analysis was developed by Ricardo at the beginning of the 19th century, and was used as an argument against the corn laws which were

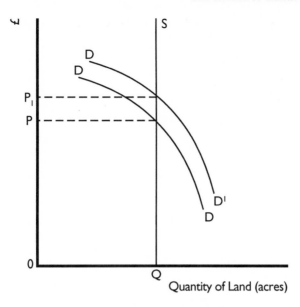

Figure 16.2 *The market for land; supply perfectly inelastic*

designed to keep wheat prices high in the UK and so created high rents. Landowners were seen as prospering, not because of some effort on their behalf, but purely as a result of a high demand for wheat.

This idea of rent being determined purely by the demand for land has important implications. Consider the observed fact that prices of theatre seats in London are higher than in other parts of the country. This is sometimes defended as being due to the fact that rents are high in London. What would happen to theatre rents if the demand for theatre tickets was to fall? It is important to remember that the demand for factors of production is a derived demand. Rents are high because the price of tickets is high.

Demand is the only influence on rent if the supply of land is fixed. If the land has alternative uses, the analysis alters.

Transfer earnings

Transfer earnings is the term given to the return which a factor of production could earn in its next best alternative use. If land has only one use, then that land will be available for that use regardless of its price. Its transfer earnings are zero. Suppose that there was a piece of land which had two possible uses. It could be a car park and earn £10 000 per annum, or it could be used to provide a street market and earn £15 000 per annum in rent. The land would be used for a market. The £10 000 which it could have earned in its next best use is known as the transfer earnings. The difference between this and the £15 000 is known as economic rent.

Economic rent

Economic rent refers to any payment to a factor of production over and above that necessary to keep the factor in its present use. In Figure 16.2, because the supply of land is fixed, all of the payment which it receives is in excess of that necessary to keep the land in production. Even if the demand for land fell to such an extent that rents were zero, there would still be OQ land in production. This concept of economic rent has an interesting property. If the part of the factor's earnings which constituted economic rent were removed from the owner of the factor, the factor would still be used in its current occupation. Thus the possibility arises of being able to tax factors of production without the tax having any impact on resource allocation.

Ricardo used this property to suggest that if all rents were removed from landowners, it would not have any impact on the use of land. This is the reason why land taxes have sometimes been advocated as a good way of raising tax revenue. If land has alternative uses, then only part of its reward in economic rent.

Economic rent can apply to any factor of production, including labour. Suppose there is an opera singer who can earn £5000 per week. Her next best occupation might be as a hairdresser at £200 per week. Her transfer earnings are therefore £200 per week and the economic rent which she earns is £4800 per week. Even if all of this £4800 were taken off her, she would still be an opera star! Thus any payment to a factor of production over and above that necessary to keep it in its current use is defined as economic rent. When we looked at super normal profits which a firm could earn, this is another example of economic rent. Normal profits are simply transfer earnings. All factors have the potential to earn economic rent. Consider the situation shown in Figure 16.3, which is on the next page.

The diagram shows the market for labour in a particular occupation. The wage rate is £200 per week and five people are employed. The supply curve of labour shows the amount of money which needs to be offered to encourage different workers to offer themselves for work. The first worker would be prepared to work for £120 a week, and so the fact that she receives £200 implies that she is earning £80 above her transfer earnings.

The second worker would work for £140 per week, and so she receives £60 above her transfer earnings. The third receives £40 economic rent and the fourth earns £20. The fifth worker receives the value of her transfer earnings since she would not work for less than £200 which implies that this is what she could earn elsewhere. Thus all five workers receive a total payment of £1000 per week, which contains £200 worth of economic rent. If the employer could have paid the five workers the minimum necessary to encourage them to work, he would only have needed to pay £800. Figure 16.4 shows the economic rent and transfer earnings.

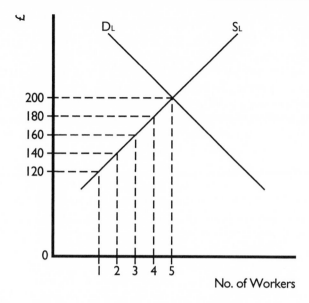

Figure 16.3 *Wages, economic rent and transfer earnings*

In diagrammatic terms, the economic rent is shown by the area AWE. The total payment is given by OWEN, and so the transfer earnings are given by the area OAEN. This is a general result for all factors of production. The diagram allows us to see what determines the amount of economic rent earned. The major factor is the slope of the supply curve of labour. If the

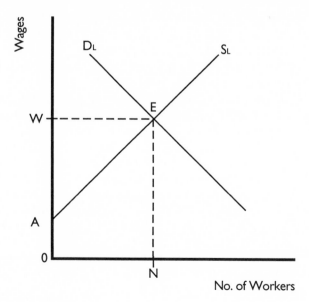

Figure 16.4 *Economic rent*

supply curve is very flat, the area representing economic rent will shrink. If the supply curve is horizontal, economic rent will be zero. The logic for this result is that if the supply curve is horizontal (perfectly elastic), this implies that all of the factors of production will transfer to their next best use if the reward they receive falls at all. Thus their transfer earnings must be equal to what they are currently earning. If the supply curve is vertical (perfectly inelastic) all of the payment to the factor is economic rent. This accords with the previous discussion on rent and land.

It is interesting to consider what are the causes of economic rent. Why should an opera singer receive £5000 per week when she would work for £200? The answer must lie in the demand for her services. It must be due to the fact that people are prepared to pay large sums of money to see her perform, that competition for her services drives the price up to £5000 per week. This is a perfectly general point. Economic rent is always demand determined.

Quasi rent

Quasi rent is the term given to any temporary earnings in excess of transfer earnings. They arise because of a short run increase in demand which allows the factor of production to earn in excess of transfer earnings, but the situation is temporary.

Summary

❏ Land is the term given to all natural resources.
❏ The payment to land is known as rent.
❏ Economic rent is the term given to the rewards which a factor earns over and above that necessary to keep the factor in its current use.
❏ This term originates from the idea that all the rent earned by landowners must be in excess of that required to keep land in production, since land is assumed to have no alternative use.
❏ Transfer earnings are the earnings available in the next best occupation.
❏ Economic rent is the difference between total rewards and transfer earnings.
❏ All factors of production can earn economic rent.

Multiple Choice Questions

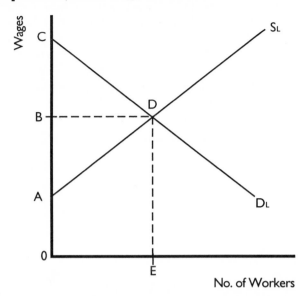

The diagram represents the market for bricklayers. Which of the areas represent the value of:

1. Economic rent earned by bricklayers?

2. The transfer earnings of bricklayers?

3. The total wages earned by bricklayers?
   - **A** OADE
   - **B** BCD
   - **C** ABD
   - **D** OBDE
   - **E** ACD

4. In order for all the earnings of a factor of production to be economic rent, which of the following must apply:
   - **A** perfectly elastic demand
   - **B** perfectly elastic supply
   - **C** perfectly inelastic demand
   - **D** perfectly inelastic supply
   - **E** demand and supply must have unit elasticity

5. Super normal profits are classed as economic rent because:
   - **A** normal profit represents the transfer earnings of the entrepreneur
   - **B** they are unearned
   - **C** normal profit is economic rent
   - **D** super normal profits are temporary
   - **E** competition will reduce profits to their normal level

Chapter Seventeen

Capital and Interest

Key concepts

- ❏ The way in which the return to capital varies as more capital is employed.
- ❏ Factors determining the demand for capital.
- ❏ The importance of the timing of receipts from new investment.

Key words

Marginal efficiency of capital, rate of interest
Present value, discounting
Investment, accelerator theory of investment

Capital and interest

Capital is the term given to all man-made resources. The reward for capital is usually referred to as interest, primarily because it is expressed as a percentage return on capital. Like the return to all factors of production, it is normally seen as being the result of the forces of demand and supply, with the demand being dependent on the marginal productivity of capital. This concept is usually referred to as the marginal efficiency of capital.

Marginal efficiency of capital (MEC)

As more and more capital is employed in an enterprise, perhaps in the form of machinery, it is usually assumed that the returns to capital will eventually start to fall. This is normally explained in terms of the most productive machinery being employed first of all, and as more and more is installed, the marginal returns start to fall.

The return on capital is normally expressed as a rate of interest. Suppose that a machine costs £100 000, and will permit output to increase by 100 units a year, with all other costs remaining the same. If the output sells for £50 a unit, the machine is yielding a return of £5000 per year. This is the same as a rate of return of 5%. If the price of the output were to rise to £60 per unit, the rate of return would rise to 6% (£6000 as a percentage of £100 000). This is shown in Figure 17.1.

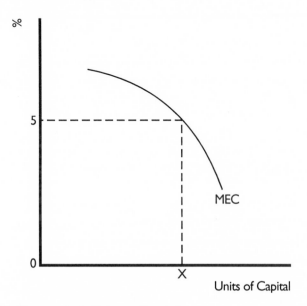

Figure 17.1 *The marginal efficiency of capital*

The unit of machinery under consideration is shown as unit OX, yielding a return of 5%. If an extra machine was installed, its return would be less, because of the idea that the more productive machinery will be employed first. Thus the curve labelled MEC is the percentage return which an extra machine will contribute. This curve is in fact the demand curve for capital, since it shows the units of machinery which it will be profitable for a firm to install, given the rate of interest which is charged for money.

The demand for capital

In the example above, it would pay the firm to install the machine if the firm could obtain the money for the machine at an interest rate less than 5%. Thus if the rate of interest which the firm must pay for money is shown on the price axis, this will identify the amount of machinery which it will be profitable for the firm to employ. The rate of interest can be thought of as the opportunity cost of the machinery, since if the firm is using its own money, it could earn 5% interest by putting the money in the bank.

A fall in the rate of interest might make it profitable to install the extra machine. If the rate falls to 4%, the extra machine would only need to make a return of 4% to make it profitable. Thus the rate of return which a marginal unit of capital would produce is shown by the line marked MEC. This is known as the marginal efficiency of capital. A profit maximising entrepreneur would employ capital up to the point where the MEC just equals the rate of interest which he has to pay. Thus the MEC represents the demand curve for capital, since it shows the amount of capital which will be employed at any particular rate of interest.

The position of the MEC will depend upon two main factors:

● If the price of new machinery falls, the return which is obtainable from that machine will rise. In the example above, if the machine only cost £50 000, the £5000 generated would represent a rate of return of 10%.
● The other factor is the value of the output which the machine produces.

This may rise because the price of the product rises. Both of these effects will cause the MEC schedule to shift to the right.

Discounting future returns

The example given above is rather simplistic since it simply expresses the annual return as a percentage of the initial cost of the machine. The problem with this approach is that it ignores the fact that money received in the future does not have the same value as money spent today. Suppose that an investment of £100 000 is expected to produce a return of £20 000 in two years time. At first sight this might appear to be a rate of return of 10% per year. However it is not!

Suppose that you had put the £100 000 in a Building Society at 10% interest for the two years. After two years it would have earned £10 000 + £11 000, which is a total of £21 000. Thus the investment in the new machinery has meant that money has been lost. The £20 000 in two years time is not an annual return of 10% on an initial outlay of £100 000.

This brings us to one of the central problems with estimating the return on capital. If money is spent buying capital equipment, the returns on this expenditure will not accrue until some time in the future. In order to see whether the outlay is justified, it is necessary to compare the sum of money spent today with the future returns.

Suppose that a machine costing £100 000 will yield a return of £150 000 in five years time, at which point the machine will be worthless. Is the outlay justified if the current rate of interest is 9%? It is necessary to compare the £150 000 in five years time with the £100 000 today. This is equivalent to asking: what sum of money today, if it were to earn 9% a year, would be worth £150 000 in five years time? This is known as estimating the present value of the £150 000. The answer is obtained by solving the equation:

$$PV = \frac{£150\ 000}{(1 + r)^5} \quad \text{where r = the rate of interest}$$

If r = 0.09 (9%), this gives a value of £97 466. What this means is that if £97 466 earned 9% interest for five years, in five years time it would be worth £150 000. Thus the return of £150 000 in five years time is not an attractive alternative to £100 000 today. Thus £150 000 in five years time would not compensate for spending £100 000 today.

A popular question which is often asked in examinations is to estimate the present value of an item which has a particular value in a year's time. Suppose you were asked to calculate the value of a Government Bond which will mature in a year's time and pay £100. If the current rate of interest is 5%, what will be the present value of the bond? This is the same as asking what is the maximum that anyone would be prepared to pay today to buy the bond which will be worth £100 in a year's time. The answer is given, by:

$$PV = \frac{£100}{1.05} = £95.24.$$

A short cut is to take the interest rate off the future value and then add a bit!

Investment and the rate of interest

The above analysis suggests that if the rate of interest falls, this will make additional units of capital profitable. The creation of additional units of capital is what economists refer to as investment. Thus the rate of interest is seen as an important factor in the determination of investment. This has important consequences for control of interest rates and the impact of monetary policy on the economy.

Investment, as we shall see later, is an important variable in economics. It represents the creation of goods not for current consumption. This includes capital equipment, and also any products which are produced and put into stocks. Most attention is normally focused on investment in terms of new capital equipment. This will be affected by several factors:

- **The rate of interest** (as discussed above)
- **Businessmens' expectations:** The returns off new capital equipment will be received at some time in the future. Thus the view of what the future holds in store will affect investment. If businessmen are optimistic about the future they will be encouraged to invest.
- **The accelerator theory of investment** suggests that firms may be forced to invest if they wish to satisfy an increase in demand for their

products, and they have little spare capacity in their factories. This makes investment depend upon changes in the level of demand and output in the economy. If the economy expands to satisfy extra demand, this will induce firms to invest. If the rate of growth of output is constant, firms will invest at a constant rate. If the growth in output accelerates, investment will rise. If output rises at a slower rate, fewer new machines will be required and so investment will fall.

● **The level of profits** may affect investment, since undistributed profits will provide a source of cheap finance.

Summary

❑   The return to capital is known as interest.

❑   The demand for capital depends upon the value which can be extracted from extra units of capital. This is known as the marginal efficiency of capital (MEC).

❑   The MEC is usually expressed as a percentage rate of return.

❑   This will increase if the cost of the capital falls, or the value of the output increases.

❑   Future returns must be discounted to obtain their present value.

❑   Money received in the future is always worth less than the same sum of money received today, because of the interest payments which it could have earned.

❑   Investment is the creation of new capital goods, and will depend upon the rate of interest, expectations, changes in the growth of output and demand, and the level of profits.

Multiple Choice Questions

1. Which of the following will cause the marginal efficiency of capital schedule of a firm to shift to the right?
   - **A** a fall in the rate of interest
   - **B** an increase in the rate of interest
   - **C** an increase in the price of capital
   - **D** a fall in the price of capital
   - **E** a fall in the price of the product produced by capital

2. The present value of an asset worth £100 in a year's time, at an interest rate of 8%, is:
   - **A** £92
   - **B** £108
   - **C** £92.59
   - **D** £100
   - **E** £87.50

3. The accelerator theory of investment suggests that:
   - **A** investment will take place if the rate of interest increases
   - **B** the growth of output is a function of the level of investment
   - **C** investment will take place if the growth of output increases
   - **D** investment will increase if the price of capital goods falls
   - **E** increased savings will increase investment

4. Which of the following would lead to a fall in a firm's investment?
   - **A** an increase in the rate of interest
   - **B** a reduction in the price of capital goods
   - **C** an increase in consumer demand
   - **D** an increase in profits
   - **E** increased optimism about the future prospects of the firm

5. Capital is the term given to:
   - **A** all human resources
   - **B** all natural resources
   - **C** money in the bank
   - **D** all man-made resources
   - **E** savings

Chapter Eighteen

The Market Revisited

Key concepts

- ☐ The circumstances in which the market mechanism will lead to an efficient allocation of resources
- ☐ The way in which monopoly and externalities might interfere with the optimum allocation of resources

Key words

Allocative efficiency, marginal benefit and marginal cost
Externalities, external costs, external benefits, monopoly
Private costs, social costs
Taxes, subsidies

Markets and productive efficiency

As we saw in Chapter Two, one of the great attractions of leaving resource allocation to the market mechanism is the belief that this will result in the efficient use of the economy's resources.

Productive efficiency is guaranteed by the existence of perfect competition which ensures that firms always operate at the lowest point on their average cost curves (see Chapter 11). Producing at the bottom of the AC curve means that products are produced as cheaply as possible. This implies that the minimum quantity of resources will be employed to produce the product. This is what is meant by productive efficiency.

This result is based on the idea of firms being motivated by the desire to make profits, by the ability of firms to enter or leave the industry, and the fact that there are many firms producing an identical product. Although these conditions are seldom, if ever, experienced in practice, this has not prevented economists, and believers in the power of markets, from advocating market forces, and competition, as the best route to ensuring productive efficiency. It is important to remember that competition plays a vital role in this process.

If competition is absent (monopoly) there is less reason to expect costs to be minimised, since a monopolist can survive even if costs are not minimised. However, if the monopolist is able to take advantage of economies of scale, it is possible that average costs might be less than those experienced in perfect competition.

Even if competition is present, any form of competition other than perfect competition will not necessarily achieve productive efficiency. Thus firms in oligopoly and monopolistic competition will not operate at the lowest point on their average cost curves, although the existence of some competition will mean that their desire to make profits will give them an incentive to reduce costs.

Markets and allocative efficiency

Allocative efficiency refers to producing the right type of goods in the right quantities. In Chapter Two, we saw that this is achieved by market forces responding to the wishes of consumers. We are now in a position to analyse the concept in more detail. Consider Figure 18.1, which represents the market position of a product in perfect competition.

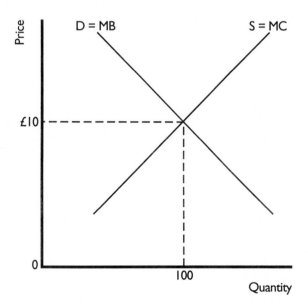

Figure 18.1 *The market equilibrium and allocative efficiency*

Market forces will create an equilibrium at a price of £10 and an output of 100 units per week. Why is this seen as allocatively efficient?

The demand curve shows the price the consumer is prepared to pay for extra units of the product. At a price of £10 the consumer is prepared to buy 100 units. This must imply that the 100th unit bought must just be worth £10 to the consumer. If it were less than this, the consumer would not have bought it. If it was worth more than £10, the consumer would have been encouraged to buy more than 100 units and would have continued purchasing the product until the marginal utility had fallen to a level which made the last unit bought just worth £10. Thus the demand curve is a representation of the marginal benefit which the consumer obtains from purchasing units of the product. The curve has therefore been labelled MB.

The market supply curve is derived from the marginal cost curves of the individual firms which make up the industry. In Chapter Eleven we saw that the firm's supply curve was its marginal cost curve. Thus the supply curve can be thought of as the marginal cost curve for the industry. The equilibrium position is thus at the point where the last unit produced (the 100th) costs just as much to produce (its marginal cost) as the price which the consumer is prepared to pay for it (its marginal benefit). Thus, the market mechanism achieves an equilibrium position where marginal cost equals marginal benefit. This is what is referred to as an allocatively efficient output.

Consider what the situation would be if the industry produced more than 100 units. The marginal cost of producing these units, as shown by the supply curve, would be above the price which people were prepared to pay. The cost of producing the extra items would be greater than the benefit which consumers derived from those items. Thus the production of those items would be a waste of resources.

Similarly, if the industry produced less than 100 units, this would mean that the last unit produced would cost less to produce than the benefit which consumers derived from that unit. This would indicate that it would be a sensible use of sources to produce more, since marginal benefits exceed marginal cost. This leads us to an important result. Allocative efficiency will be achieved when MB = MC. Since the MB is represented by the price people are prepared to pay, this result becomes the position where:

PRICE = MC

Thus allocative efficiency requires that production takes place up to the point where price equals marginal cost.

Monopoly and allocative efficiency

As we saw in Chapter Twelve, a monopolist will always restrict output and raise the price compared to a competitive industry. This must lead to allocative inefficiency since the equilibrium in Figure 18.1 will be disturbed. Output will be less than 100 units and price will be more than £10. Thus it would be possible for the monopolist to produce more of the product and the additional cost (MC) would be less than the benefit which consumers derive, as shown by the price they are prepared to pay. This is not profitable for the monopolist since he would need to drop the price of all of his product to sell the extra units, hence the marginal revenue he would earn would be less than the extra costs. Thus a monopolist will always be producing at an allocatively inefficient output. Price will always exceed marginal cost.

Externalities

Allocative efficiency requires that price equals marginal cost. This is based on the idea that the price reflects the benefit people derive from the last unit of the good and the marginal cost indicates the cost of the resources used to produce that unit of the good. As we saw in Chapter Two, there are circumstances when the price will not reflect all the benefits from a good. This is when the good confers benefits on people other than the person buying it. These are what are normally referred to as external benefits, or externalities. Similarly the supply curve may not include all the costs of producing a good, especially where some costs are felt by people other than the producer. These are known as external costs.

Let us first of all consider the case where external costs exist and see the implications for allocative efficiency.

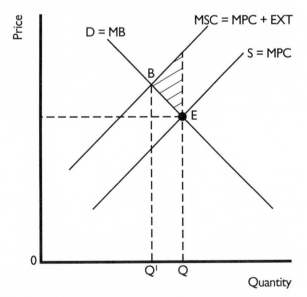

Figure 18.2 *External costs and allocative efficiency*

Figure 18.2 illustrates the market equilibrium for a particular product. The demand curve represents the price which people are prepared to pay and the supply curve shows the cost to the firms in the industry of producing extra units of the product. These costs are referred to as private costs, since they only affect the firms. The supply curve is thus also labelled as the Marginal Private Cost (MPC). Suppose that producing this product imposes costs on other people, perhaps in the form of pollution costs.

The standard textbook example is where a factory disposes of its waste products into a convenient river, which imposes costs on a fishing industry that exists downstream. These external costs might work out at £2 per unit produced by the industry. Thus the total costs to society of the product being produced is not that shown by the MPC, since this only contains the costs which the firm has to pay. The true costs are these costs **plus** the external costs. Thus the total cost to society is higher than that shown by the MPC, and is shown in Figure 18.2 as Marginal Social Cost (MSC). The difference between MPC and MSC is the extent of the external costs which exist.

Consider the implications for allocative efficiency. At the market equilibrium E, units of the product are being produced which cost society more to produce than the benefit which people derive from their production (MSC exceeds the price). In terms of allocative efficiency these units should not be produced, since they represent a loss of welfare to society. In terms of Figure 18.2, the total loss from these allocatively inefficient units is shown by the shaded area EAB. It would be allocatively efficient for the output of the product to fall to OQ', since at this point MSC equals the price consumers are prepared to pay. How can this position be reached?

The usual suggestion is that a tax should be imposed on the product. As we saw in Chapter Four, a tax has the effect of shifting the supply curve vertically upwards by the amount of the tax. Each unit produced imposes £2 worth of costs on other people. If a £2 tax was imposed on each unit produced, this will increase the firm's private costs by £2 per unit, shifting the supply curve upwards until it became equivalent to MSC. This is referred to as internalising the external cost. The key to achieving allocative efficiency in this case is to make the price of the product reflect all of the costs associated with its production.

Another possibility is that the government might regulate the behaviour of firms by legislation. Thus it may make it an offence to pollute rivers, or to impose other forms of external cost. This would force the firms to take steps to reduce pollution, which would again raise their costs, and make the price of the product rise to reflect the total costs of production.

A similar analytical framework can be used to show the problem posed by the existence of external benefits. Take the case of education for people over the age of 18. If post-18 education were left purely to market forces, there would be a certain demand for education and a certain amount of education supplied. The demand would be based upon the benefits which individuals expected to gain from education, and the supply would be from institutions interested in making profits from providing education. Hence the amount supplied would depend upon the price and the costs of providing education. These forces are shown in Figure 18.3 as demand and supply curves, and an equilibrium is established at an output of OQ units of education.

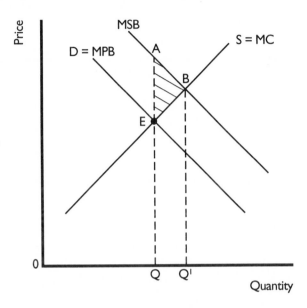

Figure 18.3 *Education, external benefits and allocative efficiency*

It is sometimes argued that education confers benefits, not only on the students who receive the education, but also to the rest of society at large. Some of the benefits will go to the student in the form of higher status, salary etc., and these will determine the students' demand for education. Other people may also benefit, perhaps from the extra knowledge which the student might generate and these benefits will not be taken into account by the individual student. Hence the demand curve may underestimate the total benefits to society from students obtaining education.

The demand curve shows the benefits which are private to the individual, the Marginal Private Benefits (MPB), since the demand curve shows the price which consumers are prepared to pay for various quantities of education. This price is taken as an indication of the benefit which the consumer expects to receive from the service. If external benefits exist, the true benefits to society will lie above the MPB.

In Figure 18.3 this Marginal Social Benefit (MSB) is shown as lying above MPB.

The allocatively efficient amount of education is shown as being OQ'.

Left to their own devices people would only purchase OQ at an equilibrium shown as point E. This is not efficient since the benefit to society of extra education (MSB) exceeds the MC. It would be in society's interests to increase the amount of education to OQ'. This could be achieved by giving a subsidy to the suppliers of education, or by giving a subsidy to the potential student. In Figure 18.3, if a subsidy equivalent to the external benefit (the distance EA) was given to the student, this would increase the student's estimate of the private benefit of education until it was equal to the social benefit. The demand curve would then become the MSB curve, and the new equilibrium would be at an output of OQ'. Alternatively, the same subsidy could be given to the supplier of education, which would reduce the marginal cost by EA and yield the same outcome. This analysis is the major justification for the taxpayer giving maintenance grants to university students and for paying their fees. If the only people who benefited from education were the students who were educated, it would be difficult to think of any reason why people who do not attend university should subsidise those who do.

The subsidy would increase the welfare of society by the area EAB in Figure 18.3.

Although we have used the examples of pollution and education as illustrations of externalities, exactly the same analysis can be applied to any good or service where external costs or benefits occur. Thus people who smoke impose external costs on non-smokers and on taxpayers in terms of costs to the NHS. Thus, the true cost of smoking lies above the cost to the smoker. Allocative efficiency requires that these costs be imposed upon the smoker, by taxation, and then the smoker can decide whether smoking is a desirable activity.

It is important to recognise that the allocatively efficient answer to pollution is not to eliminate pollution, but to ensure that the optimum amount of pollution is generated. This might seem a contradiction in terms, but what it means is that pollution is usually the by-product of some desirable activity. It is necessary to weigh up the benefits from the activity against the costs which it is imposing. A certain amount of pollution will be necessary if the benefits from the activity are to be enjoyed. Thus allocative efficiency requires weighing up the marginal costs and marginal benefits of activities and ensuring that the benefits exceed the costs.

Summary

◻ Perfect competition will guarantee productive efficiency since firms will operate at the lowest point on their average cost curves.

◻ If competition is absent, or not perfect, productive efficiency cannot be guaranteed, although private sector firms will always have some incentive to reduce costs.

◻ Allocative efficiency requires that products be produced up to the point where the benefit derived from the last unit produced, is just equal to the cost of producing the last unit. If all costs and benefits are private, this implies producing to the point where price equals marginal cost.

◻ If externalities exist, allocative efficiency requires that goods be produced up to the point where their marginal social benefit equals their marginal social cost.

◻ Allocative efficiency does not require the elimination of external costs. There is an optimum level of pollution.

Multiple Choice Questions

1. A necessary condition for allocative efficiency is that:
   A price must equal average cost
   B price must equal marginal cost
   C price must equal marginal revenue
   D price must equal average revenue
   E price should equal zero

2. Marginal social cost refers to:
   A The benefit consumers derive from consuming an extra unit of the product
   B The cost to the firm of producing an extra unit of the product
   C The benefit to society of consuming an extra unit of the product
   D The external cost incurred by producing an extra unit of the product
   E The cost to all of society of producing an extra unit of the product

3. Productive efficiency requires that:
   A all firms are in perfect competition
   B price equals marginal cost
   C price equals average cost
   D firms produce at minimum average costs
   E only normal profits are made

4. Which of the following is an allocatively efficient means of rectifying an external cost associated with the production and consumption of a particular product?
   A giving a subsidy to the producer, equivalent to the external cost
   B imposing a tax on the product, equivalent to the external cost
   C banning the product
   D Giving a subsidy to the consumer. equivalent to the external cost
   E Publicising the external costs

5. If a firm is taxed by an amount equal to the external costs which it imposes on the rest of society by its productive activity:
   A prices will rise and output will rise
   B resource allocation will suffer because of government interference with the price mechanism
   C Resource allocation will be improved because profits will fall
   D resource allocation will improve because prices will reflect social costs
   E prices will fall and output increase

Chapter Nineteen

The Circular Flow of Income

Key concepts

- ❏ The way in which expenditure and goods flow between different sectors of the economy
- ❏ Ways in which these flows can be identified
- ❏ A diagramatical representation of these flows

Key words

Households, firms, government sector, foreign sector.
Circular flow of income, real flows, money flows, income. output, expenditure
Savings, intended investment, unintended investment, government expenditure, exports, imports
Consumption

Macroeconomics

In this chapter we will begin to examine how the macro economy works. This refers to the overall economic system, rather than the study of individual markets and products. In order to examine how an economy works, economists need some way of measuring the levels of activity within an economy. This is an area of economics known as national income accounting. We shall begin by building a simple model of the circular flow of income and show how this is used as a basis for national income accounting.

The economy consists of millions of individuals all making decisions concerning economic activity. In order to analyse and measure this activity we need some way of treating people in groups. The process for doing this is known as aggregation, and it allows the economist to break the economic system down into a few, more manageable sectors.

Instead of analysing how an individual consumer might behave in certain circumstances, macroeconomics examines how the total level of spending by consumers, (known as consumption) is determined. Similarly we move away from looking at the behaviour of an individual firm, and instead group firms together, and, at the simple level those firms are then treated as one sector of the economy.

The economy is usually split into four sectors:

● **Households:** this is the sector which consists of consumers and which provides the factors of production used by firms;
● **Firms:** this is the sector which produces goods and services;
● **Government:** this is also known as the public sector, and consists of the economic activities of government;
● **Foreign sector:** This consists of the economic activities of people outside the domestic economy.

The usual way of analysing the interaction of these sectors is via a model known as the circular flow of income.

The circular flow of income

It is usual to introduce the concept of the circular flow of income by concentrating on the first two of the sectors above, and by assuming that we are operating in an economy which has no government and which does not engage in trade with other countries. This latter assumption is referred to as assuming a closed economy. Thus we will analyse a two-sector economy, and then re-introduce the other two sectors later. Thus the economy is assumed to consist of two sectors:

● **Firms**: the sector of the economy responsible for producing all the goods and services in the economy;
● **Households**: the sector which provides factors of production, or factor services, which firms use to produce goods and services.

Thus every resource which a firm wishes to employ has to be bought from someone who lives in a household. In return, the household will receive income which it can then use to purchase the goods which the firms have produced. Firms can then use this to pay income to the factors of production. One sector's receipts are always the expenditure of the other sector.

We can identify four flows which take place between the two sectors:

● spending on goods and services by households (expenditure);
● goods and services produced by firms and sold to households (output);

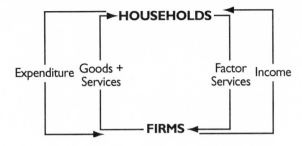

Figure 19.1 *The circular flow of income – real and money flows*

- factor services provided by households to firms
- factor incomes paid by firms to households (income).

These flows are usually shown in diagrammatic form as in Figure 19.1.

The inner part of Figure 19.1 shows the flow of real transactions between firms and households. The outer part represents the payment for these transactions. Thus in return for their factor services, households receive income. This income can then be spent to pay for goods and services produced by firms. This is why the diagram is referred to as the circular flow of income, since income flows from firms to households and back again in a circular manner.

This circular flow diagram is usually re-drawn so as to concentrate on the financial flows which occur. This is shown in Figure 19.2. The expenditure of households is normally known as consumption.

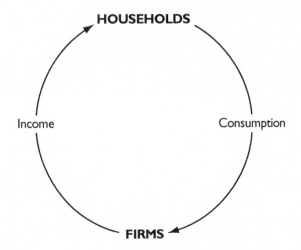

Figure 19.2 *The circular flow of income – financial flows*

Income output and expenditure

The circular flow model suggests that there are three flows which occur between the two sectors:

- Income: which is the total of all receipts earned by households;
- Output: the value of all goods and services produced by firms;
- Expenditure: the value of all spending on goods and services in the economy.

The size of these flows is what we mean when we refer to the level of activity in the economy. An economy with a low level of output will also have a low level of income and expenditure. In fact all three of the flows shown above measure the same thing.

The value of all goods and services produced in an economy will be the same as the value of all the incomes received by households in that economy. Whenever an item is produced, its value must go to somebody in the form of income. Suppose that a table is produced which has a value of £200. The table represents £200 worth of output. Where does the £200 go to? Some will be received by workers in the form of wages. Some will be received by the suppliers of the raw materials. Some will be received by the owners of the firm in the form of profit. All these payments represent income to the people who receive it. This point cannot be over emphasised. Whenever an item is produced, its value goes to someone in the form of income. Thus, in macroeconomics, income and output are the same thing. When an economy increases its output, this not only means that more goods and services are produced, but that higher incomes have been generated which enable this output to be purchased. In Figure 19.2, the flow from firms to households can be thought of as income, or output. The expenditure side of the model is less straight forward.

If households could be relied upon to spend all of the income they received, then expenditure by households would equal income and output. However, households do not spend all of their income. Some income is saved and therefore fails to return back to firms as payment for goods and services. Savings are referred to as a withdrawal from the circular flow since they represent purchasing power withdrawn from the system. Suppose that income/output had a value of £1000, and that households saved £200. Only £800 worth of goods and services would be bought by households. What would happen to the rest?

Some of them would be wanted by firms themselves. Part of the output of any economy consists of goods and services which firms themselves purchase. This may take the form of machinery and new capital. These are known as investment goods. Investment is defined as goods which are produced **not** for current consumption. Thus investment will also include any goods which firms wish to keep in the form of stocks. Suppose in the example above that firms want goods and services with a value of £150.

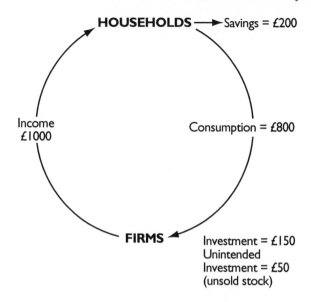

Figure 19.3 *The circular flow of income unintended investment*

This will still leave £50 worth of goods unaccounted for. These goods will remain unsold and so will show up as an unintended increase in stocks. This is shown in Figure 19.3.

Thus, output will equal the combined expenditure of households and firms, with any unintended increase in stocks counted as expenditure by firms. Investment is referred to as an injection into the circular flow since it represents expenditure which arises other than from the income which firms generate for households:

output = income = consumption + investment (intended and unintended)

consumption + investment (intended and unintended) = expenditure

thus,

Output = Expenditure.

The four-sector circular flow model

We can now re-introduce the foreign and the government sector. These sectors will influence the value of goods and services produced in the domestic economy by the way in which they influence the flow of income between firms and households. This will be through their influence on the withdrawals and injection of the circular flow. The full model is shown in Figure 19.4.

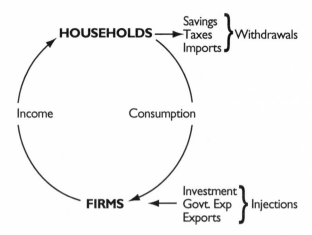

Figure 19.4 *The four-sector model of the circular flow of income*

The income of households might be lost to the circular flow through savings, taxation, or as payment for imported goods and services. Expenditure by households will only ever be a fraction of the total value of goods and services produced in the economy. In the UK it represents about 65% of total output. Additional expenditure will be acquired by the economy in the form of demand by government and the foreign sector (exports). Thus the value of goods produced must be represented by the total of expenditure on domestically-produced goods and services by households, government, foreign purchasers, and firms (including unintended stock changes).

The spending by households is known as consumption. Part of this will be spending on imports. In order to obtain the value of household spending on domestically-produced items, the value of imports must be subtracted. This yields the following result:

$$Y = C + I + Iu + G + X - M$$

where

Y = output (income)
C = total consumer spending
I = intended (planned) investment
Iu = unintended investment (unplanned changes in stocks)
G = government spending on domestically produced goods and services
X = exports of goods and services
M = imports of goods and services

The logic of this process is the idea that if an economy produces goods and services with a particular value, then these goods and services must be in the possession of someone. The only possible destinations for the goods and services are the four sectors identified above. Some will be bought by consumers (total consumption minus imports), some by government (government spending), some by people abroad (exports) and the rest by firms themselves, either in the form of capital goods, or stocks, intended and unintended.

We can now see that complicating the circular flow has not altered the basic result. The value of goods produced by the economy is equivalent to the value of all incomes earned in the economy, and also equal to the value of the total amount of expenditure in the economy. These results provide the basis for National Income Accounting which is the way in which the level of output in an economy is calculated. This forms the basis of the next chapter.

The circular flow also provides the framework in which factors that influence the level of output can be analysed.

Summary

❑ Macroeconomics aggregates the economy into four sectors: households, domestic firms, government and the foreign sector.
❑ The value of all goods and services produced in an economy must go to people in the form of income. Thus total output equals total income.
❑ This income provides the basis for expenditure on the goods and services produced and is thus returned to firms in the form of spending.
❑ Some income is withdrawn from the economy through savings, taxes and imports.
❑ Additional expenditure is injected into the economy by government spending, exports and firms' investment.
❑ All goods and services produced must be distributed between the four sectors, thus the value of all goods and services produced must be equivalent to the value of the goods and services these four sectors acquire.
❑ The acquisitions of households is known as **domestic consumption.**
❑ The acquisitions of government are known as **government spending.**
❑ The acquisitions of the foreign sector are known as **exports.**
❑ The acquisitions of firms are known as **investment** (which includes changes in stocks).
❑ Thus total output must be equivalent to total expenditure.

Multiple Choice Questions

1. Which of the following represent a withdrawal from the circular flow of income:
   - **A** investment
   - **B** imports
   - **C** exports
   - **D** government expenditure
   - **E** consumption

2. Which of the following represent an injection to the circular flow of income?
   - **A** taxation
   - **B** savings
   - **C** imports
   - **D** exports
   - **E** consumption

3. Other things being equal, an increase in the value of exports will lead to:
   - **A** output rising
   - **B** output falling
   - **C** output remaining constant
   - **D** imports falling
   - **E** savings falling

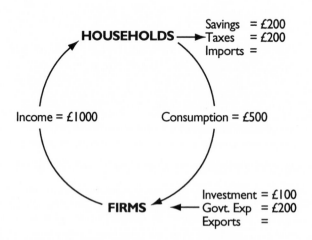

Consider the circular flow of income diagram above.

From the values given, select the value which will correspond to:

4. Exports

    A £100
    B £1000
    C £200
    D £300
    E £500

5. Imports

    A £100
    B £1000
    C £200
    D £300
    E £500

National Income Accounting

Gross domestic product (GDP)

The model we developed in the previous chapter is the basis for calculating
the value of all goods and services produced by an economy during a
particular period of time. The usual time period is taken to be one year, and
we are attempting to measure the value of all goods and services produced
in that year by the particular economy. There are a variety of terms used to
describe this value, but the most important is the concept of Gross

Domestic Product (GDP). This refers to the total output produced by economic activity in the domestic economy during a year. Statistics on GDP are often used to assess how an economy is performing. A large increase in GDP indicates that an economy has produced more goods and services, and hence more income for itself. Changes in GDP are often taken as indicating changes in the standard of living. This will be examined in more detail in the next chapter. As we saw in Chapter Nineteen, there are three ways of looking at the flow of goods and services in an economy. These provide the three ways of measuring GDP.

GDP by the income method

One method of calculating GDP is to simply add up all the incomes earned in an economy during the year in question. Table 20.1 is an example of such calculations for the UK in 1992. The key to the items is given after the table. Note that not all income is received by individuals. Some is earned by companies in the form of profit, while other income is earned by government agencies.

Table 20.1 Gross Domestic Product (income based) UK 1992

Type	£b
Income from employment	341
Income from Self-employment	58
Gross trading profit of companies	65
Gross trading surpluses of public corporations and government enterprises	3
Rent	47
Imputed charge for consumption of non traded capital	4
less stock appreciation	− 2
Gross domestic product (GDP) (income based)	514

Source: CSO, National Income and Expenditure, HMSO

Income from employment is the easiest component to measure (via the income tax system)

Income from self-employment is less easy to measure since there is more scope for under recording. It is a growing part of GDP.

Gross trading profit of companies refers to the profits made by the private sector during the year. The profits may be retained by the firms, or distributed out to households.

Gross trading surpluses of public corporations and government enterprises is income earned by the public sector. This component has been falling as a proportion of GDP because of the increased emphasis on privatisation.

Rent refers to income earned from rented accommodation.

Imputed charge for consumption of non-traded capital is an attempt to measure the fact that people who live in their own houses do not pay rent and yet they receive the benefit of housing services, although no payment is made for them. If the accommodation was rented, rent would be paid. This item is an attempt to measure the benefits. It is a hypothetical figure since it does not reflect any actual payments.

Stock Appreciation measures the fact that goods held in stocks might appreciate in value. This might then show up as an increase in profits. This does not reflect the output of any extra goods or services and so needs to be subtracted from the total.

The GDP figure which has been obtained in Table 20.1 is known as GDP at factor cost, since it represents the factor payments made as a result of producing goods and services.

Transfer earnings and GDP by the income method

One confusion which often arises when measuring GDP by the income method is in deciding what types of income to include. Suppose that a pensioner receives a state pension which is obviously part of the pensioner's income. Should it be included when measuring GDP. The important thing to remember is that GDP is measuring the value of goods and services produced. The pension is not payment for some productive activity, and should therefore be ignored. In fact, the pension is simply income which other people have earned which has been taken off them in tax and then transferred to the pensioner. These transfer payments should not be included in any GDP calculations. GDP only includes incomes earned from some productive activity.

Personal disposable income (PDI)

This is a different definition of income and refers to the total of all incomes received in an economy, including transfer payments, after income taxes and social security contributions have been removed. This is an important economic variable since it measures how much income is available to be spent. This will then be one of the major determinants of spending in an economy. Changes in PDI will indicate a change in people's ability to buy goods and services.

GDP by the output method

The second approach to measuring GDP is to simply add up all the output contributions made by the different industries in the economy. One problem which arises is the difficulty of measuring the output of some industries, especially those in services, where there is no physical output. This problem is solved by taking the value of income received in these industries as a measure of their output. Table 20.2 shows 1992's UK GDP.

Table 20.2 *Gross domestic product (output based) UK 1992*

Output	£b
Agriculture, forestry and fishing	9.3
Mining and quarrying including gas and oil	9.8
Energy and water supply	13.7
Manufacturing	114.7
Construction	32.0
Wholesale and retail trade	72.5
Transport storage and communications	41.6
Financial intermediation, real estate, renting	121.7
Public administration	36.6
Education and health services	52.5
Other services	32.9
	Total 537.7

Some of the value of the output produced by industries goes to the financial sector in the form of interest payments. This shows up as part of the output of the financial sector, and thus must be subtracted where appropriate.

Adjustment for financial services –	23.1
Gross domestic product (GDP) (output based)	514.6

Source: CSO, National Income and Expenditure HMSO.

The output method and dangers of double counting

One danger to avoid when measuring GDP by the output method is the danger of double counting. Many products go through various stages before they are finished. Suppose that a firm buys a semi-finished item for £150, and after carrying out its own production process sells the finished item for £250. What is the total value of the output of the two firms?

It would be a mistake to add up the £150 and the £250, since there has only been a product with a value of £250 produced. To obtain the value of output it is necessary to only add the value added by each firm in the production process. Thus the value of the first firm's output is £150, and the value of the second firm's output is £100, the value that it added to what the first firm produced.

The GDP figure derived from Table 20.2 gives what is known as GDP at factor cost, since it is the value of goods and services produced in terms of the factor services employed to produce those goods and services.

GDP by the expenditure method

As we saw in Chapter Nineteen, the value of goods and services produced can also be obtained by adding the expenditures of the four sectors of the economy. Three of these sectors are domestic and the fourth is the foreign sector. Total domestic expenditure (TDE) is the expenditure which comes from the domestic economy (households, firms and government). These give rise to four categories of expenditure which make up TDE:

- consumer expenditure : the total spending by households (C);
- general government final expenditure: the spending by government on goods and services produced by the economy (G);
- gross domestic fixed capital formation: demand by firms for goods and services in the form of new plant and machinery (I);
- value of physical increase in stocks and work in progress: the goods which have been produced but not sold (I). Thus,

TDE = C + I + G.

As well as expenditure arising from domestic sources, expenditure by the foreign sector, exports (X), are added to the total final expenditure (TFE).

TFE = C + I + G + X

Part of the expenditure may have been on goods from abroad. To eliminate this it is necessary to subtract imports from TFE to arrive at a figure for GDP. This is shown in Table 20.3.

GDP = TFE – M.

Thus,

GDP at market prices = C + I + G + X – M.

Table 20.3 Gross domestic product (expenditure based) UK 1992

Expenditure	£b
Consumer expenditure (C)	382.7
General government expenditure (G)	132.4
Gross domestic fixed capital formation (I)	92.9
Value of physical increase in stocks and work in progress (I)	– 2.0
Total domestic expenditure	**605.9**
Exports of goods and services (X)	139.8
less imports of goods and services (M)	– 149.2
Gross domestic product at market prices	**596.2**

This method gives the value of goods and services bought in the economy. It is valued 'at market prices' since the prices paid will be the prices which rule in the market place. These prices will have been distorted by taxes and subsidies imposed by the government. Taxes will raise the market prices and subsidies will reduce them. In order to eliminate these distortions, GDP at market prices has to be adjusted by deducting the amount of taxes on expenditure, and adding on any subsidies. These adjustments are referred to as factor cost adjustments, since they reveal the actual cost of the items produced.

This adjustment is necessary to give a clear picture of GDP because changes in tax policy will affect GDP at market prices. Suppose the government reduced income taxes and doubled expenditure taxes (e.g. VAT). This would increase the price of goods in the shops, and, hence would increase the amount of money people spend. Thus GDP at market prices would rise. This would not indicate that more goods had been produced, and, so, GDP at market prices is an unreliable indicator of what has been happening to output. Table 20.4 shows the adjustment for the UK in 1992.

Table 20.4 A factor cost adjustment

Factor	£b
GDP at market prices	596.2
Factor cost adjustment, less taxes (T)	– 87.7
plus subsidies (Su)	6.1
Gross domestic product at factor cost (expenditure method)	**514.6**

Thus,

GDP at factor cost = C + I + G + X - M + (Su – T)

This GDP figure should correspond to the two other methods of calculating GDP, since they are all attempting to measure the same thing. In practice there is often a discrepancy between the figures because of the different sources of the information, and the difficulty of obtaining accurate statistics. To overcome this problem, economists sometimes use an average of the three as an estimate of GDP.

Gross national product (GNP)

Gross domestic product is the value of all goods and services produced within the domestic economy. Income may also be earned by UK residents from economic activity which they undertake outside the UK. Thus UK firms might operate abroad and earn profits which are brought back to the UK. UK residents might invest abroad and earn interest. These are productive activities which take place outside the UK and therefore do not show up in GDP. Conversely, a foreign firm in the UK might produce goods (which will be included in GDP), but then take profits out of the UK. These earnings are known as 'property income from abroad'. If these overseas earnings are taken into account we arrive at a figure known as gross national product. Figures for the UK in 1992 are shown in Table 20.5.

Table 20.5 *Gross national product UK 1992*

Element	£b
Gross domestic product at factor cost	514.6
Net property income from abroad	5.8
Gross national product (GNP)	520.4
less capital consumption	– 64.0
Net National product (National income)	**456.4**

If more income left the UK than was earned by UK residents, the net property income from abroad figure would be negative, and, so, GNP would be less than GDP. The size of the property income from abroad depends primarily upon how much overseas investment is undertaken by UK residents. GNP can be derived by using any of the three methods of calculating GDP at factor cost, and then adding in property income from abroad.

Net national product (NNP)

A final adjustment is sometimes made to the GNP figure. Gross domestic fixed capital formation refers to the amount of new capital goods produced in a year. Some of these new machines will be simply to replace machines which have worn out or become obsolete. Thus they do not really represent an increase in the stock of capital goods. Suppose that new machines worth £100m are produced, but that machinery valued at £15m has been lost through depreciation. This only represents an increase of £85m in capital goods in the economy. Taking capital depreciation, also known as capital consumption, into account means deducting it from GNP, to arrive at a figure known as net national product. Thus,

NNP = GNP – capital consumption

Net national product is also known as national income

Summary

❏ Gross domestic product (GDP) is a measure of the value of all goods and services produced within the domestic economy.

❏ GDP by the income method consists of adding up all the incomes earned by people in the domestic economy for providing factor services.

❏ Transfer payments should not be included in GDP since they are not payments for productive effort.

❏ GDP by the output method involves adding up the output of all parts of the economy.

❏ Only the value added by a firm should count in GDP calculations, to avoid double counting.

❏ GDP by the expenditure method consists of adding up the expenditure of all four sectors of the economy.

❏ Total domestic expenditure = C + I + G.

❏ Total final expenditure = C + I + G + X.

❏ GDP at market prices = C + I + G + X − M.

❏ GDP at factor cost = GDP at market prices **less** taxes, **plus** subsidies.

❏ Gross national product (GNP) = GDP at factor cost **plus** net property income from abroad.

❏ Net national product (NNP) = GNP **less** capital consumption.

❏ NNP is also known as national income

Multiple Choice Questions

Below are national income statistics for a hypothetical economy:

Element	£m
Total domestic expenditure	5000
Exports of goods and services	1000
Imports of goods and services	800
Indirect taxes	500
Subsidies	200
Net property income from abroad	− 100
Capital consumption	100

Select the value of:

1. GDP at factor cost

   A £5200
   B £4900
   C £6800
   D £5500
   E £4700

2. GDP at market prices

   A £5200
   B £4900
   C £6800
   D £5500
   E £4700

3. National income

   A £5200
   B £4900
   C £6800
   D £5500
   E £4700

Element	£m
Consumer expenditure	1000
General government expenditure	300
Gross fixed domestic capital formation	200
Value of physical increase in stocks	100
Exports	400
Imports	500
Indirect taxes	200
Subsidies	100

Consider the national income statistics. From the options, select the value which corresponds to:

4. Total final expenditure

5. GDP at factor cost

   A £1400m
   B £1600m
   C £2000m
   D £1500m
   E £2300m

Chapter Twenty-one

GDP and the Standard of Living

Key concepts

- ❐ The use of GDP figures as an indicator of the standard of living
- ❐ Reasons why GDP figures may not be an accurate measure of economic activity
- ❐ The problem of changing prices when comparing GDP over time, and a possible solution in the use of index numbers
- ❐ Additional factors affecting the standard of living

Key words

GDP per head (per capita)
The hidden economy, the DIY economy
Current prices, constant prices, weighted price index, retail price index

GDP as a measure of living standards

An increase in GDP is usually taken as an indication of an increase in the output of goods and services produced by the economy. This implies that there are more goods and services available for people to enjoy, and that, therefore, people's standard of living will rise. Thus the standard of living is normally taken to depend upon the quantity of goods and services which the population of an economy are able to enjoy. This is obviously only true if the population has not increased more rapidly than GDP. In order to account for this, GDP per head figures are used. This is simply GDP divided by the population of the economy. Thus if GDP is £250b, and the population is 50m, the GDP per head is £5000. This is also referred to as per capita GDP. It is this figure which is often used to compare living standards over time, or between different countries. This process is flawed for two reasons:

- GDP figures may not be an accurate measure of output.
- other factors will affect living standards.

GDP and the hidden economy

In the United Kingdom, data for measuring GDP by the income and output methods is derived primarily from tax returns. If income is earned or output produced, but not declared to the tax authorities, GDP figures will underestimate the level of economic activity. This undeclared economic activity is said to have taken place in the hidden economy and there are three forms which it might take:

- legally obtained income which is not reported
- illegal income e.g. drug dealing, prostitution
- personal income in kind – taking payment in the form of goods and services rather than money.

All three of these will make an accurate measure of income, and hence output, very difficult. Estimates of the size of the hidden economy are, for obvious reasons, likely to be highly approximate. It is sometimes argued that its importance in recent years has increased, partly because of the increasing burden of taxation as more and more people have become eligible to pay income tax. This has given more people an incentive to avoid taxation. Secondly, the increased numbers of self-employed workers has made non-declaration more possible. The growth in the numbers unemployed may also have made 'moonlighting' more prevalent.

The growth of the hidden economy means that official statistics will increasingly under estimate the size of GDP. This may have important repercussions if policy decisions are taken on the basis of these figures. It is possible that an increase in unemployment and a drop in GDP might be the result of more and more activities being undertaken in the hidden economy.

Economists have tried to estimate the size of the hidden economy in various economies. Figures for the UK usually suggest that it represents 5–10% of GDP. Estimates for Italy suggest a figure nearer 30%. The problem is also severe in the Third World where, because of the difficulties involved with collecting data and the less-sophisticated taxation systems, scope for evasion and illegality is greater.

GDP and the informal (DIY) economy

GDP statistics will only include economic activity which takes place in a market where some monetary transaction occurs. Any work which takes place outside the market system, for which no payment is made will not be recorded. If you decide to have your house painted and you employ a painter, the value of the work will be included in figures of GDP (assuming the painter declares his income). If you painted the house yourself, the same economic activity has taken place, but it will not be part of GDP. Similarly, if you repair a neighbour's car in return for help with your garden, economic activities have taken place, but they cannot be recorded as part of GDP.

This aspect of GDP as a measure of output is especially important for developing countries. In the developing world many activities take place at home, for example subsistence farming. In the developed world these activities would form part of the formal economy and so would be included in GDP.

These arguments suggest that GDP figures may not provide an accurate measure of the output of an economy and that they may give a misleading idea of the size of per capita GDP. If this is the case, then these figures are an unreliable guide to the standard of living **if** per capita GDP is taken as an indicator of the standard of living. Even if GDP statistics were accurate, there would still be the problem of whether GDP is a measure of living standards.

GDP may not reflect living standards

The production of any good will increase GDP and so, if per capita GDP is taken as a measure of the standard of living, the increase in GDP would seem to indicate that the quality of life must have increased. It is possible, however, that the production of certain items might be undesirable. This is most likely to be due to the presence of externalities. If a product is produced which imposes severe costs on some section of society, it is conceivable that society may have its welfare reduced by that product, despite the fact that GDP will have risen.

GDP and the distribution of income

It is possible that a country might have a high GDP per capita, but that all of the output is captured by a very small section of the population. In these circumstances it would be difficult to argue that the country has a high standard of living, since the majority of the population might be living in poverty.

Alternative measures of the standard of living

There are many other factors which might affect the standard of living, other than GDP per head. It is possible to suggest other indicators of living standards:

- life expectancy
- levels of crime
- standards of literacy
- infant mortality.

Suppose that the level of crime rose and that more police were employed as a result. If the police were not effective at reducing crime, the quality of life would probably be seen as having fallen despite the fact that measured GDP would rise because of the increased police services being 'enjoyed'.

GDP and prices

One problem with using GDP figures over time, as a measure of living standards, is that changes in the price level will increase the value of GDP, but this will not represent an increase in the quantity of goods and services available. Thus if prices were to rise by 20%, this would increase the value of goods and services bought by 20%, but in real terms there would have been no increase. In order to overcome this problem it is necessary to adjust the GDP figures to take account of any changes in prices. This will allow us to see by how much GDP would have changed if prices had remained constant. The usual way in which this is done is to express price changes as some percentage change from some base year. This then allows a price index to be calculated. Consider the information in Table 21.1. It is difficult to see the relative increase in the price of these three items

Table 21.1 *Prices in 1985 and 1986*

Item	1985	1986
Loaf of bread	30p	33p
Kilo of potatoes	26p	30p
Pint of beer	90p	95p

from the information above (unless you happen to have a calculator). A simple way of showing the changes is to take the price in 1985, give it the value 100, and express the prices in 1986 as a percentage of the price in 1985. For example, between 1985 and 1986 the price of bread rose by 3p. This represents an increase of 10% from the price in 1985. If the price in 1985 is given the value 100, the price in 1986 would have a value of 110.

Similarly, the price of potatoes has risen by 15.4%, and the price of beer by 5.6% This information can then be presented in the form of a price index, as shown in Table 21.2.

This table introduces the idea of index numbers which show relative

Table 21.2 Prices of goods (1985 = 100)

Item	1985	1986
Bread	100	110
Potatoes	100	115.4
Beer	100	105.6

increases in the value of the items in the index. The statement (1985 = 100) indicates that prices are being shown as percentages of their 1985 value. These indices can be used to overcome the problem of price changes when output is altering, so as to permit real increases in output to be measured.

Suppose that in 1985 a brewery had an output valued at £100m. In 1986 output had risen to £110m. This would appear to be an increase of 10%. However, we know that the price of beer had risen by 5.6% and so some of the increase is simply due to the price rise. In order to determine the physical increase in output we need to know what the 1986 output would have sold for if the price of beer had remained at its 1985 level. This is calculated by dividing the value of output in 1986 by the 1986 price index and multiplying by 100

$$\frac{£110m \times 100}{105.6}$$

This gives a value of £104.2. Thus, if prices had stayed at the 1985 level, output would only have risen by 4.2%. This is referred to as the increase at constant 1985 prices, and this measure gives a much better indication of the physical increase in output, which is what GDP figures are trying to estimate.

Current and constant prices

When figures are given for the values of output based on the different price levels in the various years, this is known as expressing GDP at current prices. This is how they are collected each year. In order to allow comparisons to be made over time, it is necessary to adjust the figures for inflation. This is done by dividing by the price index for each year. This transforms the figures into output at constant prices, based on the price level ruling in the base year. This is always indicated by showing the base year = 100. In the example above this is 1985 = 100.

In order to adjust GDP figures in this way, we need a price index which can be used for GDP as a whole. This is known as the GDP deflator, and it is a type of average figure for all commodities. To show how this is calculated we will show how another price index is worked out for the economy as a whole – the retail price index.

The retail price index (RPI)

Because the prices of all goods do not change by the same amount, we need to calculate some sort of average. Some commodities will be more important in a household's expenditure than others. Suppose that the economy only produced two items. If one item doubled in price, but that item represented a very small proportion of the total output of the economy, while the other item which was a large proportion of GDP fell in price, it would not be sensible to take a straight average of the two price changes. More weight should be given to the more important item. This is achieved by weighting the price of items depending upon how important they are in terms of the proportion of total expenditure or output which the good represents.

Suppose that bread, potatoes and beer represent 25%, 25% and 50% of expenditure respectively. (We are assuming only three products exist.) The average, weighted price index is calculated in Table 21.3.

Thus the weighted price increase for all three items is 9.2% as compared

Table 21.3 General price index (1985 = 100)

	1985	proportion of expenditure (A)	1986 (B)	weighted price (A × B)
Bread	100	25%	110	27.5
Potatoes	100	25%	115.4	28.9
Beer	100	50%	105.6	52.8
GPI	100	100%		109.2

with a straight average of over 10%. The fact that beer is more important, and that its price rose by only 5.6%, has caused the weighted average to be lower.

In order to calculate the RPI, which attempts to show how prices of all commodities have risen, obviously more than three items are included. In the UK the RPI is based upon the changes in price of a 'basket' of 350 different goods and services, but the calculations follow the example in Table 21.3. Periodically the items which are considered change to reflect changes in expenditure patterns. It has been suggested that the price of skiing holidays should be included since these now represent a significant part of household expenditure.

GDP at constant prices

In order to convert GDP at current prices into GDP at constant prices, to allow meaningful comparisons to be made over time, it is necessary to deflate the GDP figures expressed in current prices by a price index, to show the changes after price changes have been eliminated. Table 21.4 gives GDP at current prices from 1976 to 1984, and the RPI (1980 = 100) for those years. The third row gives the GDP expressed in constant 1980 prices and is obtained by dividing the first row by the second, and then multiplying by 100.

Table 21.4 *GDP at constant and current prices, 1976–1984*

	76	77	78	79	80	81	82	83	84
GDP (current prices £m)	126	146	168	196	230	254	277	301	319
RPI (1985 = 100)	58	66	73	83	100	112	120	126	132
GDP (constant {1980} prices)	217	221	230	236	230	227	231	239	242

The importance of this process can be seen by examining the figures for 1981. In current prices GDP rose by £24M. This would appear to be a significant increase of 10.4%. However, in 1981 prices rose by 12%, and, so, when this is taken into account, and GDP expressed at 1980 constant prices, GDP is seen to fall. Fewer goods and services were sold in 1981 even though they had a higher value.

Summary

- ❏ GDP per head (per capita) is often taken as a measure of the standard of living.
- ❏ GDP figures are not always an accurate measure of output.
- ❏ GDP figures do not include activity in the hidden economy.
- ❏ GDP figures do not include productive activity in the informal (DIY) economy.
- ❏ Other factors, crime, education, health, can affect the standard of living.
- ❏ Over time the value of GDP will change as prices alter.
- ❏ To eliminate the affect of inflation, GDP figures must be deflated by a price index.
- ❏ The Retail Price Index (RPI) is a weighted average of the price level of a typical 'basket' of goods and services.
- ❏ The weights in the RPI reflect the proportion of expenditure which each good or service represents
- ❏ GDP at current prices reflects the actual prices charged in the shops, and so is affected by price changes
- ❏ GDP at constant prices reflects the value of goods and services produced if prices had remained at the level of the base year .

Multiple Choice Questions

In the table below, household expenditure is allocated among three products, X, Y and Z.

Product	1990		1991	
	Price index	% of total expenditure	Price index	% of total expenditure
X	100	50	110	50
Y	100	25	120	30
Z	100	25	130	20

1. Which of the following represents the value of the weighted price index for all three in 1991?

   A 120
   B 117
   C 170
   D 118
   E 110

2. An increase in the retail price index must necessarily imply:

   A an increase in the standard of living
   B a fall in the standard of living
   C an increase in the cost of living
   D a fall in the cost of living
   E an increase in the price of all goods and services

3. Which of the following would lead to an increase in per capita GDP?

   A an increase in state retirement pension
   B a fall in unemployment
   C lower income tax
   D higher income tax
   E a fall in the population

4. Consider the table which gives price indices for three countries from 1981 to 1983.

Country	1981	1982	1983
X	100	110	114
Y	100	108	115
Z	100	99	114

Select the statement which applies to these figures.

   A in 1983 prices in country Y rose by 7%
   B in 1983 country Y had the largest increase in prices
   C in 1983 country Z had the largest increase in prices
   D in 1982 prices in country Z rose by 1%
   E in 1983 country Z had an inflation rate of 14%

5. A person is given a wage increase of £2000 per year. If during the following year prices in the economy rise by 15%, other things being equal, which of the following best represents the purchasing power of the increase?

   A £1700
   B £2300
   C £1850
   D £1739
   E £2000

Chapter Twenty-two

The Determination of Output

Key concepts

☐ Factors affecting the equilibrium level of output in the economy

☐ Whether the economy can experience a deficiency in demand

☐ The possibility of the rate of interest adjusting to compensate for a lack of demand

☐ The Keynesian belief that a lack of demand was the most likely explanation for falling output

Key words

Equilibrium level of income

Market for loanable funds

Aggregate demand, paradox of thrift, the Keynesian multiplier

Equilibrium in macro economics

In Chapter Twenty we saw how economists measure the value of goods and services produced in the economy. This still leaves the question of how the level of output is determined. As we have seen, output and expenditure are the same thing if we accept that goods and services which are unsold are thought of as having been bought by firms and added to their stocks. If this did happen we would not expect firms to keep producing at the same level and at the same prices. Thus, firms would not be able to maintain their price and output decisions. This must mean that they are no longer in an equilibrium position, since an equilibrium is a position where there are no forces indicating a change and where demand and supply are equal. If firms are producing more goods than can be sold, this represents an excess supply of goods.

In order to arrive at an equilibrium the planned output of firms must just equal the planned expenditure of the four sectors of the economy. Thus equilibrium in macroeconomics is very similar to equilibrium in microeconomics. It is where demand equals supply at the macro level. This is sometimes known as the position where aggregate demand equals aggregate supply. If aggregate (total) demand in the economy does not equal total (aggregate) supply, there is either an excess supply of goods and services, or an excess demand. If this situation persists, firms will be forced to alter their price or output decisions.

Equilibrium and the circular flow of income

In order to see the basic features of the problem we will begin with a simple two sector model of the economy, and assume a closed economy (no foreign trade) and no government sector. Thus the economy illustrated in Figure 22.1 consists only of households and firms.

Suppose that output has a value of £1000 and this is distributed to households in the form of income. If households saved 20% of income, they would consume £800, and so demand £800 worth of goods and services from firms. In order for firms to be able to sell all their output they require an extra £200 worth of demand. The only sector which this can

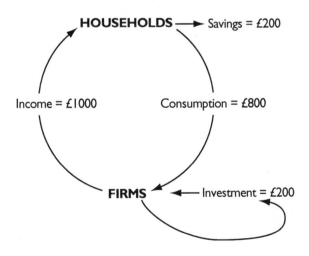

Figure 22.1 *Equilibrium and the circular flow of income*

come from is their own sector in the form of investment demand. This may take the form of capital investment (gross fixed capital formation) or through a desire to build up stocks. If these two forms of investment demand add up to £200, the economy will be in equilibrium. This means that equilibrium requires that planned investment must just equal planned savings.

We saw in Chapter Twenty that actual investment and actual savings are always equal, because of unintended investment in the form of unintended changes in stocks. Equilibrium requires that the intended behaviour of firms and households can be carried out, and so equilibrium is concerned with whether or not planned demand and supply are equal. The circular flow is said to be in equilibrium when the amount of purchasing power which is lost to the system through planned withdrawals is just compensated for by additional expenditure in the form of planned injections. This condition is a necessary aspect of equilibrium whether we are considering a two sector economy or a four sector economy; planned withdrawals must equal planned injections if the economy is to be in equilibrium.

Suppose that planned investment is only equal to £150. Firms would find that they could only sell £950 worth of output and £50 worth of output would remain unsold and so accumulate in stocks. The economy is not in equilibrium. There is a lack of demand. The way in which the economy might respond to this shortfall in demand is at the heart of many of the disputes in macro economics.

Loanable funds and the rate of interest

One view, which was current in the early decades of this century, was that any discrepancy between planned savings and planned investment would be eliminated by changes in the rate of interest. This process took place in what was known as the market for loanable funds.

Savings were seen as depending upon the rate of interest. If interest rates rose, it was assumed that this would increase the amount saved. Investment was also seen as depending upon the rate of interest. If interest rates rose, this would discourage investment in new plant and machinery (and stocks) since it would make borrowing more expensive. This is the idea we saw in Chapter 17 when discussing investment. Thus both savings and investment were seen as functions of the rate of interest, as shown in Figure 22.2.

Not only were savings and investment seen as depending upon the rate of interest, but they also determined the rate of interest in the market for loanable funds. Savings represented the supply of loanable funds and will increase as the interest rate rises, as shown in Figure 22.2. Investment represented the demand for loanable funds and is shown as increasing as interest rates fall. If people wished to save more funds than firms wished to invest, there would be an excess supply of funds, and interest rates would fall. Conversely, if savings were insufficient to meet the demand for

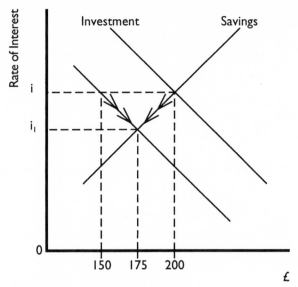

Figure 22.2 *The market for loanable funds*

loanable funds, the rate of interest would rise. Interest rates would adjust until savings and investment were equal.

In Figure 22.2 both savings and investment are shown as being equal to £200. This would put the circular flow in Figure 22.1 into equilibrium. Suppose that planned investment now falls to £150. In the circular flow this would appear to mean that aggregate demand (consumer demand plus the firm's demand for investment goods), was now only £950, whilst output was £1000. The economy appears to suffer from a lack of demand.

In the market for loanable funds the demand for funds (investment) has fallen (shown by shifting the demand curve to the left). At the original interest rate firms only wish to invest £150. The resulting excess supply of loanable funds puts pressure on the interest rate to fall. As it falls, three things happen. Savings start to fall. Consumption starts to rise (since lower savings must imply that more is being spent). Investment starts to increase. Eventually, savings and investment will equalise at £175 and an interest rate of i_1. If savings have fallen to £175, consumption must have risen to £825. Thus total demand (consumption plus investment) equals £1000, which is the output which is being produced. The circular flow is back in equilibrium, without output being disturbed.

This view of macroeconomics saw the rate of interest as the mechanism through which any shortfall in demand could be rectified. If output had a value of £1000, then the interest rate would adjust to ensure that demand was £1000. This view, which was strongly criticised by Keynes in the 1930s, had important policy conclusions for government. Consider Figure 22.3.

If we reintroduce the foreign sector and government, we can see that

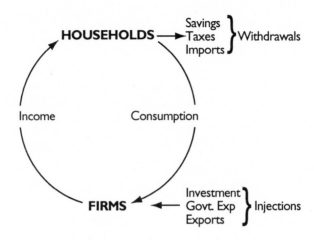

Figure 22.3 *Four sector model*

equilibrium now requires that total withdrawals equal total injections. In other words:

I + G + X = S + T + M.

If the loanable funds market ensured that S = I, and the workings of the gold standard ensured that X = M, then the only policy which the government had to follow was to ensure that G = T. This meant that governments were advised to balance their budgets and to make sure that tax revenues were equal to government spending.

This view of macroeconomics suggested that a recession could not be due to a lack of demand, but must be caused by factors which prevented firms from producing as much as they were previously. It was not an inability to sell their output which was the problem, but an inability to produce. Thus unemployment was blamed on wages being too high, or unemployment benefit reducing the incentive to work.

In the 1930s, when mass unemployment reduced taxes, and increased government spending on unemployment benefit, the budget was moving into deficit. Economists advised the government that the correct response was to raise taxes and to cut government spending. This did not appear to improve the situation.

In 1936, John Maynard Keynes, a leading economist, revolutionised the way in which economists viewed macroeconomics, by arguing that demand did not always adjust to equal whatever output was being produced, but that instead it was more likely that output would adjust to meet aggregate demand.

Keynes and the role of aggregate demand

Keynes dismissed the idea that the rate of interest could be relied upon the ensure that savings and investment would be equal. He argued that there was no real link between savings and investment. They were undertaken by different people, whose motivations were not the same. He argued that savings depended primarily on the level of income in the economy. Savings were seen as a residual, and were what was left over after households had decided their level of consumption.

Investment was seen as depending upon the rate of interest, but also upon expectations, and the rate of interest was seen as being determined by monetary factors, not the demand and supply of loanable funds.

Keynes argued that if there was a fall in demand (perhaps a fall in investment demand), firms would experience difficulty in selling their output, and that their most likely response would be to cut output. This would cut income and so would cut savings. This process would continue until savings had fallen to the same level as investment. At this point withdrawals and injections would again be equal, and the circular flow would be back in equilibrium. Thus Keynes emphasised that any changes in the level of aggregate demand would cause changes in the level of output. Keynesian economics came to be characterised by the phrase 'demand creates its own supply'. Thus Keynesian economics is based on the proposition that the level of output in an economy depends primarily upon the level of aggregate demand.

The paradox of thrift

Prior to Keynes, savings had always been seen as a desirable form of behaviour, since it would encourage investment. Keynes argued that saving might be a private virtue, but that it was a public vice. Suppose that people suddenly decide to save a larger proportion of their income. This means that the level of demand would fall. Firms would accumulate unsold stocks, and according to the Keynesian view they would be likely to cut their output. This fall in output would necessarily reduce income, and this would force people to reduce their savings. Indeed, if investment was also reduced because of the fall in demand, it is possible that demand and incomes might fall to such an extent that people might eventually be saving less than they were saving before they decided to save more! If governments wished to reduce unemployment, by encouraging firms to increase output, the solution lay in stimulating aggregate demand.

The Keynesian multiplier

Keynes also argued that if there was a fall in aggregate demand, the resulting fall in output would be greater than the initial fall in demand.

Output would fall by a multiple of the change in demand. Suppose that the economy is in equilibrium at an output level of £1000. Investment expenditure now falls by £100. Firms will only be able to sell £900 worth of output and so let us assume that they cut output to £900. This fall in output reduces income and so will also reduce consumer spending. Thus firms will not be able to sell £900 worth of output and so will be forced to reduce output below £900. This in turn reduces income even further, again reducing consumer spending. Thus output and incomes will continue falling until savings have fallen to a level where they once again equal investment. This is known as the multiplier process, and it is an important element of Keynesian economics, suggesting that a fall in investment demand of £100 causes output to fall by more than £100. This process is shown in Figure 22.4 for a simple two sector economy, with no government or foreign trade.

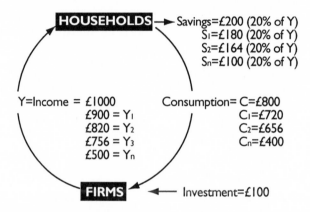

Figure 22.4 *The multiplier process*

Assume that households always save 20% of their income and that initially the economy is in equilibrium at an output level of £1000. Equilibrium requires that savings equal investment, and so investment must be £200. Investment now falls to £100. In response to this fall in demand, firms cut their output to £900, and so income falls to £900 (shown as Y_1). This fall in income means that savings fall to £180 and consumption falls to £720 (shown as S_1 and C_1). Total demand is now only £820 (consumption plus investment demand).

Firms may react to this by cutting output to £820 (Y_2). Savings will fall to £164 (S_2) and consumption to £656 (C_2). Total demand is now only £756, and income will again fall (Y_3). The process will continue, with the reduction becoming smaller until savings have fallen to £100, at which point withdrawals are again equal to injections. In order for savings to equal £100, income must have fallen to £500 (since savings are 20% of income). Thus an initial fall in investment demand of £100 has caused output to fall five times as much. In this case the multiplier is said to have a value of five. The mechanics of the multiplier will be seen in more detail in the next chapter.

Prices and equilibrium

We have seen two possible reactions to a fall in demand – a fall in the rate if interest, or a fall in income. There is a third possibility; an inability to sell all the goods which they produce, might encourage firms to cut their prices. If this happened, demand would be stimulated for two reasons:

● Falling prices would make UK goods more competitive and so would boost exports. Thus injections would increase, and restore demand to its previous level.
● A fall in the price level would increase the purchasing power of money in the economy. People's savings would be worth more, and this might encourage them to increase spending so as to compensate for the lack of demand.

Both of these mechanisms would ensure that any lack of demand was short-lived and would be offset by an increase in demand from either exports or consumption. The extent to which price changes will accommodate any changes in demand is an issue that will be examined later. It is usual to assume that the most likely reaction of firms to a lack of demand will be a fall in output.

Output and an increase in demand

In all the examples we have used so far, we have been dealing with the reaction to a fall in demand, or a situation where withdrawals exceed investment. The same processes will operate if the economy experiences an increase in demand, such that injections exceed withdrawals. If firms find that demand exceeds output, they will experience a run down in stocks. As long as the economy has spare resources available, it is normally assumed that firms will respond by increasing output. This increase in output will increase income, which in turn will raise consumption and the multiplier process will again operate. It is possible that the excess demand might put pressure on prices to rise (so reducing demand) or put pressure on the interest rate to rise (again reducing demand), but the Keynesian assumption is that the most likely reaction will be an increase in output. Thus, according to this view, the level of output is determined by the level of demand in the economy. Changes in demand will generate changes in output.

Summary

❏ Equilibrium exists when planned withdrawals equal planned injections in the circular flow of income.
❏ If withdrawals exceed injections (planned savings exceed planned investment) there will be a lack of demand in the economy.
❏ The loanable funds theory suggests that movements in the rate of interest will restore equilibrium by boosting investment and reducing savings.
❏ Keynesian analysis suggests that a lack of demand will lead to a fall in the level of income, which will reduce savings and restore equilibrium.
❏ In the case of output (income) falling, there will be further reductions in demand because of its impact on consumption.
❏ This will cause output to fall further than suggested by the original fall of demand.
❏ Income will fall a multiple of the initial fall in demand. This is known as the multiplier result.
❏ A lack of demand might cause prices to fall, which might increase consumption and reduce savings.

Multiple Choice Questions

1. The circular flow of income will be in equilibrium when:
   A savings equal income
   B withdrawals equal income
   C injections equal investment
   D withdrawals equal injections
   E income equals consumption

2. In the circular flow of income, withdrawals are equal to £1000 and injections are equal to £1000. Consumption is equal to £800. The equilibrium level of income is:
   A £1000
   B £1800
   C £800
   D £200
   E £2800

3. You are told that the multiplier has a value of 3. This means that:
   A   an increase in income of £1000 causes investment to rise by £3000
   B   an increase in investment of £1000 causes income to fall by £3000
   C   an increase in savings of £1000 causes income to rise by £3000
   D   a fall in investment of £1000 causes income to fall by £3000
   E   a fall in savings of £1000 causes investment to fall by £3000

4. A fall in the rate if interest might boost aggregate demand because:
   A   savings will increase
   B   investment will fall
   C   consumer spending will fall
   D   investment might increase
   E   prices might increase

5. The paradox of thrift suggests that:
   A   an increase in savings will boost income
   B   a fall in savings will boost income
   C   a higher income will boost savings
   D   savings are irrational
   E   higher savings will reduce unemployment

Equilibrium in the Circular Flow

The Keynesian income – expenditure model

In this chapter we will examine the Keynesian expenditure model of the macro economy. This approach is based on the belief that a fall in demand will lead to a fall in output, because there will not be strong forces correcting the lack of demand. The central idea is that firms will respond to a lack of demand by reducing output. This in turn will reduce income which will then lead to a further drop in output, until eventually, equilibrium is restored.

There are two ways of viewing the conditions necessary for equilibrium in the circular flow of income:

- income (output) must equal expenditure.
- planned withdrawals must equal planned injections.

These two conditions can be seen in Figure 23.1.

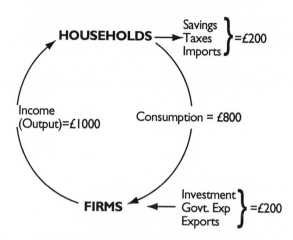

Figure 23.1 *Equilibrium in the circular flow*

If the level of output is to remain at £1000, firms must be able to sell £1000 worth of output. In order for this to occur, the purchasing power lost to the system through withdrawals (savings, taxes and imports) must be compensated for by additional expenditure in the form of injections (investment, government expenditure, and exports). If £200 is lost in withdrawals, it is necessary for injections to equal £200. Thus, as we saw in the previous chapter, for equilibrium:

$$S + T + M = I + G + X$$

Equilibrium can also be seen as requiring total output (Y) to be just equal to total expenditure. Total expenditure must arise from the four sectors of the economy. Thus total expenditure is:

C = expenditure by households on domestic
goods and services: **consumption**
I = planned expenditure by firms on
goods and service: **investment**
G = expenditure by government on
goods and services: **government expenditure**
X = expenditure by the foreign sector
on goods and services: **exports**

To create equilibrium: $Y = C + I + G + X$.

Thus in order to examine equilibrium, we can use either of these two approaches, both of which are based on the idea that equilibrium requires planned expenditure to equal output.

Withdrawals and injections – the Keynesian cross

Keynesian economics not only suggests that equilibrium requires that withdrawals equal injections, but also that if the two are not equal, there will be forces at work which will cause income to change to restore equilibrium. Consider Figure 23.2

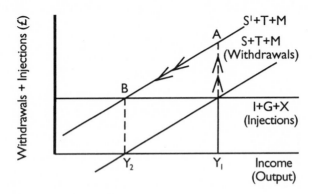

Figure 23.2 The Keynesian cross

Figure 23.2 shows the relationship between withdrawals, injections and income. As income rises we would expect withdrawals to also rise. As income rises, savings will increase, taxes paid will increase, and so will imports. Thus withdrawals are shown as a rising function of income. Injections on the other hand are usually seen as being independent of income. Investment is thought of as being governed by decisions taken by firms, which need not be related to income. Government expenditure will be determined by government, and exports will depend upon the behaviour of people abroad. Thus injections are shown as being fixed with respect to income. Withdrawals will be equal to injections at income level Y_1.

Suppose that the economy is in equilibrium and there is then a decision by households to save a larger proportion of their income. This will cause the withdrawals curve to shift upwards. (Withdrawals and injections are being measured on the vertical axis.) The new equilibrium will be at a lower income level, shown as Y_2. What is the process that will move the economy to Y_2?

At Y_1, given the increase in savings, withdrawals will now exceed injections. In other words, the level of expenditure in the economy will be less than the value of goods and services being produced, since more purchasing power is being lost to the system – in the form of withdrawals – than is being gained in the form of injections. Firms will respond by reducing output. As output falls so does income, which in turn reduces withdrawals. In terms of Figure 23.2, withdrawals start to contract from point A towards point B. Output will continue to fall until equilibrium is restored at point B, where withdrawals again equal injections.

This is the basis of the paradox of thrift – a decision to save more has led to a fall in income, which will then reduce savings. This gives the classic Keynesian argument that falls in the level of planned expenditures will cause falls in output.

A similar process will result in an increase in output if there is an increase in demand. Suppose that the economy is in equilibrium as shown in Figure 23.3 by point A.

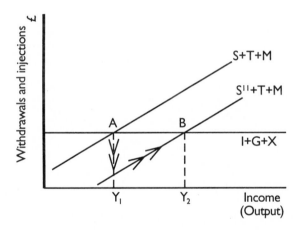

Figure 23.3 *The Keynesian cross: an increase in demand*

There is now an increase in demand, perhaps due to a fall in savings. The withdrawals line will shift downwards. This will cause injections to exceed withdrawals, and thus planned expenditure to exceed output. If there are spare resources in the economy, the Keynesian argument would be that output would rise to meet the demand. Income would rise, until it was once again in equilibrium at point B.

This analysis is at the heart of Keynesian economics and is usually characterised by the idea that 'demand creates its own supply'.

Aggregate demand and equilibrium

Equilibrium can also be illustrated by using a diagram commonly known as a 45° line diagram. This is shown in Figure 23.4.

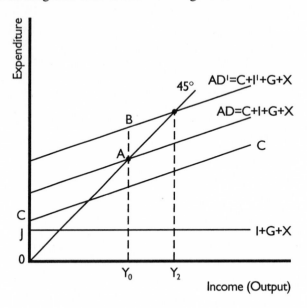

Figure 23.4 *Income-expenditure model*

The graph shows the relationship between planned expenditure and income. Planned expenditure consists of $C + I + G + X$. The last three of these terms $(I + G + X)$ constitute injections and as we saw earlier, they are assumed not to depend upon income. Thus they can be shown as a horizontal line at the required level. The distance OJ represents injections. Consumer expenditure (C) will depend upon income. Keynes suggested, and much evidence has since confirmed, that consumption would be positively related to income. This is shown by the line CC. In order to graph total demand it is necessary to add both schedules together. This gives the line labelled $AD = C + I + G + X$. This is known as the aggregate demand schedule. It simply shows that aggregate demand will increase as income rises. In order to identify the equilibrium level of income it is necessary to find the income level at which withdrawals are equal to injections, or the level where income equals total expenditure (aggregate demand). This is achieved by drawing a line from the origin with a 45° angle. This artificial device must show all points where the two axes are equal. Where the 45° line cuts the aggregate demand curve must represent the point where aggregate demand equals income. This must show the equilibrium level of income for an economy with the levels of demand shown by AD. Equilibrium is at Y_0. This diagram can be used to show the impact of a change in aggregate demand.

Suppose that the economy experiences an increase in demand, perhaps due to an increase in planned investment. This will result in the aggregate demand schedule shifting upwards by the amount of the increase and is shown as AD^1. (The shift in the injections line is not shown.) At the original equilibrium (Y_0 in Figure 23.4), aggregate demand will now exceed income by the distance AB. This excess demand for goods and services will encourage firms to increase output. This will raise income until a new equilibrium is established at an income level Y_1.

An inflationary gap

Suppose that in Figure 23.5 Y_1 was the level of output associated with the full use of resources in the economy. This is sometimes referred to as representing the full employment level of output.

If aggregate demand rose even further, say to the level shown by the schedule AD^1, it would not be possible for the economy to produce an output (income) level above Y_1. Thus demand would exceed the level necessary for full employment by the distance CD. This excess demand is likely to put pressure on prices, and so the gap CD is known as an inflationary gap. It is the amount by which aggregate demand exceeds the level necessary for full employment.

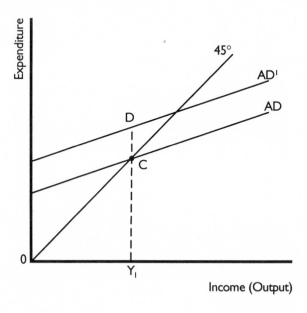

Figure 23.5 *An inflationary gap*

The multiplier

As we saw in the previous chapter, the multiplier process refers to the fact that an increase in demand will lead to an increase in output which will be a multiple of the initial increase in demand. This is because any increase in income is bound to create additional consumer spending, which will reinforce the original expansion. Consider Figure 23.6 which represents a crude estimate of the multiplier process in the UK.

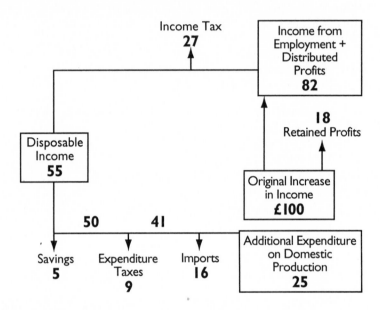

Figure 23.6 *The multiplier in the UK: an estimate*

Suppose that initially the economy experiences an increase in demand of £100, perhaps because of an increase in export demand. This is depicted in the right hand box as causing an increase in output of £100. This must represent income to people in the UK. Evidence suggests that part of this will be kept by firms in the form of retained profits, but the rest will go to households, either in the form of dividends, or as income from employment. The figures are fairly realistic estimates of the sums involved.

Households will pay tax on their gross earnings and Figure 23.5 suggests that they will only receive about 55% of the initial increase in output. Some of this will withdrawn from the circular flow in savings, some will be spent on imports, some will be paid as expenditure taxes, and only about £25 will come back to firms in the form of additional demand. This will encourage firms to produce an extra £25 of output, which again will set off around the system. If withdrawals remain the same, only 25% will again reappear as additional demand (approximately £6 of further demand). This £6 of additional demand will generate a further £6 of output and so on, until the additional increases become insignificant. In order to calculate the total increase in output it is necessary to add up £100 + £25 + £6 + £1.5 + £0.40 + ... This yields a total of about £133. This suggests that an increase in demand of £100 results in an increase in output of £133. This mean that the value of the multiplier in the UK is approximately 1.33. This example allows us to see the factors which determine the size of the multiplier.

Anything which takes the extra income out of the circular flow, (this is what Figure 23.6 actually represents), will reduce the amount of extra demand which is generated. Thus the multiplier depends upon the value of the part of any increase in income which is lost to the system through withdrawals. This is known as the **Marginal Propensity to Withdraw** and is made up of the following:

- the marginal propensity to save (MPS): the fraction of any increase in income which is saved.
- the marginal propensity to import (MPM): the fraction of any increase in income which is spent on imports.
- the marginal propensity to tax (MPT): the fraction of any increase in income which is paid in tax.

The mathematics of the multiplier means that its value is given by the expression:

$$K = \frac{1}{MPS+MPM+MPT} = \frac{1}{MPW}$$

Where MPW = Marginal propensity to withdraw = MPS + MPM + MPT.
K = Multiplier

Thus if   MPS = 0.1
             MPM = 0.2
             MPT = 0.2

The multiplier would have a value of 1/ 0.5 = 2.

The greater the value of the marginal propensities to withdraw, the lower will be the value of the multiplier. Thus an increase in the marginal rate of income tax would cause the value of the multiplier to fall. This would be because there would be less of any increase in income left for the household to spend on extra goods and services.

In terms of the formula for calculating the multiplier, the marginal propensity to withdraw in Figure 23.6 is 0.75, since 75% of the initial increase in output and income is withdrawn in the form of tax, imports and savings (including corporate saving). Hence the multiplier is given as:

1/0.75 = 1.33

Demand and prices

In all the examples given so far we have assumed that any change in demand will cause a change in output. This is based on the idea that firms will react to an increase in demand by increasing output. It is possible that firms will react to an increase in demand by increasing prices. The debate as to whether prices or output are more likely to change depends upon many factors, one of the most important being the availability of extra resources to permit an increase in output. If there are few spare resources in the economy, it is more likely that prices will alter rather than output. As we shall see in later chapters, the question as to whether output or prices will change is at the heart of many of the debates in economics. Keynesian economists stress the likelihood of output changing.

Summary

☐ Equilibrium requires that output (income) equals planned expenditure, which is the same as saying planned withdrawals must equal planned injections.

Thus, $Y = C + I + G + (X - M)$, if C is defined as consumption or domestically produced items

Or $Y = C + I + G + (X - M)$, if C is defined as total consumption

or, $I + G + X = S + T + M$

☐ If withdrawals exceed injections, output must exceed planned expenditure and output will fall.

☐ If expenditure exceeds the level necessary for full employment this will cause an inflationary gap.

☐ A change in demand will cause a change in output which will be a multiple of the original change in demand. This multiple is known as the multiplier.

☐ The value of the multiplier depends upon how much of any increase in income is spent on domestically produced items.

☐ The value of the multiplier is given by the expression

$$K = \frac{1}{MPS+MPM+MPT} = \frac{1}{MPW}$$

☐ Keynesian analysis suggests that demand affects output, not prices.

Multiple Choice Questions

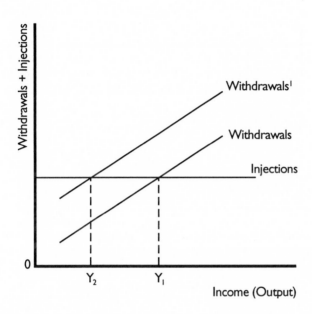

1. The diagram shows the levels of withdrawals and injections for a hypothetical economy. Initial equilibrium is at income Y_1. The movement to Y_2 could be due to:

    A an increase in savings
    B a fall in savings
    C an increase in investment
    D a fall in investment
    E none of the above

2. In a hypothetical economy, 25% of any increase in income is saved, 10% is spent on imports and 15% is taken in taxation. The value of the multiplier in that economy is:

    A 0.5
    B 60%
    C 2.0
    D 0.25
    E 4

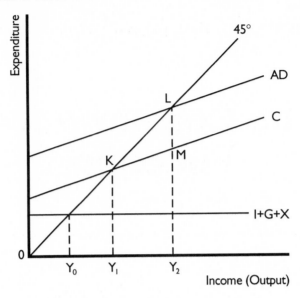

From information in the diagram, select the distance which represents:

3. The equilibrium level of income
   A OY_2
   B OY_1
   C Y_1K
   D Y_2M
   E   LM

4. The level of withdrawals at equilibrium
   A OY_2
   B OY_1
   C Y_1K
   D Y_2M
   E   LM

5. An inflationary gap is:
   A   the amount by which aggregate demand exceeds the level necessary for full employment
   B   the amount by which aggregate demand falls short of the level necessary for full employment
   C   The difference between the increase in output and the increase in prices
   D   the difference between wage increases and price increases
   E   the amount by which income exceeds output

Chapter Twenty-four

The Consumption Function

Key concepts

☐ The link between consumer expenditure and income
☐ Other factors affecting consumer expenditure

Key words

Consumption, durables, non-durables. Autonomous consumption
Consumption function, marginal propensity to consume, average propensity to consume
Permanent income, wealth

Consumption

Consumption is the term given to that part of total expenditure which is spent by households on goods and services. Consumer goods are often divided into two categories, **consumer durables and consumer non-durables.**

Non-durable consumption is quite easy to define. It consists of expenditure on goods which confer utility to the purchaser, but which are then used up very quickly. A meal is the classic example.

Durable consumption consists of expenditure on goods which confer utility on the consumer, but which continue to yield utility into the future. Washing machines and cars, are examples of durable consumer goods. This distinction between durable and non-durable consumption is important because different factors will be important in their determination. This chapter examines the factors normally seen as determining consumption.

Consumption and income: the consumption function

Keynes was the first economist to investigate the link between consumption and income. He argued that the most important factor in determining the level of consumption was the level of disposable income which the households possessed. Disposable income refers to the income which a household receives after income taxes and National Insurance contributions have been removed and any cash benefits have been added. An increase in disposable income would lead to an increase in consumption, but Keynes suggested that consumption would not rise by the full amount of any increase in income. If income rose, only a fraction of the increase would be spent on consumer goods. This fraction is called the marginal propensity to consume (MPC). It is defined as the proportion of any increase in income which is spent on consumer goods, and is measured by the following fraction:

$$\text{MPC} = \frac{\text{change in C}}{\text{change in Y}} = \frac{\Delta C}{\Delta Y}$$

Thus if income rose by £1000, and if consumption rose by £800, this would indicate a MPC of 0.8. Obviously, if the MPC is 0.8, this must mean that the MPS (marginal propensity to save) has a value of 0.2. Thus:

MPC + MPS = 1

It is usually assumed that the value of the MPC must lie between 0 and 1. It is difficult to see why consumption should rise more than income, although evidence suggests that there may have been periods in recent history when this has occurred. This is usually explained in terms of other factors stimulating consumption over and above the increase in income. *Ceteris paribus* it would seem reasonable to assume that the MPC has a value less than one.

Figure 24.1 shows two possible relationships which may exist between income and consumption. Both consumption functions in Figure 24.1 suggests that if income were zero, consumption would be positive and equal to the distance OC (a). This indicates that at low levels of income people spend more than their income. This is known as dissaving. As income increases, consumption rises. The rate at which consumption rises with respect to income is given by the slope of the line CC'. If CC' were very flat this would indicate that an increase in income had a small impact on consumption. The steeper CC', the larger the impact on consumption. The impact of an increase in income on consumption is what is shown by the MPC, so the slope of CC' gives the value of the MPC. If CC' is a straight line, this suggests that consumption and income increase at a constant rate. This means that the MPC is constant.

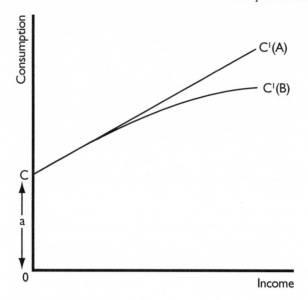

Figure 24.1 *The consumption function*

Thus the consumption function shown as CC' (A) suggests that any given increase in income brings about the same increase in consumption, regardless of whether income is high or low. The MPC is constant. This form of the consumption function, where there is a straight line relationship between income and consumption, is given by the equation:

$$C = a + bY$$

Thus when income (Y) is zero, consumption is equal to a, which is shown on the graph as the distance OC. This part of consumption, the part which takes place regardless of income, is known as autonomous consumption. The term (bY) shows how income affects consumption. If (b) had a value 0.5, this would indicate that a half of any income is also spent on consumption, as well as the autonomous element (a).

Suppose that   a = £1000
                 b = 0.5
                 Y = £1000

Consumption would be given by:

$$C = £1000 + 0.5 \,(£1000) = £1500.$$

If income rose by £1000, consumption would be given by:

$$C = £1000 + 0.5 \,(£2000) = £2000.$$

Thus an increase in income of £1000 has caused consumption to rise by £500. This indicates that the MPC must be 0.5. This is the same as the value of (b) and in fact the term (b) is the MPC. Whenever a consumption function is a straight line, it can be represented by an equation of the form:

C = a + bY, where (b) is the MPC.

The function CC'(B) indicates that as income rises, the increase in consumption begins to fall. This suggests that at higher income levels, people may save a larger proportion of any increase in income than do people on lower incomes. In terms of the diagram, the slope of the consumption function becomes smaller, and so does the value of the MPC.

Expressing consumption as a function of income allows the equilibrium level of income to be determined. Remember that equilibrium requires that:

Y = C + I + G + X.

If values I, G, X, are given, solving for Y becomes a matter of simple algebra.

Suppose that   C = 200 + 0.5 Y
and   I + G + X = 500

Solving for Y gives

Y = 200 + 0.5 Y + 500
Y = 700 + 0.5Y
0.5Y = 700
Y = 1400

The average propensity to consume (APC)

The average propensity to consume is the proportion of total income which is spent on consumption. It is measured by the expression:

$$APC = \frac{C}{Y}$$

If the consumption is a straight line, with an equation given by,

C = a + bY

then the APC is simply

$$\frac{C}{Y} = \frac{a}{Y} + b$$

The value of APC therefore diminishes as Y increases. This is an important result, since if it is an accurate reflection of actual consumer behaviour, it means that as income rises, a smaller and smaller fraction of income will be spent on consumer goods. This might indicate that total demand might be insufficient to keep output at a high level, unless other elements of

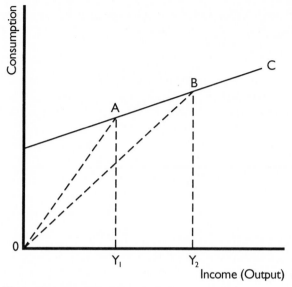

Figure 24.2 *The average propensity to consume*

demand increase to compensate. This result led Keynes to suggest that developed economies might suffer from a lack of demand as they became more affluent. This is referred to as the under-consumptiveness argument.

In terms of the consumption function it is possible to represent the APC on the graph. In Figure 24.2 the consumption function is shown as a straight line and must, therefore, have the form:

$$C = a + bY.$$

Suppose income is at Y_1. The graph indicates that consumption is given by the distance Y_1A. Income is given by the distance OY_1. Thus,

$$APC = \frac{Y_1A}{OY_1}$$

This ratio gives the angle made by the line OA. Thus the APC can be represented by the angle of a line from the origin to the point on the consumption function associated with a particular level of income. Thus at income level Y_2, the APC is given by the angle of the line OB. This angle is less than for the line OA ,and, so, the APC at income Y_2 is less than the APC at income Y_1. This accords with the result shown above.

Long run and short run consumption functions

When economists began to measure the relationship between consumption and income, they discovered a consumption function with the shape shown by CC′ in Figure 24.3. This implies that:

$$C = a + bY$$

As we saw in the previous section, this would seem to suggest that the APC declined as income rose. This would have serious implications for the level of demand in the economy, and led some economists to argue the need for expansionary policies to encourage spending. Later studies showed that when consumption/income data for a long period of time was examined, the relationship between consumption and income was better represented by the line OC″ in Figure 24.3. This implies that the relationship between income and consumption was given by the equation:

$$C = bY$$

This suggested that in the long run, there was a proportional link between income and consumption and that over time the APC was constant and equal to the MPC (b). The difference between these two views of the consumption function can be reconciled by making consumption depend upon a different concept of income – permanent income.

Consumption and permanent income

Permanent income is the term given to the average level of income which consumers expect to earn during their lifetime. The concept was intro-

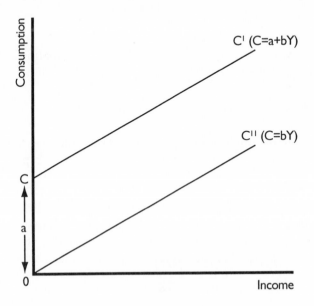

Figure 24.3 *Short and long run consumption*

duced by Milton Friedman, who argued that people did not base their consumption behaviour on their current income, but upon the level of income which they thought of as being 'permanent'. He argued that consumers would not react to a change in current income if this change was seen as transitory, but would maintain their consumption levels based on what they saw as their 'permanent' income.

Friedman tested his proposition by examining the behaviour of farmers, whose incomes fluctuate a great deal from year to year. If they were basing their consumption on current income, then their consumption levels would vary considerably. In fact Friedman found that the MPC of farmers was very low. Changes in current income had little impact on their spending. This has important implications. It suggests that people will only react to a change in their current income if they think that the change is likely to persist, since it would then affect their estimate of their permanent income. If the change was seen as temporary, people would tend to ignore it and hence the MPC-out-of-current income, would be very low.

This concept can explain the difference between long run and short run consumer behaviour. Consider Figure 24.4.

Suppose that income is at Y_1 and consumption is at C_1. Current income now increases to Y_2. In the short run people do not know whether the increase is permanent and so they only increase their consumption by a small amount, say to C_2. If income stays at Y_2, people will begin to accept the increase as permanent and their consumption will rise to C_3. Thus if the change was measured in the short run, this would give the line CC'. If the relationship was looked at over the long run, it would show up as the line OC''.

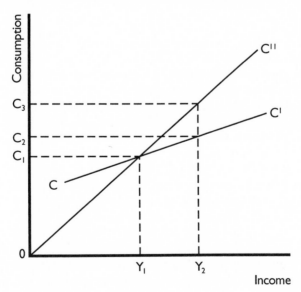

Figure 24.4 *Consumption and permanent income*

The concept of permanent income has implications for the effectiveness of tax policies. If the government wanted to reduce consumer spending, they might increase income taxes, thereby reducing disposable income. The permanent income hypothesis suggests that this will only affect consumption if consumers expect the tax increase to persist. In the short run they might simply save less and so maintain their spending levels. The policy would be ineffective.

Other factors affecting consumption

Rate of interest

Consumption will also be affected by the rate of interest. If interest rates rise, this will make borrowing more expensive and saving more attractive. This might have an impact on consumption. The impact is likely to be greater for consumer durables than for non-durables since these are the goods which normally are bought on credit.

An increase in interest rates might also affect consumption because of changes in the cost of servicing existing debt. Thus if interest rates rise, this will increase the interest payments for people who have existing debts, and this will affect their spending power. The most important aspect of this is the way in which the cost of mortgages is affected by changes in the rate of interest.

Interest rates may directly affect the disposable income of people who receive interest payments. Thus an increase in the rate of interest will increase the disposable income of some sections of society.

Wealth

Wealth may be a factor which influences consumption. If people do not simply accumulate wealth to pass on to their heirs, any increase in wealth will increase the resources which an individual is capable of spending. Thus in 1987, when the value of shares on most of the world's stock markets fell dramatically, many economists argued that this might cause consumer spending to fall. The UK government reacted to this by reducing interest rates, partly to offset the expected drop in consumption. In fact the fall in equity prices did not appear to affect consumption at all!

The importance of wealth explains that emphasis which some economists put on house prices as a factor influencing consumption, since a house represents the major asset of most households.

Inflation

Rising prices might affect consumption in several ways. If prices are rising, this reduces the purchasing power of any money which people possess. This may encourage people to save more in order to restore the value of their savings. If this did occur, higher inflation would be associated with reduced consumption.

An alternative possibility is that the possibility of higher prices in the future might encourage people to spend more immediately, to avoid the higher prices. In this case higher inflation would increase consumption. Higher inflation might, on the other hand, cause people to become uncertain about the future, which might stimulate savings.

The conclusion about inflation and consumption is that the link might be positive or negative. Evidence would seem to suggest that higher prices have a discouraging affect on consumption, possibly for the first reason given above.

Unemployment

Higher levels of unemployment might deter consumption if it causes consumers to feel that their jobs are insecure.

Taxes

Consumption will be affected by the amount of disposable income which households obtain, which obviously depends upon the level of direct taxation.

Age structure

The age structure of the population will also affect consumption. The 'life cycle' theory of consumption suggests that if people do not wish to leave assets to their heirs, they will save during their working life in order to finance their consumption during retirement. Thus, if a larger proportion of the population is retired, we would expect savings to be reduced, and hence consumption to rise.

Summary

❏ Consumption is assumed to depend primarily upon disposable income (Yd).

❏ As (Yd) increases, consumption will increase.

❏ The proportion of any increase in income which is spent on consumption is shown by the marginal propensity to consume (MPC).

❏ If the MPC is constant, the consumption function (showing the relationship between income and consumption) is a straight line.

❏ A straight line consumption function is given by the equation: $C = a + bYd$.

❏ In the equation above the term 'b' is the MPC.

❏ If the MPC declines as income rises, the consumption function will become flatter.

❏ The slope of the consumption function is given by the MPC. A higher MPC gives a steeper consumption function.

❏ The proportion of total income which is spent on consumption is given by the average propensity to consume (APC).

❏ The APC falls as income rises if the consumption function is a straight line.

❏ The value of the APC is given by the angle formed by a line from the origin to the consumption function at any given level of income.

❏ In the short run the consumption function is non-proportional (the APC falls as income rises).

❏ In the long run consumption is a constant proportion of income.

❏ Permanent income is a long run concept of income and may be a more significant factor than current income as a determinant of consumption.

❏ Consumption will also depend upon: interest rates, wealth, inflation, unemployment, taxes and age structure.

Multiple Choice Questions

1. In a closed economy with no government, consumption is given by the expression: $C = 100 + 0.6Y$. Investment is equal to 500. What is the equilibrium level of income?

   A 500
   B 600
   C 300
   D 400
   E 1500

2. The marginal propensity to consume is:

   A one minus the average propensity to save
   B the change in consumption when income increases
   C the proportion of any increase in income which is saved
   D the proportion of any increase in income which is consumed
   E the proportion of income which is consumed

3. In a closed economy with no government, consumption is given by the expression $C = 100 + 0.75Y$ the value of the multiplier is:

   A 0.75
   B 1.33
   C 4.0
   D 0.25
   E none of the above

4. Given a consumption function of the form $C = a + bY$ if income was redistributed from the rich to the poor, this would

   A reduce consumption
   B increase the marginal propensity to consume of the poor
   C increase the average propensity to save of the poor
   D increase the average propensity to consume of the rich
   E increase the marginal propensity to save of the rich

5. Autonomous consumption is:

   A that part of consumption which is affected by income
   B that part of consumption over which consumers have no control
   C consumption after taxes have been paid
   D consumption which does not depend upon income
   E given by b in the function $C = a + bY$

Chapter Twenty-five

Money

Key concepts

☐ The major functions of money, and how forms of
   money have changed over time
☐ Alternative definitions of money
☐ The ways in which the quantity of money might affect
   the level of activity in an economy, including output,
   prices and the rate of interest
☐ One way of integrating money into a macro economic
   model of aggregate demand

Key words

Medium of exchange, store of value, unit of account,
   standard for deferred payments
Deposit money, M0 (narrow money), M4 (broad money)
Quantity theory of money, MV = PT
The demand for money, transactions demand, precautionary
   demand, speculative demand
IS and LM curves, crowding out

Functions of money

Money is anything which will fulfil the following functions:

● **Medium of exchange:** the most important function of money is that it
should be generally accepted as a means of paying for goods and services.
Thus anything which allows people to purchase goods and services can be
thought of as money.

- **Store of value:** money must be capable of being stored. It would not make sense for objects to act as money if they perished overnight, since this would rob them of their fundamental function of acting as a medium of exchange.
- **Standard for deferred payment:** it is obviously useful if whatever acts as money can also be used to settle debts incurred in the past. Thus money should retain its value over time.
- **Unit of account:** again it is useful if monetary units can be used to give the relative values of different commodities.

Thus money is simply an item which permits commodities to be bought and sold without having to resort to barter. If you wish to exchange your television set for a new CD player, it is obviously more convenient to sell the TV for money and then use the money to buy the CD player than to look for someone who wishes to exchange a CD player for a TV. Thus money avoids the need to achieve a double coincidence of wants. Although it is easy to understand the functions of money, it is more difficult to define what actually constitutes money.

Forms of money: coins and paper money

The earliest form of money consisted of precious metal, especially gold and silver. These coins had intrinsic value in that the value of their metal content was equal to the value of the coins. This of course led people to attempt to 'make' money by debasing the currency, that is by adding base metals to the precious metal so as to keep the weight the same but reducing the value of the metal contained in the coins. This gave rise to 'Gresham's Law' which stated that bad money would drive out the good, which simply suggested that coins containing the more precious metal would be retained by people and not spent, and that in time only the debased currency would be in circulation. This process has continued until today, when the metallic value of modern coins is insignificant. This does not prevent them from being used as money, since they are still generally accepted as payment for goods and services.

Paper money has a much shorter history. Obviously paper money does not have any intrinsic value, and so to be acceptable initially, paper money had to be convertible into precious metal. Thus when paper money first grew up, it represented a promise to pay on demand so-much gold, the promise being made first by goldsmiths and later by banks. Since banks were in business to make profits, they were always tempted to print more notes than their gold reserves could accommodate. This gave rise to fractionally-backed paper money, and the banks were safe, so long as their depositors did not attempt to convert their notes into gold.

Suppose that a bank has £10 000 worth of gold deposited with it and issues paper money in return. It knows that it only needs to keep about 10%

of its liabilities in the form of gold, since most transactions are carried out by paper money. This means that the bank could print even more paper money, to a value of £90 000, and offer this as loans to its customers. This system would only work if people had faith in the convertibility of their bank notes, did not attempt to convert them back into gold, and simply used them to carry out transactions. In the UK this system was supervised by the Bank of England, which, when it received these notes, returned them for collection in gold. This required the banks to keep reasonable reserves of gold against their note issues.

As time went on, note issue by the commercial banks was controlled and eventually the Bank of England took over this responsibility. Initially this was still convertible into gold, but in 1931, Britain left the gold standard for the last time and since then paper money in the UK has ceased to be convertible.

Forms of money: deposit money

When the commercial banks lost their ability to print money, they did not lose their ability to create money. In just the same way that banks could print paper money based on gold reserves, they now issued another form of money, deposit money, based on their reserves of paper money! The customers of the banks sometimes deposit currency with the banks in the same way that they used to deposit gold. The bank takes the money and gives the depositor a promise to pay it back on demand. This promise to pay is not in the form of a bank note, but instead takes the form of a credit in the customer's account. The customer can use this credit by writing a cheque which is accepted by another person, and paid into that person's bank account. A transaction has been financed, and the only 'money' which has been used is the amount transferred from one account to the other.

Thus paper money plays the same role in the creation of deposit money as gold did in the creation of paper money. Suppose a bank receives a deposit of £10 000 in cash. On the basis of experience, the bank knows that at any moment it only needs to keep 10% of its liabilities in the form of cash. It could then afford to credit someone else's account by £90 000 and still feel confident that it could meet its day-to-day cash requirements. The bank has created £90 000 worth of additional bank deposits on the basis of the £10 000 cash which it received. The less cash which the banking system requires to meet its day to day needs, the greater is its ability to grant credit and to create deposit money for their customers.

Again, for the system to work, people must have faith that their money is safe in the bank. If they feel this, they will be prepared to keep their money in their account. If people lost faith and attempted to withdraw their money in the form of cash, the banking system would collapse since it would be unable to meet the cash demands. In order to avoid this risk, the Bank of England is always prepared to act as lender of last resort to the banking system, although it will ensure that such lending will be unprofitable for the banks, and so ensure that the banks act responsibly.

Definitions of money

We have concentrated above on two forms of money – notes and coins – and bank deposits. There are many other assets which people hold which might be thought of as money. The major attribute of money is that it is liquid, in the sense that it can easily be used to finance transactions.

Suppose that you inherit £100 000. There are many ways in which you might decide to hold that wealth. The most liquid asset would be to convert it to cash. The next most liquid possibility would be to place the £100 000 into a current account at the bank. This would still be available for financing transactions by cheque although you would not be holding cash, but deposit money. You might decide to place the £100 000 in a Building Society account, where you could not spend it without first of all converting the account back into cash or a current account. Should this Building Society account be classed as money?

You might decide to put the £100 000 into premium bonds. Again this cannot be spent without first being converted into another form of asset. Should premium bonds be classed as money? Suppose you converted the £100 000 into a house. Should that be classed as money?

Thus cash is simply one end of a spectrum of liquidity. There are a multitude of assets into which the £100 000 could be converted. Which of these assets is considered to be money is fairly arbitrary. In the UK there are two major definitions of money, M0 and M4.

- M0: This is also referred to as narrow money since it represents the narrowest definition. It consists of all notes and coins in circulation plus Bankers' operational deposits with the Bank of England. This is sometimes referred to as the monetary base, since it represents the liquid assets which the commercial banks can use on which to base their creation of deposit money.
- M4: This is known as broad money and consists of M0 plus bank and building society deposits.

The quantity theory of money

The quantity of money in the economy is seen as important because some economists claim that it determines the level of spending, which as we saw in Chapter Twenty One, will influence the level of output. This claim is based upon one of the oldest propositions in economics, known as the

quantity theory of money. This proposition is usually expressed in the form
of a simple equation:

$$M \times V = P \times T$$
$$\text{or} \quad MV = PT$$

where M = the quantity of money in the economy

   V = the velocity of circulation, or the number of times the
   money supply changes hands during the period.

Thus MV represents the value of money spent in the economy, since
money only changes hands when it is spent. Thus MV represents aggregate
demand.

   P = the price level
   T = the number of transactions which take place during the period

Thus PT represents the value of all goods bought in the economy.

   The quantity theory of money is thus the earth shattering conclusion that
the value of money spent in the economy must be equal to the value of
goods bought. The equation is sometimes re-written, replacing T, the
number of transactions, by Y, representing the level of output in the
economy, since these will be closely related. This gives the alternative
expression:

$$MV = PY$$

Suppose that:

   M = 100
   V = 5
   P = 10
then   Y = 50

As it stands, the quantity theory equation is fairly empty. It becomes
important when certain properties are given to the values of V and Y.

   Some economists (usually referred to as monetarists) argue that the
velocity of circulation is fairly stable and will not change dramatically or
quickly. This is claimed to be an empirically observed 'fact'. What it
suggests, therefore, is that any change in M will always show up as an
increase in MV, which, as we saw before, is simply aggregate demand.
This suggests that aggregate demand is determined by the quantity of
money in the economy. This assertion can be quite easily tested. Using the
quantity equation:

$$V = PY/M$$

PY is simply the value of all goods produced in the economy or GDP. The
proposition that V is constant is simply the idea that the ratio of GDP:

money supply is also constant, since:

$$V = GDP/M$$

In the example above:

$$PY = 500 \text{ (GDP)}$$
$$M = 100$$
$$V = 5$$

If V is constant, a 10% increase in the money supply (M) must lead to a 10% increase in GDP.

$$MV = PY$$
$$110 \times 5 = 550$$

Thus changes in GDP are the result of changes in M. This is the basis of monetarism. Unfortunately, this simple proposition is seriously flawed, because of the difficulty in establishing an agreed definition of what constitutes the money supply.

During the 1970s in the UK, it appeared that there was a definition of money (known as M3) which did go up and down with GDP, so keeping V constant. The Conservative government which came to power in 1979 thus determined to control M3 so as to control GDP. Unfortunately, as soon as M3 came targeted for control, it ceased to have a direct relationship with GDP! This gave rise to 'Goodhart's Law' which states that economic relationships will cease to exist once they become targeted by government. The reason for the breakdown in the behaviour of the M3/GDP link is easily explained. Banks are in the business of making profits. Lending money (increasing the money supply, by creating deposit money) is one of their most profitable activities. Thus if the government attempts to control their ability to extend credit in certain forms, they will simply resort to other forms of lending which fall outside the definition of money being controlled. Hence borrowing will still occur, and hence spending will still occur despite the control on M3. In terms of the quantity theory, velocity will alter. This problem will be re-examined when we look at monetary policy.

The changing definitions of money thus make the constancy of V very difficult to test. Obviously people cannot spend unless they can finance their expenditure. Whether the quantity of money determines this expenditure depends on whether a fixed money supply (if this could be defined) constrains spending. This will **not be** true in two circumstances:

- If other forms of money can be created, by the banks or other institutions extending credit;
- if the velocity of circulation rises such that a given supply of money can finance a higher level of spending.

This latter point is the basis of the Keynesian criticism concerning the link

between money and demand, and is based upon the factors which determine the demand for money (see the next section).

If velocity is constant, an increase in the money supply boosts aggregate
demand. If output is fixed, perhaps because the economy is at full employment, the change in demand will increase the price level. This is the basis
of the monetarist claim that increases in the money supply increase the
price level. It will only be true if the level of output fails to respond to the
increase in demand.

The demand for money

Keynes argued that there were three reasons for holding money as opposed
to holding other assets. Money has the virtue of being highly liquid, but it
does not as a rule pay any interest to its owner. This is a fairly general
proposition. The more liquid an asset, the lower the rate of return which
that asset earns. Keynes analysed the demand for money by focusing on the
decision to hold wealth in either the form of money or to hold bonds.

Keynes saw bonds as the major alternative to holding money. A bond is
an agreement by an institution, usually the government, to pay a fixed sum
of money at some time in the future, in return for borrowing money today.
In order to persuade people to lend to them, the institution must also pay an
agreed interest payment. Thus suppose that the government issues a bond
for £100 and agrees to pay interest of £10 a year. This represents an interest
rate of 10% per annum. The bond is to be repaid in 20 years time. Normally
one would expect this 10% interest to be an attractive alternative to holding
one's wealth in the form of money. Indeed it would seem silly for anyone
to prefer money to bonds. Keynes suggested that there were three reasons,
or motives for holding money, or in Keynes' terms, expressing a preference for liquidity:

● Transactions demand: people will need to hold money to finance their
day-to-day transactions. The level of these money balances will depend
upon the level of spending which, in turn, will depend upon the level of
income.
● Precautionary demand: people will need to keep some money available
in order to finance any unforeseen emergencies. This is also assumed to
depend upon income.
● Speculative demand: people may prefer to hold their wealth in the form
of money if they feel that other assets have become less attractive. Holding
money is riskless, while other assets including bonds have some risk
attached. The major risk associated with bonds is the risk that the price of
bonds might alter.

In the example above, the bond has a value of £100 and pays £10 a year
interest. Suppose that interest rates in the rest of the economy rise to 20%.
The bond now represents very poor value for money, since £100 would

earn £20 per annum elsewhere. Thus if the bond holder tried to sell the bond to someone else, that person would not be prepared to pay £100. In order for the £10 to compare with the 20% which could be earned elsewhere, the price of the bond would fall to £50. The bondholder would have experienced a loss of £50 if he/she were to have to sell the bond.

Thus, if interest rates are low, and expected to rise, this will discourage people from holding bonds and instead make them prefer money, which will not lose its value. Thus, the speculative demand for money depends upon the rate of interest, and will increase as interest rates fall, since this will make bonds less attractive. This demand for money functions can be shown as a demand curve for money.

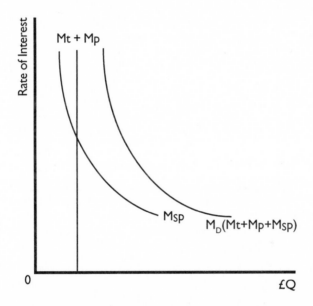

Figure 25.1 *The demand for money*

The transactions and precautionary demand for money are shown as being independent of the rate of interest, since they depend upon income. These are represented by the line Mt + Mp. The speculative demand does depend upon the rate of interest and is given by the line Msp. The total demand for money is these schedules combined and is shown as Md. This is what Keynes referred to as the liquidity preference schedule, since it shows how much money (liquid assets) people want to hold. The demand for money is seen as depending upon the rate of interest, and, it is this which gives a different view of how the money supply affects aggregate demand.

The market for money

Money is seen as a commodity like any other. There is a certain quantity of money available, and as shown above people will want to hold a certain quantity. This is simply the idea of the money market consisting of the demand and supply of money. In Figure 25.2 this is represented.

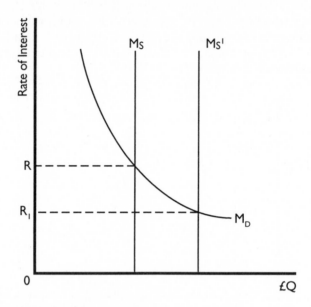

Figure 25.2 *The demand and supply of money*

The money supply is shown by the line Ms and is shown as being independent of the rate of interest. This is normally explained by suggesting that the money supply is determined by the monetary authorities. Equilibrium is shown at an interest rate of R. How is this equilibrium achieved?

Suppose that interest rates were above R. The diagram suggests that the demand for money will be less than the supply. People will have more money than they wish to hold. This suggests that they will attempt to convert these excess balances into some alternative – bonds. This increased demand for bonds will increase their price, so lowering the rate of interest. As interest rates fall, more and more people will be prepared to hold onto the surplus money, since bonds are becoming less attractive. Eventually bond prices will have risen (interest rates will have fallen) sufficiently to restore equilibrium.

Now we can examine the consequences of an increase in the money supply. An increase in the money supply would shift the line M_s to the right. This is shown as a movement to $M_s{}^1$. At the original interest rate, R, there is now an excess supply of money. People will try and convert this excess money into bonds. This will increase the price of bonds, so reducing the rate of interest. As the rate of interest falls, people are more prepared to hold money, until, when the interest rate falls to R_1, the increased supply of money is being held in speculative balances.

This is an important result. It suggests that an increase in the money supply does not show up as increased spending (as suggested by the quantity theory) but instead simply reduces the rate of interest. This fall in the rate of interest might increase spending, but this depends upon how far interest rates fall, and how responsive spending is to lower interest rates. Thus the impact on aggregate demand may be minimal. It is possible that the lower rate of interest might have no impact on demand. If this were the case, the increased supply of money would have no impact on GDP. All of the impact would have been felt on velocity. In the example in the section on the quantity theory of money, a 10% increase in the money supply brought about a 10% increase in GDP. What has happened if demand fails to respond to lower interest rates?

$$MV = PY$$
$$100 \times 5 = 10 \times 50$$

If M increases by 10%, but demand, and hence GDP, do not alter:

$$110 \times 4.54 = 10 \times 50$$

All that has happened is that velocity has altered to absorb the increased money supply. Thus Keynesian economists stress that velocity is not constant or even stable, but will respond to changes in the rate of interest as people become prepared to hold onto the increased supply of money, and it simply ends up in their speculative balances.

Thus Keynesian economists stress that money might have an influence on aggregate demand, but that this only operates indirectly via the rate of interest. Monetarists argue that an increase in the supply of money has a much more direct impact on aggregate demand, and will in fact generate a proportional increase in demand.

The difficulty in obtaining an agreed definition as to what actually constitutes money makes it very difficult to disprove either of these propositions, which explains why the debate as to the importance and nature of the mechanism through which an increase in the money supply operates, has not been decided.

Aggregate demand and money – IS and LM curves

We have seen that an increase in income will affect the demand for money and so, according to Keynesian analysis, will affect the rate of interest. A change in the rate of interest will also affect the level of aggregate demand, primarily through its impact on investment which will then affect income and hence the demand for money. This in turn will once again affect the rate of interest and hence the level of demand. Thus changes in interest rates and aggregate demand are inter-connected.

In terms of the equilibrium level of income on the economy, the level of income depends on the level of aggregate demand, and the level of aggregate demand depends upon the rate of interest. The rate of interest depends upon the demand for money which in turn depends upon the level of income. Thus we cannot solve for an equilibrium level of income unless we know the level of investment (which is an important element in aggregate demand). We cannot determine the level of investment unless we know the rate of interest, but we cannot know the rate of interest unless we know the level of income (which affects the demand for money). Thus the money market and the product market (where output is determined) cannot be treated in isolation. They must be examined together. This is what IS and LM analysis is designed to achieve.

Figure 25.3 shows a relationship between the rate of interest and the level of aggregate demand in the economy. Suppose that the rate of interest is R_1. This will give a certain level of investment, and so a certain level of aggregate demand. This is shown as a level of income Y_1. Remember that in equilibrium, income is equal to aggregate demand.

Suppose that the rate of interest falls to R_2. What will happen to aggregate demand and income? A lower rate of interest will stimulate investment (and perhaps other elements of aggregate demand), such that

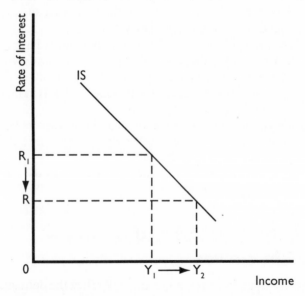

Figure 25.3 *The IS curve*

income rises to Y_2. Similarly, all other rates of interest will be associated with particular levels of aggregate demand and hence income. Thus the line IS simply illustrates the fact that lower interest rates will be associated with higher levels of demand and income.

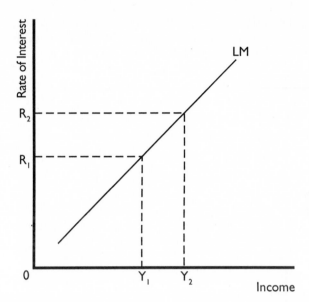

Figure 25.4 *The LM curve*

Figure 25.4 shows a relationship between the level of income and the rate of interest. Suppose the economy is at an income level Y_1. This level of income will generate a certain demand for money, which in turn will determine a particular rate of interest which will equate the demand and supply of money. This is shown as R_1.

If the level of income were to rise to Y_2, this would increase the transactions demand for money. In the money market, the demand for money curve will shift to the right, creating an excess demand for money, which will raise the rate of interest. Thus the income level Y_2 will cause a higher interest rate R_2 to be established. Similarly all other levels of income will be associated with different equilibrium rates of interest, such that higher income levels will be associated with higher interest rates. The line LM shows all such combinations.

The IS curve suggests that there are various combinations of interest and income which can combine to give equilibrium in the circular flow of income. The LM curve suggests that there are various combinations of income and rate of interest which will give equilibrium in the money market. However, there will only be one combination which will give equilibrium in both markets at the same time. This will be at the point where the two curves intersect.

For a general equilibrium solution, it is necessary that when aggregate demand equals income, that the money market is also in equilibrium at the same time. Suppose that the circular flow was in equilibrium, but the demand for money exceeded the supply. There would be an excess demand for money which would increase interest rates. This increase in interest rates would then affect aggregate demand and hence income, and so the original level of income could not be thought of as in equilibrium, since there would be forces at work causing it to change.

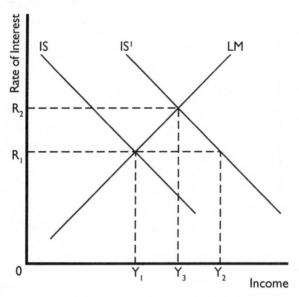

Figure 25.5 *IS and LM equilibrium*

In Figure 25.5, the original equilibrium is shown with curves IS and LM. Equilibrium occurs at income level Y_1 and interest rate R_1. Suppose that there is now an increase in the level of aggregate demand, caused by an increase in investment. What this means is that if interest rates stay at R_1, aggregate demand, and hence income will increase. The IS curve will shift to the right, shown as the new curve IS'. The diagram suggests that this will be associated with a new equilibrium, with an increase in the level of income and an increase in the rate of interest. This result will come about because the higher income increases the demand for money and so increases interest rates. Thus income does not expand to Y_2, which is what would happen if interest rates remained constant, but would only expand to Y_3. Thus any expansion of aggregate demand is dampened down by increases in the rate of interest, which choke off some of the expansion by reducing expenditure, especially investment.

The framework can also be used to show the impact of monetary policy. Suppose the money supply increases. This will have its first impact on the money market (the LM curve). At any particular level of income, the demand for money will now be less than the supply, and, so, interest rates will fall. Thus the LM curve will shift downwards. This will result in interest rates falling and income rising. This is the result which we saw in the previous section, and it is the Keynesian transmission mechanism for an increase in the supply of money.

Thus IS and LM analysis suggests that changes in aggregate demand will have an impact on the rate of interest, which in turn affects aggregate demand. Similarly changes in the rate of interest will affect aggregate demand and income, which then feed back into an impact on the rate of interest.

Crowding out

This analysis allows us to examine a phenomena which economists refer to as 'crowding out'. Suppose that in the previous section, an increase in government expenditure boosts aggregate demand. In terms of IS and LM analysis, the IS curve will shift to the right, since a given interest rate will be associated with an increased level of demand and income. This will cause income to expand, but will also put pressure on interest rates to rise. If the LM curve is steep, most of the impact of the increase in government spending will be felt on interest rates and very little on aggregate demand and income.

What this means is that the increase in aggregate demand and income boosts the demand for money and so increases the rate of interest. If the increase in interest rates is substantial, it is possible that the level of private spending in the form of investment may be reduced to such an extent that there is a very small overall increase in demand and income. Thus, the increased public expenditure might increase interest rates to such an extent that private expenditure (especially investment) is crowded out. If this result occurs, the extra government spending will have had very little impact on aggregate demand, and all that will happen is that the public sector expands, and the private sector contracts. This phenomena of crowding out is often used as an argument against the idea of using government expenditure as a means of expanding aggregate demand.

Summary

❏ Money has four functions: a medium of exchange, a store of value, a unit of account, a standard for deferred payments.

❏ Money is any asset which fulfils these functions.

❏ Deposit money is created by banks on the basis of their holdings of notes and coins.

❏ M0 is the definition of narrow money, and consists of notes and coins and deposits with the Bank of England.

❏ M4 is the definition of broad money and consists of M0 plus bank and building society deposits.

❏ The quantity theory of money is given as $MV = PY$. This states that the value of money spent is always equal to the value of goods bought.

❏ Monetarists believe that V (the velocity of circulation of money) is constant. Therefore changes in the money supply will cause changes in aggregate demand (MV), and, hence, changes in nominal GDP (PY).

❏ If output is fixed, changes in the money supply will cause changes in prices.

❏ If V is variable, changes in M may have no impact on demand.

❏ The demand for money depends upon income (transactions and precautionary demand) and upon the rate of interest (speculative demand).

❏ If income rises, the demand for money will rise.

❏ If the rate if interest rises, the demand for money will fall.

❏ The monetary theory of the rate of interest says that the rate of interest is determined by the demand and supply of money.

❏ Thus an increase in the money supply might simply reduce interest rates and increase the demand for money, which may simply reduce the velocity of circulation, and, so, have no impact on aggregate demand.

❏ IS and LM analysis can be used to show the impact of changes in aggregate demand on the rate of interest and vice versa.

Multiple Choice Questions

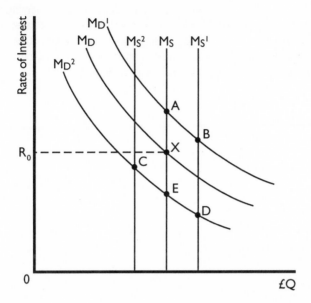

The diagram shows the demand and supply for money. The original equilibrium position is given by point X, at interest rate R0. From the points illustrated identify the new equilibrium positions in response to the following.

1. An increase in income.

2. An increase in the money supply, and a fall in the precautionary demand for money.

3. Which of the following constitute part of the broad definition of money?
   A   cheques
   B   credit cards
   C   current accounts with a commercial bank
   D   premium bonds
   E   shares

4. In a hypothetical economy, the money supply is given as 100 and the price level is 5. Output is at the full employment level and is given as 200. If the velocity of circulation is constant, what will be the new price level if the money supply rises to 120?
   A   12
   B   6
   C   5
   D   10
   E   20

5. The demand for money is a negative function of the rate of interest, because:

    A   high interest rates make money more attractive than other assets
    B   current accounts will be very attractive if interest rates are high
    C   high interest rates make holding money very attractive
    D   high interest rates make holding money less attractive
    E   high interest rates will encourage spending

Chapter Twenty-six

Fiscal Policy

Key concepts

❒ The definition of fiscal policy
❒ Ways in which fiscal policy might influence aggregate demand
❒ Ways in which fiscal policy can redistribute income
❒ Ways in which fiscal policy can affect the allocation of resources in an economy

Key words

Public Sector Borrowing Requirement (PSBR), balanced budget multiplier
Non discretionary fiscal policy and automatic stabilisers
Discretionary fiscal policy, direct and indirect taxation
Quintile groups

Definition

Fiscal policy is defined as any change in the timing, composition or level of government spending or tax revenue. Thus all tax changes are classed as part of fiscal policy, as is any change in the level of government expenditure. In the UK, these two aspects of fiscal policy used to be implemented at separate times, with the budget in April being concerned with tax changes, and the Autumn statement being concerned with expenditure. These two are now dealt with at the same time in the budget which is held in November. Fiscal policy has three possible functions:

● Influencing aggregate demand.

- Influencing the distribution of income.
- Influencing the allocation of resources in the economy.

Fiscal policy and aggregate demand

Any change in government expenditure or in taxation will have an impact on aggregate demand. An increase in taxes will represent an increase in withdrawals from the circular flow of income, and, will therefore, reduce aggregate demand. Tax revenue is purchasing power which goes to the government and is thus removed from the circular flow.

Changes in government spending will have a direct affect upon aggregate demand, since government spending is part of total domestic expenditure.

Equal changes in taxes and government spending will not have the same impact upon aggregate demand. Suppose that taxes are raised such that £1 billion is taken out of the economy, and this £1 billion is then spent by the government. How will the level of demand in the economy be affected?

The £1 billion increase in government spending will increase demand by £1 billion. However the £1 billion tax increase will **not** reduce demand by the same amount. Some of the tax increase will come out of people's savings, some may have been spent on imports anyway, and so the total amount paid in tax may not represent such a significant loss in demand for the domestic economy.

Suppose that £200m comes out of savings and £100m would have been spent on imports. The tax increase has only reduced demand for UK goods by £700m while the increase in government spending will have boosted demand by the full £1 billion. Thus the net result is an increase in demand of £300m. This £300m will then have a multiplier effect upon the economy. This example illustrates a phenomena known as the Balanced Budget Multiplier. A given change in government spending has a bigger impact on aggregate demand than an equal change in tax revenue.

The Public Sector Borrowing Requirement (PSBR)

If spending by central and local government is greater than the amount which they raise in taxation, the amount by which spending exceeds tax revenue is known as the Public Sector Borrowing Requirement because the excess has to be obtained, or borrowed, from somewhere. The PSBR is also sometimes referred to as the budget deficit, although this term should only be strictly used in connection with the deficit of central government. The government may borrow the money from one of two sources – from the banking system or from the non-bank public.

Both of these sources of funds will have implications for other aspects of the economy.

If the government borrows from the banking system, this will increase the money supply. As we saw in Chapter Twenty Five, when the banks extend credit, they increase the volume of bank deposits in the economy. This is the same whether it is the government borrowing the money, or whether it is private individuals. Hence borrowing off the banks will increase the money supply.

If the government borrows off the public, this may have implications for interest rates. In order to persuade the public to lend them money, the government must offer an attractive rate of interest. This puts the government in competition with other financial institutions. The increase in the demand for money will put pressure upon interest rates to rise. Thus any increase in the PSBR will either increase the money supply, or put pressure on interest rates to rise.

Non-discretionary fiscal policy

Some changes in taxation and government spending will occur automatically as the level of activity in the economy alters. Consider Figure 26.1. Tax revenue is shown by the line TT, and the level of government spending by the line GG. At an income level of Y_1 tax revenue and government spending are shown as OA.

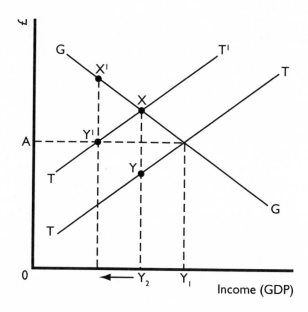

Figure 26.1 *Non-discretionary fiscal policy*

If the economy then falls into recession, the level of income will fall. This will have an impact upon both tax revenue and government spending. Lower levels of income will be associated with lower tax revenue. Since income has fallen, all taxes based on income or expenditure will fall. Lower levels of income will also be associated with increases in the level of government spending on welfare benefits, such as unemployment benefit, or income support.

In Figure 26.1 this is shown by the line representing tax revenue, TT, falling as income reduces, and the line GG rising. Thus the fall in income has caused a budget deficit (expenditure greater than tax revenue) to occur. This has happened automatically, because of the structure of the tax and benefit system, and has not been the result of any conscious policy introduced by government. These tax and expenditure changes will help to alleviate the recession, since the lower taxes and higher expenditure by government will both stimulate aggregate demand. These aspects of fiscal policy are known as automatic stabilisers since they help to overcome changes in demand and output without any policy decisions being necessary.

This phenomena has important implications for government policy. In a recession the PSBR is likely to rise automatically. Thus in Figure 26.1, a fall in income to Y2 will cause a deficit of XY in government tax revenues. If the government responds to this by increasing taxes, in an attempt to eliminate the deficit, taxes will rise as shown by the line TT'. This may cause income to fall even further and cause the deficit to reappear, shown as X'Y' in Figure 26.1. Hence, the increase in taxation will have been ineffective as a means of reducing the deficit. This process operates in reverse. An increase in income will automatically increase tax revenue and reduce government spending. Thus an expansion of the economy will improve the state of the government finances.

Discretionary fiscal policy

As we saw earlier, fiscal policy can operate through either the tax or expenditure side of the public finances. In terms of aggregate demand, tax changes are mostly directed at consumer spending. Some critics of controlling aggregate demand through fiscal policy argue that it is likely to be a very inaccurate method. This is primarily because they question the strength of the link between current disposable income and consumer spending. This scepticism is reinforced by the permanent income hypothesis which we saw in Chapter Twenty Four. This suggests that consumers base their consumption on their life time income rather than being constrained by their current disposable income. Hence changes in income brought about by tax changes may be ignored, and people may simply alter their savings to compensate, especially if the tax changes are seen as temporary.

Taxes may also be used to try and influence investment. The government may give tax allowances, or tax concessions, to firms which allow them to offset investment in new plant and equipment against corporation tax. This in effect reduces the cost of the investment to firms, and might encourage them to undertake more investment than they otherwise would, or more likely, to bring investment forward. In diagrammatic terms, the marginal efficiency of capital will shift to the right.

Direct and indirect taxation

Direct taxes are those where the burden of the tax is expected to remain with the person who actually pays the tax. Indirect taxation refers to taxes where the person who actually pays the tax is expected to pass the tax on to other people. Thus income tax is a direct tax, as is corporation tax, which is a tax on profits.

VAT is an indirect tax since the tax is paid to the government by the supplier, but is then passed onto the consumer in the final price. As we shall see in Chapter Twenty Seven, the problem of who actually pays taxes, the difference between formal incidence, the person who has the legal obligation to pay the tax, and effective incidence – the person who eventually foots the bill – is an important area of debate in economics.

Fiscal policy and the distribution of income

An important aspect of the fiscal system is the way in which government expenditure and taxation affect the distribution of income. If income distribution was solely left to market forces, people would only receive whatever income they earned from productive activity. People who did not work would receive nothing. This situation would be unacceptable since it would imply that people would starve. Thus all governments re-distribute income via the tax and benefit system. The best way to see how this operates is to look at the situation in the UK. In Table 26.1, figures are given for the distribution of income in the UK for the years 1979 and 1991.

The figures are given for quintile groups of households. What this means is that the households in the country have been split into five equal groups, with the 20% of households with the lowest household income being in the bottom quintile, and the 20% of households with the highest income being in the top quintile. The figures then show the percentage of total income which each quintile receives. If incomes were divided equally, each quintile would receive 20% of the total income. The figures indicate that this is not the case. Table 26.1 on the next page gives the distribution of total income for four definitions of income:

● Original Income is what households would receive if left to their own efforts. It shows the percentage of income which households would receive in the absence of any government intervention. Thus in 1991, left

Table 26.1 *Percentages shares of total original, disposable and post-tax incomes by quintile groups of households: 1979, 1991*

Original income

Quintile group	1979	1991
Bottom	2.4	2.0
2nd	10	7
3rd	18	16
4th	27	26
Top	43	50

Gross income

Quintile group	1979	1991
Bottom	8.5	6.7
2nd	13	10
3rd	18	16
4th	24	23
Top	37	44

Disposable income

Quintile group	1979	1991
Bottom	9.4	7.2
2nd	13	11
3rd	18	16
4th	23	23
Top	36	42

Post-tax income

Quintile group	1979	1991
Bottom	9.5	6.6
2nd	13	11
3rd	18	16
4th	23	23
Top	37	44

to their own devices, the bottom 20% of households would only receive 2.0% of income, while the top 20% would receive 50%.

● Gross Income is the income received after all cash benefits have been paid. Since the majority of these are paid to the lower income households, the percentage of income received by the bottom quintile rises to 6.7% while the top quintile only receives 44%.

• Disposable Income is the income received after all income taxes have been paid. Since the income tax system is progressive (people on higher income pay a larger proportion of their income in income tax), this again increases the proportion of income received by the bottom quintile group from 6.7% to 7.2%. Consequently the income received by the top quintile falls from 44% to 42%.

• Post-tax Income is the final definition. This shows incomes after all indirect taxes e.g. VAT, have been taken into account. Indirect taxes tend to take a larger proportion of the income of low income households. this is because these households tend to spend all their income and so pay indirect taxes on all their income. Higher income groups may save more of their income and so pay a smaller proportion in tax. Thus indirect taxes are shown to be regressive, since they reduce the share of income received by the lowest quintile group, from 7.2% to 6.6%.

Certain features of the redistributive effect of fiscal policy are worthy of comment. First of all the most redistributive aspect of the fiscal system is the payment of cash benefits. Thus it is the expenditure side of government which has most impact on income distribution. Secondly, taxes have a neutral impact on the distribution. The proportion of income going to the bottom quintile group is the same for post-tax income as it is for gross income. Taxes have made no difference. Thus the UK tax system is broadly proportional in terms if income distribution. Thirdly, the distribution of disposable income in the UK has become more unequal since 1979. The proportion of disposable income received by the poorest 20% of households has fallen from 9.4% in 1979 to 7.2% in 1991, while the top quintile has increased its share from 36% to 42%. The figures for post-tax incomes reinforce this point.

   Views as to the 'correct' distribution of income will differ from person to person. Society would find it unacceptable that the bottom 20% of households received 3% of the total income. Whether the figure of 7.2% is acceptable is a value judgement to which economics has very little to add. As we shall see in the next chapter, the desire for increased equality might have serious dangers for an economy trying to use its resources as efficiently as possible. (Consider the implications of guaranteeing every-one the same income – the incentive to work would disappear.)

Fiscal policy and the allocation of resources

If certain activities are taxed more heavily than others, this will act as an incentive for people to carry out the untaxed activity. Thus taxes will distort people's behaviour and this may be desirable or undesirable. If an activity has substantial external costs, it is sensible to use taxes to raise the price of the activity to reflect the costs it incurs. If people still wish to carry out the activity, it must mean that the benefit they receive at least compensates for the costs imposed by the activity, and hence the activity can be seen as a sensible use of resources. If the activity does not impose external costs, the tax will discourage people from enjoying the activity, and they will suffer a loss of economic welfare. (This phenomenon will be examined more closely in the next chapter.)

Thus taxes can be used to change the behaviour of economic agents, which may or may not improve the use of resources in an economy.

Summary

- ☐ Fiscal policy refers to changes in taxation or government expenditure.
- ☐ Fiscal policy can fulfil three roles: stabilisation, distribution or allocative.
- ☐ Aggregate demand can be increased through lower taxes or higher expenditure.
- ☐ A one pound increase in government expenditure has a bigger impact on demand that a one pound cut in taxes, since tax cuts may be saved or spent on imports.
- ☐ Thus the balanced budget multiplier suggests that an equal increase in government expenditure and taxation will have an expansionary effect on aggregate demand.
- ☐ Tax revenue and government expenditure will vary automatically as GDP alters, and they will tend to work so as to dampen any changes in GDP.
- ☐ Direct taxes are mostly taxes on income. Indirect taxes are mostly taxes on expenditure.
- ☐ The fiscal system redistributes income from the rich to the poor, almost exclusively through expenditure on welfare payments.
- ☐ Taxes have very little impact on the distribution of income.
- ☐ Taxes can be used to change the allocation of resources in the economy.

Multiple Choice Questions

1. Which of the following will increase the PSBR?

    A an increase in income tax
    B an fall in the level of unemployment benefit
    C a fall in unemployment
    D an increase in unemployment
    E an increase in consumer expenditure

2. In response to an increase in inflation the government decides to reduce government expenditure by £1 billion, and, at the same time, to reduce tax rates so as to reduce tax revenue by £1 billion. The effect of these measures on the economy, other things being equal, will be:

    A neutral
    B expansionary
    C contractionary
    D inflationary
    E none of the above

3. Which one of the following would you not classify as part of fiscal policy?

    A an increase in the rate of income tax
    B an increase in the rate of interest
    C a fall in government expenditure
    D an increase in VAT
    E a fall in corporation tax

4. In the UK the most redistributive element of the fiscal system is:

    A income tax
    B corporation tax
    C VAT
    D payment in kind
    E cash benefits

5. In the UK the bottom 20% of households receive approximately:

    A 10% of total disposable income
    B 20% of total disposable income
    C 5% of total disposable income
    D 15% of total original income
    E 25% of total disposable income

Taxation

Key concepts

❏ The way in which the burden of taxation may be shifted onto other people
❏ What is meant by a fair tax
❏ What is meant by an efficient tax
❏ The way in which income taxes might affect the incentive to work

Key words

Effective and formal incidence of a tax
Horizontal equity, vertical equity, progressive tax, regressive tax, proportional tax
Efficiency. Marginal rate of taxation. Income effect of a tax, substitution effect of a tax
Laffer Curve

The incidence of taxation

Incidence of taxation is a term that refers to the party who pays a tax. There are two concepts of incidence:

● Formal Incidence: this signifies who is under a legal obligation to pay the tax to the government.
● Effective Incidence: this signifies who ends up actually paying the tax.

These two are not necessarily the same person. Consider the incidence of VAT. The producer and supplier have to pay the tax to the government, and yet most people would accept that the tax is passed on to the consumer, so that effectively it is the consumer who pays the tax. In this section we will examine the major principles which determine where the effective incidence of a tax will fall.

Consider the situation shown in Figure 27.1. This represents the market for a product sold in competitive conditions, where the equilibrium price is P_1 and the industry output is Q_1 units. Suppose a tax is imposed on this product such that the producer has to pay £1 for every unit that is produced. This taxation has the effect of shifting the supply curve vertically upwards by the amount of the tax, since, to encourage firms to keep producing Q_1 units would require a price of P_1 plus £1. Similarly, in order to keep any other quantity supplied to the market, the producers would require the original price plus the tax.

Figure 27.1 suggests that the price of the product rises from P_1 to P_2. This increase is only a proportion of the tax. The tax is shown by the vertical distance between the two supply curves. Thus the tax is shown as the distance AB. The price rises by AC, and, so, CB of the tax must be paid by the producer. Thus the effective incidence of the tax falls on both the producer and the consumer. The total tax revenue is given by the area P_2ABD. The consumer pays P_1P_2AC, and the producer pays P_1CBD.

The logic behind this result is that the producer tries to pass on the tax, but trying to charge a price of P_1 plus the tax, causes demand to fall to such an extent that there is an excess supply of the product on the market. This then reduces the price until a new equilibrium is established at a price P_2.

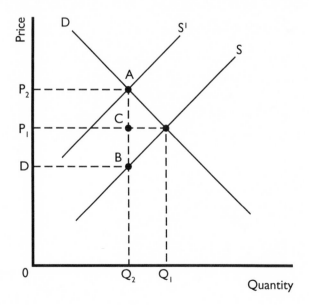

Figure 27.1 *The incidence of a tax*

The ability to pass the tax on to the consumer depends upon the elasticities of demand and supply. If demand is perfectly inelastic, the demand curve will be vertical and the price will rise by the full amount of the tax. If demand is perfectly elastic, the demand curve will be horizontal, and the price will not be affected by the tax. The producer would have to pay all of the tax. Thus the proportion of the tax paid by the consumer varies inversely with the elasticity of demand. If elasticity is high, the consumer pays less of the tax.

If supply is perfectly inelastic, that is that the same quantity will be supplied regardless of the price, all of the tax will be paid by the supplier. This result holds, because, if there is no impact on the quantity supplied, and demand does not alter, there will be no change in the price. If supply is perfectly elastic, all of the tax will be passed on to the consumer.

The incidence of income tax

The result seen in section 1 also applies to the incidence of income tax. Consider Figure 27.2.

Prior to the tax, the equilibrium wage is W_1. Income tax is paid by the employee and results in the wage received by the employee falling by the amount of the tax. Thus in Figure 27.2, in order to encourage N_1 employees to keep supplying their labour, it would require a pre-tax wage of W_1 plus the amount of income tax paid. Hence the supply curve of labour will shift upwards by the amount of the tax. What will be the impact on the labour market?

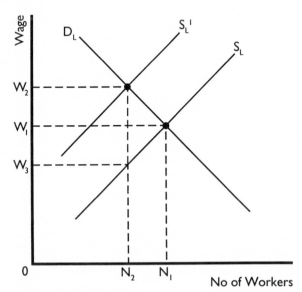

Figure 27.2 *Incidence of income tax*

The shift in the supply curve will cause the amount of labour being offered at wage W_1 to fall. This will create an excess demand for labour and, so, will put pressure on wages to rise. The new equilibrium will be at a wage of W_2. Pre-tax wages have risen (from W_1 to W_2) but post-tax wages have fallen from W_1 to W_3. The income tax is the distance W_2W_3. Thus the employer is paying W_1W_2 towards the tax and the employee is paying W_1W_3. Exactly the same analysis could be repeated for the incidence of employees' National Insurance contributions, since these are in effect an income tax.

This analysis suggests that the impact of income taxes is to reduce employment and increase pre-tax wages. The result again depends upon the relevant elasticities of demand and supply.

Equity considerations of taxation

When discussing the desirable properties of taxation there are two major considerations, those of equity and efficiency. Equity refers to the fact that most people would accept that the burden of taxation should be spread fairly throughout the economy. This is important not only on ethical grounds, but also on the practical basis that, if taxes are not acceptable, governments might find taxpayers reluctant to pay the taxes. This would create problems in obtaining the necessary tax revenues. There are two aspects of equity:

● Horizontal Equity: The idea that people in similar circumstances should be treated similarly.
● Vertical Equity: The idea that people in different circumstances should be treated differently.

While the first of these is relatively easy to understand and achieve, the second proposition is the area where disagreement arises.

There are two approaches to the problem of equity:

● The ability to pay approach
● The benefit approach.

The ability to pay approach is based on the belief that, in terms of fairness people should be expected to make the same degree of sacrifice when paying taxes, and that this sacrifice will depend upon their relative abilities to pay taxation. Ability to pay could be based on income, wealth, or expenditure, but most people take income as the best indicator of the ability to pay taxes. The question then arises as to how the tax burden should be shared between people in the economy. Horizontal equity simply requires that people on the same income should pay the same amount of tax. Vertical equity is less easy to determine. Most people would accept that people with higher incomes should pay more tax. Problems arise when trying to decide how much more they should pay. There are three possible ways in which the tax burden and income might be related:

● Progressive Taxes: These are taxes where, as income rises people pay a larger proportion of income in taxation. Thus as income doubles, the amount paid in tax more than doubles. This is necessary if the distribution of income in the economy is to be made more equal by the tax system.
● Proportional Taxes: This is when, as income rises, people pay a constant proportion of income in taxation. Thus if income doubles, so does the amount paid in taxation.
● Regressive Taxes: This is when, as income rises, a smaller proportion of income is paid in tax. Thus if income doubles, the amount paid in tax less than doubles.

It is usual to argue that equality of sacrifice should imply that taxpayers should lose the same amount of utility when they pay taxes. If one accepts the idea that money displays diminishing marginal utility, this would suggest that, in order to lose the same amount of utility, a rich taxpayer must pay more in tax than a poor taxpayer. Whether this requires taxes to be progressive, proportional or regressive is a matter of value judgement.

The benefit approach suggests that it is only fair if those people who obtain the most benefit from government spending pay the most tax. This was one of the arguments used to justify the Poll Tax or Community Charge which the Conservative government introduced to help pay for the services provided by local government. All adults were obliged to pay the same amount of money since all people benefited from local services.

There are problems associated with adopting the benefit approach. It ignores the ability to pay and so conflicts with the more generally accepted view of equity. Also, often it is difficult to determine the benefit which people receive from goods and services provided by the government. This is especially true where goods and services are provided free of charge, or where exclusion is not possible. One way in which the benefit principle can be applied is by the government charging for its services. Vehicle licences and television licences are aspects of this approach.

Efficiency considerations of taxation

Efficiency refers to the need to make the best use of resources. Government spending requires that tax revenue be raised. We have seen that, in a competitive market economy, resources will be used in the most efficient way possible, unless market failures arise. The tax system should interfere with the market allocation of resources as little as possible if this optimum is to be preserved. There are two ways in which this efficiency may be impaired:

● Costs of Collection: If a particular tax is very expensive to collect, there is an obvious waste of resources. Thus it is desirable that taxes should be cheap to collect. This should also extend to the cost of administering the tax, and the cost which the tax imposes on the taxpayer as well as the tax collector.

● The Excess Burden of Taxation: When a tax distorts consumer choice, there will be a cost to the taxpayer over and above the amount of money paid in tax. This is known as the excess burden of a tax. The test as to whether a tax imposes an excess burden is to examine how a consumer reacts to the tax. If, after reacting to the tax, the taxpayer is adopting a form of behaviour which he would not have chosen prior to the tax, then the taxpayer will be worse off even if the money paid in tax were returned to him. Consider an individual who enjoys driving a Rolls Royce motor car. If the government imposed a £1000 per year tax on running a Rolls Royce, the individual might switch to driving a smaller car to avoid the tax. The tax has still imposed a burden on this individual even though he has paid no tax. He is now driving a smaller car which gives him less satisfaction than he previously obtained from the Rolls Royce. The tax has imposed a burden over and above the amount of tax paid. (In this example no tax was paid.) This excess burden can also be shown graphically.

In Figure 27.3 the original price is P_1 and the quantity sold is Q_1. Consumer surplus is the area P_1AB. This area represents the extent to which the benefit people obtain from the product, as measured by the maximum prices they would have been prepared to pay, exceeds the amount actually paid. Suppose that the imposition of a tax causes the price if the product to rise to P_2, sales will fall to Q_2. Consumer surplus has fallen

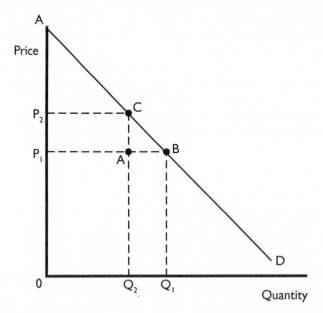

Figure 27.3 *The excess burden of a tax*

by the area P_1P_2CB, while the amount of tax paid is given by the area P_1P_2CA. This tax paid cannot really be considered as a burden since the taxpayer will receive goods and services in return. The excess burden is the area ABC since this represents the extent to which the taxpayer has lost welfare in excess of the tax paid. Even if the tax were repaid, the taxpayer has had his choices distorted by the tax and is, therefore, in an inferior position.

This result occurs because the imposition of a tax has two effects, an income effect and a substitution effect. All taxes must have the same income effect since all the taxes reduce disposable income. It is the substitution effect which causes the excess burden. If a tax alters relative prices, it will cause taxpayers to alter their consumption patterns, such that consumers do not achieve their desired pre tax positions. An efficient tax is one which minimises these substitution effects. There are several ways in which this can be achieved:

- **A Poll Tax**. If a tax is imposed such that everyone pays the same amount without it being related to any economic activity, there will be no substitution effects. This will be highly efficient, but of course highly inequitable.
- **Tax All Products**. If all products are taxed equally, there will be little change in relative prices. This will minimise the substitution effects.
- **Tax Products with an Inelastic Demand**. If products with an inelastic demand are taxed, this causes little change in consumer behaviour other than the fact that people will have had their incomes reduced by paying the tax. This is simply the income effect which causes no loss of efficiency.

It is not a solution to simply tax income, since income taxes also have an excess burden. They may alter the choice between work and leisure. This aspect of income tax is an important area of debate in economics since the disincentive effects of income tax are often put forward as a justification for reducing the burden of income tax.

There may be circumstances when it is desirable to distort consumer choice. This will be the case when external costs or benefits exist in connection with some activity. As we saw in Chapter Eighteen, taxes are a way of improving resource allocation when external costs exist, and subsidies will be allocatively efficient where external benefits arise.

Income tax and the incentive to work

An income tax will have two effects on the taxpayer, an income effect and a substitution effect. These effects will tend to operate in opposite directions on the taxpayer.

- Income Effect: If income tax rises, this has the effect of reducing the income of the taxpayer. This reduction in income will affect the incentive to work. If work is seen as an inferior good, something which is undertaken because the taxpayer cannot afford more leisure, an increase in income tax might be an incentive to work more in order to restore income. Similarly, a fall in income tax might mean that the taxpayer can now afford to work less. The income effect can be visualised as the taxpayer's reaction to receiving or losing a lump sum of money. If you won a sum of money would that make you work more or less?

● Substitution Effect: If income tax rates rise, this makes it worth less to work. Thus the cost of not working, (the cost of leisure) has fallen. If this makes not working more attractive, an increase in income tax will have proven to be a disincentive to work.

Thus on theoretical grounds an increase in income tax might make people work more because of the income effect, but work less because of the substitution effect. Which of these two effects will be dominant will determine whether higher income tax rates are an incentive or a disincentive to work. This must be a matter that can only be resolved by looking at the evidence. Unfortunately what evidence there is fails to provide an answer.

However certain conclusions can be reached. The substitution effect depends upon the marginal rate of tax since the decision about working more, or taking more leisure, is normally a decision about the relative attractions of each. This will depend upon the rewards gained from working more or less, which in turn will be affected by the tax rates imposed on working more. The marginal rate of tax is the proportion of any increase in income which is taken in the form of tax. The higher the marginal rate of tax, the less incentive there will be to engage in extra work.

The income effect depends upon the average rate of tax since it depends upon the total reward from working. The higher the average rate of tax, the more incentive there will be to work more (if work is seen as an inferior good). The average rate of tax is the proportion of total income which is taken in the form of tax. Thus if the disincentive effects of income tax are to be avoided, average rates of income tax should be high, and marginal rates should be low. Unfortunately this would tend to make income tax regressive and so would conflict with the objective of equity.

The Laffer Curve

An American economist, Arthur Laffer, put forward a proposition which bears his name and which has been influential in affecting the attitude to income tax. The Laffer Curve is simply the idea that an increase in the rate of income tax might actually reduce the amount of tax revenue which was collected. This is shown in Figure 27.4.

If the average rate of income tax was zero, tax revenue would be zero. If the average rate was 100%, tax revenue would also be zero, since there would be no point in working. Thus the revenue yield from income tax

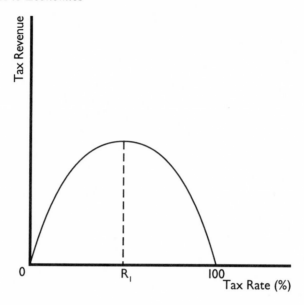

Figure 27.4 *The Laffer Curve*

must be positively related to the rate of tax when average tax rates initially increase, but there must come a point where tax revenue starts to decline as rates increase. (In Figure 27.4, this occurs beyond the rate R_1.) Unfortunately opinions differ as to what rate equates with rate R_1. People on the right of the political spectrum, who on the whole prefer lower rates of income tax, will argue that we are beyond R_1 and that reducing tax rates will boost revenue. Other people argue that an increase in rates would boost revenue.

Summary

- ❑ The formal incidence of a tax refers to who has the legal obligation to pay the tax to the government.
- ❑ The effective incidence of any tax refers to who actually pays the tax.
- ❑ The effective incidence of any tax depends upon the elasticities of demand and supply: the lower the elasticity of demand, the more the tax will be passed on. The lower the elasticity of supply, the less the tax will be passed on.
- ❑ Horizontal equity requires that similar people should be treated similarly.
- ❑ Vertical equity requires that different people should be treated differently.
- ❑ The ability to pay criteria suggests that taxes should be based on the ability to pay.
- ❑ The benefit principle suggests that equity requires that taxes be based on the benefits derived by the taxpayer from government provision.
- ❑ Taxes are efficient when they are cheap and convenient to collect.
- ❑ Taxes are efficient if they interfere as little as possible with the optimum allocation of resources.
- ❑ The income effect of a tax does not distort choice
- ❑ The substitution effect of a tax does distort choice and so imposes an excess burden.
- ❑ Income taxes impose income and substitution effects, which have opposite effects on the incentive to work.
- ❑ The Laffer Curve suggests that high average rates of tax will reduce the revenue from income tax.

Multiple Choice Questions

1. Effective incidence of a tax refers to:
   - **A** the proportion of people paying the tax
   - **B** the amount of revenue raised by a tax
   - **C** the person who has the legal obligation to pay the tax to the government
   - **D** the person who actually loses purchasing power because of the tax
   - **E** whether the tax raises enough money

2. Under which of the following circumstances would all of a sales tax be paid by the consumer?
  A perfectly elastic demand
  B perfectly inelastic demand
  C perfectly inelastic supply
  D demand and supply curves with unit elasticities
  E none of the above

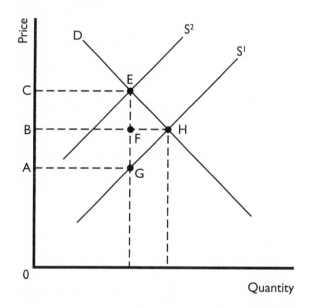

The diagram shows the market position before and after the imposition of a sales tax. Select from the following the area which represents:

  A BCEF
  B ABFG
  C BHGA
  D BCEH
  E ACEG

3. the amount of the tax paid by the consumer

4. the amount of tax revenue

5. the loss of consumer surplus caused by the imposition of the tax

Monetary Policy

Definition

Monetary policy can be defined as any change in the cost or availability of credit. Thus monetary policy is concerned with affecting the cost of borrowing, which refers to the rate of interest, and the ease with which people can obtain credit. Monetary policy operates by trying to affect the level of aggregate demand in the economy by influencing the ability of people to finance their spending. As we saw in Chapter Twenty Five, if there is an increase in the amount of money in the economy, some economists argue that this will inevitably lead to an increase in spending. If the economy is not able to increase output to satisfy this extra demand, prices will rise.

Monetary policy and the rate of interest

Changes in the rate of interest are one of the most significant aspects of monetary policy. Governments can influence the rate of interest through the Central Bank's role as lender of last resort. If the commercial banks require extra liquidity to meet their day to day requirements, the Bank of England is always prepared to act as lender of last resort. That is, they will always be prepared to allow the commercial banks to borrow cash. However the Bank of England will charge a rate of interest. If the Bank wishes to increase interest rates in the economy, it will increase the rate of interest which it charges to commercial banks. The banks will be forced to raise the rate of interest which they charge their customers in order to maintain profit margins. If the rates of interest at commercial banks increase, other interest rates in the economy will also rise, in order to maintain competitiveness. Thus rates of interest throughout the economy will increase. Changes in the rate of interest will affect the aggregate demand in a variety of ways:

• Consumer Spending: If interest rates rise, this will encourage savings and deter borrowing. Hence consumer spending will fall. In addition, if interest rates rise, interest payments on debts will also rise. Thus people with mortgages will experience increased repayments. This will also reduce purchasing power. Higher interest rates will also reduce the value of certain assets, both real and financial. An increase in interest rates is likely to reduce the value of shares and houses. Since these assets represent wealth to their owners, this fall in wealth might reduce their willingness to spend.

• Investment Spending: If interest rates rise, it will be more expensive for firms to borrow money to invest in new plant and equipment. Also firms may decide that their money will earn a higher rate of return from being placed into financial assets rather than invested in new capital equipment. Thus investment will fall if interest rates rise.

• Export Demand: If interest rates in the UK increase, the UK will become attractive as a place where financial assets pay a high rate of return. This will attract funds from abroad to invest in UK financial assets. In order to invest in financial assets in the UK, foreign currencies will have to be converted into sterling. This will increase the demand for sterling on the foreign exchange market, which will increase the foreign exchange value of sterling. If the value of sterling increases, UK exports will become more expensive abroad, which will reduce the demand for UK exports. Hence an increase in UK interest rates will normally be associated with a fall in export demand.

These channels are the main means by which an increase in the rate of interest in the UK will reduce the level of aggregate demand in the UK. The effectiveness of interest rate policy will depend upon how sensitive these three components of aggregate demand are, with respect to changes in the rate of interest. This is a source of debate within economics. Supporters of monetary policy insist that interest rate changes have a major impact on aggregate demand. Critics of monetary policy argue that interest rate changes are an unreliable way to affect aggregate demand.

Control of the money supply

The other major aspect of monetary policy is control of the money supply. As we saw in Chapter Twenty Five. it is usually argued that, if the money supply is reduced, this will reduce spending. There are two channels through which this process will occur. Monetarists stress the direct mechanism whereby a fall in the money supply will reduce spending because of the fact that the velocity of circulation of money is constant. Keynesians will argue that the reduction in the money supply will put pressure on interest rates to rise, and this increase in interest rates will then operate through the channels shown in the previous section. There are several ways in which the government may attempt to influence the supply of money in the economy:

● Special Deposits: Occasionally the monetary authorities have tried to reduce the ability of the commercial banks to lend money (which represents the most significant way in which broad money expands), by requiring the commercial banks to place 'special deposits' with the Bank of England. These deposits are then 'frozen' in that they cannot be considered as liquid assets by the commercial banks. These deposits may also be non interest bearing. Hence the commercial banks will experience a fall in liquidity and also a reduction in their profit margins. Both of these effects will put pressure on interest rates to rise. As we saw in Chapter Twenty Five, excess liquidity is also important if the commercial banks are to be able to extend extra credit. These 'special deposits' therefore may constrain the amount of extra credit which the commercial banks can offer and also increase interest rates. The UK has abandoned such controls because it feels that similar results can be achieved through open market operations.

● Open Market Operations and Funding the PSBR: As we saw in Chapter Twenty Six, the funding of a public sector deficit might have implications for the supply of money. If the deficit is financed by borrowing off the commercial banks, this will boost the supply of broad money in the economy. Thus control of the PSBR is sometimes seen as an important aspect of controlling the money supply. In the early 1980s the government deliberately sold more debt outside the banking system than was needed to finance the deficit. This overfunding reduced bank deposits and thus reduced the growth of broad money.

The sale and purchase of government debt in the money market is known as Open Market Operations. If the government wishes to reduce the amount of money in the economy, it can sell government debt (bonds) to the public. People will buy this debt with cheques drawn on the commercial banks. The volume of bank deposits will fall as money is withdrawn and paid to the Bank of England. Since the volume of bank deposits in the commercial banks is part of broad money, the quantity of broad money in the economy will fall. If the Bank of England wishes to increase the volume of bank deposits, it will purchase government debt (bonds) and so increase the volume of bank deposits, and, hence, broad money.

● Monetary Base Control: It is sometimes argued that the money supply could be controlled by controlling the amount of 'base money' in the economy. 'Base money' refers primarily to notes and coins. If the supply of these was controlled, and this could easily be achieved because the Bank of England has a monopoly of note and coin production, the ability of the commercial banks to extend credit would be curtailed since their ability to obtain the liquidity to finance those loans would also be curtailed. However this approach has been rejected by the Bank of England, since variations in the demand for base money would imply that liquidity would be a problem, and so interest rates would be volatile. Also the commercial banks would probably adapt to the shortage of cash by changing their behaviour and encouraging people to use less cash. The move towards debit cards is a step in this direction. If people can be encouraged not to use cash, the banks will obviously need to retain lesser cash reserves.

● Quantitative Controls on the Supply of Money: These are physical constraints on the amount of money which the banking system can lend. The Bank of England argues that such controls introduce rigidities and reduce competition in the financial system. Borrowers and lenders would have a strong incentive to avoid such controls, and thus, they would be likely to be ineffective.

● Interest Rates: Because of the difficulties associated with quantitative controls, the government places most emphasis on the price mechanism as a means of controlling bank lending. This means that an increase in interest rates is used to reduce the demand for money. Thus the supply of money is normally thought of as being demand determined.

Monetary policy and the exchange rate

The ability to control the domestic rate of interest depends upon the nature of the exchange rate regime which the government wishes to follow. As we shall see in Chapter Twenty Nine the rate of interest has a significant effect upon the exchange rate. An increase in interest rates will put pressure on the exchange rate to rise. If the government is trying to control the exchange rate, it will have to accept whatever interest rate is necessary to give the required exchange rate. Hence control over the exchange rate implies a loss of control over the interest rate.

Interest rates and the supply of money

As we saw in Chapter Twenty Five, a reduction in the supply of money will create an excess demand for money which will put pressure on interest rates to rise. Thus, if the monetary authorities attempt to control the supply of money, they must be prepared to accept whatever interest rate that determines. Hence control of the money supply entails a loss of control over interest rates. If the authorities wish to keep the interest rate constant, and there is an increase in the demand for money, they would be forced to allow the money supply to increase to satisfy the demand. Hence control of the rate of interest implies a loss of control over the money supply. Thus of the three variables, interest rates, money supply and exchange rate, the authorities can only ever control one of the three at any one time.

Summary

- ◻ Monetary policy is concerned with control of the cost or availability of credit.
- ◻ The rate of interest is an important part of monetary policy.
- ◻ Reductions in the rate of interest will boost aggregate demand, through its impact on consumption, investment and exports.
- ◻ Monetarists believe that increases in the money supply are inflationary and so control of the money supply is a weapon against inflation.
- ◻ Control of the money supply can be attempted by: special deposits, open market operations, control of the PSBR and its funding, quantitative controls, and by changes in the rate of interest.
- ◻ It is changes in the rate of interest which are usually seen as most important.

Multiple Choice Questions

1. Which would constitute an expansionary monetary policy?

    A   a fall in income tax
    B   an increase in the rate of interest
    C   a purchase of government bonds by the Bank of England
    D   an increase in government expenditure
    E   a fall in the money supply

2. An increase in investment is likely to be the result of:

    A   a fall in the rate of interest
    B   a fall in the money supply
    C   an increase in the cost of capital goods
    D   an increase in income tax
    E   a fall in government expenditure

3. A reduction in the monetary base (notes and coins) might control the broad money supply because:

    A   broad money (M4) consists of notes and coins
    B   if people have fewer notes and coins they will try to borrow more
    C   people cannot demand money if there is insufficient notes and coins in the economy
    D   banks may have insufficient notes and coins to allow them to extend credit
    E   people will not have enough money to spend

4. Which of the following constitute part of narrow money (MO)?

    A   current accounts with the commercial banks
    B   deposits with a Building Society
    C   commercial bank balances with the Bank of England
    D   premium bonds
    E   credit cards

5 Which of the following would you expect to increase the rate of interest?

    A   an increase in the money supply
    B   a fall in the demand for money
    C   a fall in the level of income
    D   a sale by the Bank of England of government stock to the public
    E   an increase in the exchange rate

Chapter Twenty-nine

Exchange Rates

Key concepts

❏ Factors affecting the exchange rate
❏ The importance of capital flows in determining the exchange rate
❏ The difference between a fixed and a flexible exchange rate regime, and their importance for domestic economic policy
❏ The impact of exchange rate changes on the economy: imports, exports, inflation, output

Key words

Real exchange rate, nominal exchange rate, real effective exchange rate, fundamental equilibrium exchange rate
Capital flows, capital mobility
Purchasing power parity. Fixed and flexible exchange rates, 'J' curve, elasticity of demand for imports and exports, Marshall-Lerner conditions

Definition

The nominal exchange rate is the price of one currency in terms of another. Thus an exchange rate of £1 = $2 simply says that £1 will exchange for $2. That is £1 will cost $2. The price of a currency will be determined by the forces of demand and supply in the foreign exchange market. The foreign exchange market is one of the closest examples of a perfect market. All currencies are homogeneous in that one pound sterling is identical to any other pound sterling. There is perfect communications in the market place, and there are many buyers and sellers. This means that in order to understand the determination of exchange rates, all we need to understand are the factors which give rise to the demand and supply of currency. If there is an excess demand for pounds, with more people trying to buy pounds than trying to sell, the price will rise. Conversely, an excess supply will reduce the price. The demand for pounds must represent the supply of some other currency, and pounds will be supplied in order to buy foreign currency.

There are various other definitions of the exchange rate:

● **The effective exchange rate** attempts to show how a particular currency has moved against its major trading partners.
● **The real exchange rate** attempts to show how the competitive position of one country's goods has changed when compared to that of another. It is affected by both a change in the relative price levels and also the nominal exchange rates. It is calculated by the formula:

$$\text{Real exchange rate} = \text{nominal rate} \times \frac{\text{price index for foreign country}}{\text{price index for domestic country}}$$

The importance of this term will be considered later.

● **The real effective exchange rate** attempts to show how the competitive position has altered between a country and its major trading partners.
● **The Fundamental Equilibrium Exchange Rate** (FEER) is an attempt to estimate the exchange rate which would allow the Balance of Payments to be in equilibrium.

We will first of all examine the factors which determine the nominal exchange rate.

The demand for currency – the demand for exports of goods and services

One reason why currencies are demanded is in order to buy goods and services. Hence a US importer who wishes to buy UK goods must first of all obtain sterling, since the UK exporter will probably want paying in sterling. Thus if UK exports increase, so will the demand for pounds. One of the factors which will affect the demand for UK exports will be the exchange rate. Consider Figure 29.1.

At an exchange rate of R_1, assume that the value of exports from the UK is X_1. What will be the effect of a fall in the exchange rate to R_2? If the sterling exchange rate falls, this will reduce the price of UK goods abroad. Suppose that the initial exchange rate is £1 = $2. A product which sold for £1 in the UK would sell for $2 in the US. If the exchange rate then fell to £1 = $1, the product would now sell in the US for $1. Hence a fall in the

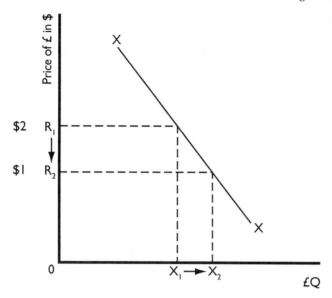

Figure 29.1 *The demand for currency*

price of the pound will cause the price of UK goods abroad to fall. This will normally cause the volume of UK exports to increase, which is bound to increase their value in terms of sterling. Selling one extra unit will bring in an extra £1. The extent to which exports will increase will depend upon the price elasticity of demand for UK exports. In Figure 29.1 this is shown by the value of exports increasing to X_2. Thus the line XX denotes the value of UK exports as the exchange rate changes. As we saw in the previous section, the value of UK exports will give rise to a demand for pounds in order to pay for these exports. Hence XX also denotes the demand for pounds for trading purposes. The slope of the line depends upon the price elasticity of demand for UK exports. The more elastic the demand, the flatter the line XX.

The supply of currency – Imports of goods and services

If UK importers wish to buy goods from the US, they will need to obtain dollars to pay for them. This will normally take place via the commercial banks, that will buy dollars in the foreign exchange market, and will sell pounds in order to do this. Hence the value of goods imported into the UK must represent a supply of pounds to the foreign exchange market. Consider Figure 29.2.

Again R_1 shows the initial exchange rate and the value of imports is given as M_1. Suppose that the exchange rate falls to R_2. A fall in the

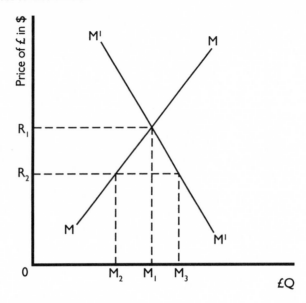

Figure 29.2 *The supply of currency*

exchange rate will increase the price of imports in the UK. At an exchange rate of $2 = £1, a $2 item from the US will sell for £1 in the UK. If the exchange rate falls to $1 = £1, a $2 item will now sell in the UK for £2. Thus a fall in the sterling exchange rate will increase the price of imports into the UK.

What will be the effect on the value of imports? Normally we would expect the volume of imports to fall, but the value depends on the price elasticity of demand. If the demand for imports is inelastic (less than one), the fall in demand will be less than the increase in price (in percentage terms). Thus the total amount of money spent on imports will rise. If demand is elastic, the value of imports will fall. In figure 29.2 we show both possibilities. The line MM shows the value of imports falling to M_2 at the lower exchange rate R_2 and so represents an elastic demand. The line M'M' shows imports increasing to M_3 and so represents an inelastic demand. It is normally assumed that the demand for imports is elastic and so we will use the line MM.

The value of imports also represents the supply of sterling on the foreign exchange market for trading purposes.

The equilibrium exchange rate

Figure 29.3 shows the market for sterling against the dollar. The schedules XX and MM are also labelled DD and SS because they represent the demand and supply of pounds. The equilibrium exchange rate will be at the

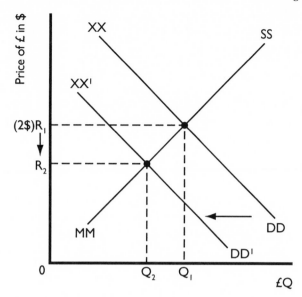

Figure 29.3 *Reduced demand for UK exports*

rate R_1. If any event occurs which changes the value of imports or exports into the UK, this will cause the exchange rate to alter, other things being equal.

Suppose that the price of UK goods rises. This will make UK exports uncompetitive and will reduce the value of exports. Hence the demand for sterling will reduce. Figure 29.3 shows the impact on the foreign exchange market.

The reduced demand for exports shifts the demand curve for sterling to XX'. At the original exchange rate this creates an excess supply of sterling and its price will fall. The process through which this occurs will be that UK importers will not be able to find sufficient dollars on the foreign exchange market because US importers do not wish to sell the same quantity of dollars to buy UK goods. Hence UK importers will have to offer more pounds for dollars in an attempt to secure the dollars they require. Thus instead of offering £1 for $2 dollars, they will offer more. In other words £1 will no longer buy $2, but instead will buy fewer dollars. The sterling exchange rate will have fallen. Thus any event which alters UK exports or imports will affect the demand or supply of pounds and so will affect the exchange rate.

The demand for currency: the demand for UK assets

There is a second reason why people may wish to buy pounds. This is in order to purchase UK assets. These assets may be physical in the form of factories etc., or they may be financial in the form of bank deposits, or shares, or government bonds. It is the demand for financial assets which is the major influence on movements in the nominal exchange rate.

Consider a US financier who has responsibility for looking after a substantial amount of money. This financier will look around the world to see where that money can earn the highest rate of return. If the UK looks an attractive proposition, the US financier will have to convert his money into sterling in order to invest his funds in the UK. This will give rise to an increase in the demand for pounds and will cause the exchange rate to rise. In Figure 29.3 XX will shift to the right. Thus anything which increases the rate of return which funds can earn in the UK will cause the demand for pounds to rise and thereby increase the sterling exchange rate. The expected rate of return on financial assets in the UK will depend upon two factors:

- **The rate of interest:** Suppose that interest rates in the UK were to rise relative to those in the US. Capital (money) would flow from the US into the UK, raising the demand for pounds and so increasing the exchange rate. Conversely a fall in UK interest rates will reduce the value of the pound.
- **Expected movements in the exchange rate:** If the exchange rate is expected to fall this will make the UK an unattractive proposition as far as foreign financial investment is concerned, since it will reduce the value of any sterling assets which foreigners hold. Thus if the value of the pound is expected to fall, foreign holders of sterling assets will sell these assets, which will increase the supply of pounds on the foreign exchange market, and so will reduce the value of the pound.

Capital flows will occur whenever one country appears more or less attractive as a home for capital than other countries. These capital flows will put pressure on the exchange rate to alter. Exchange rates will settle at the point where capital flows cease. Capital flows will cease when any interest rate differential is just offset by an expected change in the exchange rate.

Suppose that interest rates in the UK were 5% higher than in the US. Capital would flow from the US into the UK to take advantage of these higher rates. This would increase the demand for sterling and its price would rise against the dollar. As long as money flowed in from the US, the exchange rate would keep rising. At what point would the inflow of capital cease? If the value of the pound rose to such a level that people expected its value to fall by 5% in the next year, this would wipe out the attraction of the interest rate differential and capital flows would cease. The pound would cease to rise and would settle at a point 5% above its expected value. Thus any interest rate differential is just matched by an expected change in the exchange rate. This relationship is given by the following expression:

$$CF = (r - r^*) - (e - e^*)$$

where:

CF = capital flows
r = domestic rate of interest
r* = world rate of interest
e = nominal exchange rate
e* = expected exchange rate.

The exchange rate will rise until CF equals zero. Hence to the point where:

$$(r - r^*) = (e - e^*)$$
Thus, $e = e^* + (r - r^*).$

This means that the current exchange rate will be at its expected rate plus an amount equal to the interest rate differential. Thus movements in the current rate will be because of movements in either the interest rate differential, or the expected exchange rate. This suggests that an important factor in determining the current exchange rate is what people perceive as the normal or expected rate for the currency. This question is normally answered with reference to the Law of Purchasing Power Parity (PPP).

Purchasing power parity

The Law of Purchasing Power Parity states that exchange rates will adjust so as to keep the relative price of goods from different countries constant. Suppose that a particular UK commodity sold for £100 in the UK, and a similar commodity, produced in the US, sold for $200 in the US. At an exchange rate of £1 = $2, the product is selling in effect at the same price in both countries. Suppose that the price of the good in the UK rose, because of inflation in the UK, to £150. If the price in the US remained at $200, and the exchange rate stayed at £1 = $2, there would be profitable trading possibilities between the US and the UK. It would be profitable to buy the commodity in the US for $200, import it into the UK, and sell it for £150. These £150 could then be converted at £1 = $2 to give $300. This represents a profit of $100 per transaction. If the inflation in the UK has increased the price of all products by 50%, this process will be occurring extensively. There will be a dramatic increase in imports into the UK, putting pressure on the exchange rate to fall. This process will continue until the profitable trading possibilities are no longer possible. This will occur when the exchange rate has fallen to £1 = $1.33, since at this rate, the commodity sells at the same price in both countries. (If £1 = $1.33. then

£150 = $200)

PPP suggests that in the long run exchange rates will reflect differing inflation rates in different countries. In effect what this means is that, in the long run, real exchange rates will be constant, since the nominal rate will simply adjust to compensate for differences in relative inflation rates. Also the PPP suggests that the best indicator of whether an exchange rate is at its 'correct' level is to consider whether goods within one economy as compared with goods from the other country are competitive. There is no agreed basis upon which this exercise can be carried out, since it is difficult to make accurate comparisons. However the significance of whether a currency is perceived to be at its 'correct' level, is that this determines whether people expect the currency to rise or fall in the future. If the pound is expected to rise in the future because it is perceived as being 'too' low, this will encourage people to put financial assets into the UK to benefit from the rise in the value of the pound. The inflow of these assets will ensure that the value of the pound rises until it reaches the level at which it makes the UK unattractive for any more inflows.

Therefore, if any event occurs which leads people to anticipate the pound rising, it will rise immediately as people try to take advantage of this increase. Suppose people became pessimistic about inflation in the UK and expected inflation to increase. PPP suggests that this will lead to a fall in the exchange rate. If people anticipate this happening, they will withdraw funds from the UK, sell their pounds on the foreign exchange market, thereby causing the value of the pound to fall immediately. Any event which makes the UK look less attractive as a home for foreign capital will reduce the value of the pound.

Fixed exchange rates

Left to market forces the exchange rate will fluctuate from day to day and from hour to hour. These fluctuations may be quite severe depending upon the behaviour of capital flows. These capital flows have become much more important as capital has become more mobile, as restrictions on capital movements have been reduced, and as technology has improved, making the transfer of funds much easier. Fluctuations in the exchange rate are sometimes seen as undesirable because they will interfere with international trade by introducing uncertainty. If traders cannot be sure of how many pounds they will receive for goods sold in dollars, they may be reluctant to engage in trade with the US. In order to encourage trade and create stability in international trade, some countries have attempted to keep their exchange rate fixed. Consider Figure 29.4.

Suppose that the government in the UK wished to keep the value of the pound at R_1 and assume that initially this is the equilibrium rate in the market. Now suppose that interest rates in the US fall. This will encourage

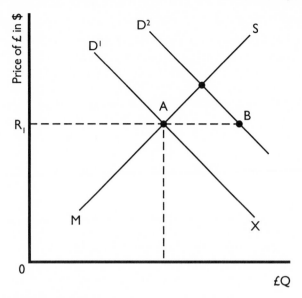

Figure 29.4 *Fixed exchange rates*

capital to flow into the UK from the US. This will increase the demand for pounds, shifting the demand to D_2. At the original rate R_1 there is now an excess demand for pounds, shown as the distance AB, and the exchange rate will rise. If the authorities wish to keep the pound at R_1, they must remove the excess demand. There are two options open to them. They could sell pounds and buy foreign currency, which would then be added to the foreign exchange reserves. This would satisfy the demand for pounds without the exchange rate rising. This process is known as intervention in the foreign exchange market. Alternatively, they could take steps to reduce the demand for pounds. The quickest and most effective method would be to reduce UK interest rates.

Both of these options can be thought of as having implications for monetary policy. If intervention is carried out, the extra pounds will be put into the UK banking system. Thus the money supply will increase. If interest rates are reduced, this has obvious implications for monetary policy. Thus attempts to control the exchange rate inevitably mean that the government loses control of its monetary policy. It is forced to carry out whatever monetary policy is necessary to keep the exchange rate at its required level. This is one reason why many people are reluctant to see the UK enter the exchange rate mechanism (ERM) of the European Monetary System (EMS), since this would entail accepting constraints on the level of the exchange rate, and so constrain the ability of the UK to implement monetary policy. The ERM is an arrangement whereby the member countries of the ERM agree to keep their currencies within certain bands against others currency.

This is an important point. A fixed exchange rate means that monetary policy has to be subordinate to keeping the exchange rate fixed. If a country wants freedom to control its own monetary policy, it cannot control its exchange rate. In the example above, a decision by the US to reduce interest rates will force the UK to follow suit if the UK wishes to keep the exchange rate fixed. If the UK wishes to follow an independent policy on interest rates it must be prepared to allow the exchange rate to vary. This implies that more emphasis will have to be placed on fiscal policy as a means of controlling aggregate demand in a fixed exchange rate system.

Flexible exchange rates

If exchange rates are left to find their own level in the market this is known as a flexible exchange rate regime. Monetary policy will now become a viable weapon in controlling the economy, since the impact on the exchange rate can be accepted. Thus a decision to raise interest rates, in order to constrain demand, will be effective and will simply cause the exchange rate to rise. This in fact would reinforce the contraction in demand because of its impact on exports. (A higher exchange rate will make exports more expensive, and so reduce their demand.) Flexible exchanges rates also mean that governments do not have to intervene in the foreign exchange market, thereby reducing the need for large foreign exchange reserves.

Impact of exchange rate changes

Another reason why governments may be concerned about the level of the exchange rate is the fact that changes in the rate will have implications for the behaviour of the domestic economy. We will examine this in the context of a fall in the exchange rate. If the exchange rate falls, this will affect the level of imports and exports in the economy. A lower exchange rate will make exports cheaper and imports more expensive. Thus exports are bound to improve following a fall in the exchange rate, both in volume and value terms. This will improve the Balance of Payments and also boost the level of aggregate demand in the economy. Export industries will expand, and this will have multiplier effects throughout the economy.

The impact on imports depends, as we saw above, on the elasticity of demand. If demand for imports is inelastic, and people keep buying them even though they are more expensive, the value of imports will rise. This would have a dampening effect on aggregate demand, since imports are a withdrawal from the circular flow of income. If demand is elastic, the value of imports will fall.

The overall effect on aggregate demand and also on the Balance of Payments depends on the combined impact on exports and imports. This

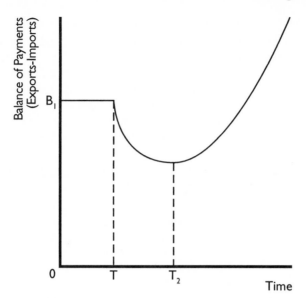

Figure 29.5 The 'J' curve

depends upon the combined value of the elasticities of demand. The Marshall-Lerner conditions state that if the combined elasticities are greater than one, the overall impact on the Balance of Payments will be positive. The importance of this result is illustrated by the phenomena known as the 'J' curve.

Suppose that at time T a fall in the exchange rate occurs. The vertical axis in Figure 29.5 represents the balance on the current account of the Balance of Payments. At time T the balance is shown as B_1. Immediately after the fall in the exchange rate, the elasticity if demand for both imports and exports is likely to be low. This is because it will take time for people to react to the price changes which have occurred. It will take time for foreigners to realise that UK exports are now cheaper, and it will take time for UK importers to find UK-sourced goods rather than the more expensive imports. This means that the value of exports will not increase very much and the value of imports will rise.

If imports rise more than exports, the Balance of Payments will deteriorate. This is shown in Figure 29.5 by the graph falling. As time progresses elasticities will increase as buyers react to the change in the relative price of UK goods. Eventually, at time T_2, the Balance of Payments will start to improve and the curve will begin to rise, giving the distinctive 'J' shape. Thus the immediate impact of a fall in the exchange rate may be to reduce aggregate demand, and to worsen the balance of payments. In the long run the impact will be to boost demand and to improve the balance of payments.

Movements in the exchange rate will also affect the rate of inflation. If the rate falls, imports will immediately become more expensive. The Retail Price Index (RPI) is calculated by examining the prices of a typical basket of goods. The 'basket' will contain some imported goods and so the average level of prices will rise. Hence the RPI will rise. Since the inflation rate is simply the rate at which prices rise, the higher RPI implies a higher rate of inflation. This will be made worse if the higher price of imports increases the cost of raw materials and components used by UK industry, since these higher costs will also push up prices. If workers see prices rising and push for higher wages, so increasing costs even further, inflation will rise again.

Thus the level of the exchange rate has implications for the level of aggregate demand (and hence will affect unemployment), the balance of payments, and inflation. These are the most important objectives which concern governments in terms of economic policy, and so the level of the exchange rate is of great importance.

Summary

❏ The exchange rate measures the price of one currency in terms of another.

❏ The real exchange rate measures changes in competitiveness.

❏ The exchange rate is determined by the demand for, and the supply of, currency.

❏ Imports of goods and services give rise to a supply of domestic currency.

❏ Exports of goods and services give rise to a demand for domestic currency.

❏ The equilibrium exchange rate will be where demand and supply are equal.

❏ The demand for UK assets, especially financial assets, gives rise to a demand for UK currency.

❏ Financial assets will be demanded if they offer an attractive rate of return.

❏ The rate of return depends upon the rate of interest which the assets can earn.

❏ The rate of return depends upon any change in the exchange rate which occurs.

❏ The expected rate of return depends upon the interest rate and any expected change in the exchange rate.

❏ Purchasing Power Parity suggests that in the long run exchange rate movements will reflect changes in the price levels of different countries, so as to keep goods and services competitive.

❏ Exchange rates can only be fixed by intervention or by accommodating interest rate policy.

❏ Fixed exchange rates make independent monetary policy impossible.

❏ A fall in the exchange rate will increase exports.

❏ A fall in the exchange rate will reduce the value of imports if the elasticity of demand for imports is greater than one.

❏ The larger the elasticities of demand for imports and exports, the greater the improvement in the balance of payments, and, hence, the bigger the boost to aggregate demand from a fall in the exchange rate.

❏ A fall in the exchange rate will increase the level of prices in the domestic economy and so will boost inflation.

Multiple Choice Questions

1. Which of the following is likely to increase the value of a country's currency, other things being equal?
    A   an increase in that country's inflation rate
    B   a fall in that country's rate of interest
    C   A fall in that country's inflation rate
    D   a deterioration in that country's balance of payments on current account
    E   political uncertainty in that country

2. Under a fixed exchange rate system, an increase in the foreign exchange reserves is likely to be associated with:
    A   downward-pressure on the value of the currency
    B   a deterioration in the trading position
    C   a fall in domestic interest rates
    D   an increase in domestic interest rates
    E   repayment of foreign debt

3. Which of the following is likely to lead to a devaluation causing the greatest improvement in the current account of the balance of payments?
    A   a high price elasticity of demand for imports and a low price elasticity of demand for exports
    B   A low price elasticity of demand for imports and a high elasticity of demand for exports
    C   low price elasticities of demand for both imports and exports
    D   high income elasticities of demand for both imports and exports
    E   high price elasticities of demand for both imports and exports

4. Purchasing Power Parity suggests that:
    A   the real exchange rate is constant
    B   inflation rates in all countries will be the same
    C   exchange rates never change
    D   the effective exchange rate is constant
    E   an increase in inflation will increase the value of the currency

5. Following a devaluation, the 'J' curve suggests that:
    A   the value exports will fall and then rise
    B   the volume of exports will fall and then rise
    C   the value of imports will rise and then fall
    D   the volume of imports will rise and then fall
    E   the value of imports will fall and then rise

Chapter Thirty

Economic Policy: Full Employment

Key concepts

❏ The major objectives of government macro economic policy
❏ The measurement, definition and causes of unemployment
❏ The costs of unemployment

Key words

Full employment, the natural rate of unemployment
Frictional unemployment, voluntary unemployment, structural unemployment, seasonal unemployment
Keynesian or cyclical unemployment
Exchequer costs, output costs, social costs of unemployment

Objectives and instruments

Objectives are what the government is trying to achieve, and instruments are the means which are being employed to achieve the objectives. The major objectives of government economic policy are:

● The achievement of full employment
● The achievement of low inflation
● The achievement of a satisfactory balance of payments position
● The achievement of economic growth.

Any policies taken to achieve any of these objectives are known as policy instruments. Thus fiscal policy and monetary policy are instruments designed to achieve these objectives. At times it might appear that certain instruments e.g. control of the money supply or maintaining an exchange rate become objectives in their own right. This is a misapprehension. The only reason certain policies become important is because they are seen as essential in achieving a particular objective. This chapter will consider the important question of whether the government can achieve full employment in the economy.

Full employment

Full employment does not mean a situation where there is no unemployment. In fact it is virtually impossible to give an accepted definition of full employment. The problem of defining full employment, and its corollary, unemployment, can be seen by considering why the phenomenon is seen as being important to the government and the economy.

Unemployment is a situation where labour resources are failing to be used productively. This is an example of economic inefficiency, since it conflicts with the idea of achieving an optimum allocation of resources. Thus any measure of unemployment is an attempt to calculate the extent to which the economy is failing to utilise its available labour resources. However, consider the position of an individual who is incapable of working. Should that individual be classified as unemployed, since he or she is not really a resource which is being wasted? What about an individual who is capable of working, but is unable to fill any of the jobs which exist in the economy? What about an individual who is capable of working, but who has made a conscious decision that he/she does not want to work? Is the lack of employment of that individual a waste of resources, given that the individual is free to choose not to work?

One definition of full employment is a situation where there are sufficient jobs available to employ all those people who are able and willing to work. This can be thought of as a situation where the demand for labour is equal to the available supply. The level of unemployment associated with this position is known as the Natural Rate of Unemployment. Consider Figure 30.1.

It is usually assumed that the overall labour market can be depicted like the market for a particular type of labour as seen in Chapter Fifteen. The demand for labour is seen as a declining function of the wage rate (lower wages will increase the demand for labour by firms), and the supply of labour is seen as a positive function of the wage rate, (higher wages will encourage more people to join the labour market). If wages respond to the overall levels of demand and supply in the market place, wages will settle at W_1 and employment will be N_1. This diagram would seem to suggest that unemployment will not exist. However it is important to realise just what is meant by the supply of labour in the context of Figure 30.1.

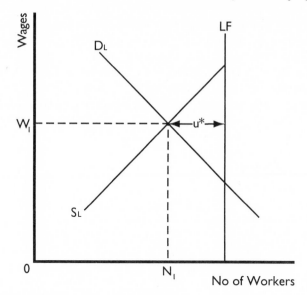

Figure 30.1 *The natural rate of unemployment*

The supply of labour contains all those individuals who are able and willing to work at the wage rates shown. It only contains individuals whose behaviour will have an impact on the labour market. Thus it does not include people who could work but who do not want to, nor people who want to work but who lack the necessary skills to be able to influence the labour market. In Figure 30.1 the line LF denotes the number of people who are eligible for work, including those unable or unwilling to work. Thus even if employment is at N1, there will still be unemployment of U*. This level of unemployment is known as the Natural Rate of Unemployment.

Measurement of unemployment

In the UK the numbers unemployed are calculated by counting all those people who are out of work and claiming unemployment benefit. This excludes from the statistics those people who are either ineligible for unemployment benefit, or those who choose not to claim it. Thus many married women, who have not made sufficient National Insurance contributions to be eligible for benefit, are not included in the unemployment figures even if they are seeking work. Men aged 60 and over, who are made unemployed, are offered higher rates of income support to encourage them to leave the working population, and so, they cease to claim unemployment benefit, and do not appear as unemployed. Several people argue that a large proportion of the people who do register as unemployed and claim benefit, are not actively seeking work and would prefer to remain unemployed. Thus they should be considered as part of the Natural Rate of

Unemployment, and their unemployment should be thought of as voluntary. Whether this type of unemployment should be part of the unemployment count is a controversial question.

Unemployment figures are either expressed in absolute terms (i.e. so many thousands) or as a percentage of the working population. The working population comprises all those people between the ages of 16 and 65, (60 for women), who are working or available for work, and so includes the numbers unemployed. Thus if there are 27 million people working, and 3 million unemployed, the unemployment rate would be 10%, and the working population would be 30 million.

In 1994, the official figures for unemployment in the UK were approximately 2.6 million. However estimates of 'true' unemployment range from about 1.6 million to 3.6 million. The reason for this spread is that some people argue that a large proportion of the official unemployed (perhaps 1 million) are choosing not to work, and, therefore, do not represent a pool of unused, available, resources. Others argue that there are perhaps an extra million people who would like to work, but who are ineligible for benefit, and so do not show up in the official statistics. Thus actual unemployment statistics are somewhat arbitrary estimates of the level of unemployment. This problem has been made worse by various changes which have taken place in the definition of unemployment in the UK during the 1980s.

The changes were made to try and give a more accurate picture of the pool of available labour in the economy, but their impact was also to reduce the numbers who appeared as officially unemployed. Thus men over 60 were removed from the count, as were school leavers. People on government training schemes are not classed as unemployed. The Department of Social Security interviews all long term unemployed to ensure that they are actively seeking work. If they are, they are offered a training course, which removes them from the unemployment statistics. If they are not, they cease to be classed as unemployed.

Categories and causes of, and cures for, unemployment

Economists distinguish between several types of unemployment, and this categorisation is useful since it gives insights into the various causes of unemployment thereby suggesting ways of dealing with unemployment.

● **Frictional unemployment:** Even if there were 27 million jobs available and 27 million people able to fill those jobs, we would not expect all jobs to be filled at any one moment. In a dynamic economy there will always be people changing jobs, and they may spend some time in between jobs. Similarly if a job vacancy occurs it will take a certain time for that job to be filled. Thus on any one day there will be vacant jobs and people in between jobs. This is what is known a frictional unemployment. It is very difficult to reduce this type of unemployment, except by trying to ensure that job vacancies and the unemployed are brought together as quickly as possible, perhaps by improving the information available at Job Centres.

● **Voluntary unemployment:** If people are choosing not to work because they prefer to be unemployed, they are classed as being voluntarily unemployed. Thus if jobs are available, at say £150 per week, but the unemployed person feels that this is not sufficient to make work attractive, that individual is choosing not to work. Some economists argue that this category makes-up a large proportion of registered unemployment, and that the solution to this type of unemployment is to either make work more attractive or to make not working less attractive. Consider Figure 30.2.

In Figure 30.2, the labour market is shown as being in equilibrium, and the wage rate is at W_1. The Natural Rate of Unemployment is U^*, and it contains people who are unwilling to work at the wage rate W_1. Cures for voluntary unemployment consist of actions which would persuade these individuals to rejoin the labour market. Two main possibilities have been suggested: reduce unemployment and other benefits, or reduce income tax. In terms of Figure 30.2 both of these measures would encourage more people to supply their labour to the labour market. The supply curve would shift to SL′, wages would fall to W_2, employment would rise to N_2, and unemployment would fall to U^{**}. This remedy for unemployment requires that the fall in wages, brought about by the new additions to the labour market seeking work, increases the demand for labour.

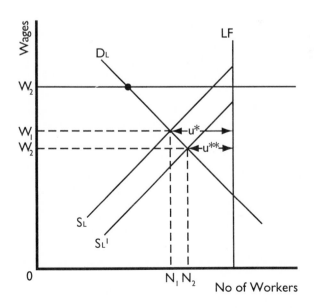

Figure 30.2 *Voluntary unemployment and the incentive to work*

In a similar vein, if wages in the economy are too high, say at W_2 in Figure 30.2, and the labour market is not reacting to the excess supply of labour by cutting wages, unemployment will result. One explanation for such a situation might be the existence of trade unions which prevent wages from falling to market-clearing level. In a sense this is still voluntary unemployment because people have priced themselves out of the labour market. An obvious solution to this situation is to weaken the power of trade unions:

• **Structural unemployment:** In a dynamic economy there will always be industries which are expanding and others which are declining. If labour is to remain employed it must be capable of transferring from the declining industries to the expanding ones. Two factors may prevent labour resources from making this transition, which may result in workers becoming unemployed and unable to participate in the labour market, thereby joining the ranks of the Natural Rate.

The first factor is **occupational immobility**. Workers leaving declining industries may not have the skills necessary to fill the jobs elsewhere in the economy. Hence labour will be scarce, wages will rise, and less people will be employed. In terms of Figure 30.2, if the labour market was initially in equilibrium at N_1, with say 27 million jobs and 27 million workers in those jobs. Now suppose that 1 million jobs disappear in one industry, but reappear in another industry. The overall demand for labour has not altered. Suppose that the 1 million who have lost their jobs are unable to fill the new jobs. The supply of labour (people able and willing to work) has fallen. The supply curve will shift to the left, reducing employment and increasing the Natural Rate.

A similar problem will arise if labour suffers from **geographical immobility**. If the new jobs are in a different area of the country, people may be unable or unwilling to move to fill the jobs, so, again, the available supply of labour will fall with the same results as seen above.

The remedy for occupational immobility is to put resources into retraining. The remedy for geographical immobility is to try and make it easier for workers to move, by perhaps giving cash incentives, or making rented accommodation more available. Another way of tackling the problem would be to encourage the new industries to locate in the areas where the spare labour is available. This policy of taking work to the workers formed an important element of regional policy in the 1960s in the UK, but has been abandoned in more recent times, since it was seen as interfering with the profit maximising behaviour of firms, and would lead eventually to inefficiency.

• **Seasonal unemployment:** Some occupations are dependent upon the weather and the season. Thus many construction workers are laid off during the winter, and the numbers unemployed always rise during this period. In an attempt to take this seasonal factor into account, unemployment statistics are sometimes referred to as having been seasonally adjusted.

What this means is that an account is taken of the amount by which unemployment is expected to change in a particular month, and this expected change is then subtracted from the actual change so that it becomes clear whether unemployment has altered more or less than expected. Thus suppose that in January, in the UK, unemployment normally increases by 100 000, but that in a particular year actual unemployment only increased by 80 000. In terms of the numbers unemployed, they have increased by 80 000, but in terms of seasonally adjusted unemployment, unemployment will have fallen by 20 000. Thus one can observe the slightly paradoxical situation where seasonally adjusted unemployment falls even though more people are unemployed.

● **Cyclical or Keynesian unemployment:** The previous categories of unemployment all form part of the Natural Rate of Unemployment. Cyclical unemployment refers to a situation whereby people are unemployed, not because they are unable or unwilling to work, but because there are insufficient jobs in the economy even though people would be prepared to accept lower wages. This approach to the problem of unemployment focuses upon the demand for labour rather than the supply, and suggests that firms will not demand more labour as wages fall, if the demand for goods and services is not sufficient to allow them to sell all their output. This approach to unemployment sees the level of aggregate demand as the key component to the problem of unemployment and is based upon the views of Keynes, who stressed the importance of aggregate demand in determining output and, hence, employment.

Keynes suggested that the economy could be faced with involuntary unemployment whereby people were able and willing to accept jobs, at virtually any wage rate, but that if the level of demand in the economy made it impossible for firms to sell any extra output, extra employment would not be generated even if wages fell to very low levels. Indeed a fall in the level of wages might cause aggregate demand to fall, which would make the problem of unemployment worse. Thus attempts to solve unemployment by increasing the supply of labour, (through retraining or increased incentives), would have no impact on unemployment. The only solution was to increase the level of aggregate demand through fiscal or monetary policy. Thus Keynes rejected the idea that the labour market would find its own equilibrium. Instead the market would be like that shown in Figure 30.3.

The supply curve for labour has the same slope as before, but the demand for labour is now constrained by how much firms can sell (determined by the level of aggregate demand). Suppose that aggregate demand will only allow the quantity of goods to be sold associated with the level of employment N_0. Employment will never exceed N_0, regardless of the wage rate. Hence the demand for labour becomes perfectly inelastic at employment N_0. In Figure 30.3 involuntary unemployment of U exists at a wage rate of W_1. Even if wages fell, no more employment would be

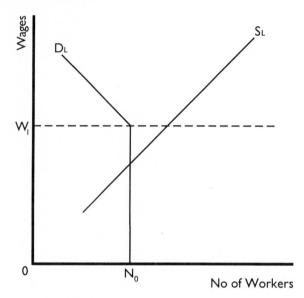

Figure 30.3 *Keynesian unemployment*

created, and it is possible that a fall in wages might reduce aggregate demand, thereby reducing the demand for labour, shifting D_L to the left and increasing unemployment. The remedy for Keynesian, or cyclical unemployment is to expand aggregate demand.

Unemployment: demand or supply factors?

It is important to identify which of the above categories best describe the unemployment faced by an economy, since different solutions are required for different types of unemployment. Suppose that unemployment consists of those categories which form part of the Natural Rate. These are all categories which explain unemployment in terms of some supply characteristic, e.g. lack of training, unwillingness to work, geographic immobility. Suppose that, in an attempt to reduce unemployment, the government decided to expand aggregate demand. This would simply create an excess demand for labour, and would result in pressure on wages and prices to rise without any reduction in unemployment. On the other hand if unemployment is due to a lack of demand in the economy, and steps are taken to increase the supply of labour, no extra jobs will be created, and any consequent fall in wages might make the situation worse by reducing aggregate demand.

The costs of unemployment

The costs of unemployment can be put under three headings:

• **Exchequer costs:** These costs refer to the fact that a person who is unemployed will be paying less tax, especially income tax, and will be receiving unemployment benefit. Both of these items represent a cost to the exchequer.

• **Output costs:** A person who is unemployed represents a factor of production which is not being employed. Therefore the economy is losing the output which that person is capable of producing. This output cost is considerable. Consider the case where GDP is £600 billion and unemployment is 10%. If these 10% were put to work, and were capable of producing the average output being produced by everyone else, GDP would rise by approximately 10%. This would be an extra £60 billion worth of goods and services, which the economy is losing every year that the unemployment rate stays at 10%.

• **Social costs:** Unemployment creates other costs. People who are unemployed tend to become ill and require health care. Some people argue that unemployment is associated with crime and social unrest. These and other costs to society are just as real as the exchequer and output costs, but are much more difficult to quantify.

Summary

❐ Full employment is a major objective of government policy.

❐ Full employment does not mean zero unemployment.

❐ The Natural Rate of Unemployment is the amount of unemployment which occurs when the labour market is in equilibrium, i.e. when the demand for labour equals the supply.

❐ The demand for labour refers to firms looking for workers.

❐ The supply of labour refers to workers able and willing to work.

❐ In the UK, unemployment statistics only include those people eligible for, and claiming, unemployment benefit.

❐ Frictional unemployment refers to people in between jobs. It is best tackled by improving the information on job vacancies.

❐ Voluntary unemployment refers to people who are unemployed because they do not want to work. It is best tackled by making unemployment less attractive, or by making employment more attractive.

❐ Structural unemployment is when people remain unemployed after the industries in which they were employed decline. It is best tackled by improving the mobility of labour, both occupational and geographic.

❐ Seasonal unemployment refers to people who are unemployed because of the weather or the time of year. Seasonal unemployment is removed from the unemployment statistics by seasonal adjustment.

❐ Cyclical, or Keynesian, unemployment occurs when labour is unemployed because of a lack of aggregate demand in the economy. It is best tackled by boosting aggregate demand.

❐ The costs of unemployment are: exchequer costs, output costs and social costs.

Multiple Choice Questions

1. The natural rate of unemployment is the level of unemployment when:

   A unemployment is zero
   B the labour market is in equilibrium
   C there is an excess supply of labour
   D frictional unemployment is zero
   E the costs of unemployment are zero

2. Which of the following sets of policies would be most suitable for a government which wanted to reduce Keynesian unemployment?

   A increase taxes and reduce government expenditure
   B reduce taxes and reduce government expenditure
   C cut unemployment benefit and raise income tax
   D reduce taxes and increase government expenditure
   E cut unemployment benefit and reduce government expenditure

3. Which of the following is most suitable for reducing the level of structural unemployment in an economy?

   A increasing aggregate demand
   B increasing levels of unemployment benefit
   C reducing levels of unemployment benefit
   D reducing the level of interest rates
   E increasing labour mobility

4. Which of the following is not a cost of unemployment?

   A the government loses tax revenue
   B the government must pay out unemployment and other benefits
   C the economy loses output
   D unemployment imposes social costs
   E none of the above

5. Suppose that the labour market was in equilibrium at the Natural Rate of Unemployment. If there was an increase in the level of unemployment benefit, the most likely impact on the labour market would be:

   A wages would fall and employment would rise
   B wages would rise and employment would fall
   C wages would rise and employment would rise
   D wages would fall and employment would fall
   E wages would rise and unemployment would fall

The Control of Inflation

Key concepts

❏ The meaning and causes of inflation
❏ The link between unemployment and inflation
❏ The costs of inflation
❏ Ways in which inflation might be controlled

Key words

Demand pull and cost push theories of inflation, stagflation
The Phillips Curve, expectations augmented Phillips Curve,
    long run Phillips Curve. Natural Rate of Unemployment
NAIRU
Prices and Incomes policy

The definition of inflation

Price inflation is simply any increase in the general level of prices in the economy. The level of prices is normally given by the value of the Retail Price Index (RPI), and so inflation is indicated by any increase in the RPI. Sometimes a slightly more sophisticated definition of inflation is employed, and this refers to a situation where there is a persistent rise in prices. These two definitions can give rise to possible confusion. If prices are rising because of excess demand in the economy, a policy which reduces demand will be considered to be anti-inflationary. One such policy might be an increase in VAT. However this gives rise to an increase in the general price level, brought about by the increase in VAT, being seen as anti-inflationary, when an increase in the price level is classed as inflation! This confusion is clarified if the increase in VAT is seen as reducing the inflationary pressure in the economy, which was causing price increases to persist, despite putting up prices on a once-and-for-all basis. Wage inflation is any increase in the general level of wages in the economy.

Causes of inflation: demand pull theories

Demand pull theories of inflation are based on the idea that prices rise when there is excess demand in the economy. Suppose that the circular flow of income is in equilibrium, in that aggregate demand is equal to total output in the economy, and there is then an increase in aggregate demand. Firms are faced with two main possibilities. Either they can increase output, or they can increase prices. The way in which an increase in demand will be shared out between output and prices is perhaps the major area of controversy in economics. We have seen two opposed views.

The basis of Keynesian economics is the idea that firms will respond to an increase in demand by increasing output if they have spare resources available. The Quantity Theory of Money, and monetarist analysis, suggests that the economy will tend to be at full employment and that any increase in demand will only increase prices with no impact on output. These two approaches seem to suggest that demand inflation will only become a problem when the economy is at or near full employment, which gives the concept of an inflationary gap seen in Chapter Twenty Three. Thus a study of demand inflation requires an analysis of the labour market, which takes us back to the causes of unemployment seen in Chapter Thirty. The usual vehicle for carrying out this analysis is one of the most famous relationships in economics – the Phillips Curve.

The Phillips Curve

The Phillips Curve depicts a relationship first identified by A.W. Phillips in 1958. He was interested in the impact of unemployment on wages. He looked at data from 1862 to 1957 and claimed to have discovered a stable relationship which had held for all that period. This was a non-linear relationship as shown in Figure 31.1.

This relationship seemed to suggest that the level of unemployment was an important factor in determining wage inflation. Phillips suggested that if unemployment was 5.5%, then money wages would remain constant. Unemployment below 5.5% would lead to increases in wages, while unemployment above 5.5% would cause money wages to fall. Phillips further suggested that increases in wages would feed through into increases in prices, but, if productivity in the economy rose by 2% per year,

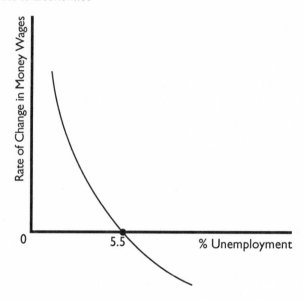

Figure 31.1 *The Phillips Curve*

aggregate demand could be at the level necessary to keep unemployment at 2.5%, without increasing prices.

Phillips explained his relationship in the following terms. If the economy experiences an increase in aggregate demand, employment will rise, unemployment will fall and output will expand. However as employment increases, some areas of the economy will start to experience labour shortages. These shortages will put pressure on wages to rise in those areas, which will increase the average level of wages in the economy. As demand keeps increasing, more and more sectors of the labour market will experience an excess demand for labour, and wages will rise more generally, while at the same time labour shortages will worsen. For both these reasons wages will rise more rapidly.

This explanation for price inflation stresses the link between wages and prices. It is through the labour market that pressure is exerted upon costs of production and hence prices. An increase in demand reduces unemployment. This creates excess demand for labour and puts pressure on wages to rise. This increases costs of production and, in order to protect profit margins, prices rise. This is the normal mechanism through which aggregate demand is seen as influencing price inflation. Demand might have a more direct impact on prices if producers use an increase in demand as an excuse to raise prices directly, but the importance of pricing policies based on costs of production suggest that prices normally rise when costs have risen.

Shortly after Phillips published his original article, other economists examined the link between unemployment and price inflation, and quickly discovered that Phillips' ideas were supported by the evidence. There did appear to be a strong link between unemployment and the rate of price inflation. Thus the Phillips Curve appeared to give governments a choice between unemployment and inflation. People referred to the 'Phillips Curve trade-off', in that higher inflation could be traded off against lower unemployment. We can see the links with the analysis of unemployment in Chapter Thirty. The level of unemployment associated with zero increase in the level of wages must be the level of unemployment associated with equilibrium in the labour market, since at this unemployment level there are no pressures on wages to change. Thus the Natural Rate of Unemployment is the rate associated with zero wage inflation, and so is the point at which the Phillips Curve cuts through the unemployment axis in Figure 31.1. This point has taken on great importance in the fight against inflation, especially when it is linked with the impact on inflation of expectations.

The expectations augmented Phillips Curve

The stable relationship which Phillips had discovered appeared to break down in the late 1960s. Instead of higher unemployment being associated with lower inflation, both unemployment and inflation increased at the same time. This problem continued into the 1970s when people began to talk about stagflation, a situation where unemployment rose as the economy stagnated, and yet inflation also increased. One possible explanation for this phenomenon was the role of expectations. Consider Figure 31.2

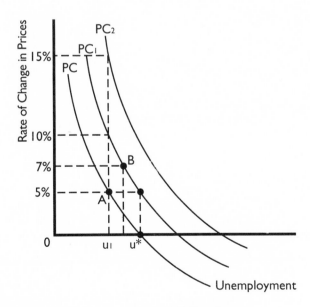

Figure 31.2 *The expectations augmented Phillips Curve*

Suppose that unemployment was at the Natural Rate U*, and that inflation was therefore zero. (We will assume that there are no productivity increases and therefore any increase in wages is passed on as an increase in prices). Aggregate demand now increases so as to reduce unemployment to U1, below the Natural Rate. The original Phillips Curve (PC) suggested that this would generate inflation of 5%. Suppose that unemployment stayed at U1, and people began to expect inflation to continue at 5%. What would happen to wage bargaining?

If employers and employees expected inflation of 5%, they would both take this into account when deciding wage increases. Thus an increase of 5% would only be enough to compensate for the expected inflation. If there was also an excess demand for labour, this would generate an increase in excess of 5%. Thus wage increases will consist of two components: one to compensate for expected inflation, and the other to reflect the existence of excess demand for labour. Thus faced with a continuing labour shortage, wages would begin to rise more than 5%. Suppose that the excess demand for labour (shown by unemployment staying at U1), still generates a 5% wage increase, in addition to the 5% inflation that everyone is expecting. Actual wages will increase by 10%, which in turn will push prices up by 10%. In effect the Phillips Curve has shifted upwards to position PC_1. Once inflation of 10% becomes expected, if the labour shortages persist (i.e. the unemployment rate stays at U1), wages will now rise by 15% (10% to compensate for the expected inflation and 5% because of the excess demand for labour). The Phillips Curve will have shifted to PC_2.

What is happening is that there is a different Phillips Curve for every level of expected inflation, such that even if unemployment reverted back to U*, the expected inflation would cause wages to keep rising at the level of expected inflation. Thus once 5% inflation becomes expected, an unemployment rate of U* will still generate 5% wage inflation.

This result gives a completely different trade-off between inflation and unemployment. Instead of lower unemployment being associated with a level of inflation, this analysis suggests that lower unemployment will be associated with continually accelerating inflation. The only level of unemployment which would give a stable inflation rate is U*, the Natural Rate. This is why this level of unemployment is sometimes referred to as NAIRU, the non-accelerating inflation rate of unemployment. At unemployment rates below NAIRU, inflation accelerates. At unemployment rates above NAIRU, inflation will decelerate as excess supplies of labour allow employers to offer wage increases below the expected rate of inflation.

This view of expectations and the Phillips Curve permits an explanation of stagflation. Suppose that unemployment fell to U1 and inflation rose to 5% which then became expected. If unemployment now increased, but kept below U*, there would still be an excess demand for labour, although of smaller size. Thus in the next period wages would rise 5% to compensate for expected inflation, and perhaps a further 2% because of the reduced labour shortage. Hence wages would rise by 7%, which would then feed through into higher inflation. Thus both unemployment and inflation would have increased at the same time. This process is shown as moving from point A to point B in Figure 31.2

This analysis shows the importance of inflationary expectations. Once inflation becomes expected, the behaviour of economic agents will guarantee that inflation occurs. If people started to expect accelerating inflation, the situation would be even worse.

The long run Phillips Curve

We have seen that attempts to run the economy below the Natural Rate will lead to accelerating inflation. Most economists accept that such a position is unsustainable in the long run, because the ever-increasing prices will be tending to reduce aggregate demand, unless the authorities are continually increasing demand to accommodate the higher prices. In terms of the Quantity Theory of Money, if P is rising, Y must be falling, unless the money supply, M, is continually expanding. This implies that, in the long run, aggregate demand will fall and unemployment will eventually revert back to the Natural Rate, but with inflationary expectations causing inflation to persist. The process is shown on Figure 31.3.

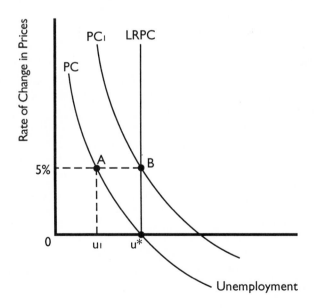

Figure 31.3 The long run Phillips Curve

Initially the economy is at the Natural Rate U*, and inflation, and inflation-ary expectations, are zero. Aggregate demand now increases to reduce unemployment to U1. In the short run inflation of 5% will be generated, and the economy will be at point A on the original Phillips curve. This 5% becomes the expected rate of inflation and the Phillips Curve shifts to PC_1. The higher prices have the effect of reducing aggregate demand, and if this reduction is not overcome by the authorities, unemployment will revert back towards U*. At U*, there is now no excess demand for labour, and so inflation remains at 5% because of expectations. The economy will move to point B on Phillips curve PC_1. Thus all that has been achieved, if this analysis is correct, is that a temporary boost to the economy has engineered a short run reduction in unemployment, but that this reduction is only short-lived, and the economy quickly reverts to the Natural Rate, with a higher inflation rate. This suggests that reducing unemployment below the Natural Rate will either be very short-lived, and inflationary, or will lead to accelerating inflation. Both these options are unattractive.

This situation will be made even less attractive if people start to anticipate inflation, before the extra demand has had time to work on unemployment. Suppose that in the example in Figure 31.3, as soon as the initial expansion in aggregate demand occurs, people anticipate that there will be 5% inflation. If wages and prices immediately rise by 5%, the extra demand will have been taken care of by the 5% inflation. Instead of moving to point A, the economy would move to point B. All that would have been achieved by the boost to aggregate demand would be an increase in prices. This is the basis of the belief that any boost to aggregate demand will only impact upon prices, because of people accurately anticipating any boost to aggregate demand. According to this view (new classical economics) the only way to engineer a reduction in unemployment is to inject an unexpected increase in aggregate demand into the economy.

These views suggest that in the long run there is no trade off between unemployment and inflation. The long run Phillips Curve will be vertical at the natural rate of unemployment. Thus, in the long run, higher inflation will not be associated with any effect on unemployment.

This has given rise to the belief that since the Natural rate is the lowest level of unemployment that will avoid these problems, and that it is the rate which the labour market tends to generate if wages are free to adjust, the best policy stance to take is to leave unemployment to the workings of the labour market and to take steps to reduce the Natural Rate.

The Natural Rate of unemployment

The above analysis suggests that inflation will increase when unemploy-ment falls below the Natural Rate. This means that any boost to aggregate demand will be inflationary if the economy is at the Natural Rate. Unfor-tunately estimates vary wildly as to what constitutes the Natural Rate. The estimates depend upon which of the unemployment categories seen in Chapter Thirty are the major causes of unemployment. If the majority of the unemployed are either unable or unwilling to work, an increase in aggregate demand will quickly generate labour shortages and so create inflation. The only way to reduce unemployment without generating inflation would be to take measures which would increase the supply of labour, that is measures which would increase the ability or willingness of the unemployed to accept jobs. This would reduce the Natural Rate of Unemployment and shift the Phillips Curve towards the origin. These are what are normally referred to as supply side measures since they affect the ability of the economy to produce goods and services rather than simply boosting aggregate demand.

Cost push inflation

A second explanation of inflation is that prices rise when costs increase independent of the state of demand. Thus if oil prices rise, this will increase the cost of producing most goods, which in turn will cause firms to raise their prices. This explanation was popular during the 1970s when OPEC caused major oil price increases.

Costs may also rise if labour costs rise. In the view of the Phillips Curve seen above, inflation is the result of increasing wages brought about by an excess demand for labour. Cost push theories of inflation stress that labour costs may rise independent of demand. If trade unions are able to exert pressure on wages, this will increase prices. Thus some economists explained the inflation of the 1970s as being the result of trade unions being too powerful. The problem with this view is that it is difficult to envisage a situation where this process could persist for a long period of time without there being sufficient aggregate demand to absorb the price increases.

Another aspect of cost inflation can be seen when the price of imports increases because of a fall in the exchange rate. This will have a direct effect upon prices, and if it then triggers off expectations of inflation and feeds through into wage demands, inflation might continue. This is one reason why governments that are concerned about inflation are reluctant to see the value of their currency fall.

The costs of inflation

Inflation imposes many costs on the economy, although these costs are often very difficult to quantify:

● **Inflation and the Balance of Payments:** If prices in one country rise faster than prices elsewhere, the goods and services of that country will become increasingly uncompetitive, unless the exchange rate varies so as to keep the real exchange rate constant. Thus under a fixed exchange rate, high inflation (or at least higher than competitor countries) will cause problems with the Balance of Payments, since exports will suffer and imports will increase.

● **Inflation and the distribution of income:** In a period of inflation, the ability of people to obtain increases in income which keep pace with inflation determines whether their incomes increase, fall or stay constant in real terms. Real income represents the purchasing power of income. If groups in society receive fixed incomes, perhaps in the form of a non-indexed pension, their real income will fall in a period of inflation. Other groups may be in a much weaker position than others in securing wage increases and, again, they will suffer a drop in real income.

This problem also affects borrowers and lenders. If interest rates fail to keep pace with inflation, real interest rates will be negative. This implies that debtors will be gaining from inflation, because the purchasing power of their repayments will be less than the purchasing power of their initial borrowing. This explains why inflation usually benefits people who have long term debts, such as house mortgages. The value of their outstanding debt falls rapidly in real terms during an inflationary period.

● **Inflation and the allocation of resources:** In a market economy, changing prices are the means by which resources are re-allocated. If all prices are rising because of inflation, it is possible that the signals being sent out by relative price changes might fail to be recognised by the market, since they are over shadowed by the rise in the general level of prices.

● **Inflation and growth:** The impact of inflation on economic growth is debatable. If growth depends upon investment, inflation will adversely affect growth if it reduces investment. This might occur for two reasons. First, inflation may create uncertainty, and this may deter investment. Secondly, inflation may encourage consumption at the expense of savings, which would encourage resources to concentrate on producing consumer goods rather than investment. The evidence on the link between inflation and savings is mixed. In the UK it would appear that inflation tends to encourage saving, perhaps because inflation reduces the real value of savings and so people save more to compensate.

● **Inflation and menu costs:** Constantly changing prices will impose direct costs upon firms. Resources will have to be employed in order to keep changing prices.

● **Inflation and political stability:** As we saw in the previous sections, one of the dangers with triggering off inflation is that, once inflation becomes expected, it will tend to accelerate if unemployment is not increased. This acceleration might lead to hyper inflation, where prices rise very rapidly. In these circumstances people might lose confidence in money, since it fails to fulfil its function as a store of value. This will simply make inflation worse as the money is spent faster and faster, and its velocity of circulation increases. The price mechanism might break down.

People with money will find that it becomes worthless. Disadvantaged groups might seek political solutions which give rise to extreme governments. Political instability might result.

The control of inflation

If inflation is seen as being caused by demand pressures, the obvious solution is to reduce aggregate demand, via fiscal or monetary policies. The problem with this approach is that it is likely to lead to higher unemployment. Elementary economic analysis suggests that another way to reduce excess demand is to increase supply. Thus if inflation is being driven by an excess demand for labour, any measures which increase the supply of labour will have a dampening effect on wage inflation. People must be made more able or more willing to work. This means reducing all the categories of unemployment seen in Chapter Thirty, with the exception of Cyclical unemployment, since this only responds to increased demand.

Cost push inflation can be tackled by reducing the cost elements of inflation. If trade union power is seen as a cause of inflation, weaken trade union power. If a falling exchange rate is pushing up import prices, try and increase the exchange rate, or at least stop it falling. This was one of the advantages seen by the UK government in joining the Exchange Rate Mechanism (ERM) of the European Monetary System (EMS). This is a fixed exchange rate system operated by most of the members of the European Union. (The problems with this system, and the reasons for its partial collapse will be seen in Chapter Thirty Six).

One other policy which has been tried in the past is for the government to introduce a **Prices and Incomes policy.** This is a situation where the government takes steps to control the increase in incomes (especially wages). This can either be a statutory policy backed by law, or a voluntary policy backed by persuasion. In the public sector such policies are more common, since the government has direct control over the pay of teachers, nurses, etc. Evidence suggests that such policies are effective, during their time of operation, at moderating wage increases, thereby reducing inflationary pressures. However there are two major problems.

When incomes policies are removed, there is usually a major 'catching up' exercise, and evidence suggests that wages simply revert back to the level they would have reached in the absence of the incomes policy. Thus the benefits are short lived. Secondly, any sort of control on the price of labour will interfere with the price mechanism. If wage increases are controlled, they cannot reflect the forces of demand and supply in the economy. Hence the allocation of resources in the economy is being affected.

Also, even if wage increases moderate, it is possible that the impact on earnings may be less impressive. Wage rates refer to the basic rate of pay.

Earnings are what individuals actually receive, and will consist of the basic wage, plus overtime, bonuses, performance related payments, etc. Thus earnings may increase even if wage rates do not. This phenomenon is known as wages drift.

Inflation and unemployment

We have seen that these two objectives are inextricably linked. Improvements in one are often associated with a deterioration in the other. Attitudes to inflation therefore often reflect views as to the costs of unemployment and vice versa. The only way to avoid this conflict is to implement policies which reduce inflation while reducing unemployment. This implies supply side policies aimed at improving the workings of the labour market. Whether this is seen as an appropriate policy stance depends upon whether the economy is seen as operating at or near its Natural Rate, and how large the various categories of unemployment are seen to be. This is an area of much dispute.

Summary

❑ Inflation is any increase in the general level of prices.
❑ Inflation may arise because of the pressure of excess demand, especially excess demand for labour.
❑ The Phillips Curve uses unemployment as a measure of excess demand, and portrays a link between unemployment and wage inflation.
❑ The Phillips Curve suggests that lower unemployment is associated with higher inflation and that there is therefore a possible trade-off between the two.
❑ Inflationary expectations will cause inflation to accelerate if unemployment is kept below the Natural Rate (an excess demand for labour).
❑ The Natural Rate is the lowest level of unemployment which avoids accelerating inflation. It is also known as NAIRU (the non-accelerating inflation rate of unemployment).
❑ In the long run, unemployment may revert back to the natural rate, and so the long run Phillips Curve may be vertical.
❑ Cost push inflation arises when prices rise because of increases in costs of production independent of the state of demand.
❑ Costs of inflation are difficult to quantify, but include: Balance of Payments problems, problems with the distribution of income, implications for economic growth and the allocation of resources, menu costs, and political instability.
❑ Demand inflation can be controlled by reducing demand. Monetarists would see this in terms of controlling the quantity of money, Keynesians by controlling any of the elements of aggregate demand.
❑ Cost inflation can be controlled by controlling costs: import costs with a fixed exchange rate, and labour costs with an incomes policy.

Multiple Choice Questions

1. The natural rate of unemployment is:
    A   the normal level of unemployment
    B   the level of unemployment which is acceptable to government
    C   the level of unemployment when there is an excess supply of labour
    D   the level of unemployment when the labour market is in equilibrium
    E   the level of unemployment associated with low inflation

2. In the diagram below, which of the following would result in the Phillips curve shifting from PC$_1$ to PC$_2$?
    A   an increase in wages
    B   an increase in inflation
    C   a fall in inflation
    D   improved training facilities for the unemployed
    E   an increase in income tax

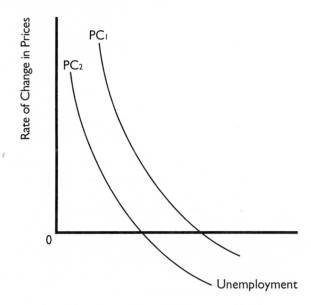

3. The Phillips Curve predicts that an increase in inflation will be associated with:
    A   an increase in unemployment
    B   a reduction in unemployment
    C   a fall in wages
    D   an increase in labour costs
    E   a lower exchange rate

4. If inflation becomes expected, this will have the effect of:

    A reducing inflationary pressure

    B reducing unemployment

    C shifting the Phillips Curve to the left

    D increasing inflationary pressure

    E reducing the Natural Rate of unemployment

5. Which of the following would you expect to reduce the rate of inflation?

    A an increase in aggregate demand

    B an increase in the money supply

    C a fall in the exchange rate

    D a reduction in unemployment benefit

    E an increase in the level of wages

Chapter Thirty-two

Balance of Payments

Key concepts

☐ The structure and meaning of the balance of payments accounts

☐ The meaning and problems associated with a deficit or surplus on the current account

☐ Measures to rectify a balance of payments disequilibrium

☐ The significance of the terms of trade

Key words

Current account, capital account, visibles, invisibles, balance of trade, balancing item

Deficit, surplus

Expenditure switching, expenditure reducing policies

Terms of trade

Definition

The Balance of Payments is a record of all the financial transactions which have taken place between one country and the rest of the world. Financial transactions take place when goods, services or assets are sold between countries. Thus the Balance of Payments is a record of the sale of goods, services and assets between one country and the rest of the world which have taken place during a particular period of time.

Any transactions which results in an inflow of pounds into the UK will show up in the UK's Balance of Payments as a (+) item. Conversely an outflow of pounds will show up as a (-) in the Balance of Payments. Thus UK exports represent an inflow of pounds (+), as will any foreign purchase of UK assets (e.g. a foreign company buying a UK firm). Conversely imports into the UK will represent an outflow of pounds (-) as will a UK firm purchasing a foreign company or purchasing foreign assets. If the UK borrows money from abroad, this will be shown as an inflow (+) of pounds, since the money will be buying an asset in the UK in the form of the debt which it is owed.

Structure of the balance of payments

The Balance of Payments accounts are divided into two accounts, the current account and the capital account.

Current Account

The current account records the transactions which have taken place in terms of goods and services. Figures for the UK in 1993 are shown in Table 32.1.

Table 32.1 *UK Balance of Payments on current account: 1993*

Elements	£ billion
Visible exports	120.9
Visible imports	− 134.3
Balance of Trade (visible balance)	− 13.4
Invisible exports	114.7
Invisible imports	− 111.9
Invisible balance	2.8
Current account balance	− 10.6

Visible imports and exports refer to the import and export of goods into and from the UK. Exports are given a positive value since they represent pounds coming into the UK. Conversely imports are given a negative value, since they represent pounds leaving the UK The overall balance between visible imports and exports is known as the Balance of Trade, and in 1993 this showed a deficit (imports greater than exports) of £13.4 billion.

The buying and selling of services is known as invisible imports and exports. These include insurance and banking services, shipping, tourism, aviation, and the payment or receipt of interest, profit and dividends. In 1993 these items gave a surplus (exports exceeded imports) of £2.8 billion. The overall balance on current is the total of visibles and invisibles, and in 1993 resulted in a deficit of £10.6 billion.

• Capital account

This account is a record of the transactions which have taken place in the purchase or sale of assets and liabilities. The figures for 1993 are shown in Table 32.2.

Table 32.2 *UK Balance of Payments on capital account: 1993*

Element	£ billion
Capital outflows	– 162.8
Capital inflows	+ 171.7
Capital account (surplus)	+ 8.9
Balancing item	+ 1.7

Capital inflows represent payment for UK assets from abroad. These may be in the form of overseas investment in the UK, borrowing by UK banks and UK residents from overseas and borrowing by government. Capital outflows to buy assets abroad are shown as negative items, since they represent pounds leaving the UK, and include lending to overseas residents by UK banks, UK investment abroad, deposits and lending overseas by UK residents and official reserves.

The balancing item exists in order to ensure that the balance of payments balances. The balance of payments always balances. This is because the balance of payments accounts, like any other set of accounts, records both debits and credits of all transactions.

Suppose that a UK importer buys a car for £5000 from France. This will show up in the current account as an import of £5000, and so will be recorded in the current account as – £5000. The French exporter now has acquired £5000 which must be disposed of. One possibility is for that amount to be placed in a sterling bank account in the UK. This will be a £5000 capital inflow into the UK and will be represented by a (+) £5000 in the capital account. Alternatively the French exporter will convert the £5000 into French francs on the foreign exchange market, probably through the banking system. The purchaser of the £5000 will now have to place the money in a sterling account, and again it will show up as a (+) item in the capital account. The whole point is that the £5000 which the UK importer has paid will eventually return to the UK as a financial asset of its holder, and as a liability for the UK financial sector or as payment for a UK export..

Any other deficit on the capital account, perhaps caused by capital inflows being less than capital outflows will have to be matched by purchases of pounds by the UK central bank, which again will show up on the capital account as a (+) item since it represents pounds being acquired by the UK. Capital outflows from the UK cannot take place unless foreign currency can be acquired to finance the outflow. The acquisition of this currency represents sterling assets being acquired by foreigners, which will then be invested in the UK. If the currency is acquired from the UK foreign exchange reserves, this will again be represented by a (+) item in the capital account.

Statistical discrepancies means that the totals for the current and capital accounts never exactly balance. The balancing item is simply a figure which must be added to the accounts to rectify any imbalance. It can be thought of as accommodating any errors and omissions in the current and capital accounts.

Most attention is normally focused upon the current account. This is because this is the account which shows whether or not the country is selling more goods and services to the rest of the world, or whether it is buying more. This is usually taken as an indication of whether or not the country is trading competitively with the rest of the world, or, as is sometimes more crudely put, whether the country is 'paying its way in the world'. A balance of payments current account deficit is often taken as a sign that the country is unable to compete with the rest of the world. As well as being a possible sign of inferiority, a deficit on the current account of the balance of payments may bring other, more tangible, problems.

Deficit problems and the current account of the balance of payments

The major problem with a current account deficit is that it must be financed. Foreigners will normally be reluctant to be paid in sterling; they require their own currency. It is the need to obtain foreign currency to pay for the deficit which causes a problem. A deficit on the current account must mean a surplus on the capital account, in order that the overall accounts balance. If this surplus comes about because of the UK being an attractive place for foreign capital, the deficit can be financed. One problem with this solution is that if foreign investors in the UK decide to take their money out of the UK, the deficit will be reinforced. However as we saw in Chapter Twenty Nine, this problem could be remedied by increasing UK interest rates, which would encourage money to stay in the UK. This of course may have damaging consequences for the UK's internal economy.

A second way of obtaining the currency needed is for the UK government to use its own foreign exchange reserves. This is the corollary of the government intervening in the foreign exchange market. In terms of the balance of payments, a deficit implies that there are more people trying to buy foreign currency to allow them to purchase foreign goods, services or assets, than there are trying to buy pounds in order to buy UK goods, services or assets. Thus there is an excess supply of pounds on the foreign exchange market. One solution is for the UK to use its foreign exchange reserves to buy the excess pounds. Thus this will show up in the capital account as a (+) item since it represents an inflow of pounds into the country. This solution to a deficit can only be short term because reserves are limited.

A third solution is to allow the excess supply of pounds to reduce the value of sterling on the foreign exchange market. As the price of sterling falls, there must come a time when the lower pound makes the UK look attractive, and so foreign capital will enter the UK. This will mean that pounds will enter the UK (after the foreign currency has been converted on the foreign exchange market). This again will show up as a (+) item in the capital account, and the overall balance will again be zero.

Therefore, a persistent deficit on the current account will imply a persistent surplus on the capital account, which will require one of three outcomes:

● High interest rates might be required to encourage capital inflows
● Foreign exchange reserves will fall
● The currency will fall in value on the foreign exchange market.

A current account deficit also means that the country is able to enjoy a higher standard of living. This is because the deficit is increasing the supply of goods and services available within the UK. This is the idea that the country would be 'living above its means'. Whether this is seen as a disadvantage or an advantage of a deficit depends upon the problems associated with paying for the deficit in the future.

Surplus problems and the current account of the balance of payments

A surplus on current account implies that the UK is enjoying a lower standard of living than is possible by consuming its own output. Take the extreme case where the country exported all its GDP and imported nothing. It would have an enormous balance of payments surplus on current account, but no goods or services to enjoy.

A surplus might put pressure on the exchange rate to rise. This would make exports more expensive and might have a detrimental effect upon industry. This is especially true if the surplus is because of short term factors, such as North Sea Oil in the UK, or the experience of the Netherlands following the exploitation of North Sea Gas. Both these led to the exchange rate of the respective country rising, with damaging consequences for other sections of their economies.

A surplus in one country must imply a deficit somewhere else in the world. Thus countries with surpluses on their current account balance of payments are always put under great pressure by the deficit countries to do something about their surpluses. Thus the US is continually pressing Japan to take steps to reduce Japan's current account surplus.

Measures to rectify a deficit in the current account

The current account can be improved, and a deficit reduced, by either taking measures to reduce total expenditure, which will include expenditure on imports, or by taking measures to persuade consumers to switch expenditure from imports to domestically-produced items, and to persuade foreigners to buy UK goods rather than their own. Consider Figure 32.1.

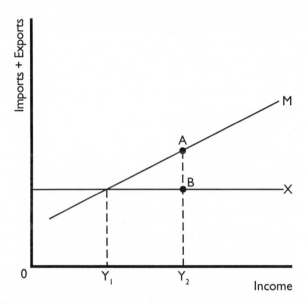

Figure 32.1 *Income and the current account*

Expenditure reducing policies

Exports will not normally be affected by the level of income in the domestic economy, and so are shown in Figure 32,1 as being constant (X). Imports will depend upon domestic income. As income rises, more will be spent on imports. Hence imports (M) are shown as rising with income. Equilibrium on the current account will be at income Y_1. If income rises to Y_2, the current account will move into deficit, shown by the distance AB. This is because imports will increase, while exports will remain unaffected. Conversely, if income fell, the current account would move into surplus. Thus changes in the level of income, which are associated with changes in the level of expenditure, will affect the current account. Thus a deficit could be removed by reducing income and expenditure. Such a policy is known as expenditure reducing. The need to deflate the economy to rectify a balance of payments problem was a major cause of the stop-go cycle which plagued the UK in the 1960s.

Expenditure switching policies

Expenditure switching can be achieved by making UK-produced goods more attractive, by reducing their price relative to the price of goods from other countries, or by physically preventing people from being able to import all the goods they would like. Any measures which affect the relative price of imports and exports will affect the value of imports and exports. The impact of a change in prices will depend upon the elasticities of demand for imports and exports. Such changes can be brought about in various ways. A depreciation in the value of the currency will make exports cheaper and imports more expensive.

As we saw in Chapter Twenty Nine a fall in the exchange rate will only improve the current account if the sum of the elasticities is greater than one (the Marshall-Lerner conditions). Another way to increase the price of imports is to impose a tariff on imports. This has the effect of rising the price of the imported good, and will, therefore, reduce the demand. Again the impact depends upon the elasticity of demand. If tariffs and reducing the exchange rate are rejected as policies, the only other way to improve the price competitiveness of UK goods is to somehow reduce their price. The only way to improve competitiveness is either to increase productivity, or to reduce costs of production, especially wage costs.

A final policy which will achieve expenditure switching is to impose quotas on imports. Quotas are quantity restrictions on imports whereby only a fixed amount of any specified product is allowed to be imported. This will reduce the volume of imports, but will raise the price of the item which has had its supply curtailed. One problem with taking direct action to curtail imports by imposing tariffs or quotas is that such policies might invite retaliation. Another problem is that interfering with free trade will also reduce living standards throughout the world, since free trade is usually seen as increasing world output. This will be considered further in Chapter Thirty Three.

The terms of trade

The terms of trade measure the relative price of imports and exports. It is given by the expression:

$$\text{Terms of trade} = \frac{\text{index of export prices}}{\text{index of import prices}} \times 100$$

If the terms of trade increase, this shows that export prices have risen faster than import prices. This is usually referred to as an 'improvement' in the terms of trade, because it indicates that fewer goods need to be exported to purchase a given quantity of imports. Thus when the price of oil rose in the 1970s, oil exporting countries experienced an improvement in their terms of trade and became more prosperous.

However an increase in the terms of trade may also represents a deterioration in the competitiveness of exports, and so may not indicate an improvement in either the performance of the economy or in the balance of payments. Whether an increase in the terms of trade is beneficial depends to a large extent upon the reason for the increase. The impact of any change in the terms of trade on the balance of payments will obviously depend upon the relevant elasticities of demand.

Summary

❏ The Balance of Payments is a record of all the transactions between one country and the rest of the world.

❏ The current account deals with transactions in goods (visibles) and services (invisibles).

❏ The capital account deals with transactions in assets, both real and financial.

❏ The overall balance of payments always balances, and the balancing item ensures this balance by making up for any errors and omissions in the statistics.

❏ A deficit on the current account is only a problem in that the deficit must be financed.

❏ Financing a deficit on current account will either reduce reserves, lower the exchange rate, or require interest rates to be attractive for foreign investors.

❏ A deficit implies that the country is enjoying a higher standard of living than could be obtained by the country's own GDP.

❏ A surplus implies a lower standard of living than could be obtained from its own GDP.

❏ A deficit can be rectified by expenditure reducing policies.

❏ A deficit can be rectified by expenditure switching policies.

❏ The terms of trade measure the relative price of imports and exports.

Multiple Choice Questions

1. Suppose that the invisible balance on the current account of the balance of payments shows a deficit of £200m. The over-all current account is in deficit by £450m. These figures suggest that:

   A   the capital account is in deficit
   B   the balance of trade is in surplus
   C   the visible balance is in deficit
   D   the balancing item is £250m.
   E   the country has a balance of payments deficit

2. An improvement in the terms of trade represents:

   A   an increase in the ratio of imports to exports
   B   a fall in the ratio of export to import prices
   C   an improvement in the current account of the balance of payments
   D   a fall in import prices in relation to export prices
   E   a fall in the exchange rate

3. Which of the following would be classed as an increase in exports in the invisible account in the balance of payments?

   A   an increase in the exports of wheat
   B   increased investment in the UK by overseas companies
   C   an increase in the expenditure of overseas tourists in the UK
   D   an increase in the expenditure of UK tourists overseas
   E   a reduction in the overseas earnings of UK firms

4. Which of the following would you class as an expenditure switching policy as far as the current account of the balance of payments is concerned?

   A   an increase in income tax
   B   an increase in the exchange rate
   C   an increase in government expenditure
   D   a reduction in the rate of income tax
   E   restrictions on bank lending

5. The balancing item in the UK balance of payments represents:

   A   the amount by which imports exceed exports
   B   a figure to compensate for errors and omissions in compiling the statistics
   C   the amount by which exports would need to rise to give a balance of payments equilibrium
   D   the sales or purchases of sterling by the Bank of England
   E   net property income from abroad

Chapter Thirty-three

Aggregate Demand and Aggregate Supply

Key concepts

- ❏ The nature of the conflicts between government macro economic policies
- ❏ The way in which time lags create a problem for demand management
- ❏ The use of aggregate demand and supply curves to illustrate the impact of policies on output and prices
- ❏ The argument behind supply side policies

Key words

Incomes policy, import controls, demand management
Inside lags, outside lags
Aggregate supply curve, aggregate demand curve
Stagflation, supply shocks, supply side economics
The Natural Rate of unemployment

Problems of demand management – conflicts between objectives

As we have seen in the previous chapters, all of the three most important economic objectives of government will respond to changes in aggregate demand. Unfortunately, the three objectives, full employment, controlling inflation, and avoiding a balance of payments deficit, conflict, in the sense that an increase in aggregate demand will cause an improvement in some objective, but a deterioration in another. Thus an increase in aggregate demand will reduce unemployment (by reducing Keynesian unemploy-ment), but will put pressure on prices to rise, and also increase imports. A reduction in demand will increase unemployment, but ease inflationary pressure, and improve the balance of payments. These conflicts imply that attempts to run the economy by demand management, necessarily will require governments to give priority to certain objectives, and less priority to others.

Thus the Conservative government elected in 1979 gave priority to controlling inflation by imposing restrictions on aggregate demand, both through monetary and fiscal constraints, which led to the recession of the early 1980's. Once inflation had been controlled, aggregate demand was allowed to increase, partly through a relaxation of fiscal and monetary policy, and partly through the deregulation of the financial system which permitted the banking system to expand credit. This expansion brought about the consumer boom of the late 1980s, which halved unemployment from over 3 million to just over 1.5 million. This expansion brought about a deficit on the current account of the balance of payments, and also caused inflation to rise to over 10%. In order to correct the inflation, the UK raised interest rates to reduce demand. This deflationary policy was reinforced by joining the ERM at an exchange rate which made UK exports uncompeti-tive. The consequent reduction in demand reduced inflation, but brought about the recession of the early 1990s, with unemployment rising towards the 3 million mark again.

This cycle of expansion followed by contraction is what economists refer to as the 'stop-go' cycle, and it has been a feature of the UK economy since 1945. Many people argue that it is the inevitable outcome of allowing politicians to use demand management techniques to control the economy, and that it has damaged the long run performance of the economy by creating uncertainty that deters investment.

Some economists argue that the problem can be overcome by using additional policy tools to counteract the worst of the conflicts which occur. Thus incomes policies are sometimes suggested as a way of avoiding the inflationary consequences of expansionary policies. A depreciation in the currency is sometimes seen as a way of protecting the current account of the balance of payments. Import controls have also been suggested. Thus demand management policies need to be reinforced by other policies if they are to avoid the inconsistency between the major objectives.

The problem of conflicts between policy objectives is made worse by the problem of trying to implement demand management policies at the most appropriate time. This is the problem of time lags in fiscal and monetary policy

Problems of demand management – time lags

Suppose that the economy moves into recession and the government wishes to take policy measures which will stabilise the economy and avoid the recession. In terms of demand management, the economy requires an increase in demand. Unfortunately the timing of the impact of such a policy might be such as to actually destabilise the economy.

Left to itself, there is strong evidence to suggest that the economy would not follow a smooth growth path, but would experience booms and slumps. This is the idea of the trade cycle which will be examined in Chapter Thirty Four.

If demand management policy is to be successful, the changes in aggregate demand must take effect at the right time. Consider Figure 33.1.

Left to its own devices, the economy would follow the path shown as GDP, with GDP rising and falling in a cyclical fashion. In order to prevent such fluctuations, demand management policies would need to be counter cyclical. The required policy would look like the curve 'required policy', with demand being boosted when GDP was falling, and being reduced when GDP was expanding. Time lags might prevent this from being achieved. Time lags are simply delays which occur before the policy takes effect, and they can be put under two headings:

● **Inside lags:** These refer to time delays which will occur before any policy is put into operation and consist of the following:

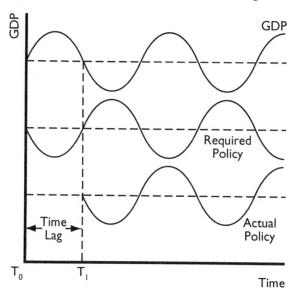

Figure 33.1 *The trade cycle and stabilisation policy*

Recognition lag: it will take time for the government to recognise that the economy is going into recession. Economic statistics are always at least one month out of date.

Decision lag: it will take time for the government to decide what are the most appropriate steps to take.

Legislative lag: it might take time to seek legislative approval for any changes (e.g. a change in income tax rates).

Administrative lag: it will take time for changes to be implemented. Hence the Inland Revenue might be unable to implement tax changes immediately.

These delays imply that a period of time will elapse between a policy measure being required and the policy being implemented. One of the advantages which is sometimes credited to monetary policy (changing interest rates) is that the last two of the above lags will be avoided. Once a policy is implemented, other delays will occur, however:

● **Outside lags: Income lag**: it will take time for the policy to affect people's disposable income; perhaps people only get paid at the end of the month, or their mortgage payments are monthly.

Expenditure lag: it will take time for the change in income to affect spending, which is the whole point of the exercise.

Output lag: it will take time for firms to react to the change in spending by altering output. Thus GDP may not respond to the policy measures until some considerable time after such a response is required.

Suppose that in Figure 33.1 the policy does not take effect until time T_1, with the total time lags shown by the distance T_0 to T_1. Instead of stabilising the path of GDP, the actual policy will reinforce the changes in GDP. Thus by the time the deflationary policy takes effect (time T_1), the economy is already contracting by itself, and so the cut in demand will simply cause the economy to contract even more rapidly, fuelling unemployment. Similarly, when the economy requires a reduction in demand to offset an increase in GDP, the time lags might imply that the economy simply feels the impact of inflation policies designed to correct the previous slump, thus causing unemployment to rise.

The only way to overcome such problems is to put faith into the accuracy of economic forecasts which would allow the government to take steps to correct fluctuations in economic activity before such fluctuations actually occur. The problem with this solution is that there is very little evidence to suggest that economic forecasts are accurate enough to permit such policies to be reliable.

The problems seen above have persuaded some economists that governments should not practice demand management, but instead should accept that the economy will fluctuate around some equilibrium level (normally associated with the Natural Rate of unemployment). Other economists argue that the problems are not insuperable and that there are additional policy tools which government could use to combat the inherent conflicts between objectives. They also argue that economic forecasts are accurate enough to avoid the pitfalls of time lags.

The problems of demand management have led economists to investigate policies designed to boost the supply side of the economy rather than demand. This requires an investigation of the concept of aggregate supply.

Aggregate supply

Macro economists in the period following 1945 concentrated almost exclusively on the concept of aggregate demand, and simply assumed that an increase in aggregate demand would lead to changes in output, unless the economy was at full employment, in which case an increase in demand would cause inflation. The Phillips Curve suggested that this view was too simplistic and that wages and prices would rise over a range of unemployment. This led economists to investigate how the supply side of the economy would react to changes in demand, and required an examination of what determined the output of firms.

Microeconomics suggests that firms will produce up to the point where marginal cost equals marginal revenue. In other words, firms will be trying to maximise profits. Thus anything which alters costs or revenue will affect their output decisions. One of the most important factors will be the price which they can receive for their output. This is the basis for the aggregate supply curve which shows the output which firms produce at various price levels, other things being equal. Consider Figure 33.2.

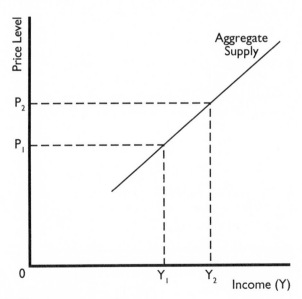

Figure 33.2 *The aggregate supply curve*

At a price level of P_1, firms in aggregate are prepared to put output Y_1 on the market. The total output of firms represents GDP, and so the bottom axis measures GDP, or as more conventionally presented, income (Y). Suppose that prices in the economy rise to P_2, with all other aspects of the economy held constant. An increase in prices will make output more profitable. The demand for labour will rise as its marginal revenue product rises. Employment and output will rise. In Figure 33.2 this is shown by the aggregate supply curve sloping upwards, indicating that the higher price level will be associated with a higher output Y_2. Any event which makes output more attractive to firms will shift the aggregate supply curve to the right. Any event which makes output less profitable will shift aggregate supply to the left. Thus the aggregate supply curve will behave in a very similar fashion to the market supply curve seen in Chapter Four. Of course a supply curve is of little use without a demand curve, and so to complete the picture, we construct an aggregate demand curve.

Aggregate demand

We have already seen the basis of aggregate demand in previous chapters. How will aggregate demand vary as the price level alters? Consider Figure 33.3. An increase in the price level will reduce aggregate demand for the following reasons: If prices rise, and wages do not, the purchasing power of wages will fall, and the level of profits will rise. If the marginal propensity to consume (MPC) of workers is greater than the MPC of

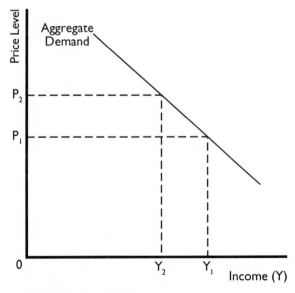

Figure 33.3 *The aggregate demand curve*

employers, aggregate demand will fall. In addition, a rise in prices will reduce the purchasing power of money in the economy, and this fall in the real value of money will again reduce demand. In terms of the Quantity Theory of Money, $(MV = PY)$, any increase in P must reduce Y, if M and V are constant. In an open economy, higher prices will also reduce export demand.

For all these reasons a rise in the price level from P_1 to P_2 will reduce aggregate demand from Y_1 to Y_2. Thus the aggregate demand curve slopes downwards from left to right. Note that it slopes downwards for reasons other than those associated with a demand curve for a particular product.

Equilibrium between aggregate demand and supply

Equilibrium in the economy will occur when aggregate demand equals aggregate supply. This is shown in Figure 33.4.

Suppose the economy has a price level P_1 and output Y_1. Aggregate demand equals aggregate supply and so the economy is in equilibrium. Suppose that there is now an increase in aggregate demand, caused by an increase in injections or a fall in withdrawals. This will shift the AD curve from AD_1 to AD_2. In the economy there will now be an excess demand for goods and services, shown by the gap BC. The simple Keynesian assumption is that this excess demand will simply boost output. This implies that the AS curve is horizontal and that output and employment would rise (and

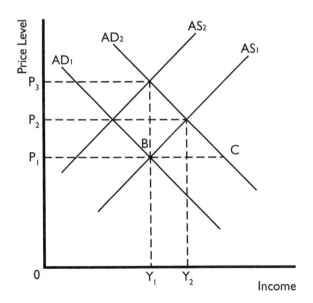

Figure 33.4 *Aggregate demand and supply and equilibrium*

unemployment fall), without any impact on prices. This result is inconsist-
ent with the Phillips Curve which suggests that as output rises, and
unemployment falls, prices will rise.

The aggregate supply curve in Figure 33.4 suggests that it is the increase
in prices which is necessary to encourage firms to increase output. As
prices rise, because of the excess demand for goods, output expands, and
a new equilibrium is achieved at a higher price level, P_2, and a higher
output, Y_2. Thus an increase in aggregate demand boosts both output and
prices. This is simply the Phillips Curve result, since the increased output
will reduce Keynesian unemployment.

This however will only be a short run equilibrium if the analysis is
combined with the concept of the Natural Rate of unemployment seen in
Chapter Thirty One. Suppose that Y_1 was the level of output associated
with the Natural Rate of unemployment. In other words, it corresponds to
the point on the Phillips Curve where inflationary pressure in the labour
market is zero. The expansion of demand and the increase in output and
employment shown by the move to Y_2 will have caused an excess demand
for labour. This excess demand for labour will put pressure on wages to rise
(as the original Phillips Curve suggested). As wages rise, the profit
maximising output of firms will fall. Any increase in costs of production
will reduce supply. Hence the aggregate supply curve will start to shift to
the left. As it does so, prices will rise even further, output will fall and
unemployment will rise until the economy has reverted back to the Natural
Rate (Y_1), at which point wages and prices will cease to rise, aggregate
supply will be at position AS_2, and the price level will be at P_3.

This analysis suggests that any boost to aggregate demand will only
bring about a temporary expansion of output, and this will then be eroded
by rising wages and prices. This is the story which we told in Chapter
Thirty One concerning the short run effects of taking unemployment
below the Natural Rate.

Stagflation

Aggregate demand and supply analysis allows an explanation for a phenomenon which caused great concern to economists in the 1970s, the
phenomenon of rising prices being accompanied by rising unemployment.
The 1970s was a period when oil prices rose dramatically because of the
actions of OPEC. How would this impact on aggregate demand and
supply?

Suppose that the economy is at the Natural Rate of unemployment at an
output Y_1, and a price level of P_1, as shown in Figure 33.5. An increase in
the price of oil will raise the costs of production of most firms in the
economy. Some firms will find it difficult to keep in production while
others will reduce output or be prepared to keep producing only if a higher
price can be obtained. For all these reasons the aggregate supply curve will

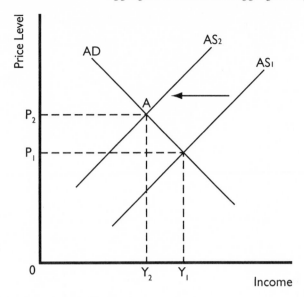

Figure 33.5 *An oil price rise: stagflation*

shift from AS_1 to AS_2. This creates an excess demand for goods and prices will rise. A new equilibrium will be established at a lower level of output (and hence a higher level of unemployment) and a higher price level, shown as point A in Figure 33.5. This is the phenomenon of stagflation – higher unemployment and higher prices. Again this will be a short run problem if the unemployment puts pressure on wages to fall, since lower wages will reduce costs, thereby increasing aggregate supply back towards AS_1, and the level of output back towards the Natural Rate, Y_1.

Supply side economics

Suppose that the economy goes into recession. This could either be because of a fall in aggregate demand, which would be accompanied by a lower price level, or a fall in aggregate supply, which would imply a higher price level. Figure 33.6 shows the aggregate demand curve shifting to the left, showing a fall in aggregate demand. Output falls to Y_2 and prices fall to P_2, shown as the equilibrium position moving from A to B. Unemployment will have risen. What is the correct policy response?

Keynesian economists would stress the need for demand management policies designed to boost aggregate demand back to AD_1. Such a policy would be successful, but would increase prices, and would restore equilibrium to position A.

Economists who dispute the effectiveness of demand management policies would argue that the economy would revert back to Y_1 under its

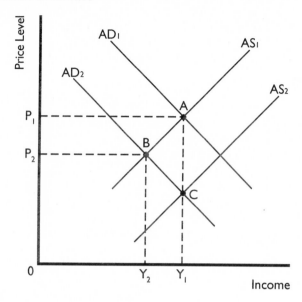

Figure 33.6 *A fall in aggregate demand*

own steam, as long as the unemployment puts pressure on wages to fall. Workers could price themselves back into jobs which would shift the AS curve from AS_1 to AS_2. Thus Y_1 would be achieved at a lower price level, as shown by equilibrium position C.

If there were forces in the economy preventing wages from falling (perhaps trade union pressure, or generous unemployment benefits), then the economy would stay at point B. Thus the best way to restore full employment, in the context of this view of the economy, would be to take steps to ensure that wages were flexible in a downwards direction.

A second strategy would be to take steps to encourage firms to increase output, regardless of the level of demand. This could be achieved by increasing their profitability, perhaps by reducing their tax burdens, or removing restrictive pressures from trade unions or government regulations, or by encouraging investment to increase efficiency. These measures are what are normally referred to as supply side measures and are increasingly seen as an alternative to demand management.

The Natural Rate of unemployment

The above analysis suggests that any movement away from the Natural Rate will be short lived. An expansion of the economy beyond the Natural Rate creates inflationary pressures which through their impact on costs and aggregate demand, will move the economy back to the Natural Rate. Similarly any contraction in the economy will create an excess supply of labour, which, if wages are flexible downwards, will again restore demand and supply back to the Natural Rate. This implies that any long run reduction in unemployment can only be achieved by reducing the Natural Rate itself.

As we saw in Chapter Thirty, the Natural Rate consists of all those people unable, or unwilling to work. Thus long run reductions in unemployment can only be secured by reducing the number of people unable or unwilling to work. These measures include: reducing the level of unemployment benefit, increasing the net wage by reducing income tax, and so increasing the incentive to work, retraining programmes designed to improve skills, encouraging people to move to find employment, perhaps by increasing the supply of rented accommodation available, interviewing all long-term unemployed people to motivate them to find work, job clubs designed to give the unemployed the encouragement to seek employment.

If these supply side measures are successful, they will shift the aggregate supply curve to the right by reducing wages (because of the increased supply of labour), thereby permitting an increase in output and employment and a reduction in the price level. In effect the major basis of supply side measures aimed at the labour market is to reduce wages by increasing labour supply.

Demand or supply side policies?

The debate surrounding the choice between demand and supply side policies depends primarily upon the slope of the aggregate supply curve. If the aggregate supply curve is horizontal, or very flat, then demand management policies will be the most effective way of stimulating output, with very little impact upon prices. If the aggregate supply curve is steep, changes in aggregate demand will have most of their impact on prices, and little in output. The Natural Rate hypothesis suggests that the long run aggregate supply curve is vertical at the Natural Rate, and, so, in the long run, any change in aggregate demand will only affect prices. To a large extent this depends upon the way in which wages respond to unemployment being taken above or below the Natural Rate.

If wages always adjust very quickly to any excess demand or supply of labour, the aggregate supply curve will be steep. If wages respond immediately to a change in prices, the aggregate supply curve will be vertical, and firms will not be encouraged to produce more even if prices rise, since wage costs would increase at the same time. Thus the slope of the aggregate supply curve is closely connected to the behaviour of the labour market.

Keynesian economists argue that in a recession, even if unemployment is high, and excess supplies of labour exist, it is unlikely that falling wages will restore output and employment. This is because there are strong reasons to believe that the labour market does not behave like the market for oranges, and that an excess supply of labour will not reduce wages. Several reasons have been put forward to explain this wage rigidity. Employers may not like to be associated with lowering wages, a lower wage might reduce the quality of the worker attracted. The unemployed 'outsiders' exercise little influence on the wages set by 'insiders' who are in employment. If wages are very slow to fall in the face of recession, a much quicker way to increase output and employment would be to boost aggregate demand, even though this would be at the expense of higher prices. This brings us back to the idea of having to choose between the various economic objectives.

Summary

☐ An increase in aggregate demand will improve unemployment, but worsen the balance of payments and the rate of inflation.

☐ These conflicts between objectives mean that priorities must be assigned to objectives.

☐ Changing priorities may give rise to a 'stop-go' cycle.

☐ Time lags make the correct timing of policy impossible, unless accurate forecasts can be made.

☐ Aggregate supply shows the total output which firms will produce at various price levels.

☐ A higher price level will result in a higher output, because profitability will have increased if wages do not rise by the same amount.

☐ The aggregate demand curve shows the level of demand in the economy at various price levels.

☐ The aggregate demand curve slopes downwards because lower prices stimulate aggregate demand.

☐ Equilibrium will occur when aggregate demand equals aggregate supply.

☐ The Natural Rate of unemployment occurs when the labour market is in equilibrium.

☐ If aggregate demand increases and equilibrium output expands, prices will rise because of the excess demand for goods and services.

☐ If the economy expands beyond the level associated with the Natural Rate, excess demand for labour will cause wages to rise.

☐ Increases in wages will reduce aggregate supply (supply is less profitable).

☐ Reduced aggregate supply will increase prices and reduce output back to the Natural Rate.

☐ Deviations from the Natural Rate will be temporary.

☐ Supply side policies are aimed at increasing aggregate supply, and at reducing the Natural Rate of unemployment.

☐ This model suggests that the only way to achieve a long run expansion of output is to reduce the Natural Rate of unemployment.

Multiple Choice Questions

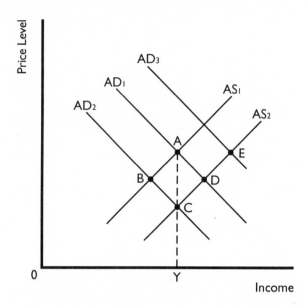

1. In the diagram above the economy is at the output level (Y), associated with the Natural Rate of unemployment at the equilibrium position shown as point A. The economy experiences a fall in aggregate demand. Given flexible wages and prices, the long run equilibrium position of the economy will be shown as point:

    A
    B
    C
    D
    E

2. Which of the following measures would you expect to shift the aggregate supply curve of an economy to the right?

    A   an increase in the price of oil
    B   an increase in the rate of income tax
    C   an increase in wages in the economy
    D   an increase in the supply of labour
    E   an increase in VAT

3. The Phillips Curve suggests a conflict between full employment and price stability because:

    A   high employment will reduce wages
    B   high wages will reduce unemployment
    C   low unemployment will reduce prices
    D   high unemployment will increase prices
    E   low unemployment will increase wages

4. Which of the following might be classed as a supply side policy?
   A an increase in government expenditure
   B an increase in VAT
   C a cut in income tax
   D a fall in the exchange rate
   E the imposition of import controls

5. Other things being equal, an increase in the price level will increase aggregate supply because:
   A real wages will fall
   B the real rate of interest will fall
   C the level of profits in the economy will fall
   D aggregate demand will fall
   E inflation will increase

Chapter Thirty-four

Economic Growth

Key concepts

☐ The nature of the trade cycle (business cycle)
☐ The meaning of economic growth, both short term and long term
☐ Factors causing the trade cycle
☐ The relationship between long term growth rates and productive potential
☐ Factors affecting economic growth
☐ The importance of economic growth for the standard of living

Key words

Trade cycle, business cycle. Productive potential
Multiplier-accelerator interaction, political trade cycle
Land labour capital and the production possibility curve

Fluctuations in economic activity

We have seen that the level of economic activity in an economy is affected by changes in the level of aggregate demand. An increase in demand will increase income and output, while a reduction in demand will cause output to fall. This suggests that changes in the level of output may be caused by changes in demand. It is an accepted fact of economic history that economies seem to experience cycles in economic activity which occur at fairly regular intervals. Over time one would expect output to increase because of improvements in productivity and technology. In terms of the production possibility curve (PPC) seen in Chapter One, the PPC moves outwards.

Experience suggests that this does not happen at a steady rate, but that periods of rapid expansion are followed by periods of slow or negative growth in a regular pattern. This phenomenon is what is known as the trade cycle, or as it is more recently known, as the business cycle. Consider Figure 34.1.

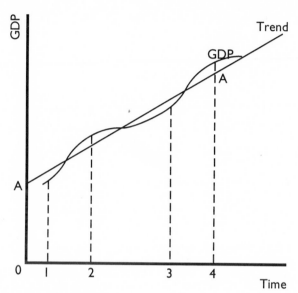

Figure 34.1 *The business cycle*

The growth of GDP is shown as increasing over time but at a changing rate. The straight line AA shows the trend in GDP over the period. During the period 1–2, GDP is shown as increasing faster than the over all trend. This is referred to as an expansionary period. At period 2 the growth of GDP ceases to grow faster than trend and this is known as the peak of the cycle. Growth then takes place at less than the trend rate, and the economy enters a period of slow growth from period 2–3. Eventually growth accelerates, and from period 3–4 rises, once again faster than trend. Period 3 is the trough of the cycle.

Figure 34.1 has been expressed in terms of deviations from trend growth, and until very recently the term 'recession' was applied to a period of growth below trend. This definition has changed and now governments only acknowledge the existence of a recession when GDP growth has become negative. This means that recessions are now much rarer than they were before, since a period of falling GDP is an uncommon event.

This regular process of fast growth, followed by slow, or even negative, growth, has been a consistent feature of UK economic history for the last 150 years. Table 34.1 gives figures for the growth of GDP in the UK since

1950. These figures are at constant 1985 prices and thus represent real changes in GDP.

Table 34.1 UK GDP and growth 1970–1992

Year	GDP (£b)	Growth (%)
1970	232.3	–
1971	236.2	1.7
1972	242.8	2.8
1973	260.9	7.5
1974	257.0	– 1.5
1975	255.0	– 0.7
1976	261.7	2.6
1977	268.4	2.6
1978	276.3	2.9
1979	284.0	2.8
1980	278.2	– 2.1
1981	275.0	– 1.2
1982	279.7	1.7
1983	290.1	3.7
1984	296.0	2.0
1985	307.9	4.0
1986	319.7	3.8
1987	334.4	4.6
1988	349.4	4.5
1989	356.7	2.1
1990	359.0	0.6
1991	350.2	– 2.5
1992	348.5	– 0.5
Total		41.4
Average		1.9

Annual growth has varied over the period from 7.5% in 1973, to – 2.5% in 1991. On average the UK economy has grown by 1.9% per year since 1970. Over a longer period the average rate of growth is usually accepted as having been about 2.5%.

It is usually seen as desirable to achieve as high a rate of growth in GDP as possible. This is because GDP is closely connected with the calculations of the standard of living. An increase in GDP implies an increase in GDP per head (unless population is rising). GDP per head is the major indicator of living standards in an economy. Thus economic growth is an important objective of government economic policy. An important distinction needs to be made concerning long run and short run rates of growth, however.

Growth rates and productive potential

The rate of growth in any one particular year or any short period is fairly irrelevant in determining the standard of living in an economy. Consider the years 1983 to 1988 in Table 34.1 above. Over this period the average growth rate was 3.8%, which on a historical basis is an exceptional increase. This was achieved by the 'Lawson boom' in which the Chancellor of the Exchequer, Nigel Lawson, expanded the economy by fiscal and monetary means. Unfortunately, as we saw in the previous chapters, an expansion of aggregate demand is likely to cause problems with inflation and the balance of payments. Because of these problems, especially inflation, the government was forced in the following years to adopt a deflationary policy. Growth rates from 1989 to 1992 were low, as were the growth rates in the period prior to the boom. Thus to some extent the high growth rates of the mid 1980s were simply allowing the economy to climb out of the hole into which it had sunk in the early 1980s. Over the whole period 1980 to 1992 the average growth rate was only 1.6%, which is below average for the post-war period. Thus, although governments tend to stress annual growth rates, especially when they are high, what is important to living standards is the long run performance of the economy. This point can be illustrated by using a production possibility curve.

The PPC in Figure 34.2 shows the total output which the economy is capable of producing. Suppose the economy is at point A inside the frontier. This means that the economy is not producing all it could. There

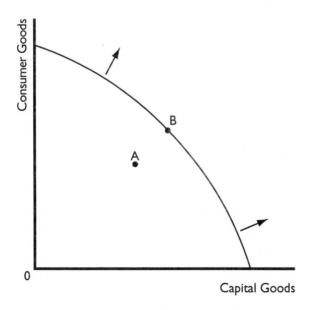

Figure 34.2 Production possibility curve (PPC) and economic growth

334 Access to Economics

are unemployed resources in the economy. If aggregate demand were to increase, these resources might be put to work, and the economy would grow to point B on the frontier. If the amount of unemployed resources is large, the movement from A to B might be substantial, as it was in 1973 (7.5%). However such expansion must be short lived, because, once the frontier has been reached, the rate of growth must depend upon how quickly the frontier itself shifts to the right. It is this growth in productive potential which will be the determining factor in the long run rate of growth. Thus in discussing economic growth there are two issues which need explaining: why do short run growth rates fluctuate so much, and what determined the long run growth in productive potential?

Short run growth: the trade cycle

Several explanations have been put forward to explain the booms and slumps which economies experience:

● **The multiplier – accelerator interaction**

Suppose that the economy starts to expand because of an increase in aggregate demand. As we have seen an increase in output will increase incomes which in turn will boost consumer spending. This extra consumer spending will cause output and incomes to expand further. Thus any expansion will continue. This is the multiplier process. This process will be reinforced if the increase in output also has an effect on investment. The accelerator theory of investment suggests that, when firms expand output to meet an increase in demand, they will be induced to invest in extra machinery and other capital equipment. This extra investment will itself set up a multiplier process, by boosting aggregate demand even further. The expansion will therefore continue.

Eventually the economy will approach full employment, whereby there will be very few labour resources available to expand output. Eventually the rate of expansion will have to slow down. As soon as this occurs, firms will no longer require as much additional machinery as they were requiring, and so investment will fall. As soon as investment falls, aggregate demand will fall. The multiplier process will move into reverse. Output and incomes will fall. Firms will require even less new machinery. Investment will decline further, reinforcing the slump. Eventually investment will be zero, and the downward spiral will end.

Over time machinery will wear out and depreciate, and firms will need to invest again. Once investment restarts, aggregate demand will increase and the whole process will repeat. Thus the economy has expanded, declined and started to expand again. A trade cycle has been generated.

● **The Natural Rate hypothesis**

As we saw in Chapter Thirty Three, if the economy expands beyond the Natural Rate, market forces will increase wages. This will have the effect of contracting the economy back to the Natural Rate, by making production less profitable. Similarly, any negative shock to the economy which takes output below the level associated with the Natural Rate will put pressure on wages to fall, which in turn will restore the economy back to the level of output associated with the Natural Rate, because of the effect of lower wages on profitability. Thus growth rates in excess of the growth in productive potential will expand the economy, reducing unemployment, which will then put pressure on wages to rise, putting a brake on the expansion.

These output changes will occur irrespective of whether the movement away from the Natural Rate is caused by demand side factors or supply side factors.

- **The political trade cycle**

Given the conflicts which exist between inflation, unemployment and the balance of payments, it is inevitable that governments will have to give priority to some objectives over the others. It is possible that approaching elections, a government might attack that objective which it felt would give most electoral benefit. Most people would argue that faced with an election, governments will have a temptation to adopt expansionary policies which will increase consumption and reduce unemployment. These policies would also encourage a faster rate of growth by making a fuller use of resources. In terms of Figure 34.2, it would imply a movement from A to B. After the election the government might face a higher rate of inflation and a balance of payments problem. In order to correct these problems, aggregate demand may be reduced, which would reduce growth and move the economy back towards A. Thus the trade cycle might be the result of deliberate actions taken by governments for political reasons.

Long run growth – growth in productive potential

In the long run, the ability of the economy to grow will be constrained by the growth in the productive potential of the economy. This means the growth in what the economy is capable of producing when all its resources are fully employed. In terms of the PPC it depends upon the rate at which the frontier moves outwards. The frontier will only move outwards if there is an increase in the resources available to the economy, or if existing resources increase productivity. There are three categories of resources: land, labour and capital:

- **Land**: This refers to all natural resources, and the ability to increase these is obviously limited. The UK was able to increase its natural resources by the discovery of North Sea Oil.
- **Labour**: Labour resources depend upon population and the age structure of the population, and this is again difficult for the government to

influence. In the 1950s the UK made extensive use of immigration policies to boost the labour force because of labour shortages. There is more scope for influencing the productivity of labour. Much emphasis is placed upon increasing the quality of the labour force through education and training. If successful this will increase the ability of the economy to produce goods and service. The PPC will move outwards and higher growth will be possible.

• **Capital**: This is the resource which is often seen as the most important in determining growth rates. The quantity and quality of the capital stock can be changed through investment. Thus, many economists see investment as the key to increasing growth rates. Countries with high growth rates are often countries which also have high levels of investment. Unfortunately the UK has found it difficult to increase the level of investment. This has been put down to many factors. The UK banking and financial system places great emphasis on short term profits to the detriment of returns from investment, which are always long run. Also, increases in investment imply fewer resources being devoted to consumer goods, which in turn implies a lower level of spending on consumer goods, and increased savings. However, UK consumers appear to save only a small part of their incomes. The 'stop-go' cycle may have deterred investment because of the uncertainty which it generates, coupled with a political system in which two parties take turns to be in power, with differing views on how to run the economy.

Economic growth and the standard of living

Small differences in the rate of growth can make substantial differences in living standards over time. Consider Table 34.2.

Table 34.2 Growth rates and income

Year	2%	3%	5%	7%
0	100	100	100	100
10	122	135	165	201
30	182	246	448	817
50	272	448	1218	3312
100	739	2009	14841	109660

Thus if the growth rate could be increased from 2 to 3%, in ten years time the level of GDP would have risen by 35% instead of only 22%. Over longer periods the differences become even more pronounced. Thus if one accepts GDP per head as a good indicator of the standard of living, an increase in the long run rate of growth will have a significant impact upon living standards.

Some people argue that the costs of economic growth outweigh the benefits and so an increase in GDP per head may be a poor way of calculating living standards. The costs of economic growth usually refer to the pollution costs, or the externalities associated with growth. Suppose that every family in the UK had two cars. This would often be taken as an indicator of a high standard of living. If the roads were unable to cope with the number of cars, and travel times were very low, it is not obvious that people are better off than when they used public transport which travelled much quicker. Faster economic growth is also sometimes criticised because it will use up more of the earth's resources, and may result in fewer resources being available for future generations.

Summary

- ❏ Economic growth refers to the rate of increase in GDP.
- ❏ Growth rates fluctuate over time and give rise to the trade cycle.
- ❏ Growth in the short run can be achieved by making fuller use of existing resources.
- ❏ Growth in the long run is constrained by the growth in productive potential.
- ❏ In the short run growth rates will be affected by changes in aggregate demand or supply.
- ❏ The interaction of the multiplier and the accelerator theory of investments can explain short run trade cycles.
- ❏ The political trade cycle refers to changes in aggregate demand for electoral purposes affecting aggregate demand in a cyclical fashion.
- ❏ The Natural Rate Hypothesis suggests that output will fluctuate around the Natural Rate.
- ❏ Long run growth depends upon increasing the quantity or quality of the economy's resources.
- ❏ Education and training will improve the economy's labour resources.
- ❏ Investment is necessary for improving the economy's stock of capital.
- ❏ Small differences in long run growth can have major impacts on the long run level of GDP.
- ❏ Economic growth imposes costs as well as benefits.

Multiple Choice Questions

1. Economic growth is seen as a desirable objective of economic policy because:

    A economic growth automatically increases the welfare of everyone in society
    B economic growth increases pollution
    C economic growth reduces unemployment
    D economic growth increases GDP per head
    E economic growth reduces inflation

2. The multiplier-accelerator theory of the trade cycle suggests that:

    A any fall in investment pushes the economy into recession
    B any fall in income increases investment
    C any increase in investment reduces unemployment
    D any increase in demand reduces investment
    E changes in demand must be caused by changes in investment

3. Which of the following will result in an increase in productive potential?

    A a reduction in unemployment
    B a reduction in inflation
    C an increase in investment
    D a fall in population
    E an increase in GDP per head

4. Consider the following table and select the answer which corresponds to the information in the table:

    UK GDP and Growth 1988 to 1992

Year	GDP	Growth %
1988	349.4	—
1989	356.7	2.1
1990	359	0.6
1991	350	− 2.5
1992	348.5	− 0.5

    A in 1991 GDP per head fell by 2.5%
    B GDP increased by 3.1% in 1991
    C GDP fell by 3.1% in 1991
    D economic growth 1988 to 1992 was negative
    E the standard of living was lower in 1992 than in 1989

5. Faster economic growth will always:

    A reduce unemployment
    B increase inflation
    C increase imports
    D increase GDP per head
    E increase GDP

International Trade

Reasons for trade

On a very simple level, trade is necessary if one country wishes to obtain goods or services which its resources are unable to produce. Thus certain metals are only found in certain areas of the world. If other countries wish to obtain these metals, trade must take place.

However the most important reason for international trade is that it allows a more efficient use of the world's resources. Instead of all countries trying to be self-sufficient, they can concentrate on producing what their resources are best able to produce. This is simply an extension of the case for specialisation being carried into the international sphere. Two circumstances can be identified in which such specialisation will be beneficial to the world: where absolute cost advantage exists between countries, and where a comparative cost advantage exists.

Absolute cost advantage

If two countries are capable of producing two commodities, but if one country is better at producing one, and the other country is better at producing the other, simple logic would suggest that if the countries specialised in what they had the advantage in producing, the total output of both products would increase. Thus both countries could enjoy higher consumption of both goods than they could have enjoyed if they had attempted to be self-sufficient. This example is known as absolute cost advantage because it represents a situation where one country has an absolute advantage in producing one product, and the other country an absolute advantage in the other.

Comparative cost advantage

This situation occurs when one country is more efficient at producing both products, but is comparatively more efficient at one than the other. In this case, trade and specialisation will still also offer a potential gain to both countries. This idea, which owes its origins to David Ricardo in the early 19th century, has provided the basis for free trade ever since. It may not appear logical that a country which is relatively inefficient at producing all products may still obtain a benefit from engaging in free trade with other, more efficient countries, but the theory of comparative advantage is generally accepted as providing the justification for just such an assertion.

Suppose that there are two countries, Moreland and Lessland. Moreland has a much more efficient economy and is able to produce goods and services in a more productive fashion than Lessland. Assume that both countries have the same labour force, and prior to trade taking place, both countries produce two products, pens and paper, and employ half of their labour force in each industry. The output of both countries is shown in Table 35.1.

Table 35.1 *Moreland and Lessland: outputs prior to trade*

Country	Pens	Paper
Moreland	1000	1000
Lessland	800	400
Total output	1800	1400

Let us consider what these figures mean and how trade might improve the use of resources. In Moreland, every pen that is produced means giving up one unit of paper (since a unit of labour can produce the same quantity of pens as paper). This is the concept of opportunity cost seen in Chapter Two, and we could say that in Moreland the opportunity cost of one unit of paper is one unit of pens. In Lessland a unit of labour produces less pens and paper than in Moreland. However in Lessland labour can produce twice as many pens as units of paper. Thus the opportunity cost of producing one unit of paper in Lessland is two units of pens. Thus in terms of the optimum allocation of resources, the world loses two pens every time that Lessland produces a unit of paper. It would seem sensible for Lessland to concentrate on producing pens and to give up paper production. This will allow Moreland to concentrate its resources on producing paper, since every time it produces a unit of paper the world only loses one unit of pens. Table 35.2 shows the results of complete and partial specialisation.

Table 35.2 *Moreland and Lessland: outputs after specialisation*

Country	Complete specialisation Pens	Paper	Partial specialisation Pens	Paper
Moreland	–	2000	300	1700
Lessland	1600	–	1600	–
Total output	1600	2000	1900	1700

Partial specialisation on the part of the more efficient country (Moreland), and complete specialisation by Lessland, has allowed the total output of pens to rise from 1800 to 1900, and the output of paper to rise from 1400 to 1700. The world has more of both goods to enjoy, and, so, potentially both countries could consume more of both products than they could have enjoyed if they had not engaged in trade. This is the result which is used to justify free trade since it indicates that the total output of the world (in this case the two countries combined) will increase if countries do not attempt to be self-sufficient, but instead allow trade and specialisation to improve the allocation of resources.

The key to this result lies in the different opportunity costs, which exist in both countries, of producing pens and paper. The implication is that countries should specialise in commodities which have the lowest opportunity cost. If the opportunity costs are the same in both countries, there will be no gain from trade.

A useful analogy is to consider the case of an individual who could either paint his house or write an article for a magazine. It may be in his interests to employ his neighbour, who is an inferior author and an inferior painter, to paint his house, even though he will carry out an inferior job, so that the individual can concentrate on the activity where he can make the most return, writing the article. Thus the inferior painter will still secure gainful employment despite his relative inefficiency.

Economies of scale

The allocation of resources between countries might also be improved by trade if specialisation allows economies of scale to be enjoyed. Economies of scale arise when increased output is associated with a reduction in long run costs of production. In the example above, the output of the paper industry in Moreland increases from 1000 units to 1700 units. This expansion of output, or increase in scale, might allow the firms within the paper industry in Moreland to secure cost reductions through economies of scale. Thus fewer resources will be needed to produce paper, thereby improving productive efficiency. In the less efficient economy, Lessland, the output of pens rises as resources are concentrated on pen production. This larger output might also permit firms in the pen industry in Lessland to enjoy economies of scale, again improving the allocation of resources.

The process of trade

In the example above, it is shown that the process of specialisation can increase the total output of all goods. This leaves open the question of how this specialisation comes about. Once free trade is possible, resources will move to the activities which return the highest profit. In Moreland, where paper can be produced 2.5 times as efficiently as in Lessland, the opening of the paper market in Lessland will provide a highly profitable export opportunity. Resources will flow into the paper industry, which will expand. Given that resources are limited, there will be fewer resources available to produce pens in Moreland. Exporters in Lessland will seize the profitable opportunity provided by this demand in Moreland and will export pens to Moreland. The pen industry in Lessland expands. Consider the figures in Table 35.3 which show the supply and demand conditions in both countries for paper, both prior to, and after, trade.

Table 35.3 *Supply and demand for paper*

Price (£)	MORELAND Demand	Supply	LESSLAND Demand	Supply	COMBINED Demand	Supply
10	400	2700	100	600	500	3300
9	600	2500	300	500	900	3000
8	750	2300	400	400	1150	2700
7	850	2100	600	200	1450	2300
6	600	1900	800	100	1400	2000
5	700	1700	1000	0	1700	1700
4	900	1400	1200	0	2100	1400
3	1000	1000	1400	0	2400	1000

Prior to trade the equilibrium price in Moreland is £3 and in Lessland it is
£8, (where demand equals supply in each market) Output in Moreland is
1000 units and in Lessland it is 400 units. This corresponds to the figures
in Table 35.1. If trade takes place, the supply and demand conditions will
simply be the combined supply and demand. This will yield an equilibrium
price of £5, which will be common in both countries. In Lessland the price
has fallen from £8 to £5, and at this price, there is no output, since the paper
industry there is unable to produce profitably at this price. In Moreland
output has expanded to 1700 units, but only 700 units are bought by
consumers in Moreland. The other 1000 units is exported to Lessland. This
process is shown in Figure 35.1 below.

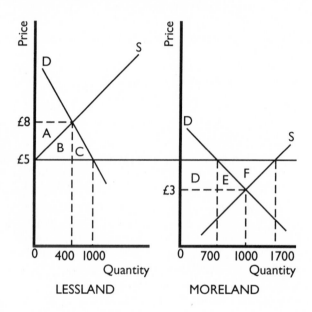

Figure 35.1 *The gains and losses from trade*

The original prices and quantities are shown in both diagrams. Trade leads
to a common price of £5 being established, which reduces supply in
Lessland to zero, and expands supply in Moreland to 1700 units. This
diagram is useful because it allows us to illustrate the gainers and the losers
from trade. In Lessland the consumers gain, because prices fall and more
paper is consumed. The gain to consumers can be illustrated by the gain in
consumer surplus. This is shown as the areas A + B + C. The logic behind
this is that there are 400 consumers who bought paper at £8 per unit. They
now can buy the paper at £5, thus they have gained by £3 × 400. This is area
A + B. There are 600 extra consumers who now buy paper who previously
did not because of its high price. Some of these 600 would have been
prepared to pay nearly £8 while others were only prepared to pay £5. On

average they may have been prepared to pay £6.50. Thus a crude approximation would suggest that their gain is 600 × £1.50, (represented as area C in Figure 35.1). This yields a total gain to consumers in Lessland of £2100, shown as area A+B+C.

In Lessland producers lose. Prior to trade they earned a producer surplus shown as area A. This represents the extent to which price exceeded marginal cost. (Remember that the supply curve is the marginal cost curve.) This could be approximated as consisting of 400 units at an average producer surplus of £1.50, giving a total of £600. After trade this area disappears. Thus, in the less efficient country, consumers gain, but producers lose from trade. The gain to consumers is greater than the loss to producers. In the example above the net gain is £2100– £600, a net gain of £1500 shown as areas B + C.

In Moreland, the more efficient country, exactly the opposite occurs. The price of paper rises from £3 to £5 and so consumers lose because they buy less paper at a higher price. Producers gain because they sell more paper at a higher price. The loss to consumers is shown by area D+E, while the gain to producers is area D + E+F. Thus there is a net gain of area F. The reader can work out the approximate value of area F from the diagram. I make it about £1000.

Thus the total gain in both countries is areas B + C + F. On my calculations the net benefit to producers and consumers in both countries is £2500. This example is useful because it illustrates two important points:

● Free trade confers benefits to some groups, but imposes costs on others.
● Free trade will reduce prices in countries where goods are produced inefficiently by the domestic industry, but might increase prices in the domestic market of the efficient country. The possibility of economies of scale also affecting this result should be recognised.

Limitations of free trade

As we have seen, where comparative advantages occur, there is always a potential gain from free trade. However there are circumstances in which free trade may not be of mutual benefit to countries.

● **Factor immobility:** If free trade occurs, inefficient industries in some countries will decline. In order to reap the gains of comparative advantage, the resources released from these industries should transfer into other, more efficient occupations. It is possible that factor immobility, whether occupational or geographic, may prevent resources from securing alternative employment. These resources may remain unemployed, in which case the advantages of free trade will not be realised. It is sometimes argued that some temporary protection might be desirable to allow resources to be reallocated over a period of time.

● **Terms of trade:** In order that both countries should benefit from trade, the relative prices of the two products must be such as to allow each country to obtain more of both products than they could have obtained without trade. In other words for free trade to be mutually beneficial, one country must not be in a position to buy all the output of the other country with a small proportion of its own output. In the example above, Lessland's exports of pens must bring in enough revenue to allow it to purchase the paper imports from Moreland. The terms of trade is the term given to the ratio of export to import prices. If export prices rise, this is known as an improvement in the terms of trade, since it means that more imports can be bought for a given volume of exports.

● **Infant industries:** It is possible that a country might have the potential to be highly efficient at producing a particular product, but that the industry is not well developed, and is what is known as an infant industry. If free trade is permitted, the infant industry may not be able to compete and may therefore fail to develop, despite its long run potential. In these circumstances it would be in every country's interests that the industry be protected to allow it to develop and achieve its potential. The problem with this approach is that once an industry has been protected, it is usually very difficult to remove the protection, because the domestic producers will always insist that the industry requires protecting for a little longer.

● **Dumping:** Sometimes countries sell their products to other countries at prices which are below the costs of production. These products are likely to be very popular and will cause the other country's industries to decline. This decline is not because of some inherent inefficiency, but because the dumping country is trying to undermine these industries, for political or strategic reasons. In these circumstances it is usually argued that measures should be taken to keep out such 'dumped' products.

● **Balance of payments:** Free trade is sometimes questioned if one country is running a large balance of payments deficit. Protection in the form of tariffs or quotas is often advocated as a way of reducing imports. This of course will prevent the gains of comparative advantage, and will simply encourage the protected industries to remain in business, and perpetuate the misallocation of resources which the prevention of free trade implies.

● **Strategic reasons:** Specialisation implies reliance on other countries for many goods and services. Some countries feel reluctant having to rely on others. This is especially true in agriculture, where many advanced countries are reluctant to allow free trade.

Arguments for protection

As we have seen above, free trade yields benefits to some sectors of society, but will impose costs on others. Although the net gains will be positive, if resources are mobile, and if the terms of trade are compatible with free trade, there will always be some groups arguing for barriers to trade to be erected. These arguments will be supported by the idea of protecting infant industries, or protecting the balance of payments, or defending the strategic interests of the country, or preventing dumping.

The majority of the voices advocating protectionism, (obstructing free trade), will come from producer groups, either employers or employees. This is because some industries, in some countries, will be adversely affected by free trade. One of the major arguments employed will be the idea that free trade destroys jobs, by allowing cheap imports into the country. If these imports come from countries where wages are low, this fact will be used to reinforce the arguments for protection. These arguments are usually thought of as being invalid. If products can be produced more cheaply in another country, why should consumers be denied the opportunity to purchase these cheaper products, and be forced to buy more expensive home-produced items?

The logic of comparative advantage is that the imports should be accepted gratefully, and the resources moved from the uncompetitive home industry and put to work producing goods or services which are not available from cheaper foreign suppliers. If resources are not mobile, then temporary protection might be justified, to allow a gradual run down of the home industry, which would allow resources to gradually adjust. One reason why protectionist arguments are often successful is that producer groups are easy to co-ordinate in order to put pressure on government. Consumers, who will be the major beneficiaries of free trade will be much more difficult to organise into pressure groups.

Summary

❐ Trade improves the world allocation of resources by allowing specialisation.

❐ Absolute cost advantage occurs when one country is more efficient at producing good A and the other country is more efficient at producing good B.

❐ Comparative advantage occurs when one country is more efficient at producing both products, but is relatively more efficient in one than the other. This implies that the opportunity cost of producing both goods in each country will differ.

❐ Under comparative advantage, there is a potential gain to both countries from trade, including the inefficient country, since the total supply of goods and services will increase by specialisation. Countries will specialise in the goods where the opportunity cost of producing the good is lowest.

❐ If economies of scale exist, the gains from specialisation will be reinforced.

❐ In countries where free trade reduces the price of products, consumers gain and producers lose. If trade raises prices, consumers lose and producers gain. The net gain to consumers and producers will be positive.

❐ If factors of production are immobile, the gains from trade may not be realised.

❐ The terms of trade will determine whether a particular country benefits from trade and specialisation.

❐ The protection of infant industries, avoidance of dumping, protecting the balance of payments, and strategic factors, are all put forward as arguments for protection

❐ The protection from cheap imports is an invalid argument for protection.

Multiple Choice Questions

1. Increased specialisation by countries in those activities in which they have a comparative advantage will necessarily:
    A increase foreign trade
    B reduce the standard of living in less efficient economies
    C reduce unemployment
    D bring about greater equality in the distribution of income
    E reduce inflation

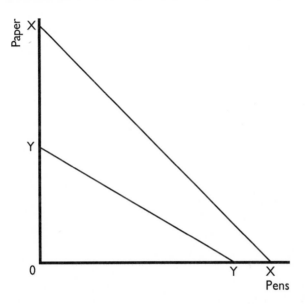

2. In the diagram, XX and YY represent the Production Possibility Curves of two countries, X and Y respectively. Each country only produces two goods, paper and pens. From the information provided it can be deduced that:
    A country X has a higher GDP per head than country Y
    B given free trade, country X would import paper
    C given free trade, country Y would export paper
    D country Y has an absolute cost advantage in both paper and pens
    E country X has a comparative advantage in the production of paper

3. Which of the following is not a barrier to free trade?
    A tariffs
    B quotas
    C immobile factors of production
    D customs duties
    E fluctuating currencies

4. The domestic costs of producing a ream of paper and a box of pens in countries X and Y are given below.

	Country X		Country Y	
	Paper	Pens	Paper	Pens
Domestic costs	$20	$20	£5	£10

According to the theory of comparative advantage which of the following is correct?

A country Y has an absolute advantage in paper and pen production
B trade is of no benefit to country X since the cost of producing pens and paper is the same
C paper in country X is four times as expensive as in country Y
D country X has a comparative advantage in producing pens
E in country Y the opportunity cost ratio of paper to pens is 1:1

5. The following figures denote the domestic prices of five products in two countries A and B. At an exchange rate of £1 = $2, which products would country A export to B?

	Pen	Paper	Cloth	Wine	Plate
Country A	£1	£2	£3	£4	£5
Country B	$1	$3	$7	$7	$11

A pens and paper
B paper and cloth
C cloth and wine
D wine and plates
E cloth and plates

Chapter Thirty-six

The Economics of European Integration

The European Economic Community (EEC)

The European Economic Community (EEC) was set up in 1958 following the signing of the Treaty of Rome in 1957. The UK did not seek membership in 1958, but finally became a member in 1973. The fundamental economic idea behind the creation of the EEC was the creation of a customs union between the member countries. A customs union exists when countries join together and abolish all tariffs between themselves erecting a common external tariff against the rest of the world. The benefits of such a union will arise from the gains associated with free trade seen in Chapter Thirty Five. Most of the economic debates within Europe are concerned with the steps which are needed to be taken in order to ensure that these gains are realised. The EEC was also designed to promote greater political cohesion within Europe, to avoid the conflicts which have riven the continent during the 20th century. As we shall see, the economic steps necessary to create a customs union have political connotations which may prove extremely unattractive to some people.

Free trade and currency stability

In order to allow free trade to be encouraged, currency stability is usually seen as preferable to a situation where the value of currencies fluctuates from day to day. This is the argument for fixed exchange rates seen in Chapter Twenty Nine. The members of the EEC set up the European Monetary System in 1979, which was designed to promote currency stability and to create a new European Currency Unit (ECU). This was a unit of account, and it was calculated as a weighted average of the value of all member currencies. The UK did not join the EMS in 1979, but the value of sterling was still included as part of the ECU calculations.

Although the ECU does not exist as notes or coins, transactions can be carried out in terms of ECUs, and they are becoming established as an international unit of account. It is possible to open a bank account in ECUs in the majority of member countries of the EEC, and to carry out transactions using ECUs. The domestic currencies of the member countries can all be valued against the ECU, and members of the EMS were obliged to keep their currencies within certain bands against the value of the ECU. This arrangement is known as the Exchange Rate Mechanism (ERM) of the EMS. As members of the ERM, countries had to keep currency within very small bands (+/-) 2.5% against the ECU, although occasional realignments were allowed. The UK joined the ERM in 1990, but was allowed a wider band within which the pound could move. (Italy was also given the same dispensation.) In 1992 the UK was unable to keep the pound within its bands and the UK left the ERM. The instability of currencies which followed, led to the permitted bands being widened to (±) 15% for all currencies.

Implications of membership of the ERM

A system of fixed exchange rates is usually seen as beneficial to international trade, and this is the major rationale behind the ERM in Europe. However fixed exchange rates imply that countries lose control over domestic monetary policy. This is because the rate of interest has to be at a level compatible with the desired exchange rate. This was the reason for the UKs withdrawal from the ERM in 1992. At that time conditions in Germany were such that inflation had become a possibility, and the German authoritised were determined to eliminate the threat. Thus interest rates in Germany were increased, and the value of the German Mark rose against the pound. In the UK, unemployment was increasing and the economy was in recession. In order to keep the pound within the ERM, UK interest rates were at a high level and this was one of the factors contributing to the recession. This problem was exacerbated by the fact that the UK had joined the ERM at an exchange rate which some people felt was uncompetitive and above its Purchasing Power Parity. International financiers become concerned that the UK would be unable or unwilling to take the steps necessary to keep the pound at its ERM level. (This would have involved further increases in UK interest rates.) Thus holders of assets denominated in sterling sold those assets, and converted the currency out of sterling. This created an even larger excess supply of pounds on the foreign exchange market which the UK authorities tried to remove by using their foreign exchange reserves. The reserves proved ineffective, despite assistance from other European central banks, including a large loan from Germany, and eventually the UK left the ERM, and the value of the pound was allowed to fall to a new equilibrium level against the other

European currencies. This fall in the value of the pound is generally seen as being a factor in the economic recovery which occurred in 1993/4.

The Single European Market (SEM)

In 1986, the member states of the EEC signed a Single European Act. This act committed member states to completing a customs union by January 1st 1993. This came to be known as the movement towards 1992, and implied a completely free market within the EEC. The creation of this free market required the removal of all trade barriers between member states. These barriers consisted of both tariff and non tariff barriers:

● **Tariff barriers** are barriers caused by the imposition of tariffs on goods being taken into a particular country. On 1st January 1993, customs barriers were removed and there are now no customs duties to be paid on goods being moved between countries within the EEC. This should mean that traded goods prices will be equalised throughout Europe, since it will not be possible for goods which can be traded to sell at higher prices in one country than another, because people will simply buy the goods in the part of the single market where they are cheapest. This has given rise to a large trade in wine between the UK and France. The different rate of duty which the UK government imposes on wine sold in the UK means that wine in France is much cheaper than in the UK. As a consequence many people are travelling to France, buying wine and returning with it to the UK. The UK authorities have attempted to prevent the resale of such wine, but it is questionable whether this is legal given the commitment to the single market. This reveals another requirement of the creation of a single market.

● **Tax harmonisation** is advocated by some economists as a necessary part of the single market. In order for the gains from comparative advantage to be realised, goods should sell at prices which reflect the costs of production. Thus the more efficient producers will expand their market share. If prices are distorted by countries imposing different rates of tax on goods produced domestically, comparative advantage may be obscured.

● **Non tariff barriers** are factors which work against the free movement and trade, of goods and services. Thus filling in forms at frontier crossings is expensive in time and money. The Single European Act abolished customs controls thereby removing the need for much 'red tape'.

● **Common standards** across Europe are necessary, to prevent one country from protecting its domestic industry by requiring expensive alterations in goods before they are allowed to be imported. The Single European Act also required that countries had to ensure that **government procurement** of goods and services was always carried out on the basis of buying from the cheapest supplier. This was to prevent countries from favouring domestic producers when government purchases were made. This is likely to have most impact in the field of expenditure on defence equipment. One final barrier to trade within Europe is the need to change currencies when transactions are carried out. This creates expense as well as some uncertainty. To overcome these barriers, the EEC is committed to working towards the establishment of a common currency within the EEC.

A common currency – Economic and Monetary Union (EMU)

In order that trade between France and the UK could be carried out as easily as between England and Scotland (which is what the single market is trying to achieve), many people argue that a single currency, used in both countries, is required. This is the ultimate goal of European integration, the creation of a single currency, which would imply economic and monetary union between the member states of the EEC.

In 1992 the members of the EEC signed the Maastricht Agreement which committed all the signatories to the creation of a single currency by 1999. The UK government secured an 'opt out' to this part of the agreement, and will only move to a single currency when it has been approved by the UK Parliament. The establishment of a single currency will have several implications for the EEC.

Economic convergence and EMU

A common currency means that the option of devaluation will have been completely removed for those countries using the common currency. Thus countries which find themselves uncompetitive with other countries will have to improve their competitiveness by increasing productivity, or by reducing costs (especially wage costs).

Suppose that inflation in one country is greater than in another. The products of the inflating country will be uncompetitive. Sales will fall. Unemployment will rise. This process will continue until the inflationary pressure has been removed and prices fall until they are once again competitive with other countries. Thus inflation rates within the common currency area will converge. This shows the importance of inflation rates being the same before the common currency area is established. If countries wish to avoid the painful process described above, they will need to have the same inflation rate as other countries before they enter into the single currency. This is the reason behind the convergence criteria which were laid down in the Maastricht agreement as being necessary before EMU takes place. Maastricht laid down four criteria:

● Inflation rates should be similar. (No more than 1.5% above the average of the three best performing members)
● Currencies have to be held within ERM bands for a two-year period before EMU takes place

● Interest rates have to be similar. (No more than 2% above the average of the lowest)
● The proportion of GDP accounted for by the PSBR should be less than 3% of GDP, and the National Debt (which is the sum of all government borrowings in the past), should be no more than 60% of GDP.

The logic behind these criteria are as follows:

● Inflation rates must be similar to prevent countries from becoming uncompetitive immediately after EMU
● If currencies have been held fixed against each other for a long period, this implies that the exchange rates are at a sustainable level. The single currency is in effect an extreme example of a fixed exchange rate
● Once a single currency is established, with no possibility of exchange rates altering, interest rates throughout the common currency area must be the same. (It is impossible for Scotland to have higher interest rates than England, because people will simply borrow money from the cheapest source if there is no exchange risk attached.)
● The PSBR requirement is an attempt to force countries to adopt similar fiscal stances prior to EMU, both to ensure similar inflation rates, and also to control the need for government borrowing, which some economists see as inflationary.

EMU and the need for inter-regional transfers

As we saw in Chapter Thirty Five, free trade will create winners and losers. The net gains outweigh the losses, but the creation of a single currency and the single market may have serious implications for countries of Europe. Within the UK, if an area of the country becomes depressed because of declining industries, and this creates structural unemployment, the fiscal system of the UK will automatically alleviate the problem by increasing the level of unemployment benefit being paid to the area, thereby reducing the amount of money paid in taxes. Thus aggregate demand within the depressed region will be boosted.

Suppose that within the single market, the UK economy as a whole suffers from a decline in demand for its products and structural unemployment rises throughout the economy. If devaluation was an option, the government could restore competitiveness, but within an EMU, this option is not possible. Hence the UK economy will enter recession. There are no automatic transfers which will alleviate the problem. Thus the UK economy might enter recession for a long period of time, until resources have moved to other, more competitive industries, or until wages have fallen. Some people argue that if these problems are to be avoided, there is a need for the countries which gain from the single market to compensate those which lose. This requires a transfer of funds between countries. This requires taxes to be levied at a European level. This may prove unpopular.

European Central Bank

If a common currency is established, this will require some sort of central bank to regulate the supply of the currency. This is especially true if the control of the money supply is seen as the way to control inflation. Thus countries will have to pool their sovereignty over monetary control (although as we have seen this is also an implication of fixed exchange rates even without EMU).

The European Union (EU)

It is instructive to chart the changes which have taken place in the name given to the European integration which we have described. In the early stages the organisation was known as the European Economic Community (EEC), or, less formally, as the Common Market. This stressed the economic case for integration, which were based on the arguments for free trade seen in Chapter Thirty Five. In the mid 1980s there was a subtle change and the organisation became known as the European Community (EC). This dropped the reference to 'economic', and, instead, simply stressed the idea of a community of countries which had come together for some undefined purpose. Some argued that this downgrading of the economic aspect of integration showed a move towards political union. By 1994 the organisation was officially known as the European Union (EU), again placing less emphasis on the economic benefits of integration. Critics of integration see this as a creeping move towards some form of United States of Europe with a Federal government, with political integration replacing the economic logic given by free trade.

Gains from European integration

The gains from integration can be classified under the following headings:

● **Micro economic gains**: This refers to the gains associated with comparative advantage and the realisation of economies of scale within the EU. Cost savings will also arise from the abolition of frontier controls, the introduction of common standards, and the increased competition which should ensue. These micro gains will allow more goods and services to be enjoyed by the consumers within Europe, as output increases and prices fall.
● **Macro economic gains**: This refers to the idea that if increased competition and specialisation within the EU reduce price levels and increase employment, the countries within Europe will be able to run their economies at higher levels of activity without the fear of inflation. Public finances will improve with a reduction in unemployment, which will allow more expansionary fiscal stances to be taken. Both these effects will permit higher levels of output to be achieved.

● **Dynamic gains** might arise if the boost to activity triggers off an increase in investment which will increase growth rates within Europe. Monetary union will confer further cost savings by eliminating the need for different currencies.

Summary

☐ The EEC was set up in 1958 to secure the gains of free trade within its member countries.

☐ Free trade is encouraged by currency stability.

☐ The EMS was set up and the ECU created as a step towards currency stability. This was formalised in the ERM which is a system of relatively fixed exchange rates within the EEC.

☐ Membership of the ERM involves a loss of sovereignty over domestic monetary policy.

☐ The SEM involved the elimination of all barriers to trade, both tariff and non tariff barriers.

☐ The SEM may require the harmonisation of all indirect tax rates in Europe.

☐ If exchange rates are to be increasingly fixed, the logical conclusion to this process is a single currency. This is known as EMU.

☐ EMU will require a European Central Bank.

☐ EMU will bring about convergence in inflation rates and in interest rates.

☐ Within an EMU, some countries may gain and others lose. Compensation will require inter regional transfers if tensions are to be avoided within the EMU.

Multiple Choice Questions

1. The creation of a customs union will:
    A improve resource allocation both inside and outside the customs union
    B promote trade between the customs union and the rest of the world
    C increase trade within the customs union
    D benefit all producers in the customs union
    E raise living standards for every person in the customs union

2. Which of the following will result from a single currency within the EU?
    A inflation rates will diverge within the EU
    B interest rates within the EU will be the same in all countries
    C unemployment rates will be the same in all countries
    D GDP per head will be the same in all countries
    E increased trade with the rest of the world

3. Which of the following might rise if the creation of the European Single Market increases trade within Europe?
    A inflation
    B voluntary unemployment
    C structural unemployment
    D seasonal unemployment
    E money supply

4. Which of the following is not part of the convergence criteria laid down at Maastricht?
    A convergence on unemployment rates
    B convergence on inflation rates
    C convergence on interest rates
    D convergence on the scale of budget deficits
    E convergence on the scale of the National Debt

5. In an Economic and Monetary Union, with a single currency, which of the following is a viable means of increasing aggregate demand?
    A devaluation
    B lowering interest rates
    C increasing interest rates
    D cutting income tax
    E increasing the money supply

Standard Topics and Suggested Answers

Assessment by essay question

In any assessment in economics it is quite easy to identify topics or areas which are popular with examiners. This is because the subject matter of economics focuses on particular issues, and the major problem which examiners face is how to test students' grasp of the issues without setting the same questions year after year. The best form of revision which a student can undertake is a perusal of past exam questions in an attempt to identify the type of question which a particular examiner or board prefers when examining these issues.

In an attempt to show what is required, I have identified ten topics which experience has shown provide the majority of questions when examining economics students. Several questions of a discussible nature are then suggested which show the various ways in which such issues may be approached, and an indication is given of the ingredients of a reasonable answer.

Finally a model answer, or at least the best answer I can produce, will be provided for a specimen question. This answer has been written under exam conditions and represents the sort of approach that will be acceptable as an exam answer. It is NOT a perfect answer!

These questions and answers are presented as part of the learning process. Reading them should indicate the ways in which the contents of the text can be used to answer questions, but also as a way of indicating and reinforcing the analysis which you have studied. It is often easier to grasp the basic ideas behind some aspects of economics when you see them applied to a specific question. Thus these questions should be treated as part of the learning process.

The important thing to remember when answering economics questions is that there will always be a body of theory or specific information required in each answer. The trick is to identify the body of theory, explain the theory and its implications, and then to critically discuss the issues raised. It is not a good idea to answer a question because:

a) you think it is interesting
b) you saw a programme on the television about the topic
c) you think you can make something up which might be relevant.

Unless you can recognise the body of knowledge required in a question, move on and do another. This section of the book is an attempt to show you how to identify the necessary theory in a variety of questions.

One way you might like to use this section is to look at the various questions I have selected, draft out your own answers, and then compare these with mine. If your answers are different, this does not mean that you are wrong. When comparing you will be able to tell whether your answer is relevant. If my answer suggests that you have used the wrong information in your answer, check to see how I have interpreted the question. The most popular way of failing examinations is to answer questions which do not appear on the exam paper. Do not put down an answer which you have prepared but which fails to address the question!

Topic one: the market mechanism

This topic appears on all exam papers, and is usually trying to discover if the student can explain how the market mechanism operates, why it is seen as a desirable way of solving the economic problem, and any problems which the market may fail to solve. In recent years this topic has been linked to the idea of privatisation and the economic benefits which privatisation is supposed to bring. Privatisation is simply allowing the market mechanism to operate in running the industries involved rather than the public sector.

The key theoretical framework to employ concerns the concepts of productive and allocative efficiency, since markets are usually seen as being highly efficient at solving the economic problem of scarcity. However examples of market failure – monopoly, income distribution, public goods, merit goods, externalities – need to be understood, as do the steps needed to rectify them. There are a few general diagrams that shed light on these areas:

- The production possibility curve (Figure 2.1), to illustrate the idea of scarcity and opportunity cost
- The marginal cost and marginal benefit curve (Figure 18.1), to illustrate the concept of allocative efficiency in a competitive market. This should be linked to the idea of P = MC
- Competitive firms producing at minimum average cost (Figure 11.3), to illustrate the concept of productive efficiency.

Sample questions

❑ **Explain the increasing reliance which the countries of Eastern Europe are placing upon the market mechanism as a means of solving the economic problem.**

This involves a definition of the economic problem and the idea of scarcity as well as the idea of achieving an optimum allocation of resources. Efficiency and the concepts of productive and allocative efficiency are involved. Problems of a planned economy in achieving an efficient allocation of resources require illumination as do ways in which a market might achieve efficiency: in terms of productive efficiency (desire for profits, pressure of competition, threat of being taken over) and allocative efficiency (providing the right level of service - in technical terms operating where P = MC). The importance of competition needs to be stressed.

❑ **Examine the role played by prices in the market solution to the economic problem.**

This involves a definition of the economic problem and an explanation of how the market allocates resources as well as an identification of the role of prices – which is best achieved by giving an example of the market mechanism in action. Describe how the market would react to an increase in demand. Prices reflect the cost of producing the item and the benefit which consumers derive (concept of allocative efficiency). The profit motive ensures that firms respond to changes in demand, if this affects prices, and also changes in costs, since these will also be reflected in price changes. Thus prices act as signals indicating changes in demand or cost conditions.

❑ **In what sense is pollution part of the economic problem? How can the government attempt to solve the problem of pollution?**

Define the economic problem. Pollution affects allocative efficiency since it ensures that price does not reflect the true marginal cost of production. (Figure 18.2)

Governments can tackle the problem by making the price reflect the true costs to society of goods production. This can be achieved through taxation, or by forcing the firm to internalise the cost by reducing the pollution through regulation.

This question may take the form of examining other types of externality: traffic congestion, destruction of wildlife or ecology, noise pollution. Sometimes external benefits may be examined, eg the case for subsidising higher education, providing public libraries. The important thing to remember is that they all require an examination of how externalities interfere with the allocative efficiency of the market, and therefore are all dealing with the same issue. That is the divergence between private and social costs and benefits.

❏ **Examine the economic case for privatisation**

This takes into account a definition of privatisation and necessitates outlining the major argument in terms of improving economic efficiency. Define productive and economic efficiency.

Examine how market forces will encourage each type of efficiency. Stress the importance of competition. Examine whether privatisation has increased competition (concept of natural monopolies), and whether there is a need for regulation to prevent monopoly power being exploited. Also decide the macro impact of privatisation in terms of reducing the PSBR.

All of the above questions are variations on the same theme; what is meant by an optimum allocation of resources, and under what circumstances is such an allocation likely to be achieved? Thus all the four questions rely on an appreciation of what is meant by economic efficiency. A grasp of the issues involved will pay great dividends, because this topic is at the heart of much of economics, and any question which asks about the solutions to the economic problem, efficiency, arguments for privatisation, problems caused by externalities, are all asking for variations on the theme of efficiency.

Specimen answer

❏ **What is meant by an economic system and what are the main types of economic system? Why have planned economies become less and less popular in recent years?**

An economic system simply refers to the way in which a society decides to solve the economic problem. The economic problem consists of the fact that all societies suffer from a lack of resources. This means that all economies only have a finite supply of factors of production. These consist of labour (all human resources), land (all natural resources), and capital (all man-made resources). Given that human wants are usually seen as insatiable, this means that decisions have to be made as to which goods and services should be produced with the available resources. A decision to produce more of one product implies that resources are not available to produce some other product. This is known as the opportunity cost of producing an item. Thus resources are scarce.

An economic system refers to how these decisions are taken, so solving the economic problem. This is sometimes known as the problem of deciding what goods should be produced, how these goods should be produced and for whom these goods should be produced.

There are three approaches to solving the economic problem, which give rise to three types of economic systems. A market system solves the economic problem by allowing individuals to make decisions about what, how, and for whom to produce on the basis of each individual attempting to make themselves as well-off as possible. All resources are owned by private individuals and all decisions are the outcome of market forces determining the relative prices of resources and goods, which are then bought and sold in the market place.

A planned, or command, economy is an economic system where the decisions of what, how and for whom, are taken by some central planner. The planner decides which goods are to be produced, and so the means of production must be owned, or at least controlled, by the planner. Prices are not used as a means of rationing the goods and services available, and they are controlled by the planners. Thus consumers are not able to influence prices or outputs by expressing their choices.

A mixed economy tries to use the best features of both of the other systems. Market economies suffer from several problems which may require government intervention and control.

Planned economies have become less popular in recent years because the countries which used central planning, Russia, China, Rumania, and the other countries of Eastern Europe, found that their standards of living, as measured by GDP per head, were falling relative to the market-orientated economies. This is explained in terms of the more efficient way in which a market economy will utilise resources.

Given that resources are scarce, they should not be wasted. They can be wasted in two ways. If more resources are used to produce an item than is strictly necessary, then this is a waste. In a planned economy there is no incentive to save resources. As long as the production target is met, the planner will be satisfied. In a market economy, the producer is trying to maximise profits. This requires reducing costs to a minimum, especially if there are other firms in competition. Thus a competitive firm will never use more resources than are necessary. It is said to achieve productive efficiency.

Resources will also be wasted if they are used to produce goods and services which are not the ones most required by consumers. In a planned economy, the only way that the planners can know which goods are required is by some form of guesswork, or via market research. This is both wasteful of resources and likely to be inaccurate. Thus planned economies are characterised by the production of surpluses of certain items and acute shortages of others. In a market economy the consumer is able to signal preference by spending money, which in turn affects the relative prices of goods and services. Goods which are more popular will increase in price. This will make these goods more profitable for producers to supply.

Goods which are unwanted will fall in price and producers will very quickly stop their production. Thus market economies are more likely to be allocatively efficient. Competition will ensure that, if the price which a person is prepared to pay for an item (which must reflect the marginal benefit received) exceeds the cost of producing an extra unit of the item (known as the marginal cost), then an extra item will be produced. Goods will be produced up to the point where marginal cost equals price. This is the technical condition necessary for allocative efficiency.

The freedom of choice which market economies offer has also been linked with the idea of freedom of choice in the political sphere. Hence the move towards a market economy has been accompanied by moves toward political democracy. Some people argue that the two are inextricably linked, and so some of the movement away from planned economies can be explained by the demands for political democracy which arose in many of the countries of Eastern Europe.

However market economies do suffer from several problems which require some form of government intervention; market forces cannot be allowed to operate in all areas of the economy. Thus market economies may fail to use resources efficiently if monopolies exist since monopolies may fail to be efficient, and still survive. Thus government must control or at least supervise monopolies. Externalities interfere with the efficient use of resources, since society may not benefit from the production of an item if it imposes severe external costs. Again government may interfere. Income distribution cannot be left to market forces, since this would imply that people who had no income or savings would perish. Thus the government must play a role in income redistribution, which again will involve interfering with individual freedom of choice.

The movement away from planned to market economies is in order to become more efficient. However some degree of central control will still be necessary to permit the examples of market failure to be overcome.

Topic two: theory of the firm

One popular question asked on this topic is usually about the advantages and disadvantages of monopoly and competition. The basic argument against monopoly is that it leads to productive and allocative inefficiency. Price exceeds marginal cost (allocatively inefficient) and costs need not be at a minimum (productive inefficiency). The argument in favour of monopoly depends upon the existence of economies of scale, which if they are substantial, will permit a monopolistic entity to produce at lower costs. This is linked with the concept of a natural monopoly, and the idea of a minimum efficient scale.

Other questions ask about the pricing behaviour of firms faced by different market structures, or simply ask for an analysis of the equilibrium positions of firms in different forms of competition.

Sample questions

❒ Is competition always preferable to monopoly?

Go over the ways in which competition ensures productive and allocative efficiency. The diagrammatic representation of the impact which monopolisation would have on a competitive industry is at Figure 12.3. Price would be higher (and above MC, and hence allocatively inefficient), and output would be lower. Supernormal profits can be earned in the long run, and so there is less incentive to operate at minimum average cost (hence not necessarily productively efficient). Consumers have a restricted choice of products.

The arguments in favour of monopoly rely on economies of scale. If an increase in scale reduces costs, shown by a declining long run average cost curve (Figure 12.4), then a natural monopoly exists if Minimum Efficient Scale is more than 50% of the total market. Competition would increase costs.

A pure monopoly is difficult to envisage since almost all products have some substitutes. Thus consumers cannot be ignored, eg British Rail has a monopoly of rail transport, but is in competition with other forms of transport. Thus one cannot always say that competition is preferable.

❒ Compare the price and output policies of a firm in perfect competition with firms in other market situations.

Firms in perfect competition do not have a pricing policy. They are price takers. Price is determined in the market (Figure 11.3). The output of the firm will be where profits are maximised, where MC = MR. In the short run firms may make super normal profits, but in the long run, the freedom of new firms to enter the market will reduce profits to normal and will force price down to the point of lowest average costs.

In monopoly firms can control their price or output. If they are concerned with profit maximisation, they will again produce where MC = MR. This will be at a lower output and higher price than the competitive firm (unless economies of scale exist), as pictured in Figure 12.3.

In oligopoly, firms will not engage in price competition because of the fear of retaliation (Figure 14.1). Prices will be set by the industry, but usually in excess of the competitive level, since firms in oligopoly can earn super normal profits. Non-price competition will be practised. Firms may collude or practice price leadership, in which case the industry will act as a monopoly.

In monopolistic competition, freedom of entry means that in the long-run prices will equate with average costs of production, although not at the lowest point of average cost. Thus prices will be higher than in competition. Output will be lower, since firms will not be able to operate at their optimum output (Figure 13.2).

❐ **Explain when it becomes uneconomic for a private firm to remain in business.**

Review the definition of normal profit. In the short run firms will remain in business if variable costs can be covered (Figure 11.4) This applies to all forms of market structure. If losses are made, in the long run some firms will leave the industry which will raise price. The firms that survive must be able to cover all their costs. If the firm is a monopoly, it must be able to increase its price to cover all costs or it will cease trading. Thus in the long run, survival depends on being able to earn at least normal profits. These will depend on the transfer earnings of the firm.

❐ **What economic factors would you consider to be most important in determining the price of carrots? a) in the long run? b) in the short run?**

Carrots (and most other primary products) are produced in a competitive market. Price will depend upon demand and supply. In the long run, firms in perfect competition can only earn normal profits. The price of carrots will be determined by the position of the lowest point on the average cost curve of firms in the industry (Figure 11.3). Thus in the long run it is supply factors (the costs of production) which determine the price. In the long run the supply curve is horizontal at the lowest point of the average cost curve. If something occurs to alter the long run costs, this will affect the long run price.

In the short run, price will be affected by any change in demand or supply. Thus any factors which lead to an increase in demand (Figure 5.3) will boost the price, and factors causing an increase in supply (Figure 5.4) will reduce the price. The cobweb model suggests that it may take a considerable time for the long run price to be re-established (Figure 7.4) and that prices may continue to fluctuate.

Specimen answer

❐ **How might the economic efficiency of an industry be affected by the presence of economies of scale? What is the importance of this for the privatisation of the electricity supply industry?**

Economic efficiency refers to making the best use of the economic resources available to an economy. This means that resources should not be wasted. Economic efficiency requires that resources (land, labour and capital) should be used so as to ensure productive and allocative efficiency. Productive efficiency requires that products are produced using the minimum possible resource. Allocative efficiency requires that the products which are produced should be the ones which confer most benefit to society. Both these types of efficiency will be achieved if there is perfect competition in the market. Competition will ensure that firms are forced to be productively efficient, and will produce at the lowest point on their average cost curves. They will also produce where marginal cost equals the price, which guarantees allocative efficiency.

Economies of scale refer to cost advantages which a large firm experiences over a smaller firm. These advantages may arise because of several factors, eg the ability to practice division of labour, the ability to attract better qualified staff, the ability to raise finance more cheaply, the ability to utilise machinery more fully, the ability to obtain economies in buying raw material, the ability to exercise marketing economies. These economies suggest that the long run average cost curve will fall as output increases (Figure 12.4). If long run costs fall as output expands, the industry will be characterised by larger and larger firms. Inevitably this implies fewer and fewer firms. It is possible that economies of scale may be so important that only a few, or perhaps only one, firm dominates the industry. Thus the industry will be characterised by oligopoly, or monopoly.

Firms in oligopoly and monopoly will not achieve allocative efficiency. Allocative efficiency requires that, if extra units of a product confer more benefit to society than they cost society to produce, then more of that product should be produced. This process should continue until the last unit produced confers the same benefit to society as it imposes costs on society. The price reflects the benefit which is obtained; and the marginal cost is the cost of producing the last unit. Hence allocative efficiency requires that price equals marginal cost. A monopoly will be equating marginal cost with marginal revenue, since this creates maximum profit. Because the demand curve is downward sloping, marginal revenue is always less than the price which is being charged. Hence in monopoly price always exceeds marginal cost and this is not allocatively efficient. This is shown below:

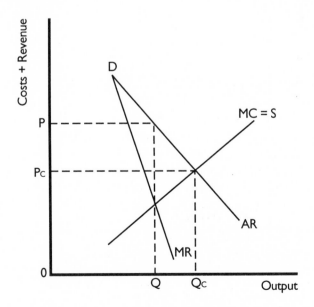

Profit maximisation occurs where MC = MR at output OQ. Price is given by the demand curve and is shown as OP. Price exceeds marginal cost. If this industry was in perfect competition, price would be OPc and output would be OQc. Price would equal marginal cost, since the marginal cost curve is the supply curve in perfect competition.

Firms in a non-competitive environment will also have less incentive to reduce costs, since they can make super normal profits, and the existence of economies of scale means that new firms are unable to enter the industry such that these profits may be sustained in the long run. This may permit the firm to survive even if it is operating at less than peak productive efficiency.

Electricity supply is normally thought of as an industry which has the characteristic of a natural monopoly. Electricity generation by coal-powered stations has large economies of scale, as does nuclear power. This suggests that small organisations will be unable to compete with existing producers.

Privatisation is designed to increase economic efficiency. In the case of a natural monopoly this depends upon the monopolistic entity responding to the desire to make profits by eliminating productive inefficiencies. Allocative efficiency would not be achieved, since equating price with marginal cost would entail running at a loss if economies of scale meant that long run average costs were falling. If average costs are falling, this must mean that marginal cost is below average cost. Thus putting price equal to marginal cost would mean that price was below average cost, and so total costs would exceed total revenue. This is shown below.

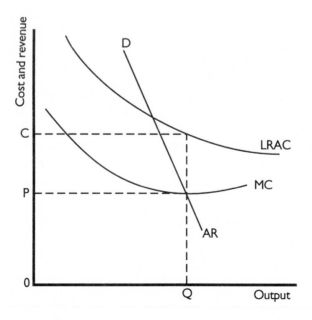

Allocative efficiency is at output OQ, but at this output total revenue is given as OP x OQ. Total cost is given by OC x OQ. Hence the area PCxOQ shows the losses made by the firm. If the firm is run by the public sector, this loss could be subsidised out of taxation, but it is impossible for it to be incurred by a private firm.

Thus if natural monopolies are privatised, they should be regulated to ensure that the firm does not use its monopoly power to raise price and profits too far above the economically efficient levels.

Topic three: wages

The usual questions either ask for an economic analysis of what determines wages, or why different groups receive different wages, or how various factors affect the labour market. The basic theoretical ingredient is the marginal productivity theory of wages.

Sample questions

❐ **What determines the wages earned by a particular group of workers?**

Wages, the price of labour, is determined by the forces of demand and supply. Supply is assumed to depend upon the wage rate. Higher wages will increase the supply of labour for a particular occupation. Demand depends upon the profit maximising decisions of employers. Workers will be hired up to the point where their marginal cost equals the marginal revenue they generate. The law of diminishing returns implies, that eventually, extra workers will display diminishing returns. Their marginal product will start to fall. The extra revenue generated by these workers will fall. Wages will be determined where demand equals supply (Figure 15.3).

Wages set by marginal productivity will differ for three reasons:

a) people differ, not everyone is capable of doing a particular occupation. The supply of labour will be restricted in those occupations
b) jobs differ, not all jobs will be equally attractive (non-pecuniary advantage) which will be reflected in the wage people are prepared to accept
c) people may not be able to enter certain labour markets.

Some wages are not set by market forces, e.g. workers in the public sector (teachers, nurses) and some top executives who set their own pay.

❐ **How might Trade Unions affect the labour market?**

Left to market forces, wages will be determined by demand and supply (Marginal productivity theory of wages). Unions are usually seen as attempting to increase wages. In the unionised sector this will normally reduce employment. Higher wages will reduce the demand for labour. The extent of the fall in employment will depend on the elasticity of demand for labour (Figure 15.4).

The price elasticity of demand for labour will depend upon: the ease of substituting capital for labour, the proportion of total costs represented by wages, the elasticity of demand for the product. These factors will vary from industry to industry. The greater the elasticity of demand, the greater the reduction in employment, the less the power of the Trade Union. Whether increases in wages can be sustained above the market level depends on the ability of Unions to prevent the excess supply of workers from exerting downward pressure on wages.

Wages will also be affected in the non-union sector (Figure 15.5).

☐ What will be the impact of the introduction of a statutory minimum wage?

The main points in this answer are the same as the question on Unions, since a minimum wage has the same effect of increasing the wage above the level set by the market. Thus, this too, depends on elasticity of demand.

Additional points concern the impact of a minimum wage on other wage rates and hence inflation, and the impact on aggregate demand.

Specimen answer

☐ Discuss the causes of the differences in the wages earned by people in different occupations.

Wages are normally seen as being determined by the forces of demand and supply. The demand for labour will depend upon the profitability of employing extra workers. The law of diminishing returns states that eventually returns to a variable factor will start to fall when it is used in conjunction with a fixed factor. Thus in the short run the marginal product of labour will start to fall after a certain level of employment is reached. This is shown below on the next page.

After 10 people are employed, the marginal product of extra workers, which is the extra output which additional workers are able to produce per week, begins to decline. Thus the eleventh worker adds 200 units of extra output, whilst the fifteenth worker only adds 120 units. Suppose that the product which these workers produce sells for £1 per unit. The marginal product in units now represents the value of their marginal product in pounds. This value is known as the marginal revenue product. Thus the fifteenth worker now adds £120 per week to the revenue of the firm. Suppose that the wage rate is £120 per week. The firm will employ 15 workers. Thus firms will employ workers up to the point where their marginal revenue product is equal to the wage. Thus the marginal revenue product curve is the demand curve for labour since it identifies the number of workers who will be employed at various wage rates. If the wage rose to £200 per week only 11 workers would be employed.

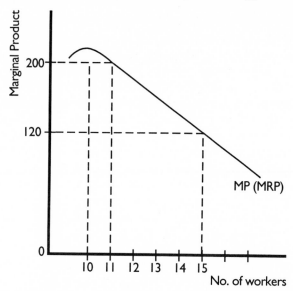

The supply of labour is determined by the number of people able and willing to work at various wage rates. An increase in wages is assumed to make work more attractive and thus to increase the supply of labour to any particular occupation. The demand and supply curves for a particular occupation is shown below.

The equilibrium wage will be OW. Wages will increase if there is an increase in the demand for labour or a fall in the supply. An increase in the demand for labour will come about if labour becomes more productive, or if the price of the product increases. Whether these higher wages will be

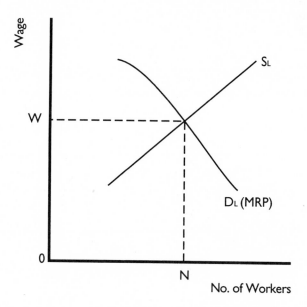

sustained depends upon whether new workers will be able to enter that particular labour market. If there are no barriers preventing new workers being able to enter that occupation, then the higher wages will simply attract workers from other occupations who will drive the wage back down. Thus long-term wage differentials must be due to factors which prevent workers from moving from low wage occupations into high wage occupations. This may be due to people not having the necessary ability, training, or education, or because existing workers put up barriers to entry in the form of minimum qualifications, physical characteristics, educational background. Additionally workers may not be attracted from other occupations if the work in question has some unpleasant aspects. Thus workers on North Sea oil rigs can earn a premium because of the hazardous nature of the job.

Thus the marginal productivity theory of wages suggests that workers are paid the value of their marginal product. If some occupations have a high marginal product, and there are factors preventing labour supply to the occupation expanding, wages in that occupation will be high. Thus accountants, solicitors, doctors could be thought as falling into this category. If there are no restrictions on labour entering an occupation, wages in that occupation will be at the average level. Wages will be lowest in occupations where the marginal product is low, and there is a large enough pool of workers prepared to accept jobs in that occupation at the low wage.

There will be some workers whose pay is not determined in the market place. Thus public sector employees will have their pay determined by government, and, although market forces cannot be ignored, in the short run wage differentials may appear. Similarly some executives appear to determine their own remuneration, and, although they may appeal to market forces to justify the salaries earned, it is often difficult to accept the justification.

Topic four: demand and supply, elasticities
Sample questions

❑ **What is meant by the term 'elasticity of demand' in economics? Why is the concept important to a) producers? b) government?**

Elasticity of demand refers to how demand responds to a change in some other variable. Various aspects of elasticity of demand, include: price elasticity of demand, income elasticity of demand, cross elasticity of demand. Producers will be affected because price elasticity determines the impact of price changes. Inelastic demand will mean that higher prices boost revenue. Price elastic demand suggests that lower prices will boost revenue. Price elasticity has implications for the practice of price discrimination. Income elasticity determines how demand will change as incomes vary, and is important for demand over time. Cross elasticity determines whether a commodity has close substitutes or complements, and how a firm will be affected by a change in other firms' prices.

Government will be affected because: price elasticity determines how much of an indirect tax is passed on to consumers, and how much sales will fall if a tax is imposed (Figure 27.1). This has implications for the amount of revenue raised. Cross elasticity will allow estimates to be made of the impact of taxes on one commodity on demand for another. Price elasticity has implications for the excess burden of a tax (Figure 27.3).

❐ **What factors will determine the price elasticity of demand for rail transport? What is the significance of this for the pricing of rail transport if it became privatised?**

This question involves a definition of price elasticity of demand (PED). PED is affected by availability of substitutes, proportion of income spent on the good. The more the number and closeness of substitutes, the larger the PED. Rail transport is in competition with other forms of transport: motor cars, buses, air travel. PED will vary depending on the ability to switch from rail to these other forms. At times when roads are very congested, road transport (cars and buses) will be a poor substitute. eg commuters into London. Competition will be greater on other routes and at other times.

The proportion of income spent on the good will affect PED. Thus companies may see transport as a small item of total costs, in which case it will have a low PED. For other groups (poor, elderly) it may represent a high proportion, implying a higher PED.

If privatised rail operators are interested in maximising profits, differing PEDs suggest that rail operators could practice price discrimination. Prices should be higher on routes with low PED and lower on routes with higher PED. The markets could be kept separate by time or by age. Thus in the rush hour when PED will be low, higher prices should be charged. Low income groups (pensioners, students) should face lower prices (Figure 12.5). If PED was ever found to be less than one, prices should be raised until demand became elastic, since higher prices will reduce demand, and raise revenue.

If the government wished to encourage rail usage, it could give a subsidy to the rail operators to reduce prices.

❐ **Price controls will always lead to less of a product being sold and are therefore never in the interests of the consumer. Discuss this proposition.**

Price controls lead to maximum or minimum prices. Minimum prices reduce demand but increase supply (Figure 5.6). Thus less will be sold. All consumers are worse off because they buy less at a higher price. Minimum prices lead to a loss of consumer surplus (Figure 8.10). Size of loss depends on price elasticity of demand. If demand is inelastic, there will be little impact.

Maximum prices will reduce price below equilibrium. This will increase demand but reduce supply. Less will be sold. Some consumers will benefit, those who can obtain the product at the lower price. Some will be worse off since they cannot obtain the product. It is impossible to judge whether the gains exceed the losses. If supply is price inelastic, consumers will be better off, since there will be a small drop in supply and more consumers will benefit from the lower price. If supply is elastic, more consumers will be unable to obtain the product.

Thus minimum prices cause a loss of welfare to consumers. Maximum prices cause gains and losses.

◻ Why do the prices of agricultural products fluctuate more than those of manufactured items?

Agricultural products are bought and sold in competitive markets. Prices determined by demand and supply. Supply of agricultural products are affected by weather, and thus variable. Manufactured products have prices determined by producers and are thus less volatile, especially if oligopoly exists.

The extent of price changes is determined by PED. If PED is low, changes in supply will have large impact on price, since a large change in price will be needed to reduce the excess demand.

Price change is also affected by Elasticity of supply. If supply is inelastic in the short run, prices will rise more for a given drop in supply, since extra output will not be supplied as prices rise. In manufacturing industry it is much easier to boost supply if prices start to rise; thus the price increase will be smaller.

Agricultural products may be affected by the cobweb. If a price change occurs, prices may continue to fluctuate if supply takes time to respond (Figure 7.4). This is often seen as a feature of agricultural output.

Specimen answer question

◻ "A bad harvest or a bloody war". Why should both these events improve the economic well-being of farmers?

The output of the farming industry is bought and sold in competitive markets. This makes farmers price takers in that they are forced to accept the ruling market price. This price will be determined by the forces of demand and supply in the market place. The amount of income which farmers receive will be determined by the amount of money which consumers spend on agricultural produce. The amount which consumers spend will vary as the price of agricultural produce alters. If the price of agricultural produce increases, the impact on total spending depends upon the concept of price elasticity of demand. Consider the diagram on tne next page.

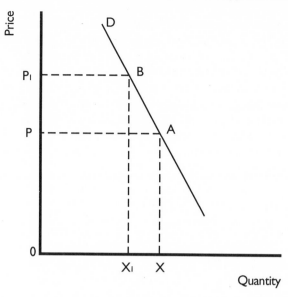

At a price of OP, farmers can sell OX. This gives a total income to farmers equal to the area OPAX. Suppose that some event occurs which causes the supply of agricultural produce to fall, for example a bad harvest. This is shown by the quantity coming onto the market falling to OX1. We shall assume that the supply has fallen because of a bad harvest, and that it will remain at this level. This implies that the short run elasticity of supply of agricultural produce is zero.

The fall in supply will cause the price to rise until demand has fallen to OX_1. This will happen when the price has risen to OP_1. The new expenditure of consumers, (and hence the income of farmers), will be given by the area OP_1BX_1. What will determine whether this area is larger or smaller than the original expenditure?

This will depend upon the value of price elasticity of demand. Price elasticity of demand (PED) is defined as the responsiveness of demand to a change in price and is measured by the expression:

PED = % change in quantity demanded

—————————————————————

% change in price.

If the value of this expression is less than one, this suggests that a 10% increase in price will be associated with a less than 10% change in demand.

Agricultural produce is normally assumed to have an inelastic demand. This suggests that demand does not respond a great deal to a change in price. The major factor which affects price elasticity of demand is the availability of substitutes. If there are close substitutes, then an increase in the price of a particular item will encourage consumers to switch to an alternative. If a bad harvest has a damaging effect upon all foodstuffs, it is not possible for consumers to switch to any other products, unless imports are included. Thus the PED for agricultural products is low. This means that any fall in supply will increase the amount spent by consumers and hence boost farmers' incomes. Suppose that supply fell by 10% because of the bad harvest, and that the PED for agricultural products is 0.5. The fall in supply will create an excess demand which will cause the price to rise. Price will continue rising until demand has fallen enough to eliminate all of the excess demand. In order for demand to fall by 10%, price must rise by 20%. If farmers are selling 10% less, but are receiving 20% higher prices, the amount of money they will receive, which is their income, will increase.

In the diagram below, the quantity coming onto the market falls from 100 units to 90 units (10%). The original price was £1. If PED equals 0.5, then price will rise by 20% to reduce demand by 10%, thus the new price is shown as £1.20. At the original equilibrium total expenditure was £100. After the fall in supply the expenditure rises to £108. Farmers will receive more income for selling a smaller output.

A war will have a similar impact. During war time domestic food production is often disrupted, and imports of food may be difficult. Thus the supply of food will fall and food prices will rise, giving the same result as shown above. This is one reason why food prices are often controlled during war time, to prevent some consumers from being unable to afford food. This usually requires some form of direct rationing to allow food to be distributed more evenly.

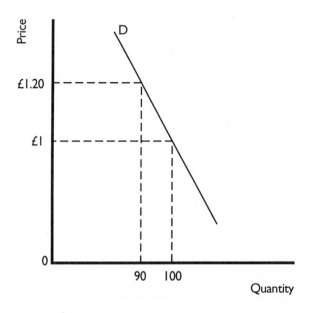

Topic five: consumer theory
Sample questions

❏ **Why do economists assume that a demand curve slopes downwards? Under what circumstances will this assumption be false?**

A change in price has two effects: an income effect and a substitution effect. A substitution effect always works in favour of the good whose price has fallen (marginal utility analysis and equilibrium of consumer). An income effect depends on whether the good is an inferior good or a normal good. If an inferior good, a lower price will boost income, which will tend to reduce demand. If an income effect of an inferior good exceeds the substitution effect, the demand curve will slope upwards. Both effects can be shown by indifference curves (Figure 8.8). The demand curve can be derived (Figure 8.9).

❏ **Under what circumstances will a consumer be in equilibrium when allocating his/her income between alternative products? How will this position be disturbed by an increase in the consumer's income?**

Consumers are assumed to want to maximise utility. Diminishing marginal utility suggests that, as more of a product is bought, extra units of the product confer less and less utility to the consumer (Figure 8.1). Consumers will not buy beyond the point where MU = Price. If income is insufficient to achieve MU = Price for all products, consumers will try and obtain the same utility for the last unit of money spent on each product. Thus it is in equilibrium when:

$$\frac{MUa}{Pa} = \frac{MUb}{Pb} = \frac{MUc}{Pc}.....$$

An increase in income will allow more of all goods to be bought; still , it is necessary t to ensure that ratios are equal in new equilibrium. A problem with MU analysis is that it cannot deal with income effects.

Utility maximisation can also be shown on indifference curves. Consumers will allocate income to reach highest indifference curve (Figure 8.5). Increases in income will shift budget line (Figure 8.6) and may increase demand for both goods. If a good is an inferior good, an increase in income might reduce demand. The result depends on slope of indifference curves.

❏ **What is the purpose of consumer theory? Does it matter that consumers may be unaware of the concepts of marginal utility and indifference curves?**

Theories may have two functions, to explain behaviour or to predict behaviour. Consumer theory tries to do both. Explanation lies in the idea of maximising utility and the need to equate ratios of MU and price for all goods. This is an attempt to rationalise a process which consumers carry out subconsciously. This theory also allows predictions to be made as to how consumers will react to changes in prices. If the predictions work, then the theory has worked and is therefore valid.

Indifference curve analysis again tries to describe what must occur if consumers maximise utility, allowing income and substitution effects to be isolated and understood. They are not real predictions since results depend on the assumptions made about the slope of indifference curves. But they can show different predictions of different assumptions concerning preferences.

Theories do not need to be realistic in order to predict accurately. Predictive content may excuse unrealistic theories.

❐ **How does the presence of advertising affect the equilibrium of the consumer?**

Advertising is an attempt to boost demand. Consumers are said to be in equilibrium when ratios of MU to price are equal for all goods. Advertising is an attempt to increase the perceived MU which consumers obtain from a particular good. If successful, and MU rises, to maintain equilibrium the consumer will increase purchases, reducing MU (law of diminishing MU), and restoring equality of ratios.

In terms of indifference curve analysis, advertising is an attempt to alter the slope of the indifference curve. The curve will become flatter with respect to the advertised product. The MRS of the advertised product will have fallen. The consumer will need more of the unadvertised product in order to be compensated for giving up a given amount of the advertised product. This will change the equilibrium and cause more of the advertised product to be bought.

Responding to advertising is a rational response to changes in the perceived utility of a particular product.

Specimen answer

❐ **Explain the conditions necessary for a consumer to be in equilibrium when faced with a given income and goods which have different prices. How will this equilibrium be altered by an increase in the price of one good, and by an increase in the general price level.**

The consumer is assumed to be interested in maximising utility. The consumer will be in equilibrium when he is allocating his income in such a way as to obtain the maximum amount of utility from his expenditure. It is normally assumed that, as the consumer obtains more of one product, extra units of that product will yield less and less utility. This is known as the law of diminishing marginal utility. It is this proposition which allows an equilibrium to be obtained.

The consumer will be in equilibrium when he is unable to re-allocate his expenditure to bring him more utility. This implies that the last unit of money spent on each product must yield the same amount of utility. This is because, if this was not the case, units of money could be transferred from the product that gave least utility to the product that gave the most, thereby increasing the amount of utility obtained by the consumer. The amount of utility obtained from the last unit of money spent on a product is given by the ratio of marginal utility to price: MU/P. Thus if the last unit bought of product A gave 50 units of utility, and its price was 25p, this would give 2 units of utility for a penny. If the price of product B was 30p and the last unit bought gave 90 units of utility, the last penny spent on B yields 3 units of utility. Thus if we assume that products A and B could be infinitely divisible, the consumer's utility would increase by spending a penny less on A (losing 2 units of utility) and an extra penny on B (gaining 3 units of utility). The consumer will be in equilibrium, and will have no incentive to alter his purchases, only if the ratio of marginal utilities to price is the same for all products ie

$$\frac{MUa}{Pa} = \frac{MUb}{Pb} = \frac{MUc}{Pc}.....$$

If the price of product A was to increase, this would disturb the equilibrium.

In order to restore the equilibrium position, the consumer would need to raise the MU of A (or reduce the MU of other products). The MU of A will increase if the consumer buys less of it, because of the concept of diminishing marginal utility. Conversely the MU of other products will reduce if the consumer buys more. Thus the restoration of the equilibrium position will be brought about by a fall in the demand for product A whose price has increased and an increase in the demand for the other products which are now relatively cheaper. This is known as the substitution effect of a change in relative prices. As well as a substitution effect, the fall in the price of A will also have an income effect.

If the consumer spent a large proportion of his income on product A, the increase in price will have left the consumer with less income if he continues to buy roughly the same amount. This reduced spending power will cause the consumer to change his purchases of all goods. The impact on product A will depend upon whether the product is an inferior good or a normal good. An inferior good is one where the consumer buys the product because of an income constraint which prevents him from buying superior products.

The reduced purchasing power brought about by the increase in the price of A might force the consumer to buy less of some more expensive product and more of A, even though its price has risen, since the reduced purchasing power means that the consumer can only afford to buy A rather than its superior substitutes, even though these substitutes are now relatively cheaper. If product A is a normal good, the reduced purchasing power will cause less of it to be bought.

If there is a rise in the general price level there will be no substitution effect because relative prices are unaltered, and so the ratios are still being satisfied. However the increase in all prices will still have an income effect. In fact the impact on the consumer will be the same as if the consumer had experienced a reduction in income. Nothing has changed to affect the relative attractiveness of different products, but the consumer will be unable to continue purchasing the same quantities, assuming that the consumer was spending all his income in the first place. This situation can be analysed using indifference curves.

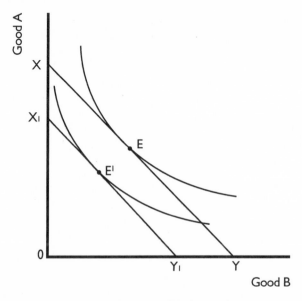

The diagram represents the initial equilibrium of the consumer with his budget constraint being given by the line XY. Equilibrium is at point E. If the price of both goods increases by the same proportion, the budget line will shift to position X_1Y_1. The new equilibrium is shown as E'. The slope of the budget line reflects the relative price of the two goods and so is not affected by an increase in the general price level which affects both goods. In the diagram, both goods are shown as normal, since the demand for both will fall. If the indifference curves were as shown in the diagram on the next page, the demand for product A is shown as falling whilst the demand for B increases. Product B is an inferior good.

Thus the equilibrium of a consumer will be affected by both income and substitution effects if faced with a change in relative prices, but will only be affected by an income effect if all prices rise because of an increase in the general price level, assuming that all prices rise by the same amount.

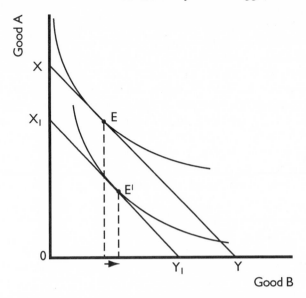

Topic six: money and monetary policy

The are various aspects of money which are examined:

a) questions concerning the theoretical way in which money affects the economy. Often this is split into Keynesian and Monetarist views, although this distinction is becoming very old fashioned

b) questions concerning the forms which money may take, and the ways in which the government may control the supply of money

c) questions concerning the impact of monetary policy on the economy.

❑ **What is meant by the demand for money? Discuss the significance of alternative views of the demand for money for the impact on the economy of a change in the supply of money.**

The demand for money is the amount of wealth that people wish to hold in a liquid form. Keynes suggested there would be three motives for holding money: the transactions demand, the precautionary demand, and the speculative demand. The first two depend on income, and consider money as a medium of exchange. The speculative demand depends on the rate of interest, and considers money as a store of value.

The demand for money is shown as a declining function of the rate of interest (Figure 25.1). The slope depends on the interest elasticity of the demand for money. The rate of interest is determined by the interaction of the demand and supply of money (Figure 25.2). An increase in the supply of money will reduce the rate of interest, because the excess money will be spent on financial assets (bonds). Extent of the fall depends on elasticity. Fall in the rate of interest boosts aggregate demand. Size of boost depends on how aggregate demand responds to lower interest rates.

Monetarists stress that the speculative demand is less important;, therefore, the demand for money curve is very steep. The demand for money depends primarily on income. An increase in money supply will create an excess supply, which will be spent directly on goods and services, or cause a large change in the rate of interest. Both will have a bigger impact on aggregate demand. Thus demand will respond more directly to an increase in the money supply. Excess money will be spent, due to the constant velocity of circulation (quantity theory of money). If interest rates affect the demand for money, velocity will alter as people change their speculative holdings.

The Keynesian link is indirect. Monetarists are more direct and powerful.

❐ What is meant by the supply of money? Why are there more than one definition of the money supply?

Money is any asset which performs the functions of money: medium of exchange (primary function), store of value, standard for deferred payments, unit of account. Primarily it must be generally acceptable as a means of payment. The supply of money is the total value of all the assets which have been classed as fulfilling these functions.

There are various forms of assets in which wealth can be held. Money raises the concept of liquidity. Some assets perform some functions, some perform others. Many assets can act as a medium of exchange: cash, current account (via cheques), any other account which can be used by writing a cheque. Other assets are easily transformed into liquid form eg deposit accounts.

Measurement of money supply gives a measure of the purchasing power in the economy. Which assets give this measure? It depends on the degree of liquidity.

In the UK there are two main definitions: M0 (narrow money), notes and coins and bankers deposits with the Bank of England. These represents perfectly liquid assets which can be used as a medium of exchange. The M4 (broad money) is M0 plus accounts with banks and building societies. These are less liquid, but still represent potential purchasing power.

In advanced economies there are many forms of financial assets which fulfill roles of medium of exchange and store of value. There is no one accepted definition of money supply. Thus the definition has changed and will continue to change as other assets become used as a medium of exchange or as a liquid store of value.

❐ What are the ways in which the government may attempt to control the money supply and what problems might prevent such attempts from being successful?

First there are problems of defining the money supply. One major factor in the increase in money supply is the extension of bank lending, for which banks require excess liquidity. There are various methods of control:

- Open market operations (selling government stock). This is linked with the concept of over funding. It also directly reduces bank deposits.
- Special deposits. These reduce the liquidity of the commercial banks, thereby reducing their ability to extend credit. Banks usually have excess liquidity and can still expand credit. Credit creation is the most profitable bank activity. Alternatively special deposits may act as a financial penalty on banks if they extend too much credit. Banks may create new forms of credit to avoid controls.
- Monetary base control. This is done to reduce the amount of notes and coins, again reducing the liquidity of the banking system. This strategy would make interest rates volatile, and might cause problems with bank liquidity.
- Interest rates. Increased rates will reduce the demand for money, thereby reducing the demand for bank credit. This is the most popular and effective method.

Banks always have incentive to avoid controls. They create new forms of money, credit cards, etc.. Reduction in use of cash relieves problems of liquidity.

◻ **Trace out the ways in which monetary policy might affect the economy.**

Define monetary policy. This would include an analysis of the impact of an increase in interest rates, which would affect aggregate demand through its four components:

- Consumption reduced, because; savings increase, debt repayments increase, reducing spending power, house prices may fall, reducing wealth
- Investment reduced, because the opportunity cost of investment increased. This may have long-run consequences for economic growth
- Government expenditure. Little impact although debt servicing will rise, which may put pressure on other forms of expenditure
- Exports reduced, because higher interest rates will boost the value of the exchange rate, with exports becoming cheaper, imports more expensive. This might increase inflation (higher import prices)

One impact of the control of the money supply will be its affect on the rate of interest. This may also directly reduce bank lending if government can control credit creation. Reduced credit will reduce aggregate demand.

Thus contractionary monetary policy will reduce aggregate demand, increase unemployment, reduce demand inflation, improve balance of payments and reduce economic growth.

Specimen answer

☐ **What do you understand by 'monetary policy'? How has monetary policy changed in the UK since 1979?**

Monetary policy consists of policies designed to control the cost or availability of credit. That is, it is designed to alter the rate of interest or to alter the supply of money in the economy. The authorities attempt to control the supply of money by restricting the ability of the commercial banks to lend money to their customers, since this is the major way in which the money supply increases. There are two definitions of the money supply which can be targetted by the government. Narrow money (M0) consists of mainly notes and coins in circulation, and in theory this must be under government control since the Bank of England has a monopoly on printing bank notes. However the commercial banks can always obtain notes and coins if they become illiquid since the Bank of England would never allow the commercial banks to be unable to honour demand for cash. Broad money (M4) consists of narrow money plus all bank and building society deposits. Changes in these mainly come about when people borrow from the banks or the building societies. Hence control of broad money is in effect control of bank lending. This can be attempted through a variety of means.

The Bank of England might try and reduce the liquidity of the commercial banks to prevent them from having sufficient liquidity to extend credit and to create deposit money. However as mentioned above, the Bank of England will always act as lender of last resort to boost liquidity.

The commercial banks may have a financial penalty imposed in the form of special deposits which are monies deposited with the Bank of England paying no interest, if they lend more than the authorities would like. However, the commercial banks always have an incentive to avoid such measures because lending money is their most profitable activity. Thus new forms of credit may come into operation to avoid the penalty. This suggests that the supply of money is demand determined since the commercial banks will always be able and prepared to meet any demands for credit. Thus the most effective way of controlling the supply of money is to control its demand. This can be achieved by using the other instrument of monetary policy, the rate of interest. The Bank of England can affect the rate of interest by forcing the money market to borrow money. This can be achieved through Open Market Operations whereby the Bank sells government debt, removing liquidity from the financial system. When the Bank is asked to lend money to restore liquidity, it can raise its interest rate which will increase all other interest rates in the economy. When interest rates rise, it becomes more expensive to borrow money and the demand for bank lending will reduce. Thus the money supply will stop expanding. Open market operations may be used on their own to take money out of the banking system, thus reducing the money supply.

Since 1979 the approach to monetary policy has switched from attempting to control the supply of money directly to controlling it via the rate of interest. The problem of targetting and controlling the money supply was made worse by the inability to agree on an accepted definition of the money supply. In 1979 a definition known as M3 was targetted, which was the current broad money definition, minus building society deposits. Once this became targeted it became uncontrollable and also ceased to be related to the level of spending in the economy. This gave rise to Goodhart's Law, which states that any variable which becomes the target for control will cease to be related to the activity which it is being controlled to influence. The reason given for this is the incentive which the commercial banks have to avoid any controls. Thus, even if certain forms of money are controlled, the banking system will allow expenditure to continue by extending credit in other forms.

In the 1980s M3 was abandoned as a target and was replaced by narrow money M0. This still proved an unreliable indicator of spending, and the government finally abandoned control of the money supply and instead began to control the rate of interest. This was partly due to the impact of the rate of interest on the exchange rate, since membership of the ERM meant that monetary policy had to be directed at maintaining the exchange rate at its required level. In a fixed exchange rate system the government cannot carry out an independent monetary policy, and so the interest rate policy which was implemented had little to do with controlling the domestic economy, and instead was directed at keeping the exchange rate at its required level.

Since leaving the ERM, the UK government has established an inflation target and appears to be using interest rates as a weapon for regulating aggregate demand to keep within the inflation target. Thus interest rates are once again the dominant aspect of monetary policy.

Topic seven: fiscal policy and taxation

Topics include:
a) the incidence of taxation
b) the PSBR and its significance
c) taxation and the supply of labour
d) desirable properties of taxes.

Sample questions

❑ **Examine how the impact of a tax on a particular commodity will be affected by elasticities of demand and supply.**

In a competitive market, a commodity tax will shift the supply curve vertically upward by the amount of the tax (Figure 27.1). Price elasticity of demand (define) will determine how much the price increases, thereby determining the extent to which the tax is paid by the consumer or the producer. An inelastic demand will cause the price to rise more than if demand is elastic.

Elasticity of supply also affects this result. An inelastic supply will cause prices to rise by less, since there will be less impact on quantity supplied. If supply is perfectly elastic, all of the tax will be paid by the consumer.

Thus price elasticities have implications for the consumer, the producer and for sales. Government will be affected because price elasticities of demand will affect tax revenues. If demand is elastic, tax revenue will be lower, and more consumer surplus will be lost (Figure 27.3). Cross elasticity of demand will determine the impact on other commodities of an increase in price of the taxed commodity.

☐ What factors will determine the size of the PSBR? Is the size of the PSBR of economic significance?

Define the PSBR. The PSBR will be affected by any changes in tax revenues or government spending. These may be discretionary or non-discretionary.

- Discretionary: Government may decide to cut taxes or boost government spending to increase aggregate demand. This is usually done if the economy is in recession. It is known as deficit financing if it pushes the PSBR into deficit.
- Non-discretionary: the level of activity in the economy will affect the PSBR. A recession will automatically boost spending on benefits and cut tax revenues, thereby increasing the PSBR (Figure 26.1).

The significance of the PSBR depends on the cause of the deficit and the need to finance it. If deficit is cyclical (caused by non-discretionary changes), its significance is reduced.

The need to finance the deficit is met in two ways; borrowing off the public or borrowing off the commercial banks. Borrowing off the public will put pressure on interest rates to rise, may crowd out private spending, or increase the exchange rate and crowd out exports. Borrowing off banks will expand the money supply, a practice which is sometimes seen as inflationary.

The PSBR will increase the size of the National Debt, which will increase future interest payments by the government.

☐ How might a reduction in income tax affect the level of unemployment and the level of inflation in the economy?

There are two mechanisms by which to understand this, via aggregate demand and aggregate supply. A reduction in income tax might cause aggregate demand to increase. A disposable income increase should boost consumer spending. Impact depends on the nature of the Consumption function and the importance of permanent income as a determinant of consumption. Higher spending will reduce unemployment. Lower unemployment will increase pressure on wages and prices to rise. This is shown by the Phillips Curve (Figure 31.1). Expansionary effects would be temporary as the higher inflation eroded the value of money and reduced aggregate demand.

On the other hand, aggregate supply might increase. If lower income tax increases the incentive to work, voluntary unemployment might fall. (Depends on income and substitution effects). The increased labour supply will put pressure on wages to fall. Employment will rise and pressure on inflation would reduce. The Phillips Curve would shift inwards. This effect would be permanent. Both mechanisms could be shown via aggregate demand and supply curves. (Figure 33.4).

❐ What are the desirable properties of a good tax? Is income tax a good tax?

Taxes are necessary to finance government expenditure, to redistribute income or to affect the allocation of resources.

Taxes are judged against the criteria of equity and efficiency. Equity refers to fairness. There are two approaches; ability to pay and benefit.

- Ability to pay is normally related to income, although other indicators are possible. Income tax can be made as progressive, or as regressive as desired to achieve whatever equity considerations are required
- The benefit approach suggests that taxes should relate to the benefit people derive from the expenditure. This is closer to a price mechanism. Income taxes do not satisfy the benefit approach.

Efficiency refers to various aspects of taxation; taxes should be easy and convenient to collect, and provide government with a predictable source of revenue. Income taxes satisfy most of these requirements. Efficiency also relates to minimising the excess burden of taxation (Figure 27.3). Income taxes cause no distortion between commodities and thus seem efficient. However they may cause a distortion between work and leisure. Increased income tax might increase voluntary unemployment, or reduce the work effort of people in employment. These depend on the relative strengths of income and substitution effects. The disincentive effect is greater if marginal rates of tax are higher, since these affect substitution effect at the margin. Average rate of tax determines income effect. The evidence on disincentive effects is mixed.

Theoretically all taxes should have the same impact on work incentives, but income tax is more noticeable (A possible advantage?).

Specimen answer

☐ **Compare the relative merits of direct and indirect taxation. Explain the trends which have taken place in the relative importance of these taxes in the UK since 1979.**

Direct taxation refers to taxes for which formal and effective incidence are deemed to be the same. Formal incidence refers to who has the legal obligation to pay the tax to the government. The effective incidence refers to who actually pays the tax. Income tax is a direct tax since the income earner has the obligation to pay the tax and he/she is normally assumed to be unable to pass the tax on to any other member of society. Other examples of direct taxes include corporation tax, national insurance contributions and capital gains tax.

Indirect taxes are intended to be passed on to other members of society. Thus VAT is paid by the producer/retailer, but is added onto the consumer's final bill, and so the effective incidence falls on the consumer, depending upon the relative elasticities of demand and supply. Other examples of indirect taxes are taxes on alcohol and tobacco and duty on petrol.

Taxes are normally judged against various criteria, especially the criteria of fairness and efficiency.

Fairness refers to the fact that it is generally accepted that taxes should display vertical equity. This implies that people in different circumstances should be treated differently by the tax system. This is often linked to the idea that taxes should be based on the ability to pay. If income is taken as an indicator of the ability to pay, vertical equity is usually taken to imply that people on higher incomes should pay more tax. If the amount paid in tax as a proportion of income increases as income rises, taxes are said to be progressive. If the proportion paid in tax stays the same, the tax is proportional; and if the proportion paid in tax falls as income rises, the tax is defined as regressive. It is generally accepted that taxes should not be regressive. Direct taxes are normally related to income, and take income as the tax base. Hence rates of tax can be levied to satisfy any ability-to-pay criteria.

Indirect taxes are normally taxes on expenditure, and since people on lower incomes tend to spend a larger proportion of their income, they will pay a larger proportion in tax. Thus indirect taxes tend to be regressive. This will be reinforced if the indirect taxes are levied at the same rate on all items of expenditure.

Another possible criteria of equity is the idea that taxes should be based on the benefit which the taxpayer receives from the expenditure which the tax finances. Taxes which fall into this category are the road fund tax, and the television licence. Whether these are defined as direct or indirect is unclear.

Efficiency criteria relate to the way in which the tax affects the workings of the economy. The basic economic problem concerns making the best use of the economy's resources. The tax system should interfere as little as possible with the best use of resources. In the absence of any taxation it is usually assumed that a competitive economy will generate an optimum allocation of resources. If the tax system distorts this allocation, this may be inefficient.

Indirect taxes distort the choices between products which are taxed at higher and lower rates. Consumers will be encouraged to buy products with low or zero rates of tax, and discouraged from buying highly taxed items. There may be circumstances in which such a distortion might be desirable. If products impose external costs on society, the imposition of an indirect tax will improve the use of resources. Other distortions will be minimised if the rate of taxation is the same on all products. Thus indirect taxes will be more efficient, other things being equal, if the same rate of tax is imposed on all products.

Direct taxes, which tend to be taxes on income, either corporate or individual, do not distort choices between products, but may distort the choice between work and leisure. Thus it is often argued that income tax is a disincentive to work, and so a switch from income tax to indirect taxation would improve work incentives, and so improve the use of resources in the economy. Evidence on the incentive effects of income tax is inconclusive.

Other desirable properties of taxation are that taxes should be difficult to avoid and easy to collect. The first point is important since it allows government to predict its tax revenues, whilst the second is connected with efficiency. It is inefficient to use more resources than are necessary when collecting taxes since resources are scarce. This includes the time and effort spent by the taxpayer as well as the tax collector. One criticism of VAT is that it places a burden upon the taxpayer, especially small businesses, who need to fill out tax returns.

Although both direct and indirect taxes have advantages and disadvantages, it is only possible to come to a conclusion as to which is preferable if one can decide as to which criterion is most important.

Since 1979 there has been a shift in the emphasis between direct and indirect taxes in the UK. Income tax has been reduced as a proportion of total taxation, and indirect taxes, especially VAT, have increased. This change has been a deliberate act of policy by government.

The government has decided that high rates of income tax are a disincentive to effort and have therefore reduced the marginal and average rates of income tax. In order to maintain tax revenue this has meant an increase in indirect taxes, especially VAT. This has meant that the overall tax system is now less progressive than it was in 1979, but the government has argued that the boost which lower income taxes give to the economy in terms of improved work incentives, will allow all sections of society to become better off, and so offset the increased tax burden on lower income households. One further rationale for the change is that income tax is a much more noticeable tax than VAT. It is doubtful whether people appreciate the total amount which they pay in VAT and so opposition to higher rates of VAT will not be as strong as for income tax which impacts directly onto disposable income.

It is often argued that indirect taxes give increased freedom of choice to individuals since they receive more disposable income if income tax is reduced. This is an invalid argument. Taxes cannot be thought of as voluntary unless a distortion of choice is classed as voluntary. Raising the price of all commodities by 10% will have the same impact as reducing disposable income by 10%. The only difference is that income which is saved will escape taxation until it is spent.

Thus the argument concerning the relative merits of direct and indirect taxes cannot be resolved by economic analysis. The increased emphasis on indirect taxation since 1979 can be explained as the government placing more emphasis on the incentive effects of lower income tax, and ignoring the regressive nature of VAT.

Topic eight: unemployment and inflation

Unemployment and inflation are often linked together because the Phillips curve suggests that lower unemployment will be associated with higher inflation. Sometimes the topics are treated separately. This section gives examples of both types of question.

Sample questions

❐ **What is meant by the Natural Rate of Unemployment? What steps can a government take to reduce the natural rate?**

The Natural Rate of unemployment is the level of unemployment when the labour market is in equilibrium, when the number of people able and willing to work just matches the available jobs (demand equals supply). There is no pressure on wages to change because of excess demand or supply of labour. Unemployment consists of frictional unemployment plus people unable or unwilling to work (Figure 30.1) The Natural Rate is also the level of unemployment where the Phillips curve cuts through the bottom axis, generating zero inflationary pressures (Figure 31.1).

The Natural Rate can be affected by policies aimed at the various categories of unemployment: Voluntary (reduce benefits, cut income tax), Structural (make labour more mobile, retraining and education), Frictional (improve efficiency of labour market). These are known as supply side measures. They will not be affected by increasing aggregate demand.

❐ **Is it possible to reduce unemployment without increasing inflation?**

The Phillips curve suggests that unemployment and inflation are linked (Figure 31.1). This is because the level of unemployment is taken as an indicator of the excess demand or supply of labour. If aggregate demand rises and Keynesian unemployment falls, some labour markets will experience excess demands for labour, raising wages. This is the mechanism behind the Phillips curve.

Inflationary pressure can be avoided if unemployment can be reduced without increasing the demand for labour, but instead by boosting the supply (eg Figure 30.2). This requires the measures seen in the previous answer. Impact will be to shift the Phillips curve inwards, allowing a fall in unemployment with no inflation.

Also a reduction in inflationary expectations might permit unemployment to fall and inflation to remain static.

❏ **Compare the relative costs of unemployment and inflation.**

Itemise the costs of unemployment; exchequer costs, output costs, social costs. The first can easily be quantified. The second can be guessed; the third is subjective.

Costs of inflation – international competitiveness, distribution of income, menu costs, interferes with the price mechanism, political instability, and dangers of hyper-inflation. All are difficult to quantify.

Comparison is difficult; choice a matter of political judgement.

❏ **Inflation is always and everywhere a monetary phenomenon. Explain what is meant by this statement.**

Define inflation. There are two views of inflation, demand pull or cost push. Demand inflation is associated with increased demand for goods causing increased demand for labour, raising wages, and hence prices. Monetarists would see any increase in demand as resulting from an increase in the money supply. This is due to the belief that the velocity of money is constant, and so an increase in money supply is necessary to allow the demand to increase. Hence an increase in the money supply will boost demand and put pressure on prices.

If inflation is fuelled by cost push pressures, prices may rise. If prices rise, and the supply of money does not, this creates an excess demand for money. This would put pressure on interest rates to rise (Figure 25.2). This would reduce demand and create unemployment, putting pressure on wages to fall, reducing inflationary pressure. If prices rise, aggregate demand will fall (Figure 33.3). This will create stagflation (Figure 33.5). Thus if money supply does not expand higher prices will reduce demand and create unemployment which will reduce inflationary pressure. Thus an increase in the money supply is necessary to allow inflation to continue.

❏ **What explanations can you give for the increase in unemployment which has occurred in the UK since 1979?**

Examine the various categories of unemployment and suggest reasons why these categories might have increased.

- Frictional unemployment: The benefit system might have encouraged more people to spend a longer period of time looking for work
- Voluntary unemployment: Again the benefit system might have encouraged people to remain unemployed. High rates of income tax might make work less well paid and also make unemployment more attactive
- Structural unemployment: The process of change in industry has been rapid. New skills have been required. Occupational immobility might explain much of an increase in unemployment. Industries in certain regions have declined, causing regional problems.
- Keynesian unemployment. Since 1979 a major priority has been the control of inflation. This is best achieved by controlling demand, especially via restrictive monetary policies as seen in the early 1980s. These may have increased Keynesian unemployment.

Additional points; there might now be increased numbers seeking employment, and employers may be substituting capital for labour. Both these should have put pressure on wages to fall. If wages remain high, this might encourage increased mechanisation.

Specimen answer

❐ **Examine the possible causes of inflation. Why has the control of inflation proved so difficult?**

Inflation is defined as any increase in the general level of prices, but more usually the term is given to a situation where prices rise continually. Economists identify two major explanations for inflation: demand pull and cost push theories.

Demand pull inflation is said to exist when prices rise because of an increase in aggregate demand. Monetarists would explain the increase in aggregate demand in terms of an increase in the money supply. An increase in aggregate demand may boost prices through two mechanisms. First firms may take the opportunity to raise prices in order to increase profit margins. This will increase the profitable maximising output of the firm, and so the firm will also try and increase output. Secondly, firms may respond to the higher demand by simply increasing output, which will increase the demand for labour. Thus an increase in aggregate demand may raise prices directly, but will also be associated with an increase in the demand for labour. It is this increase in the demand for labour that most economists see as generating inflationary pressure.

This link between the demand for labour and prices has been explored by the Phillips Curve. This was a relationship discovered in 1958 by A.W. Phillips between unemployment and the rate of change in wages.

This showed that if unemployment fell below a certain level (5.5% according to Phillips), wages would rise. The more unemployment fell below this level, the faster wages would rise. This was explained as the

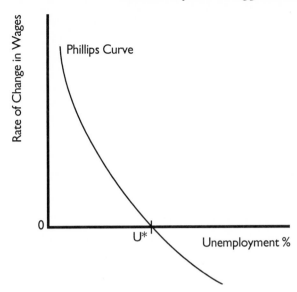

lower levels of unemployment being associated with excess demand for labour in various labour markets. This would put pressure on wages to rise in those markets. As unemployment fell further, more and more labour markets would experience greater and greater excess demand, and wages would rise even faster. If one accepts that wage increases are likely to be passed on as price increases, the Phillips Curve can be reinterpreted as a relationship between unemployment and price inflation. The level of unemployment shown as U* is known as the natural rate of unemployment, and is associated with equilibrium in the labour market, such that there is no pressure on wages or prices to alter.

This analysis would suggest that the control of inflation simply requires control of unemployment via control of aggregate demand. The problem is complicated by the effect of expectations on the Phillips Curve.

Suppose that in the diagram on the next page, unemployment falls to U_1, and this generates wage and price inflation of 5%. If unemployment stays at U_1 for any length of time, people may come to expect inflation of 5%. This means that in the next time period, wage and price increases of 5% will be built into people's expectations. Since employers expect prices to rise by 5%, they will grant wage increases of 5% simply to keep real wages constant. If unemployment stays at U_1, and so labour shortages persist, the employer might have to grant higher wage increases to prevent workers from moving elsewhere. Thus U_1 might be associated with wage increases of 10%, 5% to compensate for the expected inflation and 5% due to the excess demand for labour. This has the effect of shifting the Phillips Curve to the position shown as PC_1. Even if unemployment was to revert to the level U*, because of inflationary expectations, inflation would stay at 5%. In order to eliminate inflation, unemployment would have to rise to U_2, so that, even though 5% inflation was expected, the amount of unemployment

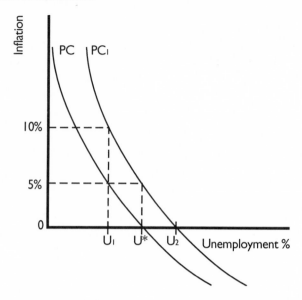

created sufficient excess supply of labour that employers need grant a
zero increase in wages.

This explains why inflation, once it becomes expected, becomes very
difficult to eradicate. If people can be convinced that inflation will be low,
their actions will assist in reducing inflation. If people expect inflation to
rise, it will be increasingly difficult to reduce inflation. It is possible that
people may even anticipate inflation if they anticipate an increase in
aggregate demand. If this occurred, there would be no reduction in
unemployment and the increased demand would simply be inflationary.

This demand pull view of inflation suggests that reducing unemployment below the Natural Rate will have severe consequences for inflation.
If the Natural Rate of unemployment increases, due to changes in the
nature of unemployment, this will make the control of inflation even more
difficult. If more and more people become unemployed because they lack
the necessary skills in the labour market, labour shortages will arise at
higher levels of unemployment. This will increase inflationary pressure in
the economy. Many people would argue that this has happened in the UK
in recent years.

The second theory of inflation suggests that it is the result of costs of
production rising independent of the state of demand. Thus import prices
might rise, or Trade Unions secure large wage increases. These cost
increases will generate a once and for all increase in the price level, but for
the inflationary pressure to persist, either the cost increases must continue, or the initial price rises might trigger off inflationary expectations,
with the consequences seen above. To prevent such cost increases, Trade
Unions must be deterred from pushing for higher wages, and the exchange
rate kept high, to prevent import prices from rising.

Thus control of inflation requres that inflationary expectations are not created. If inflationary pressure and expectations do arise, inflation will only reduce if unemployment is taken above the Natural Rate so as to create an excess supply of labour. The consequences of high unemployment may be severe, especially if the electorate decides that this is not a price worth paying for reduced inflation.

Topic nine: the balance of payments and exchange rates

Questions on this area are concerned with the causes and consequences of a balance of payments deficit (usually limited to the current account), and measures which can be taken to alleviate the deficit. Exchange rate questions focus on the determination of exchange rates, the impact on the economy of a change in the exchange rate and the merits of fixed/flexible rates, especially in the context of the ERM.

Sample questions

☐ **What are the possible causes and consequences, of a deficit on the current and capital account of the Balance of Payments?**

A current account deficit means that the value of goods and services imported exceeds the value of goods and services exported. A capital account deficit means that the value of assets (both real and financial), bought by UK residents overseas, is more than the value of UK assets bought by people overseas. The sum of current and capital accounts should balance. Thus a current account deficit implies a capital account surplus.

- Current account: Demand depends upon relative prices and income. Ultimately these will depend upon price competitiveness, exchange rate, quality of exports, nature of imports, level of income in the UK and level of income abroad. Level of income in the UK is a major determinant of imports. Higher income translates into higher consumption, which translates into higher imports.
- Capital account. This will relate to the relative attractiveness of UK assets. Long term investment (eg foreign investment in UK industry) depends on profitability in the UK. Financial assets depend upon relative interest rates and expected exchange rate movements.

Current account deficit implies higher living standards but a capital account surplus. It also implies increasing indebtedness to the rest of the world, while suggesting a lack of competitiveness. At the end of the day, deficit may require higher interest rates or a lower exchange rate or a fall in foreign exchange reserves to create a capital account surplus.

Capital account deficit suggests current surplus.

❏ **What relationship would you expect between the terms of trade and the balance of payments on current account?**

Terms of trade refer to the relative price of exports and imports. If export prices rise, there is an improvement in terms of trade. The relative price of imports and exports will affect the current account. The impact of terms of trade depends on the price elasticities of demand.

If export prices rise because of inflation in the UK, the value of imports will rise since they are relatively cheaper. The value of exports depends on the elasticity of demand. If inelastic, the value of exports increases, if elastic, it will fall.

If export prices rise because of a rise in the exchange rate, the impact on current account depends on Marshall-Lerner conditions (If sum of elasticities greater than one, current account will deteriorate).

❏ **How might the government attempt to rectify a deficit on the current account of the balance of payments?**

Define current account deficit. There are a certain number of measures that can be used.

Expenditure-switching policies:
● Engineer a lower exchange rate (perhaps by lowering interest rates). The impact on the current account depends on Marshall-Lerner conditions.
● Impose imports controls (tariffs or quotas). Import controls may encourage inefficiencies and encourage retaliation.

Expenditure reducing policies:
● Deflate the economy via fiscal or monetary policy. Reduced aggregate demand will reduce imports. May encourage firms to put more emphasis on exports, leading to increased unemployment and reduced inflation, making exports more competitive.

❏ **Assess the case for the UK being a member of the ERM.**

ERM is a system of fixed exchange rates. The exchange rate is determined by the demand and supply of currency on the foreign exchange market. Floating rates are allowed to find their own level. Fixed rates imply that the government must take steps to keep the equilibrium rate at the desired level.

Benefits of membership of European Union are based on gains from trade. Fixed rates encourage trade because of increased certainty. But, if the UK becomes uncompetitive, a fixed rate prevents devaluation from restoring competitiveness, which will then have consequences for employment and output. Thus the case for entry depends on: a) entering at right rate, b) ensuring inflation is not higher than competitors.

Membership also implies loss of control over domestic monetary policy. The rate of interest will affect the exchange rate; thus interest rates will be determined by rates in rest of the ERM.

Specimen answer

☐ **What factors will determine the value of the pound? How will an increase in the level of domestic interest rates affect the level of the pound?**

The value of all currencies is determined by the forces of supply and demand in the foreign exchange market. This has the characteristics of a perfect market, where individual traders are unable to affect the price of a currency. Thus any changes in the price of the pound will be because of changes in its demand or supply.

The demand for the pound will be based on people abroad wanting to buy UK goods, services, or assets. In order to buy these, the foreign purchaser will need to convert a domestic currency into pounds. This will generate a demand for pounds. Conversely if a UK resident wishes to buy goods services or assets from abroad, he or she will need to buy the foreign currency by selling pounds. Thus an examination of the factors affecting the demand and supply of pounds requires an examination of the factors affecting the purchase of UK goods and services and assets from abroad.

The export of UK goods and services will generate a demand for pounds. Anything which boosts the UK current account of the balance of payments will boost the demand for pounds. Exports may rise because of lower prices in the UK, because of a fall in the exchange rate, because of higher incomes and hence spending, abroad, or because of some increase in the resources at the UK's disposal (eg North Sea Oil).

The import of goods and services from abroad will generate a supply of pounds. This will increase if any factor boosts UK imports. Consider the diagram below:

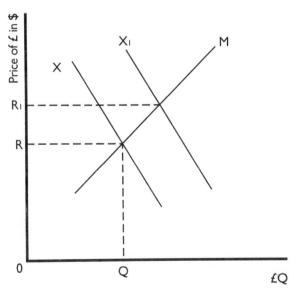

The demand for pounds is given by the export schedule, labelled X. This is shown as increasing as the exchange rate falls, since a lower exchange rate will make UK goods more competitive. Imports are shown as falling as the exchange rate falls, since a lower exchange rate will make imports more expensive; and if the price elasticity of demand for imports is greater than one, this will reduce the value of imports.

The exchange rate will adjust until demand and supply are equal, at an exchange rate of OR. Suppose that there is an increase in export demand. This will increase the demand for sterling and the demand curve will shift to the right. This is shown above as the new demand curve X_1. The equilibrium exchange rate will rise to OR_1. Thus anything which increases UK exports, or reduces imports, since this will shift M to the left, will increase the exchange rate.

The demand and supply of the pound will also be affected by the demand for assets in the UK and abroad. This will depend upon the relative attractions of UK assets as compared with assets abroad. The major demand will be for financial assets. The expected return on financial assets will depend upon two factors, the rate of interest and the expected change in the exchange rate. Suppose that interest rates in the UK increase. This will increase the return which can be earned on financial assets in the UK. Foreign investors will transfer funds into the UK to take advantage of these higher rates. In order to buy the UK asset, the investor will need to convert a domestic currency into pounds, thereby boosting the demand for pounds. In the diagram above the demand for pounds will shift to the right. This will raise the equilibrium exchange rate. Thus an increase in the rate of interest will boost the value of the pound.

However the return on assets will also depend on any expected change in the exchange rate. If the exchange rate is expected to fall, foreign investors will take their money out of the UK, since the value of their pounds would otherwise fall. This withdrawal of funds will have the effect of causing the pound to fall. If the increase in the rate of interest is seen as a sign of a fundamental weakness in the value of the pound, which the rise in interest rates is designed to offset, this might reduce the attraction of UK assets since it may be an indication that the pound is overvalued. In these circumstances the pound might fall. An increase in interest rates might also affect the value of the pound if it reduced the level of spending in the UK which would reduce the demand for imports.

Topic ten: international trade

The questions on trade have increasingly focused on the arguments for free trade within Europe. This is simply an extension of the normal arguments concerning the desirability of free trade. This question may become linked with the idea of monetary union within Europe, since this is the logical conclusion of a customs union.

Sample questions

❏ **How will the creation of the Single European Market affect the standard of living in the UK?**

Define the standard of living, which is usually taken as GDP per head. The SEM will not affect population (unless people move countries) but will affect GDP. The SEM is a customs union designed to promote free trade within Europe. The gains from trade are connected with comparative advantage and economies of scale. Comparative advantage suggests that specialisation will boost output.

Specialisation will encourage economies of scale, so reducing costs and improving productive efficiency, unless monopoly power interferes. Increased competitions will reduce costs where economies of scale are less important. Increased output may confer macro advantages, lower inflation, reduced unemployment.

Gains require that factors are mobile and that exchange rates permit gains to be realised. Both factors may be relevant for the UK.

❏ **Assess the argument that import controls are never justified since they prevent the gains from free trade.**

Free trade will generate potential gains from trade (brief summary of arguments for free trade).

Benefits depend on factor mobility and correct terms of trade. If factors are immobile, free trade may lead to unemployment. Protectionist measures may permit time for adjustment to take place. Dumping may create damage which is not due to comparative advantage, protection thus justified. Infant industries may need protection.

If a country is facing a balance of payments crisis, a reduction in imports may be necessary for policy reasons. Deflation (expenditure reduction) is one possibility. Import controls are another; this will avoid the increase in unemployment.

Some countries may impose tariffs to raise revenue, or for strategic reasons to protect key industries, eg agriculture.

Specimen answer

❏ **Assess the view that the costs of UK membership of the Single European Market will exceed the benefits. How will this situation be affected by the creation of a single currency within Europe?**

The creation of the Single European Market (SEM) is designed to promote the benefits of free trade within Europe. These benefits derive from the idea of international specialisation based on the law of comparative advantage. This suggests that if countries specialise in producing those commodities in which they have a comparative advantage, the total output of goods and services will increase and therefore it will be possible for all countries to increase their GDP and hence their standard of living. Comparative advantage is based on the idea of different opportunity costs of producing different items in different countries. Consider the case of two countries which can both produce two items, but where one country (country A) can produce both commodities more efficiently than country B. Suppose that one unit of labour can produce the outputs shown below:

	Wine	Cloth
Country A	2	3
Country B	1	2

In country A every time that a unit of wine is produced, the labour which is used could have produced 1.5 units of cloth. Thus the opportunity cost of producing one unit of wine in country A is one and a half units of cloth. In country B, every time one unit on wine is produced, the labour could have produced two units of cloth. Thus the opportunity cost of producing one unit of wine in country B is two units of cloth. Thus country B has a larger opportunity cost of producing wine and should therefore concentrate on producing cloth. Country A should concentrate on wine production. This is what would happen if trade between the two countries was allowed to take place. The fact that wine production in A is twice as efficient than in B would indicate that wine exports to B would be profitable. Resources would flow into wine production on A. The wine industry in B would shrink because of this competition. The cloth industry in A would shrink because of the greater profits to be earned by producing wine. Thus cloth could be exported from B to satisfy the demand in A. Both countries would become more specialised in their most efficient commodities.

This process lies behind the move for economic integration in Europe. The gainers and losers from free trade are shown below on the next page.

The diagrams show the industry for wine in both countries. Before trade, the price in A will be OPa and the price in B will be OPb. After trade prices are equalised, the price of wine in A will rise and in B will fall to the level shown as OP. Thus consumers in A will lose from trade, but producers will benefit, since output will increase from OX to OX_1. In country B the consumers benefit from the lower price of wine, but wine producers will lose since production will fall from OY to OY_1.

This analysis shows the impact on the UK of the SEM. Industries in which the UK has a comparative advantage will expand. These are often suggested as being financial services and chemicals. Industries in which other countries have an advantage will decline. In order for the benefits of free trade to be realised, resources, especially labour must be free to move from the industries which decline, to the industries which expand. If these resources are immobile, either geographically or occupationally, the benefits

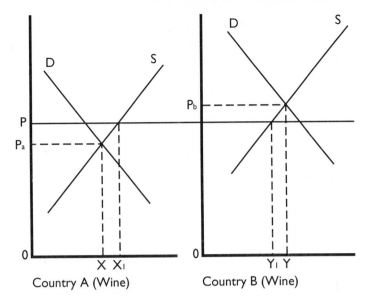

Country A (Wine)   Country B (Wine)

may not be realised, since the resources may remain unemployed. Thus the SEM may impose substantial adjustment costs upon sectors of UK industry.

If the exchange rate is at such a level that much of UK industry is uncompetitive, a large proportion of the workforce may become unemployed. One way of restoring competitiveness would be to allow the exchange rate to fall. If the UK enters into a single currency, this option will no longer be available, and so large parts of the UK economy might suffer severe decline, and other industries may be unable to expand because of the unfavourable price level. This is the great danger behind the move towards a single currency. If relative prices cannot be altered through the exchange rate, any uncompetitiveness has to be removed by UK prices rising more slowly than in the rest of Europe. This will be brought about by prolonged unemployment, which will reduce the rate of inflation.

This means that the advantages to the UK of the SEM and a single currency depend upon the exchange rate being at a competitive level when the single currency is introduced, and also upon the ease with which resources can move within the UK from declining to expanding industries. A further implication of a single currencies that the UK would lose control over its domestic monetary policy. Interest rates could not be altered in response to a change in the domestic economy. This would again prevent the UK from taking policy decisions to rectify problems caused by uncompetitiveness.

Answers to Assessment Questions

Chapter Two

1. **D;** Merit goods are those which society has deemed should be available to everyone, even though they are capable of being denied people. Washing machines are private goods which are denied to people who cannot/will not pay for them Motorway maintainance and defence are public goods, in that their benefits cannot be denied to people once they are provided.
2. **C;** The PPC shows the output which the economy is capable of producing when all resources are being used as efficiently as possible.
3. **D;** Every time the output of X rises by 20 units, the output of Y falls by 40 units.
4. **C;** It is difficult to define what is meant by needs. Even if all needs were met, if people wanted more goods and services than could be produced, resources would be said to be scarce.
5. **B;** Imposing costs on society over and above the benefits derived, leads to an inefficient allocation of resources, since if less of the good were produced society would benefit.

Chapter Three

1. **C**
2. **A;** All the others cause demand to fall (the demand curve to shift to the left) except C, which would increase demand, but this would be shown by a movement along the existing demand curve, since all that has changed is the price, which is measured on the vertical axis.
3. **C;** Petrol and cars are complementary goods.
4. **E**
5. **B**

Chapter Four

1. C

2. D; A shift to the left implies that less will be supplied at all prices. This must be because something other than the price, has made the product less attractive to producers, or reduced output. Increased costs of production are one such event.

3. A; Quantity is measured along the bottom axis.

4. C; Nothing has happened to affect the profitabilty of producing potatoes, or their supply. If the tax reduces the demand for crisps this might affect the demand for potatoes, which might reduce their price. This would not cause the curve to shift, since at any particular price, the same quantity would be supplied. A change is supply brought about by a price change simply takes us to a new point on the original supply curve.

5. D; If supplers are prepared to keep producing additional units of the product at a price of £5, these additional units must be profitable and so must be capable of being produced for £5.

Chapter Five

1. C
2. A
3. D
4. B
5. E

Chapter Six

1. C

$$PED = \frac{\% \text{ change in quantity demanded}}{\% \text{ change in price}} = -\frac{10}{20} = -(0.5)$$

2. C
3. D
4. C
5. B

Chapter Seven

1. A
2. C
3. D
4. D
5. E;

$$\text{If } D = 100 - 5p$$
$$\text{and } S = 5p$$
$$\text{In equilibrium } D = S$$
$$\text{therefore } 100 - 5p = 5p$$
$$\text{thus } 100 = 10p$$
$$\text{thus } 10 = p$$
$$\text{If } p = 10 \text{ then } D = 50 \text{ and } S = 50$$

Chapter Eight

1. D
2. C
3. A; In equilibrium   Question says

$$\frac{MUx}{Px} = \frac{MUy}{Py} \qquad \frac{MUx}{Px} = \frac{1}{2} \text{ and } \frac{MUy}{Py} = \frac{1}{3}$$

Thus equilibrium requires that MUy increases and MUx falls. Therefore buy more of x and less of y.

4. E
5. C

Chapter Nine

1. C
2. E; The diagram illustrates economies of scale. In the long run all costs are variable and so the curve cannot show falling average fixed costs.
3. D; Average fixed costs are £2. (ATC = AVC + AFC)
   Total fixed costs are £10 000.
   AFC = TFC divided by Q. Thus Q = 5000
4. E
5. C; Increasing output from 100 to 200 requires an extra 110 units of capital. Increasing output from 200 to 300 requires 120 units of capital. Thus returns to capital diminish. Increasing output from 100 to 200 units requires 90 units of additional labour. Increasing output from 200 to 300 only requires 80 units of labour. Thus labour is becoming more productive, returns to labour increase.

Chapter Ten

1. **C**
2. **E**
3. **C**
4. **E**
5. **A**

Chapter Eleven

1. **D**
2. **E**
3. **B**
4. **D**
5. **E**; In perfect competition all units are sold at the market price, regardles of how many units the firm produces.. Hence the price is £10 per unit. In order to make normal profit, total revenue must equal total cost. Total revenue is price × quantity.

   Thus $TR = P \times Q = 10 \times Q$
   and $TC = 150 + 5Q$

   Thus require

$$10Q = 150 + 5Q$$
$$5Q = 150$$
$$Q = 30$$

Chapter Twelve

1. **E**
2. **Q_4**
3. **B**
4. **C**
5. **C**; If the monopolist sells 10 units at 50p, total revenue is 500p. If PED is –(2.0) then quantity demanded changes twice as much as the price, in % terms, but in the opposite direction. If price falls to 47.5p. this represents a 5% fall. Thus demand will increase by 10%, from 10 to 11. Thus new sales will be 11 at 47.5p. This gives a total revenue of 522.5p. Hence marginal revenue from selling the extra unit is 22.5p.

Chapter Thirteen

1. D
2. E
3. B
4. D; Since demand is elastic, an increase in price will reduce total expenditure on the product.
5. B; Since only normal profit can be made in the long run.

Chapteen Fourteen

1. C; Elasticity of demand depends upon the pricing decisions of competitors. These are unknown.
2. C
3. B
4. B
5. E; Revenue will be maximised when it is not possible for it to increase. Hence marginal revenue must be zero. When price changes are associated with no change in revenue, price elasticity of demand is one.

Chapter Fifteen

1. C
2. B
3. D
4. C; Labour will be hired up to the point where the wage (£200) equals the marginal revenue product (Marginal product × price)

$$\text{Thus } £200 = MP \times £5$$
$$\text{Or} \quad 40 = MP$$

The marginal product of the sixth worker is 40. To check: the sixth worker produces 40 units which sell at £5, thus producing £200. He is just worth employing. The seventh worker only produces 30 units, which only yields £150 revenue.
5. E

Chapter Sixteen

1. C
2. A
3. D
4. D
5. A

Chapter Seventeen

1. D
2. C
3. C
4. A
5. D

Chapter Eighteen

1. B
2. E
3. D
4. B
5. D

Chapter Nineteen

1. B
2. D
3. A
4. C
5. A

Chapter Twenty

1. A
2. B
3. E
4. C
5. A

Chapter Twenty One

1. B
2. C
3. E
4. C
5. D

Chapter Twenty Two

1. D
2. B
3. D
4. D
5. B

Chapter Twenty Three

1. A
2. C; The value of the multiplier is given by the expression 1/MPW where

   $$MPW = MPS + MPT + MPM$$
   $$= 0.25 + 0.1 + 0.15 = 0.5$$

3. A
4. E; Since in equilibrium, withdrawals equal injections, which are shown as LM
5. A

Chapter Twenty Four

1. E; In equilibrium $\qquad Y = C + 1$

   therefore
   $$Y = 100 + 0.6Y + 500$$
   $$Y = 600 + 0.6Y$$
   $$0.4Y = 600$$
   $$Y = 1500$$

2. D
3. C; Given that $C = 100 + 0.75Y$, the MPC is 0.75.
   In a closed economy with no government, the only withdrawals are savings, hence the MPW = MPS.
   If MPC = 0.75, the MPS = 0.25. (MPC + MPS = 1)
   The multiplier is given by $1/MPW = 1/0.25 = 4$
4. D; Given the function $C = a + bY$, the average propensity to consume (APC) is given by $APC = C/Y = a/Y + b$. Thus as Y increases, the value of APC falls. Since the redistribution of income has increased the income of the poor, their APC will fall. The income of the rich has fallen and so their APC will rise.
5. D

Chapter Twenty Five

1. B
2. D
3. C
4. B
5. D

Chapter Twenty Six

1. **D;** Since this will increase government expenditure on unemployment and other benefits
2. **C;** Since the government expenditure multipler exceeds the taxation multiplier. In other words, some of the tax cut will be saved and so will not affect aggregate demand.
3. **B**
4. **E**
5. **C;** In 1991, the bottom quintile of households receved 7.2% of disposable income. This is the nearest correct figure of the possible answers.

Chapter Twenty Seven

1. D
2. B
3. A
4. E
5. D

Chapter Twenty Eight

1. **C;** The purchase of government bonds will expand the money supply.
2. **A**
3. **D**
4. **C**
5. **D;** This will reduce the quantity of money in circulation, if the government does not spend the money it receives from the sale of stock.

Chapter Twenty Nine

1. **C;** A fall in inflation will improve the trading prospects of the country and will increase the purchasing power parity of the currency. If this encourages more people to invest in ther currency, its price will rise.
2. **D;** An increase in reserves suggests that the central bank has been selling its own currency and buying foreign exchange. This is necessary if there was an excess demand for the currency. This will occur if some event makes the currency more attractive. An increase in domestic interest rates will increase the demand for a currency as foreign investors try and take advantage of the increased interest rates.
3. **E;** This is the basis of the Marshall-Lerner conditions.
4. **A**
5. **C**

Chapter Thirty

1. **B**
2. **D**
3. **E**
4. **E**
5. **B**

Chapter Thirty One

1. **D**
2. **D;** This would reduce structural unemployment and so reduce unemployment without generating any excess demand for labour.
3. **B**
4. **D**
5. **D;** Since this might increase the supply of labour and so relieve any pressure on wages caused by an excess demand for labour.

Chapter Thirty Two

1. **C**
2. **D**
3. **C**
4. **B**
5. **B**

Chapter Thirty Three

1. **C**; In the long run, wages will fall if unemployment stays above the natural rate. This will reduce costs of production, and cause the aggregate supply curve to shift to position shown as AS_2, so returning the economy to its natural rate of unemployment.
2. **D**
3. **E**
4. **C**; If the fall in income tax increases the incentive to work, and hence results in a fall in the numbers of people voluntarily unemployed.
5. **A**

Chapter Thirty Four

1. **D**
2. **A**
3. **C**
4. **E**
5. **D**

Chapter Thirty Five

1. **A**
2. **E**; Because line XX is steeper than YY, any change in the output of pens in country X will cause a larger change in its output of paper than in country Y. Thus an increase in pens output in X has a larger opportunity cost in terms of paper foregone, than in Y. Thus country X should not produce pens and should concentrate on paper production, since it has a comparative advantage in producing paper.
3. **C**; Immobile factors do not prevent free trade, although they may prevent a country from reaping the full benefits of trade.
4. **D**
5. **E**

Chapter Thirty Six

1. **C**
2. **B**
3. **C**; Since increased specialisation will require that resources, especially labour resources, will need to be mobile, both occupationally and geographically. If they are not mobile, structural unemployment will increase.
4. **A**
5. **D**

Index